Implementing Environmental and Resource Management

Michael Schmidt • Vincent Onyango
Dmytro Palekhov
Editors

Implementing Environmental and Resource Management

Springer

Editors
Professor Dr. Michael Schmidt
Vincent Onyango, Ph.D.
Dmytro Palekhov
Brandenburg University
of Technology (BTU), Cottbus
Department of Environmental Planning
Erich-Weinert-Straße 1
03046 Cottbus
Germany
michael.schmidt@tu-cottbus.de
vin_onyango@yahoo.com
palekdmy@tu-cottbus.de

ISBN 978-3-540-77567-6 e-ISBN 978-3-540-77568-3
DOI 10.1007/978-3-540-77568-3
Springer Heidelberg Dordrecht London New York

Library of Congress Control Number: 2011928782

Cover design: SPi Publisher Services

Printed on acid-free paper

Springer is part of Springer Science+Business Media (www.springer.com)

Preface

The environmental challenges of the modern era cannot be faced with scientific knowledge alone. Additionally, experience of how such knowledge can be communicated and applied, an understanding of the inherent social factors as well as knowledge of the economic causes and effects, are all of equal importance. It is therefore important that practitioners of Environmental and Resource Management (ERM) combine the fields of environmental science, engineering, management and sociology. Environmental and resource managers may be found in all industry sectors, as well as in politics, commerce and academia, thus must be fundamentally transdisciplinary. This volume illustrates the broad range of work currently being performed by practitioners of ERM by presenting a collection of papers written by ERM Alumni from the Brandenburg University of Technology, Cottbus, Germany.

The work in this volume, which has been divided into three distinct sections: Energy Efficiency and Innovation; Planning and Decision Making; and Limits to Managing the Environment, demonstrates the wide reaching implementation possibilities of ERM as well as the range of knowledge and experience of it's practitioners. The need for such a broad expertise in global environmental issues has been demonstrated repeatedly over recent years. Consider for example the damaging disconnect between climate scientists and climate change-denying politicians in the USA or the need to negotiate an accord on cash benefit sharing for genetic resource exploitation before any agreement on biodiversity protection could be reached at the COP10 in Nagoya Japan. These examples demonstrate a very current and serious breakdown in communication between socio-political and scientific bodies. Clearly there is a need for politicians who can communicate with ecologists, economists who understand scientific dialogue and scientists who can argue their case with social advocate groups. Graduates in ERM can provide a method of bridging these seemingly incompatible issues or even become specialists in one field while retaining sufficient knowledge and experience in others to make that bridge unnecessary.

This volume is the result of the 2008 BTU ERM Alumni Conference and represents the collected works of ERM Alumni as well as young professionals and researchers who are involved in the field of ERM. The connecting theme of these works is the successful implementation of environmental and resource management in a wide range of issues including energy management, climate change response, fossil fuels, sustainable development and the economic, social and legal aspects of resource management in developing countries.

The completion of this volume leaves us indebted to many people. First of all we wish to thank all authors from the various countries for their valuable articles, which made possible this comprehensive publication. We thank the German Academic Exchange Service in Bonn (DAAD – Deutscher Akademischer Auslandsdienst) for its generous support in organising the ERM Alumni Conference and in publishing the resulting book. We are very grateful to Gerhard Wiegleb for his help in preparing this volume and for the comprehensive review of all chapters.

We also wish to express our gratitude to Ernest Fongwa, Ingmar Lippert and Satyanarayana Narra for their special assistance in the initial stages of the preparation of this book project and we are very thankful for their help at such a crucial time. We are particularly indebted to the excellent work provided by Robert Atkinson without whom the finalising of this volume would have been much more difficult.

We hope that researchers, academics, students as well as teachers of ERM will find the content of this book valuable in their work, research and studies.

Michael Schmidt, Vincent Onyango and Dmytro Palekhov
Cottbus, December 2010

Table of Contents

List of Contributors

Robert Atkinson is a current student of the ERM MSc programme at the Brandenburg University of Technology (BTU) Cottbus. His move to environmental management came after five years working as a production chemicals specialist in the oil industry. His master's thesis will deal with the social and technical aspects of the terrestrial application of carbon capture and sequestration technology.

Department of Environmental Planning, Brandenburg University of Technology (BTU) Cottbus, P.O. Box 101344, 03013 Cottbus, Germany; Email: Rob.Atkinson01@googlemail.com

Adeline A. Awemo holds a BSc in Environmental Science from the University of Buea, Cameroon and an MSc in Environmental Resource Management from Brandenburg University of Technology (BTU) Cottbus. She is a doctorate student of Environmental Geology in BTU Cottbus. She is currently researching on ground water contamination from waste sites in Cameroon.

Chair of Environmental Geology, Brandenburg University of Technology (BTU) Cottbus, P.O. Box 101344, 03013 Cottbus, Germany; Email: abimnwi@yahoo.com

Peter Ay is a professor and Head of the Chair Mineral Processing and Biogenic Resources. He has broad experience in the field of mineral processing, solid and liquid waste management and mechanical and physicochemical unit operations in environmental engineering. He leads international cooperation with several universities and develops projects regarding the upgrading of raw materials and biomass residues.

Head of the Chair Mineral Processing and Biogenic Resources, Brandenburg University of Technology (BTU) Cottbus, Siemens-Halske-Ring 8, 03046 Cottbus, Germany
Tel: +49 (0) 355 69 3536; Email: ls-at@tu-cottbus.de

Jordi Cadilla works since March 2010 as International Cooperation Officer in the field of Infrastructure for the European Commission (DG Development and Cooperation) and the European External Action Service (EEAS) at the Delegation of the European Union in Rwanda. He holds a MSc degree in Environment and Resources Management from the Brandenburg University of Technology (BTU) Cottbus, Germany. His Master's thesis was on "Technical and economic aspects of grid-connected solar photovoltaics in Brazil".

EU Delegation in Rwanda, Infrastructure Section. Bd. Umuganda 1807, BP515 Kigali, Rwanda
Tel: +250 252 585739; Fax: +250 252 585736; Email: jordicadilla@yahoo.com

Maurício Ferreira Silva Corrêa graduated in 2005 in Mechanical Engineering at the Mackenzie University in Sao Paulo, Brazil. In 2010 he obtained a Master degree in Technology and Innovation Management at the BTU Cottbus with the topic "Perspectives of Sugarcane as Raw Material for Ethanol Production in Brazil".

Tel: +49 (0)160 209 8853; Email: mauricio.ferreirasilvacorrea@tu-cottbus.de

Victor Ngu Cheo is a Senior Lecturer at the department of Journalism and Mass Communication, Faculty of Social and Management Sciences in the University of Buea, Cameroon. In 2010, he defended a PhD in Environmental and Resource Management at the Brandenburg University of Technology (BTU) Cottbus, Germany. He has contributed several scholarly articles in international journals and also published a number of book chapters. His current research interests are environmental policy and environmental communication, sustainable development and political ecology.

Department of Journalism and Mass Communication, Faculty of Social and Management Sciences, BP 63, University of Buea, South West Region, Cameroon; Email: v_cheo@yahoo.com

Bibek Das holds a Masters degree in Environment and Resources Management from Brandenburg University of Technology (BTU) Cottbus, Germany, majoring in Loss Prevention in Process Industries. At the time of authoring his chapter he was working with Bureau Veritas as a Risk & Safety Engineer where he worked for 4.5 years in Abu Dhabi, Paris and Houston. He recently joined American Bureau of Shipping in Houston as a Senior Risk Engineer and is involved with various R&D projects with the marine and offshore oil & gas facilities. His research interests are Hydrocarbon Fires and Vapour Cloud Explosion modelling.

American Bureau of Shipping, ABS Plaza, Houston, Texas, USA
Tel: +1 281 8776185; Email: bidas@eagle.org; dbibekd@yahoo.co.in

Şebnem Düzgün is senior lecturer, professor and vice-chair person of Mining Engineering Department and also senior lecturer and professor of Geodetic and Geographic Information Technologies (GGIT) Division at Middle East Technical University (METU), Ankara – Turkey. In 2000 she received her PhD degree in on Reliability-Based Design of Rock Slopes Mining Engineering at METU. Her main research areas are landslide hazard and risk assessment and management, use of geographical information systems (GIS) and RS in mining, probabilistic modelling of rock slopes, use of probabilistic methods in rock engineering, uncertainty modelling in geotechnical engineering, natural hazard risk assessment through GIS, geostatistics, spatial statistics in GIS and its applications, spatial data analysis and GIS, spatial data mining, modelling spatial uncertainty.

Department of Mining Engineering, Middle East Technical University, 06531, Ankara – Turkey
Tel: +90-312-2102668, Email: duzgun@metu.edu.tr
Web page: http://ggit.metu.edu.tr/full_time_members/sebnem_duzgun.htm

Ernest Anye Fongwa is research and teaching assistant, and a PhD candidate at the Department of Ecosystems and Environment Informatics at the Brandenburg University of Technology (BTU) Cottbus, Germany since 2008. He holds a MSc degree in Environment and Resources Management from BTU. His Master's thesis was focusing on corporate finance for investing in business development for protecting environmental goods and services which is still his main research area, but concentrating on modelling and simulation. Beside he has been an administrator and project coordinator at ERIMON Ltd in Cameroon from 1999 to 2001.

Department of Ecosystems and Environmental Informatics, Brandenburg University of Technology (BTU) Cottbus, Konrad-Wachsmann-Allee 1, D- 03046 Cottbus-Germany
Tel: +49 (0)355 69 2831; Fax: +49 (0)355 69 2743; Email: enibks@yahoo.co.uk

Albrecht Gnauck is the Head of the Department of Ecosystems and Environmental Informatics at the Brandenburg University of Technology (BTU) Cottbus since 1993. He studied Mathematics and Physics at Humboldt University of Berlin. In 1970 he received a doctorate degree in hydrobiology, and 1988 a doctorate degree in biology, including ecology, from Technical University of Dresden. Since 2003 he is a member of the Managing Board of the International Society for Environmental Protection at Vienna, and since 2005 he works as member of the Editorial Board of the international journal "Ecological Indicator". He published over 200 scientific papers and is the editor of a workshop series on "Modelling and Simulation of Ecosystems".

Brandenburg University of Technology, Department of Ecosystems and Environmental Informatics, Konrad-Wachsmann-Allee 1, 03046 Cottbus, Germany
Tel: +49 (0)355 69 2713, Fax: +49 (0)355 69 2743, E-mail: umweltinformatik@tu-cottbus.de
http://www.tu-cottbus.de/fakltaet4/umweltinformatik

Abdurrahman Belel Ismaila is a graduate assistant at Department of Urban & Regional Planning of Federal University of Technology Yola, Nigeria since 2006 and currently a PhD candidate at Department of Geodetic and Geographic Information Technologies, Middle East Technical University (METU), Ankara – Turkey. His research interests include spatial analysis, GIS and Remote Sensing applications, renewable energy, and uncertainty analysis in spatial data and models.

Department of Geodesy & Geographic Information Technologies, Graduate School of Natural & Applied Sciences, Middle East Technical University, 06531, Ankara – Turkey
Tel: +905064195822; +905349551124; Email: belelismaila@yahoo.com; belelismaila@gmail.com

Franz Krause works at the Countryside and Community Research Institute and the Centre for the Study of Floods and Communities, University of Gloucestershire, UK. He holds a Doctoral Degree in anthropology from the University of Aberdeen, UK. His research interests include human interaction with rivers and water, political ecology and phenomenological anthropology.

Countryside and Community Research Institute, University of Gloucestershire, Oxstalls Campus, Oxstalls Lane, Gloucester GL2 9HW, UK
Email: fkrause@glos.ac.uk

Hans Joachim Krautz is a professor and Head of the Chair of Power Plant Technologies. He has experience in the combustion of lignite and the maintenance of power plants. The investigation of oxyfuel combustion in a 500 kW pilot plant and the Hydrogen Test Rig at the BTU Cottbus are cutting edge projects in these fields worldwide. He commits himself for a German – Brazilian cooperation aiming research in renewable energy such as biomass combustion.

Chair of Power Plant Technologies, Brandenburg University of Technology (BTU) Cottbus, Universitätsstr. 22, 03046 Cottbus, Germany
Tel: +49 (0)355 69 4600; Email: krautz@tu-cottbus.de

Paul Pinamang Kyei is a PhD student at the Department of Environmental Planning, Brandenburg University of Technology (BTU) Cottbus since 2008. In 2004, he received his MSc in Environmental Management from the Department of Planning, Aalborg University, Denmark. He also holds M.Phil in Environmental Science from the University of Ghana, Legon. Before Starting the PhD programme, he had worked as a research scholar at UNEP/ETC in Murdoch University, Australia and as a hydrologic data analyst at Intelligentsia International, Inc., Florida, USA. His main research interests are Strategic Environmental Assessment, Environmental Impact Assessment and Land Use Planning.

Department of Environmental Planning, Brandenburg University of Technology (BTU) Cottbus, P.O. Box 101344, 03013 Cottbus, Germany; Email: kyeippin@hotmail.com

Christine Laures is a research assistant at the Department of Water Resources Management and Rural Engineering, Water Supply Networks Section, University of Karlsruhe. She holds a BSc in Environmental and Resource Management from the Brandenburg University of Technology (BTU) Cottbus and an MSc in Water Engineering and Management from the University of Stuttgart. Her Master thesis was about Benchmarking of Selected Yemeni Water Utilities.

Universität Karlsruhe (TH), Institut für Wasser und Gewässerentwicklung, Bereich Wasserwirtschaft und Kulturtechnik, Geb. 10.63, Kaiserstraße 12, 76131 Karlsruhe, Germany
Tel: +49 (0)721 608 45698; Email: Christine.Laures@kit.edu

Ingmar Lippert is a social scientist engaged with an ethnography of environmental managers in the financial services sector. He is affiliated to the Chair of Sociology of Augsburg University (Germany) and an alumnus of the Institute of Advanced Studies on Science Technology and Society (Graz, Austria). He graduated in Environmental and Resource Management (BSc) with studies at Brandenburg University of Technology (Cottbus, Germany) as well as at Bosporus University (Istanbul, Turkey) and completed his postgraduate studies in Environment, Culture and Society (MA) at Lancaster University (UK).

Chair of Sociology, Faculty for Philosophy and Social Science, University of Augsburg, Universitätsstraße 6, 86159 Augsburg, Germany
Fax: +49 821 598 4218; Email: lippert@ems-research.org; Web: http://lippert.ems-research.org

Bruna Missagia started studying Biology in 1997 in the Federal University of Minas Gerais, Brazil. From October 1999 to December 2006 she studied Environmental and Resource Management at BTU Cottbus. Her Master thesis was on Land Use Management in the Brazilian Atlantic Rainforest. Since 2007 she is working at the Chair of Power Plant Technologies. She coordinates projects with Brazilian universities regarding the generation of energy from biomass residues.

Chair of Power Plant Technologies, Brandenburg University of Technology (BTU) Cottbus, Universitätsstr. 22, 03046 Cottbus, Germany
Tel: +49 (0)355 69 3541; Email: missagia@tu-cottbus.de

Satyanarayana Narra is a senior scientist at the Chair of Mineral Processing at the Brandenburg University of Technology (BTU) Cottbus. In 2008 he perceived his doctorate degree at the BTU Cottbus.

Chair of Mineral Processing, Brandenburg University of Technology (BTU) Cottbus, P.O. Box 101344, 03013 Cottbus, Germany
Tel: +49 (0)355 69 4325; Fax: +49 (0)355 69 2929; Email: narra@tu-cottbus.de

Balgah Sounders Nguh is the current head of Geography Department at the University of Buea, Cameroon. He holds a PhD from the University of Buea; an MA and a BA from the University of Lagos, Nigeria. He is a specialist in remote sensing and its application to natural resources and resource management. His works centre on land use/land cover types and land use dynamics. He is author to a number of book chapters and scientific articles in scholarly journals. He is a co-author of Population Resources Scarcity and Conflict Trinity: Analysis of North West Cameroon, and the Urbanization Process in Cameroon: Patterns, Implications and Prospects. His current research interest is on population, natural resource management, remote sensing and GIS, and development studies.

Department of Geography, Faculty of Social and Management Sciences, P.O Box 63 University of Buea; Email: juniorsa2002@yahoo.co.uk

Anup Sam Ninan is currently a Fellow at the Bremen International Graduate School of Social Sciences (BIGSSS), Bremen, Germany. A former Fellow of Institute for Advanced Studies on Science, Technology and Society (IAS-STS), Graz, Austria, he earned his Masters degree in Sociology and M.Phil in Science Policy Studies from Jawaharlal Nehru University (JNU), New Delhi, India. At BIGSSS, he is in the thematic field of Global Integration, working on the framing of sustainability in climate change discourse.

Bremen International Graduate School of Social Sciences (BIGSSS), Postfach 330 440 FVG-West, Wiener Straße/Ecke Celsiusstraße, 28334 Bremen, Germany
Tel: +49 (0) 421 218 66418; Email: asninan@bigsss.uni-bremen.de

Sören Noack holds a BSc and MSc degree in Environmental and Resource Management from the Brandenburg University of Technology (BTU) Cottbus, Germany. In 2007 he participated in a project on "Cleaner Production for Jeans Laundries in Northeast Brazil" in cooperation with Training and Development Centers of the Bavarian Employers' Associations, the ASA programme and local Brazilian organizations. His Master's thesis focused "Challenges and Opportunities for Developing Countries by Emission Trading after 2012".

Sternstr. 24, 01968 Senftenberg, Germany
Tel. +49 178 5399 707; Email: soeren.noack@gmx.net

Vincent Onyango is a researcher on environmental planning and strategies and is currently associated with the North Yorkshire County Council's planning team working on preparation of the Council's next Rights of Way Improvement Plan. He received his PhD in Environmental Resources Management, specialising in

Strategic Environmental Assessment. His current research interests are in the use of Ecosystem Services concept within national Low Carbon Strategies.

58 West Farm Wynd, Newcastle Upon Tyne, NE12 8UE, UK
Tel.: +44 (0)7980 136 07; Email: vin_onyango@yahoo.com

Dmytro Palekhov is a lecturer and research associate at the Department of Environmental Planning, Brandenburg University of Technology, Cottbus, Germany. He obtained a doctorate degree in law from the V.M. Koretsky Institute of State and Law of the National Academy of Sciences of Ukraine (2009), holds a LL.M. degree from the National Mining University, Dnepropetrovsk, Ukraine (2003) and BSc in Environmental and Resource Management from the BTU Cottbus (2003). His research interests are on environmental assessment (EIA and SEA) and environmental law.

Department of Environmental Planning, Brandenburg University of Technology (BTU) Cottbus, P.O. Box 101344, D-03013 Cottbus, Germany
Tel: +49 (0)355 69 3054; Fax: + 49 (0)355 69 2765; Email: dmitry.pal@gmail.com, palekdmy@tu-cottbus.de; Web: www.tu-cottbus.de/environment

Wolfgang Schluchter is a professor and Head of the Chair of Environmental Issues in Social Sciences since 1993 and the Director of the Human Ecology centre at the BTU Cottbus. His research interests include issues of public participation in environmentally relevant planning and decision-making processes, psychological effects and the social impact assessment, principles of environmentally acceptable and socially responsible technology design, environmental protection in education, training, and professional development.

Chair Environmental Issues in Social Sciences, Brandenburg University of Technology (BTU) Cottbus, Erich Weinert Str. 1, 03036 Cottbus, Germany
Tel: +49 (0) 355 69 3036; Email: schluchter@tu-cottbus.de

Michael Schmidt is a professor and Head of the Department of Environmental Planning at the Brandenburg University of Technology (BTU) Cottbus. At the BTU Cottbus, he initiated the international study programmes "Environmental and Resource Management" and "World Heritage Studies". In 2002 he received the "Award for Excellence in International University Cooperation" by the German State Federal Ministry of Education and Research, and in 2005 the Dr. h.c. of the National Mining University, Dnepropetrovsk, Ukraine. Since 1997 he is consultant of the German Agency for Technical Cooperation (GTZ) in Jordan, Lebanon, Syria and Yemen. His scientific research and lecturing fields include environmental planning, environmental assessment, strategies for sustainable development, techniques for combating desertification as well as monitoring and evaluation.

Head of Department of Environmental Planning, Brandenburg University of Technology (BTU) Cottbus, P.O. Box 101344, D-03013 Cottbus, Germany
Tel: +49 (0)355 69 24 54; Fax: + 49 (0)355 69 27 65; Email: michael.schmidt@tu-cottbus.de;
Web: www.tu-cottbus.de/environment

Hannah Strauss is a PhD candidate at Thule Institute, University of Oulu, Finland. Funded by the Academy of Finland through the Finland Distinguished Professor initiative she contributes to research on "Human-environment relations in the North" by investigating the negotiation of Nordic and circumpolar energy resource exploitation. She obtained an MSc in Science and Technology Policy and Management (UK) and an MA in Sociology and Social Psychology (Germany) and recently submitted her PhD thesis "For the Good of Society: public participation in the siting of nuclear and hydro power projects in Finland".

Thule Institute, P.O. Box 7300, 90014 University of Oulu, Finland
Tel: +358 40 853 2412, Email: hannah.strauss@oulu.fi;
Web: http://thule.oulu.fi/englanti/about/hannahstrauss.html

Shrinivas Tukdeo is working as a manager in Ecolutions Carbon India Pvt. Ltd. in India, where he is dealing with Clean Development Mechanism offering his advisory services. He holds a MSc degree in Environmental and Resources Management from Brandenburg University of Technology (BTU) Cottbus.

Ecolutions Carbon India Pvt. Ltd, Unit No. 15, Ground floor, Mahindra Chambers, 619/28, W.T. Patil Marg, Opp. Dukes Factory, Chembur, Mumbai – 400071, India
Tel: +91 (0)22 25200500; Fax: +91 (0)22 25201743; Email: info@ecolutions.in

Onur Uşkay is a software development engineer at Acls Systems. He holds an MSc degree in Geodetic and Geographical Information Technologies from the Middle East Technical University (METU), Ankara - Turkey. His master's thesis was on "Route Optimization of Solid Waste Transportation Using Parellel Hybrid genetic Algorithms".

Department of Geodesy & Geographic Information Technologies, Graduate School of Natural & Applied Sciences, Middle East Technical University, 06531, Ankara – Turkey
Tel: +90 536 2594608, Email: onuruskay@gmail.com

Shouke Wei is a scientist of Department of System Analysis, Integrated Assessment and Modelling in the Swiss Federal Institute of Aquatic Science and Technology (Eawag) in Switzerland. In 2008 he got his PhD in Environmental and Resource Management from Faculty of Environmental Sciences and Process Engineering at Brandenburg University of Technology (BTU) Cottbus, Germany. His research interests are interdisciplinary modelling and simulation techniques and data analysis methods in the fields of socio-economic, environment, resources and energy.

Eawag, Swiss Federal Institute of Aquatic Science and Technology, Überlandstrasse 133, P.O.Box 133, CH-8600 Dübendorf, Switzerland
Tel: +41 (0)44 823 5364; Fax: +41 (0)44 823 5028; Email: shouke.wei@eawag.ch

Gerhard Wiegleb is professor of General Ecology at BTU Cottbus. His current research focuses on ecological and socio-economic driving forces of biodiversity change in disturbed landscapes. Recent research is dealing with the legal framework of biodiversity protection under the EU liability directive.

Department of General Ecology, Brandenburg University of Technology (BTU) Cottbus, P.O. Box 101344, D-03013 Cottbus, Germany

Tel: +49 (0)355 69 2291; Fax: +49 (0)355 69 2225; Email: wiegleb@tu-cottbus.de;
Web: www.tu-cottbus.de/environment

Angkarn Wongdeethai holds a PhD in Environmental and Resource Management from the Brandenburg University of Technology, Cottbus, Germany, since 2006. His research interests are on Sustainable Development, with particular emphasis on Industrial Ecology, Recycling and Design Analysis, and Environmental Protection.

Email: wongdeethai@hotmail.com

Evren Deniz Yaylacı is co-founder and business development coordinator at KCM Consultancy Ltd. in Ankara - Turkey since 2005 and PhD candidate at Mining Engineering Department, Middle East Technical University (METU), Ankara – Turkey. He holds BSc degree in Mining Engineering (METU - 2003) and MSc degree in Environmental and Resource Management from Brandenburg University of Technology Cottbus (BTU) Cottbus since 2005. His main research interests include mine closure and reclamation; spatial analysis, spatial statistics in GIS and its applications for decision making and environmental management.

KCM Project & Consultancy Ltd., Ahmet Rasim Sk. 29/6, 06520, Çankaya, Ankara – Turkey
Tel: +90 312 440 22 88, +90 533 518 28 09;
Email: evren@kalkinmacalismalari.com, evrenyaylaci@gmail.com

1 Editorial - Environmental Challenges and Management of Natural Resources

Michael Schmidt, Vincent Onyango and Dmytro Palekhov

Department of Environmental Planning, Brandenburg University of Technology (BTU), Cottbus, Germany

1.1 Introduction

Today, we live in a world in which the issues of environmental protection and sustainable management of natural resources are of significant concern. Globally, several challenges of various severities to sustainable environmental and natural resources management have been reported (EIA 2008; IPCC 2007; FAO 2006; MEA 2005; WCED 1987). These include problems significantly affecting land, atmosphere, water, and biodiversity, at various spatial and temporal scales. These challenges take several forms e.g. pollution, degradation, decreasing biodiversity and degraded ecosystem services (MEA 2005; IPPC 2007; Taylor and Buttel 1992). Hence, the world's societies are facing the crucial task of developing corrective, adaptive and coping mechanisms (Clini et al. 2008; Clark and Noin 1998). Policy-makers and practitioners have aimed at transforming these problems into manageable challenges (Pepper 1996). This is aptly exemplified by current efforts to meet the challenges posed by climate change and global warming, and the potential attendant impacts (Ranganathan et al. 2008; FAO 2006). Other efforts can be found in the conventions and norms, policies, programmes and projects, at various levels of governance (Albrecht et al. 2007; Hendricks and Guruswamy 1997).

Moreover, to facilitate environmental conservation and sustainable development, various study programmes have been introduced. Subsequently, studies in environmental assessments, impacts and integrated planning provide a significant linkage between human socio-economic interactions and the natural environment. Whether these programmes constitute an emerging or a fully-fledged field of study and management science can be debated. The study programme Environmental Resources Management (ERM) was started at the Brandenburg University of Technology (BTU), Cottbus, Germany in 1998. The objective was to produce interdisciplinary professionals versed in the science, practice and management of environmental and natural resources (www.tu-cottbus.de/environment). Similar study programmes, going under various names, today constitute a fully-fledged field of study and management science, offered at many universities worldwide. It was envisaged that ERM graduates would contribute to ensuring a more sustainable environment.

1.2 Aim of this Volume

A decade after the ERM programme was initiated at BTU, an alumni conference was held in October 2008. It had two objectives: 1) Facilitate networking among ERM alumni and, 2) Distil experiences, challenges and perspectives of alumni in applying their knowledge and skills. Subsequently, this volume has two aims: 1) Expose some of the research outputs of BTU ERM alumni and, 2) Present perspectives and critical questions of alumni as agents of change in ERM, focusing in what they perceive as limits to ERM application. Whilst the former contribution is a snap window to showcase research applications of BTU ERM alumni, the latter is more novel. This is because it is questioning how agents of ERM interact with phenomena and other actors within the arena in which ERM is practiced. This represents a level of awareness and perception that is often lacking, as agents of ERM have traditionally been subsumed into the existing and dominant perspectives, without significant scrutiny of their roles and reality (see Huber 2008; Davidson and Frickel 2004). Dominant perspectives in this case refer to the prevailing knowledge, attitudes and practices held within ERM working and researching environments.

Through these two aims, the editors hope not only to distribute output from ERM alumni, but also to start an earnest debate into the agency of ERM actors in managing the environment and its resources. In this context, it is assumed that systematic research interest will develop in the field of unpacking the fundamentals, constraints and driving forces that determine the application and subsequent effectiveness of ERM agents. The research results can provide empirical bases on which ERM study programmes and/or working environments can be problematised and/or reviewed in order to more effectively deliver the objectives of ERM. The intended audience of this volume is wide and includes not just potential ERM students who want to understand how ERM is being applied but also targets teachers of ERM who want to understand the roles and perceptions of ERM alumni at work. The volume is also relevant to researchers who can take up the challenge of unpacking the constraints and limitations that may inhibit the effectiveness of ERM agents. This is important if ERM graduates are to be re-tooled as more effective agents of change towards sustainable stewardship of the environment and its natural resources.

1.3 Outline of this Volume

This volume brings together twenty-one ERM-related chapters with 17 (81%) of them focusing on various issues of energy e.g. innovative technologies, wind, solar and bio-energy. Four of the chapters (19%) focus on environmental and sustainability planning; and five (24%) present critical review of ERM and its actors, highlighting limits to ERM application. The chapters in this volume contain studies from at least 10 countries on five continents; while one adopts a rather global approach i.e. Ecosystem Services as a potential target for mitigating carbon emissions (Chapter 12). This diverse selection reflects the scope defined by the conference organisers, the varied interests of ERM alumni and the multi-national character of the studentship within the BTU ERM programme.

The volume is structured into three parts according to focal themes of the chapters. Part I consists of chapters dealing with energy efficiency and innovative production. Part II consists of chapters addressing various aspects of decisions-making and planning for sustainability, proposing how this can be promoted. Part III consists of chapters presenting limits to managing the environment, in terms of theory and practice. The chapters question the knowledge perspectives as well as application of ERM and apply ethnography in trying to understand cognitive contradictions and phenomena as ERM agents interact with the modifying influences of technological, institutional and social factors, while at work.

The volume ends with a final chapter by Gerhard Wiegleb on the outlook of ERM. He is a long-time researcher and experienced teacher in ERM, and offers thoughts on how ERM graduates can be better integrated into social and institutional environments, in a way that enhances their potential to effectively address environmental problems. Potential themes for future ERM-related research are also presented.

References

Albrecht E, Hoffmann J, Knopp L (2007) Selected Conventions and Treaties on International Environmental Law, 3rd ed., expanded and updated edition. Aktuelle Reihe 3/2007

Clarke J, Noin D (1998) (eds) Population and Environment in Arid Regions. UNESCO/Partenon Publishing Group, Paris

Clini C, Musu I, Gullino ML (2008) Sustainable Development and Environmental Management – Experiences and Case Studies. Springer, Dordercht

Davidson DJ, Frickel S (2004) Understanding Environmental Governance: A Critical Review. In: Organization and Environment 17(4): 471-492

EIA – Energy Information Administration (2008) International Energy Outlook 2008. Energy Information Administration, Office of Integrated Analysis and Forecasting, U.S. Department of Energy Washington, DC

FAO – Food and Agricultural Organisation (2006) World Agriculture: Towards 2030/2050. Prospects for Food, Nutrition, Agriculture and Major Commodity Groups. Global Perspective Studies Unit. FAO, Rome

Hendricks BR, Guruswamy LD (1997) International Environmental Law in a Nutshell. Westgroup Publishers, Carlifornia

Huber J (2008) Pioneer Countries and the Global Diffusion of Environmental Innovations: Theses from the Viewpoint of Ecological Modernisation Theory. In: Global Environmental Change 18: 360-367

IPCC – Intergovernmental Panel on Climate Change (2007) Climate Change 2007: Synthesis Report. Internet: http://www.ipcc.ch/pdf/assessment-report/ar4/syr/ar4_syr.pdf, last accessed on 21.04.2010

MEA – Millennium Ecosystem Assessment (2005) Ecosystems and Human Well-being: Synthesis. Island Press, Washington

Pepper D (1996) Modern Environmentalism – An Introduction. Routledge, London

Ranganathan J, Munasinghe M, Irwin F (2008) (eds) Policies For Sustainable Governance of Global Ecosystem Services. Edwarg Elgar Publishing Ltd, Cheltenham

Taylor PJ, Buttel FH (1992) How do we Know we have Global Environmental Problems? Science and the Globalization of Environmental Discourse. In: Geoforum 23(3): 405-416

WCED – World Commission on Environment and Development (1987) Our Common Future. Oxford University Press, Oxford

Part I - Energy Efficiency and Innovation

Vincent Onyango

Department of Environmental Planning, Brandenburg University of Technology (BTU), Cottbus, Germany

The world is focused on the urgent need to use energy efficiently, produce it from more sustainable sources and reduce the adverse impacts of energy generation and use. Within this context, Part I of this volume presents various research results and opinions on how energy efficiency in various areas of application can be innovatively achieved. Chapter 2 shows the potential of biomass pellets for energy generation in Brazil. It presents the polluting and combustion behaviour of several blends of residual biomass, the goal being to search for the most efficient biomass mixture. Chapter 3 shows how rice husks can be used to produce energy in India. It argues that instead of the rice husks being dumped as waste, fermenting and producing global warming methane, the rice husks may instead be converted into electricity and thermal energy at relatively high efficiencies. In Chapter 4, case studies from 3 countries are used to show how the energy efficiency of central water supply systems can be increased through energy efficient ways of transporting water to consumers. These are reduction of water losses, optimised operational strategies, energy recovery within the distribution system and use of renewable energy for the water pumps. It concludes that the scarcer energy as well as water resources become, the more often these concepts will find an application. In Chapter 5, it is concluded that innovative use of technology in local reclamation of wastewater offers a cost effective alternative for improving the efficiency of water-use in agriculture. In this chapter, opportunities and potentials for improved energy efficiency within wastewater treatment are identified. In Chapter 6, the Brazilian energy sector is reviewed and a hypothetical case study with three configurations of solar modules is used to highlight the environmental, technical and economic aspects of grid-connected solar photovoltaics.

Chapters on the Kyoto Protocol's Clean Development Mechanism (CDM) follow those on energy efficiency and technological innovation, albeit within energy-related aspects. In Chapter 7, CDM application in wind power projects in India is presented. It is stated that the decline in registration of CDM wind projects has resulted in the creation of a Voluntary Emission Reduction (VER) market in India. This presents a realistic option for investors to avail themselves of additional benefits, thus encouraging the development of new wind power parks. Chapter 8 discusses CDM projects worldwide and then focuses in detail on a Brazilian case study. It highlights inequitable distribution of CDM projects and outlines the theoretical conception of the Flexible Mechanisms and critiques criteria such as additionality, sustainability and distribution of CDM projects.

Chapter 9 moves away from CDM and presents the adverse environmental impacts of jeans laundries in Brazil. Aspects of water consumption and pollution are discussed and the potential for energy efficiency in jeans laundries analysed. The chapter concludes that there is a market for producing high quality and ecologically friendly textiles; by establishing a clear link between economic benefits and environmental improvements.

Discussions on the future of sustainable energy in Thailand and China are also presented. In Chapter 10, Thailand's energy sector is reviewed in terms of future energy alternatives and sustainability. It proposes that for Thailand to have a successful sustainable energy programme, it is important to have a holistic view of the energy sector. This should focus on securing and stabilizing the energy situation; reducing dependence on imported oils; reducing inefficient logistics and lack of energy-saving behaviour among consumers; and, reducing the energy consumption, enhancing energy efficiency and the use of more alternative energy. Chapter 11 analyses strategies for sustainable energy in China and highlights the key challenges i.e. insufficient energy supply, environmental pollution and rural energy shortage. It also explores China's main problems in energy structure, energy consumption efficiency, energy policy, energy market, technology and energy saving awareness. The study proposes five strategies for addressing China's energy challenges. Part I concludes with Chapter 12, which argues for greater focus on the concept of Ecosystem Services when setting targets for mitigating Climate Change. It is herein argued that since emissions from fossil fuels are likely to continue; and since Kyoto Protocol mechanisms are currently inadequate; that Ecosystem Services (ES) can play a vital role in fighting climate change. However, the challenge remains, how can Ecosystem Services be market-based whilst avoiding the free rider problem and 'the tragedy of the commons' involved in the consumption of public goods.

2 Comparative Analysis of Brazilian Residual Biomass for Pellet Production

Bruna Missagia[1], Maurício Ferreira Silva Corrêa[2], Islam Ahmed[3], Hans-Joachim Krautz[1] and Peter Ay[4]

1 Chair of Power Plant Technology, Brandenburg University of Technology (BTU), Cottbus, Germany
2 Department of Technology and Innovation Management, Brandenburg University of Technology (BTU), Cottbus, Germany
3 Department of Environmental and Resource Management, Brandenburg University of Technology (BTU), Cottbus, Germany
4 Chair of Minerals Processing, Brandenburg University of Technology (BTU), Cottbus, Germany

2.1 Introduction

Brazil is an important producer and the largest exporter of sugar, ethanol, coffee, orange juice, and tobacco. The country's availability of land, water and labour has allowed for increased production and exports. Continuing the trade expansion and diversification of markets and products remain at the core of Brazil's agricultural growth strategy (Valdez et al. 2006). The increase in crops generates a biomass residue surplus. It is known that approximately 30% of the sugar cane production is bagasse (Rosillo-Calle et al. 2007) and 22% of rice is constituted of husks (Eriksson and Prior 1990). This residual biomass can be transformed into a valuable fuel, becoming an important local energy source. There are several conversion technologies for biomass, based on the type, available residues and the market demand. Pressing of residues increases storage and transport efficiency. Pellets, briquettes, or any other pressed form can be used as a fuel. Recent research shows different combustion technologies for biomass: gasification, pyrolysis and combined heat and power (Rosillo-Calle et al. 2007).

In Germany, Austria and Scandinavian countries, the compressed biomass, mostly wood pellets, is widely used for household heating. Moreover, the conversion of pellets into electricity has also been studied in decentralized power plants (Thek and Obernberger 2002). In Brazil, where heating is not necessary due to a tropical climate, the demanded product of biomass conversion is electricity. Here hydropower accounts for approximately 77% of the energy supply (Ministério de Minas e Energia 2008). Nevertheless, it has been documented that Brazil's annual production of sugar cane bagasse can supply inhabitants with as much electricity as Brazil's largest hydropower plant Itaipú (Ministério de Minas e Energia 2008). Other kinds of residue, like wood saw dust and coffee husks, also have a great potential, either for covering the local energy demand or for export in form of pellets.

The aim of this work is to study and evaluate the implementation of pellet production using residues like rice husks and sugar cane bagasse for energy generation in Brazil. Some properties of residual biomass were analysed at the Brandenburg University of Technology (BTU) in Cottbus, Germany. The first parameters investigated were moisture, ash content, calorific value, and ash melting point. The analysis helped the authors to determine optimal pellet mixtures of different raw biomasses with their best characteristics. Besides, the resulting blends were also based on the geographical and agricultural aspects of the crops. The conversion of biomass into pellets and pellets into energy could be applied for Brazilian biomass. This potential should foster research towards new power plant technologies for decentralized energy generation. Furthermore, the socio-economic feasibility of pellet production should be taken into consideration.

2.2 Situation Description

In Brazil, agricultural production is located within the humid and warm semitropical latitudes of the South and Centre-West regions (Figure 2.1). The urban centres, as well as the good access to the main ports, facilitate the access to markets for producers (Schnepf et al. 2001). The Federal State of Rio Grande do Sul is the core of irrigated crop acreage and produces an important share of Brazil's rice. The Federal State of Minas Gerais is the leading producer of coffee. The main sugar cane production is located on the Federal State of São Paulo, which has modern industrial technology and the lowest production costs. Besides that, sugar cane crops are closer to consumers, to research centres, and to the ethanol machinery sector. During the last five years, ethanol production has been growing and exports increasing. According to the Instituto Brasileiro de Geografia e Estatística, the yield of 2007 was of approximately 550 million tonnes of sugar cane, of which around half was used for ethanol production (15.3 billion of litres). In 2007, there were 70,000 farmers planting sugar cane all over Brazil and 393 ethanol plants, distributed mainly to the Centre-south region (IICA 2007).

The fast-growing tree species *Eucalyptus sp.*, originally an Australian plant, occurs all over Brazil's geographical regions (Müller et al. 2005). Most of the post-lignite mining areas are reforested with this tree species. Opposing the current environmental policy in Brazil, areas where native vegetation was illegally exploited have been recovered with *Eucalyptus sp.* monoculture (Müller et al. 2005). *Eucalyptus sp.* wood is mostly employed in the paper industry, as charcoal in the pig iron furnaces and broadly used for carpentry.

Fig. 2.1. Map of Brazil showing the regions Minas Gerais, Sao Paulo and Rio Grande do Sul which are respectively leading coffee, sugar cane and rice production (Source: www.limasolucoes.com.br/images/mapaBrasil.gif)

2.3 Materials and Methods

Four types of Brazilian biomass - rice and coffee husks, sugar cane bagasse and sawdust from *Eucalyptus sp.* wood - were investigated. The residues were collected in the Federal State of Minas Gerais, where the Federal University of Viçosa, a partner university, is located. The coffee husks were from a large-scale farm located in the region called Zona da Mata. Rice husks and sugar cane bagasse were also collected in the same region, although from small-scale agriculture. The local furniture and carpentry industry uses mostly *Eucalyptus sp.* wood, producing a high quantity of sawdust, which was also used in the experiments. The research consisted of three steps:

- Collection, drying and transporting of samples
- Analysis of biomass properties
- Pelleting

During the months of May and June, the residues were collected, stored and dried in order to decrease moisture content and avoid decomposition. Thereafter, the samples were packed and transported to Germany with a moisture content value of approximately 13%. The analysis of the transported material was carried out in August at the BTU Cottbus. This investigation covered some chemical-physical aspects, such as: moisture content, ash content, heating value and ash melting point. These preliminary results are important to characterize the efficiency of the pellets as a fuel. Although the elementary analysis and the emission analysis of CO_2, SO_2, NOx and dust are not included here, further investigations are planned.

Thereafter, the agglomeration properties of the residues have been investigated by pellet formation. The pelleting process was performed with the Laborkompaktor Bepex L 200 / 50 G + K compressor producing approximately 20 kg of pellets per hour. This was carried out after crushing and moistening (17.5%) the material.

The initial task was to verify the feasibility of converting the above mentioned residues into pellets.

2.4 Results and Discussion

The results presented in this paper are part of an extensive research process, analyzing the viability of pelleting Brazilian biomass. Since some experiments are still in process, we described the preliminary properties of the residues. The water content analysis of the studied biomass was used to determine the processing feasibility of the material. After the harvest, the biomass moisture varied from 14 to 16%. Such high moisture content can cause the decomposition of the material and increase the transport costs. Hence, reducing the water content of the biomass was a necessary step before pelleting. In Brazil, drying the residues was done with minimum costs, due to the availability of space and workforce. However, processing biomass with high moisture could be a time, energy and money consuming activity. The biomass was exposed to air and constantly revolved for approximately six weeks during the dry season. The material could be then transported with a moisture value of maximum 13%. Figure 2.2 shows the moisture content for different types of residues. Coffee husks and saw wood had satisfactory moisture values after the drying period. Sugar cane bagasse presented the lowest value despite its high juice content. Considering that bagasse and rice husks presented moisture content varying from 7 and 9% respectively, this biomass would need a shorter drying period.

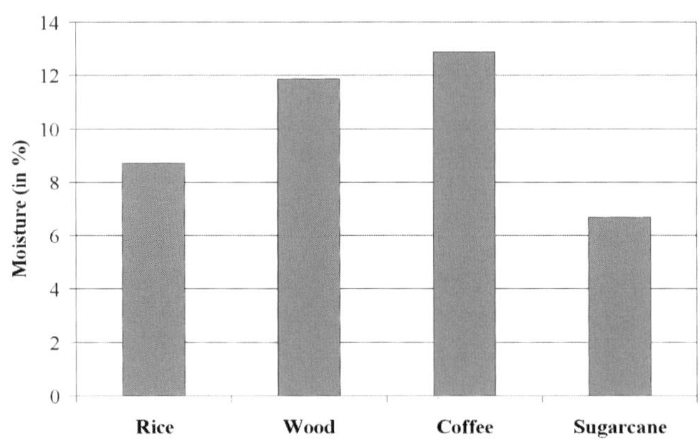

Fig. 2.2. Moisture content for different types of residues

The percentage of ash formed by the combustion process related to the total water free weight of the used material and is a relevant parameter for determining the pellet mixtures. As shown in Figure 2.3, rice husks presented high ash content. This hinders the economic feasibility of the fuel, due to the high costs of removing and transporting the ashes. Nevertheless, the development of a blend using lower quantities of this material could be feasible.

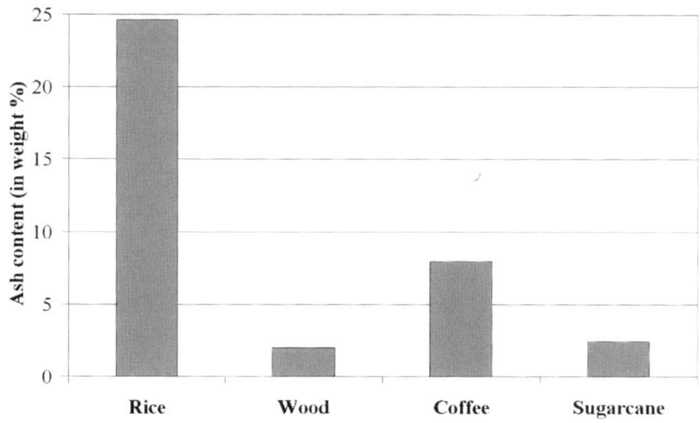

Fig. 2.3. Ash content (water free) for different types of residues

The lower heating value shown in Figure 2.4 was used to define how much energy is generated per amount of dried biomass. Rice husks presented the lowest heating value. This was due not only to its high ash content (Figure 2.3), but also due to its low quantity of elementary carbon (36.5%) and hydrogen (6.3%) compared to the other biomass. In contrast, *Eucalyptus sp.* wood presented the best heating value. This was due to its low ash content (Figure 2.3) and high quantity of elementary carbon (46.9%) and hydrogen (8.1%) in water free conditions.

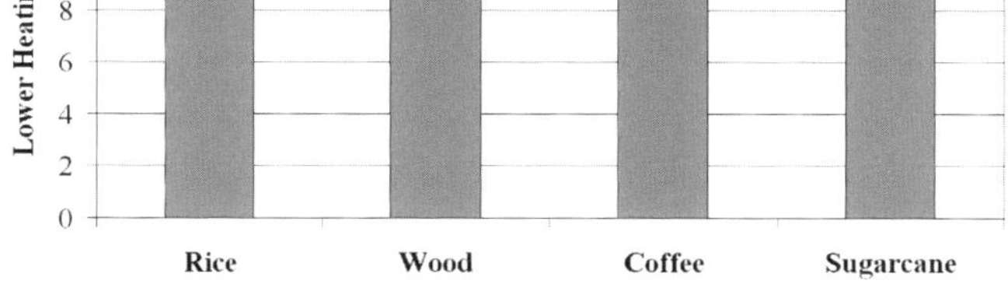

Fig. 2.4. Lower heating value for different types of residues

The ash melting point has a direct effect on the slag formation. Furthermore, the melting of ashes at low temperatures may cause corrosion in the furnaces. As shown in Figure 2.5, rice husks have a comparably low ash melting point. This allied to its high ash content limited the use of this residue in the biomass mixtures.

On the other hand, sugar cane bagasse, sawdust and coffee husks presented satisfactory ash melting points. This enables the use of these biomass types as main components in the pellet mixtures (Table 2.1).

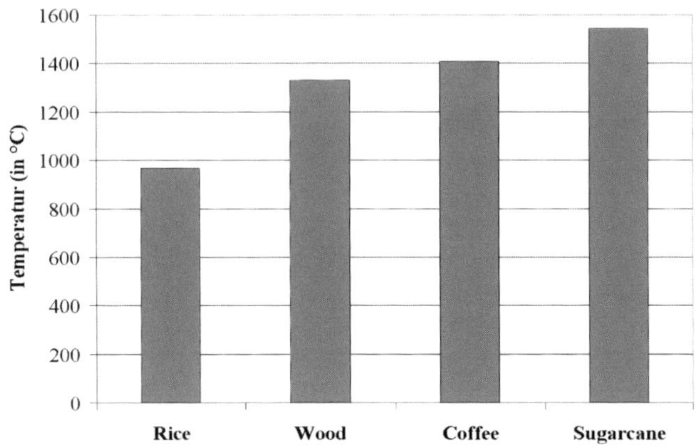

Fig. 2.5. Ash melting point

The broad geographical occurrence of *Eucalyptus sp.* and its outstanding properties would allow this species to be used as main component in the pellet mix. However, its poor agglomeration characteristics limited the use of sawdust in the mixtures to a maximum of 40%. Moreover, rice husks could not be compressed at all due to the limitations of the available devices and due to its unsatisfactory ash content and melting point.

Table 2.1. Brazilian pellet biomass mixtures

Material	Blend 1	Blend 2	Blend 3	Blend 4	Blend 5
Sugar cane	80%	60%	-	-	50%
Coffee husks	-	-	80%	60%	50%
Eucalyptus sp. saw dust	20%	40%	20%	40%	-
Rice husks	-	-	-	-	-

Sugar cane bagasse can be used as main component in the pellet blends due to its outstanding ash melting point and satisfactory heating value, however the location of the crops should be taken into consideration. Mostly, sugar cane grows near to coffee plantations and to *Eucalyptus sp.* trees, but not to rice. Furthermore, sugar cane bagasse and coffee husks have compatible physical-chemical properties. This allows the production of a 50/50% coffee-sugar blend pellet with suitable physical properties and crop logistics.

2.5 Conclusions

Although the resulting pellets presented technical and physical- chemical limitations, improvement of both processing and physical properties is possible. For example, the percentage of *Eucalyptus sp.* sawdust weight could be increased in the pellet blends using an industrial scale machine. However, conversion of residues into pellets as well possible utilisation methods are also dependent on the purpose for using the mentioned goods. Sugar cane bagasse pellets combined with the application of new technologies for its combustion in decentralized energy systems could be one alternative. On the other hand, unprocessed bagasse could be efficiently used in a combined system for heating and power generation. Considering the increasing production of sugar cane, another option is the export of surplus pellets. All the alternatives mentioned could be applied, supporting local economies by generating jobs and opening new markets. Nevertheless, it is up to the society to accept the viable technologies, adapting them to the existing socio-economic and environmental conditions. These are issues to be further investigated in socio-economic feasibility studies.

References

EPE – Empresa de Pesquisa Energética (2007) Balanço Energético Nacional 2007: Ano Base 2006, Rio de Janeiro

Eriksson S, Prior M (1990) The briquetting of agricultural wastes for fuel. Food and Agriculture Organization of the United Nations, Rome, Italy. Internet: http://www.fao.org/docrep/T0275E/T0275E08.htm, last accessed on 21.04.2010

IICA – Instituto Interamericano de Cooperação para a Agricultura (2008) Situação e Perspectivas da Agricultura no Brazil 2007: Inclui a Linha do Tempo. Internet: http://www.iica.org.br/Docs/Publicacoes/Agronegocio/Perspectivas_2007.pdf, last accessed on 21.04.2010

Ministério de Minas e Energia (2008) Resenha Energética Brasileira 2007. Internet: http://www.mme.gov.br/mme/menu/todas_publicacoes.html, last accessed on 21.04.2010

Müller MD, Tsukamoto AA, doVale RS, Couto L (2005) Biomass Yield and Energetic Content in Agroforestry Systems with Eucalyptus in Vazante-MG. Biomassa e Energia 2:125-132

Rosillo-Calle F, de Groot P, Hemstock SL, Woods J (eds) (2007) The Biomass Assessment Handbook - Bioenergy for a Sustainable Environment. Earthscan, London

Schnepf D, Dohlman E and Bolling C (2001) Agriculture in Brazil and Argentina: Developments and Prospects for Major Field Crops. Market and Trade Economics Division, Economic Research Service, U.S. Department of Agriculture. Internet: http://www.ers.usda.gov/Publications/WRS013/, last accessed on 21.04.2010

Thek G, Obernberger I (2002) Wood pellet production costs under Austrian and in comparison to Swedish framework conditions. In: Swedish Bioenergy Association(ed) Proceedings of the 1st World Conference on Pellets. Stockolm, Sweden, pp 123-128

Valdez C, Lopes IV, Lopes MR, Oliveira MS, Bogado PR (2006) Factors Affecting Brazilian Growth or Are There Limits to Future Growth of Agriculture in Brazil?" Getulio

Vargas Foundation, Rio de Janeiro. Internet: http://www.ers.usda.gov/AmberWaves/November06/, last accessed on 21.04.2010
Van Loo S, Koppeja.n J (eds) (2008) The handbook of biomass combustion and co-firing. Earthscan, London

3 Bioenergy Production: Special Emphasis on Rice Husks Usage in India

Satyanarayana Narra

Chair of Mineral Processing, Brandenburg University of Technology (BTU), Cottbus, Germany

3.1 Introduction

Rice is a staple food crop. Its annual production in India and the world is about 90 and 400 Million Tons (MT) respectively. Rice is a major cereal in India accounting for about 40% of food grain production and over 30% of its cropped area. India's share in world rice production is about 22% (Baruah and Jain 1998).

Rice is the edible form of paddy and in the process of conversion from paddy, rice husk and rice bran are generated as by-products. The rice husk is generally used as a fuel the form of bricks, furfural and many others. The use of husk in industries involves handling and transportation. Rice husk has a very low bulk density (112-144 kg/m^{-3}), which increases the handling and transportation costs. In the past, rice husk was mostly dumped as waste causing a waste disposal problem for the mills (Beagle 1981). Also, when rice husk is fermented by microorganisms, methane is emitted contributing to global warming problem (Bhattacharya et al. 1999). Rice husk is a fine and light particle and can cause breathing problems (Beagle 1981). Hence, rice mill owners must find the proper way to deal with this waste.

The onsite usage of rice husk would reduce the handling and transportation costs. Technology for the conversion of rice husk into electricity and thermal energy is available at relatively high efficiencies. Under the best operating conditions, an efficiency of up to 65% can be achieved. The usage of rice husk would also reduce the greenhouse gas emissions as rice husk is considered as carbon neutral fuel. The CO_2 released is much less as compared to the amount of CO_2 sequestrated during the growth of the rice. Thus, the net amount of CO_2 added to the atmosphere during energy production through the use of rice husk over the entire life cycle is nearly zero (Mann and Spath 1997; Hall and Scrase 1998).

The availability of rice husk depends on the paddy production. The availability of this material is only 7 months (June to December) in a year. Total energy potential would depend upon the calorific value (12.1-15.2 MJ/kg) (Beagle 1981). The potential of rice husk depends on the quality (different varieties of rice husk) and quantity available. Variations in rice husk availability are dependent on the geographical distribution, seasonal distribution and also on the capacity of rice mills. The basic idea of rice husk as an energy source relates to its thermo-chemical conversion. Gasification of rice husk to produce a gas has a high potential in India. The produced gas can be used to generate electricity (15% efficiency) using an internal combustion engines. Another usage of rice husk would be the generation of thermal energy (55% efficiency). However it is expected that the efficiencies of over 40% could be achieved for electricity generation through rice husk gasification. Cogeneration of electrical and thermal energy using rice husk may be the best option for rice processing industries. Cogeneration has been practiced in India especially in rice mills of higher capacities (>120 t/hr).

In section 3.2 a case study of a Clean Development Mechanism (CDM) project based on rice husks is presented. In section 3.3 the results of the case study are analysed and discussed. The case study compares pre-project and post-project scenarios. The emission reductions achieved by the project described in the case study were about 14,744 tonnes of CO_2 equivalent. The project was successfully registered as a CDM project in year 2006 with a 10 year (2001-2011) crediting period. In section 3.4 it is concluded that rice husk has a high potential for use as a feedstock for electricity production. It performs better than fossil fuels in terms of environmental emissions and may help mitigate climate change and limit dependence on fossil fuels.

3.2 Case study: Rice-husk Based Cogeneration Clean Development Mechanism Project

This case study describes a project by Shree Bhawani Paper Mills Limited (SBPML). In this case study the usage of rice husks will be explained and thoroughly researched. The purpose of the project is to supply electrical and thermal energy to the paper mill. Paper manufacturing is a continuous process requiring both thermal and electrical energy for the drying of paper and running the dryers respectively. The purpose of the project activity is to have Combined Heat and Power (CHP) generation to meet the energy requirements and improve the overall energy efficiency of the paper mill and reduce greenhouse gas emissions.

3.2.1 Pre-project Scenario

The paper mills' thermal energy requirement was supplied with the rice husk fixed boilers and the electrical demand with Diesel Generators (DG). A maximum power of 2.4 MW was required to run the paper mill operations. The power requirement was fulfilled by running 3 DG continuously while 2 DG were kept in stand-by. In total 5 DG each with 1000 kVA were used to run the paper mill. The rice husk was procured exclusively from rice shellers operating in the Rae Bareli district and the potential of rice husk from farmers practising manual de-husking was not realized.

3.2.2 Post-project Scenario

The proposed cogeneration plant accomplishes both the thermal and electrical energy requirements of the paper mill. The cogeneration plant displaces DG, which reduces greenhouse gas (GHG) emissions. The only fuel used in the project activity was rice husk. The total CHP output is utilized by the paper mill. The usage of carbon neutral rice husk results in GHG reduction compared to the DG sets. The project produced 3 MW which is more then the demand (2.4 MW) of the paper mill. About 0.4 MW has been utilized by the power plant auxiliaries. There was no change in the process of thermal energy. All the 5 DG sets were kept as stand-by. Over a period of time the number of rice shelling units (Allahabad, Sultanpur and Pratapgarh) has increased in the region indicating a higher availability of rice husk (Table 3.1).

Table 3.1. The summary of Paddy crop production in tonnes district wise

Year / District	Rae Bareli	Allahabad	Sultanpur	Pratapgarh
1997-1998	240,099	264,382	334,187	228,671
1998-1999	240,025	334,437	317,796	174,882
1999-2000	252,465	431,418	340,777	228,834
Average	244,196	343,412	330,920	210,795
Rice husk (0.25%) of the Paddy	61,049	85,853	82,730	52,699

The total rice husk requirement is around 34,000 tonnes per annum in the post project scenario. Around 29,000 tonnes were collected from the district's rice shellers and the remaining 5,000 tonnes were collected from the farmers practicing manual de-husking. The rice husk collected from various districts was analyzed for different elements which could play a major role in the usage of rice husk.

Table 3.2 gives information about the elements present in rice husk which play important role in GHG emissions (carbon, sulphur and nitrogen). It can be observed that the rice husk has very low concentration of nitrogen and sulphur. The presence of carbon in rice husk was about 38%.

The project considers the sustainable development indicators:

- Social well being: removal of social disparity and improvement in the quality of life of people;
- Economic well being: reduction in total energy consumption due to the increased efficiency achieved with CHP;
- Environmental well being: sustainable usage of natural resources, reduction in GHG ; and
- Technological well being: environmentally safe technology.

Table 3.2. Components analysis of rice husk sample (source: Mahajan and Mishra 1992; Grover 1989)

Parameter	Proportion (%)
Carbon	38.1
Hydrogen	4.7
Oxygen	29.3
Nitrogen	1.5
Sulphur	0.1
Moisture	8.9
Ash	17.4
Volatile matter	60.6
Fixed Carbon	19.9

3.2.3 Methodology

The methodology 'AMS-I.D. – Renewable electricity generation for a grid' was applied. The methodology is approved by the United Nations Framework Convention on Climate Change for the small scale 'Clean Development Mechanism' projects (UN 2010). This category comprises renewable energy technologies that supply electricity to an electricity distribution system that is or would have been supplied by at least one fossil fuel or non-renewable biomass-fired generating unit. Biomass based CHP systems supplying electricity to a grid are included in this category. For CHP systems to qualify, the energy output should not exceed 45 $MW_{thermal}$ energy equivalents. The development is a rice husk based CHP project for on-site use only. The project clearly qualifies the above category as only 38.44 $MW_{thermal}$ energy is produced:

$$\text{Boiler Capacity} = 24\ \text{tph} = \frac{24*1000kg}{3600s} = 6.67\frac{kg}{s} \quad (3.1)$$

Energy of steam = 3300 kJ/kg = 3.3 MJ/kg (at 45 kg cm^{-2} pressure and 440°C temperature) (3.2)

Energy of water at 100 °C = 418 kJ/kg = 0.418 MJ/kg (3.3)

$$\text{Boiler rating} = 6.67\frac{kg}{s}*(3.3-0.418)\frac{MJ}{kg} = 19.22MW_{thermal} \quad (3.4)$$

$$\text{2 Boilers were used} = 2*19.22MW_{thermal} = 38.44MW_{thermal} \quad (3.5)$$

3.2.4 Baseline Emissions

For a system where all generators use exclusively fuel oil and/or diesel fuel, the baseline is the annual kWh generated by the renewable unit multiplied by an emission coefficient for a modern diesel generating unit of the relevant capacity operating at optimal load. Table 3.3 gives the emission coefficient values depending on the load factors. The project activity has a load factor greater then 200 kW, therefore the emission factor of 0.8 kg CO_2 equivalent per kWh was selected.

Table 3.3. Emission factors for diesel generator systems (in kg CO_2 eq./kWh) for three different levels of load factor

Cases	Mini-grid, 24-hour service	Mini-grid, temporary service (4-6 hr/day); Productive applications; Water pumps	Mini-grid with storage
Load factors	25%	50%	100%
< 15 kW	2.4	1.4	1.2
>= 15 < 35 kW	1.9	1.3	1.1
>= 35 < 135 kW	1.3	1.0	1.0
>= 135 < 200 kW	0.9	0.8	0.8
> 200 kW	0.8	0.8	0.8

The baseline emissions are calculated using equation (3.6) and the CO_2 emission reductions from the project was calculated using equation (3.7).

$$Baseline\ emissions = \frac{kWh}{yr}\ generated{*}emission\ factor\,(0.8\frac{kgCO_2}{kWh}) =$$

$$= (18.43{*}10^6){*}0.8 = 14744000\ kg\ \frac{CO_2}{yr} = 14744\ t\ \frac{CO_2}{yr} \quad (3.6)$$

$$CO_2\ emission\ reductions = Baseline\ emissions\text{-}Project\ emissions =$$

$$= 14744\text{-}0 = 14744\ t\ \frac{CO_2}{yr} \quad (3.7)$$

3.2.5 Project Boundary

The project boundary extends from the point of rice husk storage to the point of electricity supply to the paper mill and covers rice husk storage, boilers, steam turbine generators and all other accessory equipments (see Fig. 3.1).

3.3 Results and Discussions

There was no policy existent in the state of Uttar Pradesh (UP) for the promotion of renewable energy source based power generation at the commencement of the project in year 2001. Due to this lack the paper industry suffered from the implementation of emission reducing technologies. At the time of the project activity, 71 paper mills were operating in the state of UP. 94% of the power required for the paper mills was provided through the state grid or from captive diesel generator sets producing high GHG emissions. There were hardly any rice husk based cogeneration units in the state of UP in year 2001. This project activity is first of its kind in the state of UP using only rice husk as a fuel. Thus the project clearly demonstrates an opportunity to introduce the practice and also reduce GHG emissions.

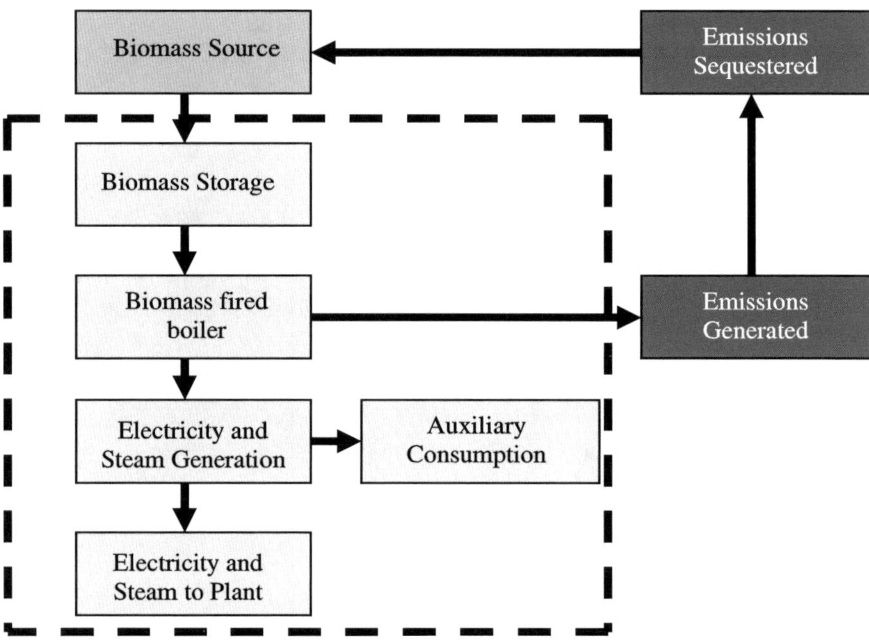

Fig. 3.1. Project boundary represented by the dashed line

The project activity has replaced the fossil fuel consuming diesel generators with carbon neutral rice husk to generate power. The CO_2 emitted by the project is from biomass combustion and hence, being part of the global carbon cycle, does not contribute to global warming. This is a distinct advantage of biomass-based energy production.

SO_2 emissions of the project were less then the emissions from coal and oil power plants, which is due to the very low presence of sulphur in rice husk. Similarly NOx emissions were also less compared to coal and oil power plants. This is to be anticipated as combustion temperatures are lower than 900 ºC implying that all the NOx generated will only be from the N-content in the rice husk and not from the air. It must be noted here that the rice husk power plant performs better than conventional electricity production even though there are NOx and SO_2 removal equipment (bio-filters) installed in the latter. Both these emissions contribute to acidification and in addition, NOx contributes to photochemical ozone formation and nutrient enrichment. Thus, the electricity production from rice husk is better than the conventional electricity production on these counts.

Total Suspended Particulates (TSP) from rice husk energy is quite large when compared to conventional electricity production. Dust emissions from rice husk power plant are higher than coal and gas power plants, but slightly less than oil power plants (Chungsangunsit et al. 2005). It is known from previous research that rice husk combustion produces significant amounts of particulate matter (Chungsangunsit et al. 2005). However, the rice husk power plant had a built-in multicyclone and electrostatic precipitator for dust removal. Hence the dust emissions were reduced.

The emission reductions achieved with the project were about 14,744 tonnes of CO_2 equivalent. The project was successfully registered as a CDM project in year 2006 with a 10 years (2001-2011) crediting period.

3.4 Conclusions

In India, a large portion of the electricity production is from fossil fuels causing concern for energy security as well as environmental emissions of CO_2, SO_2 and NOx. Biomass has been proposed as one of the alternative sources of energy which could offset the use of fossil fuels to a certain extent. This project, with the usage of rice husk, is especially suitable for India where one-fourth of the worlds rice is produced. The study shows that the emissions of SO_2 and NOx are lower in comparison to coal and oil-fired power generation. The emissions of CO_2 from combustion of rice husk are considered zero since they do not contribute to global warming. Overall, the study indicates that rice husk has a high potential for use as a feedstock for electricity production as it performs better than fossil fuels in terms of environmental emissions.

References

Baruah DC, Jain AK (1998) Distribution of agricultural residues in India. In: Journal of Agricultural Engineering 35(1):7-12

Beagle EC (1981) Rice husk conversion to Energy. FAO, Rome, Italy

Bhattacharya SC, Joe MA, Kandhekar ZP, Salam A, Shrestha RM (1999) Greenhouse-gas emission mitigation from the use of agricultural residues: the case of rice husk. In: Energy 24(1): 43-59

Chungsangunsit T, Gheewala SH, Patumsawad S (2005) Environmental Assessment of Electricity Production from Rice Husk: A Case Study in Thailand. In: International Energy Journal 6(1): 347-356

Grover PD (1989) Biomass: Thermo-Chemical Characteristics of Gasification. Indian Institute of Technology, New Delhi

Hall DO, Scrase JI (1998) Will biomass be the environmentally friendly fuel of the future? In: Biomass and Bioenergy 15(4): 357-367

Mahajan KC, Mishra J (1992) Energy from Paddy Husks - An Overview. In: Energy Management 16: 5-14

Mann MK, Spath PL (1997) Life cycle assessment of biomass gasification combined-cycle system. National renewable energy laboratory, USA.

UN – United Nations (2010). Indicative simplified baseline and monitoring methodologies for selected small-scale CDM project activity categories. Internet portal of the United Nations Framework Convention on Climate Change (UNFCCC). Internet: http://cdm.unfccc.int/UserManagement/FileStorage/SJI52M6QXGKFNOZABTHDYP U789EV3C, last accessed on 11.11.2010

4 Innovative Energy Concepts in the Water Supply Sector

Christine Laures

Institute for Water and River Basin Management (IWG), Water Supply Network Section, University of Karlsruhe

4.1 Introduction

The world's energy consumption is mainly dependent on the supply of fossil energy sources. In 2006, more than 80% of the world's total primary energy demand was covered by oil, coal and gas (IEA 2008). While fossil resources are a phase-out model, experts are not able to predict exactly when fossil energy resources will be exhausted. Nevertheless the effects of resource shortages are already leading to considerable rises in the cost of energy. Furthermore, topics such as political instabilities due to energy dependencies and insecurities as well as the challenges of global climate change should not be neglected. A reduction of fossil energy demand can be achieved by two means: either by the development of alternative energy resources or by an increase in energy efficiency. In the industrialised world, drinking water from a house connection is taken as granted. Most people do not think about the question where the water is coming from or how much energy is used to make the required amount of water at good quality and sufficient pressure available. In this chapter, the question of how much energy is used in central water supply systems will be discussed – by means of some selected examples – and how the energy efficiency of central water supply systems can be increased through innovative energy concepts.

4.2 Concept of a Central Water Supply System

In the year 2004, 78% of the urban and 30% of the rural world's population profited from water supply via house connection (JMP 2006). It can be assumed that a high percentage of this group was supplied via a central water supply system. Taking goal 7 and target 10 of the Millennium Development Goals (MDGs) of the United Nations ("Halve, by 2015, the proportion of people without sustainable access to safe drinking water and basic sanitation") (United Nations Millennium Declaration 2000) as well as the numerous national poverty reduction strategy papers into account, it can be further assumed that the coverage of water supply via central water supply systems will continue to rise during the forthcoming years.

The generalised concept of a central water supply system is as follows: a water source – such as groundwater or surface water – is captured and treated. Afterwards the water is transported via a main system to storage tanks. From there, it is conveyed via primary and secondary distribution pipes to the customers. Usually, the water source is situated at a lower elevation than the end consumer. Therefore, energy is needed to pump the water from lower to higher situated geographical points. At the house connection level, a pressure of at least 1.5 bar (15 m water column) is recommended in Germany (DVGW 2004). Additionally, energy is needed for the treatment of the water. The energy intensity of the treatment depends mainly on the method used. Within this chapter, only the energy demand of the water transport will be discussed.

4.3 How Much Energy is Used in the Water Supply Sector – Some Selected Examples

It is difficult to find literature on the overall energy consumption of water transport in central water supply systems. It seems that this question has been more or less neglected in scientific literature (Zhou and Tol 2004). In general it can be said that four factors influence the energy intensity of water distribution systems. These are (1) the vertical elevation difference between the source and the consumer; (2) the horizontal distance between the source and the consumer in combination with the physical properties of the system (wall roughness, pipe diameters, pipe bending, etc.); (3) the quantity that is consumed per capita, and; (4) the efficiency of the transport system (operational strategy, water losses, etc). The installed power needed by a water supply system can be calculated as follows:

$$P = \eta * \rho * g * H_f * Q \tag{4.1}$$

Where

P	=	Power	(W)	g	=	Gravity constant	(m/s²)
η	=	Efficiency	(-)	Q	=	Discharge	(m³/s)
ρ	=	Density	(kg/m³)	H_f	=	Elevation	(m)

The elevation H_f consists of the vertical elevation distance and the frictional head losses during the transport. In general it can be said that lifting water in the vertical direction is much more energy intense than in the horizontal direction. A vertical lift of 100 m is approximately as energy intense as a horizontal transport of 100 km (Zhou and Tol 2004). The influence of the water quantity is linear.

According to information provided by pump manufacturers, about 30% of the industrial electricity demand within the European Union is used for pumping systems (includes all kind of industrial systems) (Broderson 2006). This equals to approximately 9% of European Union's overall energy consumption. In the United

States, the more than 60,000 water systems and 15,000 wastewater systems are among the country's largest energy consumers, using about 75 billion kWh/a nationally. This makes up about 3% of the annual U.S. electricity consumption (EPRI 1999). To give a further impression of exactly how energy intense the transport in central water supply systems can be, some selected examples will be given in the following subsections. Although this will not provide an overall picture of the energy situation, potentials for improvement possibilities will become clear.

4.3.1 Lake Constance Water Supply System (BWV)

One example of an energy intense water supply system is the Lake Constance system (Bodenseewasserversorgung, BWV) in the South-West of Germany. The long distance water supply system was constructed back in the 1950s, since the region was suffering from water shortages due to karst undergrounds. Nowadays, the system supplies approximately four million customers in about 180 member communities (BWV 2006). The primary network consists of around 1,700 km of pipes. The system source is Lake Constance, from which water is abstracted at a depth of 60 m. To transport the average quantity of 4.2 m^3/s to all member communities, as well as to lift the water, in some cases nearly 400 m, high amounts of energy are needed. In 2006, 164 GWh/a were consumed by the long distance system (BWV 2006). To compare this with the average annual electricity consumption of a German single household – which amounts 2,000 kWh/a (EnergieAgentur.NRW 2006) – a total of 82,000 single households could cover their energy demand with this amount of energy. The responsibility of the BWV ends at a transfer point at the communities. To transport the water from there to the customers, the communities often have to make use of additional energy. For example within the city of Stuttgart, elevation differences are up to 320 m, making 58 independent pressure zones and 50 additional pumping stations necessary (Kober 2008).

4.3.2 Mexico City Metropolitan Area Water Supply (MCMA)

The central water supply system of Mexico City Metropolitan Area supplies, at present, around 66 m^3/s to about 16 million customers. The primary network consists of 1,074 km of water pipes and the secondary network of 12,278 km (Tortajada 2006). About 68% of the drinking water is abstracted from 'internal sources' (mainly from the Mexico city aquifer) and 32% from 'external' distant water sources. From the external sources, 23% is taken from Cutzamala River with a transport distance of 60-154 km and 9% from the Lerma well field, which is situated at a distance of 60 km from the metropolitan area with a well depth of 50-300 m. The water from the Cutzamala River has to be pumped to a height of more than 1,000 m, requiring 102 pumping stations to reach the supply area. To realise the transport of the drinking water from the Lerma well field as well as from the Cutzamala River into the city, a pumping power of more than 800 MW was installed.

The average energy consumption amounts to about 7,000 million kWh/a, which equals the overall energy demand of the Mexican city Puebla (1.5 million inhabitants) or 3.5 million already mentioned German single household equivalents. Further Tortajada estimates that about 20% of the national electricity production is used for the water supply and waste water disposal of the Mexico City Metropolitan Area. Due to high water losses caused by leakages in the network – estimates go up to 40% – the water supply system can be described as very inefficient in terms of energy use (Tortajada 2006). If water losses would be reduced by only one percent, another 160,000 customers could be supplied while using the same amount of water and energy.

4.3.3 California State Water Project (SWP)

The California State Water Project (SWP) is another example of an energy intense long-distance water supply system. To supply approximately 60 million customers in Southern California, water is transported from the San Francisco Bay-Delta in a system which consists of $\approx$1,000 km open canals and pipelines. Although the system uses measures, such as energy recovery, the net energy consumption of the transport system amounts to approximately 5,100 GWh/a, which equates to 2-3% of the state electricity consumption (Cohen et al. 2004).

4.4 Innovative Energy Concepts in the Water Supply Sector

There are several possibilities to save energy in water supply systems. Within the following section two examples of projects of the Institute for Water and River Basin Management (IWG), Water Supply Network Section of the University of Karlsruhe that make use of several energy saving strategies, will be described.

4.4.1 Integrated Water Resources Management (IWRM) in Gunung Kidul

The Integrated Water Resources Management (IWRM) project in Gunung Kidul (Java/ Indonesia) is a research project financed by the German Federal Ministry for Education and Research (BMBF) and executed by the Forschungszentrum Karlsruhe. Several universities as well as industry partners are participating within the framework of this project. Motivation for the project is the water shortage of the Indonesian region Gunung Kidul. Although rainfalls are high (about 2,000 mm/year), water leaves the area fast via the perforated karst underground. This leads to a lack of drinking water, especially during the dry periods of the year. Within the framework of a previous project (Water Resources Management of an underground River in a Karst Area) the development and implementation of a regenerative water pumping station via the construction of an underground dam in a karst system was initiated (Figure 4.1). Within a karst cave, water is dammed up to a height of 10-15 m. The main part of the captured water is used to run an inverse operating pump (PAT, pump-as-turbine), which is coupled via a mechanic drive directly to the pumps that are lifting the water (Nestmann et al. 2008). Under full load conditions about 65 litres/second can be pumped over a 220 m distance to an elevated tank. This amount of water is sufficient to supply a population of 80,000 people with 70 litres/day. The innovative character of this approach is that the pumping station becomes independent from external energy sources, using 100% 'renewable' energy. Additionally, the use of a PAT instead of a turbine leads to reduced costs, an increased robustness and easier maintenance of the equipment.

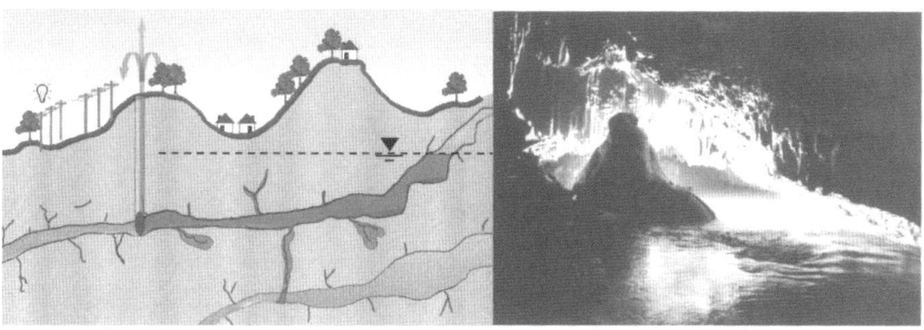

Fig. 4.1. Schematic overview of the planned retention and lifting of the cave water (left), underground water sources of the karst cave Bribin (right) (source: IWG)

Since it is not sufficient to pump the water to the surface, the project also takes care of the distribution of the drinking water within the supply area. The Water Supply Network Section is involved in this part of the project. Within the project area a distribution system already exists. The objective of the sub-project is to perform a rehabilitation planning for the existing system. The decisive factor in achieving a positive energy balance is the development of an optimised operational strategy. Pump manufacturers predict an energy saving potential for pumping systems of between 20-40% worldwide by means of optimised operational strategies (Broderson 2006). Therefore attention has to be drawn to the selection of the 'right' pumps in terms of appropriate pumping head and quantity of water. Additionally, the pumping schedules have to be well designed. To develop an optimised operational strategy, the use of a numeric model of the water supply network is of advantage. The setup of the numeric model is therefore one of the first steps during the work of the Water Supply Network Section. Further, it is planned to implement a SCADA system (Supervisory Control And Data Acquisition system) in combination with the control technology of an industrial partner. The final goal will be to develop an operational management tool, which will be able to analyze the data of the control system and the calculation results of the numeric model. The tool will provide the operator with recommendations on operational strategies, adapted to the real-time state of the system.

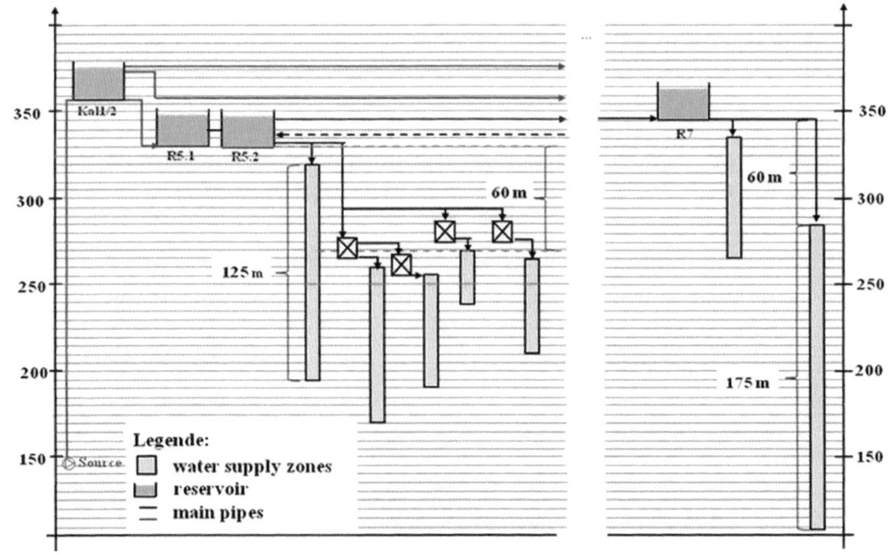

Fig. 4.2. Simplified schematic sections of the water supply system Bribin, highlighting areas with potentials of energy recovery (source: Käser 2008)

Additionally an analysis of the potential for decentralised energy recovery and the implementation of a pilot installation shall be done. Decentralised energy recovery in a water supply system is possible if the pressure within the systems becomes too high. For example, in Germany a maximum system pressure of 8 bar (80 m of water column) is recommended (DVGW 2004). If the pressure becomes higher due to elevation differences, usually pressure reduction valves (PRVs) are used to prevent damage of the system elements. The water supply system of Gunung Kidul consists of a main water transport system that transports the water to intermediate storages. From there, water flows via gravity into the numerous water distribution systems. For example, one of the pressure zones shows elevation differences of up to 235 m (compare Fig. 4.2). Thus, a considerable head might be used for energy recovery. This concept is also implemented at the Lake Constance water supply system, which led to the generation of 16.1 million kWh/a in 2006 (BWV 2006). In the case of Indonesia, the potential still has to be investigated in more detail. Special attention shall be given to the potential of installing cost efficient PATs (pumps-as-turbines).

4.4.2 Integrated Water Resources Management (IWRM) for Oases

The Integrated Water Resources Management (IRWM) for the Oases project in Algeria is another example of a water supply rehabilitation project. The project is funded by the German Federal Ministry for Economic Cooperation and Development (BMZ) and executed by the German Technical Cooperation Agency (GTZ)

GmbH. The first phase of the project took place from 2004 until 2006. The second phase started in July 2007 and will last until the end of 2009. Target of the project is the development of an integrated water resources management concept for oases in the Saharan zone on the basis of a participative process including drinking water, sanitation, irrigation, socio-economic aspects and the implementation of the concept in the Béni Abbès Oasis. The oasis has about 13,000 inhabitants (Klingel and Deuerlein 2008). A central water supply system exists, which can be described as deficient. The water is fed via four storages into the distribution system. At the moment, no pressure zones exist and a clear network structure is missing. Further, the water supply is not continuous but intermittent, which makes intermediate storage in private tanks necessary for the customers (see Fig. 4.3).

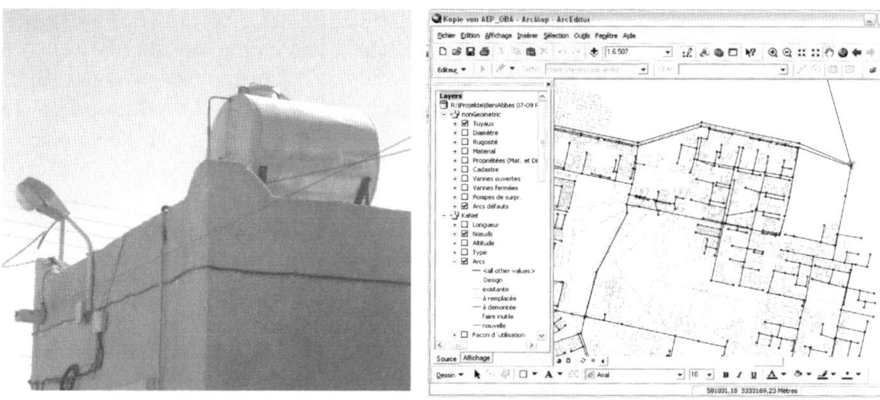

Fig. 4.3. Private tank on a roof in Béni Abbès (left) (source: photo by Deuerlein J.); overview of the GIS integrated network register of the water supply system (right)

Due to long storage times in private tanks and high temperatures, the storages should be emptied regularly which leads to a high wastage of water. No measuring devices are installed within the system, which makes estimating water losses rather difficult. Due to the current state of the system, water losses of up to 50% were estimated in the framework of the efficiency analysis. At the same time the analysis showed that sufficient water would be available to supply all inhabitants within the next 20 years with $\approx$ 80 l/hab/day (Klingel and Deuerlein 2008). The target of the drinking water module is the introduction of a sustainable and continuous water supply. This shall be realised by a holistic rehabilitation of the water supply system. A clear network structure – based on a main, primary and secondary network structure – will be introduced. Three fixed pressure zones and additional sectors that can be further subdivided will be created. Water measuring devices will be installed at important points for the supervision of the system. The operation will be improved by the set up of a GIS integrated network and defect register (see Fig. 4.3).

The working approach of the project can be described as participative. Expected achievement is an overall improvement of the water supply system. This shall finally lead to improved energy efficiency due to an optimised operation of the main system and a significant reduction of water losses. The water supply system of the Béni Abbès Oasis shows several characteristics – such as intermittent supply, capturing of water in private tanks, absence of a clear network structure, lack of measuring devices – that are typical for developing countries. The applied concept may not be described as 'innovative' in terms of energy reduction, since the relation between reduction of water losses and energy efficiency is well known. Nonetheless, this approach still offers significant potential for improvement.

4.5 Conclusions

Within this chapter the connection between energy use and water supply transport was highlighted and important measures on how energy efficiency of water distribution systems can be increased were introduced. These are: (1) reduction of water losses; (2) introduction of an optimised operational strategy; (3) the utilisation of energy recovery within the distribution system, and; (4) the utilisation of renewable energy sources for the operation of the system pumps. Several examples showed that the potential for improvement is still high. For the future, it can be assumed that these concepts will be applied more frequently, since energy as well as water resources will become scarcer.

References

Broderson S (2006) Lebenszykluskosten für Förderanlagen – Auswahlkriterien für wirtschaftliche Entscheidungen, KSB Frankenthal AG, Frankenthal, 2006

BWV – Bodenseewasserversorgung (2006) Geschäftsbericht Bodensee-Wasserversorgung. Geschäftsleitung Zweckverband Bodensee-Wasserversorgung, Stuttgart

Cohen R, Wolff G, Nelson B (2004) Energy Down the Drain – The Hidden Costs of California's Water Supply. Pacific Institute, Oakland, California, August 2004

DVGW – Deutsche Vereinigung des Gas und Wasserfaches (2004) Arbeitsblatt W 400-1, Technische Regeln Wasserverteilungsanlagen (TRW V), Teil 1: Planung, Oktober 2004

EnergieAgentur.NRW (2006) Presseinformation der EnergieAgentur.NRW: Stromverbräuche von Privathaushalten unterschiedlicher Größe, 06.04.2006

EPRI – Electric Power Research Institute (1994) Energy Audit Manual for Water/Wastewater Facilities, CEC Report CR-104300, July 1994

IEA – International Energy Agency (2008) Key World Energy Statistics, Paris, 2008

JMP – Joint Monitoring Programme (2006) Meeting the MDG Drinking Water and Sanitation Target – The Urban and Rural Challenge of the Decade, World Health Organisation/ UNICEF, 2006

Käser G (2008) Erstellung eines hydraulischen Modells des Wasserversorgungsnetzes Bribin, Diplomarbeit, Juli 2008

Klingel P, Deuerlein J (2008) Rehabilitation Strategy for Water Supply Systems in Developing Countries - Case Study IWRM Oasis Béni Abbès, Algeria, 10th Intern. Water Distribution System Analysis conference, Kruger National Park, South Africa, August 17-20, 2008

Kober E (2008) Integrierte Betrachtung von Wasserverlustmanagement und Rehabilitationsplanung, Symposium Instandhaltung von Trinkwasserund Abwasserleitungen TU Graz, 9 - 10. Juli 2008

Nestmann F, Oberle P, Ikhwan M, Singh P (2008) Bau eines Höhlenkraftwerks zur Trinkwassergewinnung auf Java, Teil 1: Gesamtkonzept zur energetischen Nutzung unterirdischer Wasserressourcen in Karstgebieten, Symposium Betonbauwerke im Untergrund – Infrastruktur für die Zukunft; 5. Symposium Baustoffe und Bauwerkserhaltung, Univ. Karlsruhe, S. 109-120, 13. März 2008

Tortajada C (2006) Water Management in MCMA, Water Resources Development, Vol. 22, No. 2, 353-376, Third World Centre for Water Management, Atizapán, Mexico, June 2006

United Nations Millennium Declaration, (18 September 2000) Resolution A/55/L.2, General Assembly, Fifty-fifth session

Zhou Y, Tol R (2004) Evaluating the costs of desalination and water transport. Working paper, December 9 2004. Internet: http://www.mi.uni-hamburg.de/fileadmin/fnu-files/publication/working-papers/DesalinationFNU41_revised.pdf, last accessed on 05.07.2010

5 Energy Conservation in Aerobic Wastewater Treatment Units

Paul Pinamang Kyei

Brandenburg University of Technology (BTU), Cottbus, Germany

5.1 Introduction

A study was conducted by the author on existing aerobic wastewater treatment units to increase their energy efficiency while improving nutrient removal performance. This chapter provides the results of an experimental design to investigate the effect of two different aeration regimes on the nutrient removal performance of the treatment units. The paper was conceptualised and deemed relevant at a time when there was so much global outcry to look out for an alternative source of energy as a mechanism for climate change adaptation.

Section 5.2 describes what the system looks like and the requirements for which it can successfully be applied. It also describes how the aerobic treatment units work. Section 5.3 highlights the material and the methodological approach employed for the study. In this section, emphasis was placed on the two different experimental set-ups. Section 5.4 presents the results for each experimental set up by determining the mean values for both influent and effluent qualities of the measured parameters, and calculating for the actual percentage removal efficiency. It also highlights the quantity of energy saved and how much this could be quantified in monetary terms. This is followed by a discussion in Section 5.5.

The chapter ends with conclusions in Section 5.6, highlighting that sound aeration control of the aeration regime promotes simultaneous nitrification and denitrification in the aeration chamber. It also concludes that there is an appreciable energy saving that equates to monetary savings.

5.2 Aerobic Wastewater Treatment Units (ATUs)

These are small-scale systems for onsite wastewater treatment and disposal designed principally for single dwellings and small community applications. They are similar to the conventional septic system in the sense that both use natural processes to treat wastewater. The difference is that the aerobic treatment system requires oxygen to aid aerobic bacterial breakdown of the organic constituents in the wastewater (NSFC 1996). The aerobic system employs biological processes for wastewater treatment. During these processes, the microbes in the wastewater feed on the organic substances and convert them to non-polluting substances. Dissolved and solid pollutants are also converted to cell mass, non-degradable material and gases such as carbon dioxide, hydrogen and methane (Lesikar 1999). According to NSFC (1996), the ATUs are very useful in environmentally sensitive areas that are less suitable for proper use of the conventional septic system. Such areas include; those with inappropriate soil conditions where the water table is too high to allow the drain field to operate effectively, areas of insufficient availability of land for septic systems and areas where high level of treatment is required by regulation.

5.2.1 How the ATUs Work

There are many types of ATU, but the most common household units use a process called suspended growth. These units have a main compartment (aeration chamber) in which air is forced and mixed with the wastewater (Figure 5.1). This creates an environment where bacteria are free-floating in the liquid and grow as they digest the solids (Lesikar 1999). Many units include a second chamber (settling chamber) where solids that the bacteria are unable to digest, settle. The two chambers are connected, so these undigested solids can be returned to the aeration chamber, either by gravity or a pump. It is this process of return and mixing that is important for effective operation.

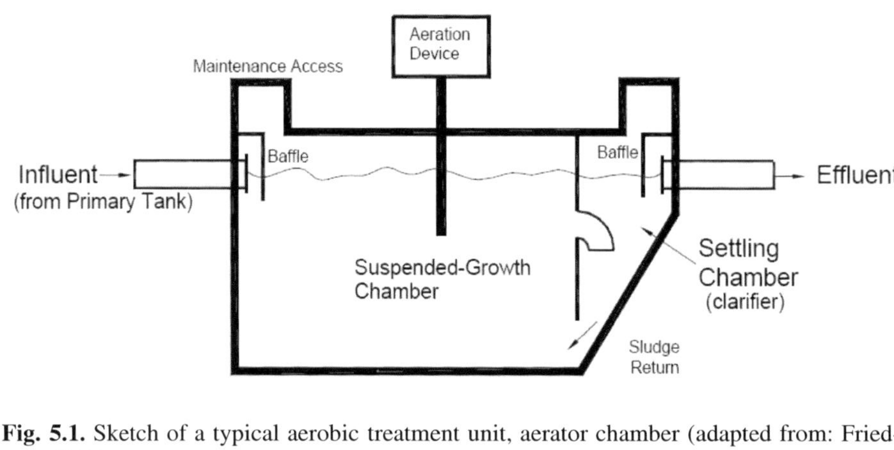

Fig. 5.1. Sketch of a typical aerobic treatment unit, aerator chamber (adapted from: Friedman 2010)

The wastewater leaving these two chambers is not ready to be returned to the environment and must receive final treatment or disinfection in the disinfection chamber. Methods for final treatment include discharge to a soil absorption field, a sand filter or an evapotranspiration bed.

5.3 Materials and Experimental Method

The BioMax C10 ATUs at the Environmental Technology Centre of Murdoch University in Perth, Western Australia, were used for this investigation. The BioMax ATU was chosen for this investigation due to its effective operation and good quality of the treated effluent. The experiment was conducted in two stages, with the first stage comprising intensive sampling and testing to collect the background data required for comparing performance of treatment units before and after modification to the aeration regime. Initially, the power of the aerator device and its operational time was recorded to be able to quantify the electrical energy consumption for that aeration period. The aerator was allowed to operate for 24 hours each day and sampling between 9.00 and 10.00 a.m. for a period of four weeks was carried out. The second stage involved the implementation of the proposed modification to the aeration unit. This involved connecting an aeration controller and timing device to the existing aeration unit to provide intermittent aeration in every other hour so that within a 24 hour period, there were only 12 hours of aeration. Intensive sampling and testing of effluent sample to collect data required for comparison of performance before and after modification of the aeration period followed this operation.

5.4 Results

The performance of the BioMax ATUs were determined for each of the experimental set-ups by determining the mean values for both influent and effluent qualities of the measured parameters, and calculating for the actual percentage removal efficiency using the formula below:

$$\left[100 - \left(\frac{Effluent}{Influent} x100\right)\right] \tag{5.1}$$

5.4.1 The BioMax ATUs Performance Characteristics before Modification

The typical operational parameters prior to the modification trial are given in the table below. These were generated by four weeks of sampling and laboratory analysis using the analytical method described in APHA (1998).

Table 5.1. Influent and effluent qualities of the BioMax ATUs before modification of the aeration regime

Parameters	Influent (mean value)	Effluent (mean value)	Removal efficiency (%)
Nitrate-N	36.3 mg/l	41.1 mg/l	-
Ammonia-N	8.54 mg/l	14.6 mg/l	-
Phosphorus	5.9 mg/l	5.4 mg/l	8.5
Suspended solids	39.2 mg/l	25.0 mg/l	36.2
BOD_5	77.2 mg/l	22.2 mg/l	71.2

Table 5.1 lists the mean results of influent and effluent qualities before modification. It indicates that phosphorus, suspended solids and BOD showed some amount of decrease in the effluent whereas there was an appreciable increase in the nitrate and ammonia concentration levels. The mean values indicated that, nitrate levels increased from 36.3 mg/l to 41.1 mg/l. Ammonia concentration also increased from 8.54 mg/l to 14.6 mg/l. However, there was some decrease in phosphorus concentration from 5.9 mg/l to 5.4 mg/l. This represents about 8.5% removal efficiency of the influent concentration. Suspended solids also decreased from 39.2 mg/l to 25.0 mg/l indicating 36.2% removal efficiency. BOD on the other hand showed a decrease from 77.2 mg/l to 22.2 mg/l. This represents 71.2% removal efficiency indicating that the most significant difference was in BOD removal.

5.4.2 The BioMax ATUs Performance Characteristics after Modification

Table 5.2 lists the mean results of influent and effluent qualities after modification. During this experiment the aeration timer was set to operate intermittently for 12 hours per day for four weeks. The modification showed some amount of changes in the effluent quality.

Table 5.2. Influent and effluent qualities of the BioMax ATUs after modification of the aeration regime

Parameters	Influent (mean value)	Effluent (mean value)	Removal efficiency (%)
Nitrate-N	36.3 mg/l	18.7 mg/l	48.5
Ammonia-N	8.5 mg/l	12.4 mg/l	-
Phosphorus	5.9 mg/l	3.6 mg/l	40.0
Suspended solids	39.2 mg/l	9.4 mg/l	76.4
BOD_5	77.2 mg/l	12.6 mg/l	83.7

During all periods of this experiment a high degree of the BOD removal was noted. The effect of BOD removal as a function of the decrease in the aeration time was evident in this experiment. Table 5.2 shows BOD removal from a mean value of 77.2 to 12.6 mg/l, indicating about 83.7% removal efficiency of the influent quality. Nitrate nitrogen concentrations showed in Table 5.2, indicates an appreciable decrease from 36.3 to 18.7 mg/l. This represents about 48.5% removal efficiency. Ammonia nitrogen (NH_3-N) concentration showed an increase in concentration from 8.5 to 12.4 mg/l after modification, whereas in the existed system, it increased to 14.6 mg/l. Due to the low concentration of nitrate and ammonia after the modification it could be assumed that some amount of nitrification and denitrification occurred. Phosphorus removal efficiency was very high. It can be inferred that a decrease in the influent concentration was from 5.9 to 3.6 mg/l indicating removal efficiency of 40% (Table 5.2). Suspended solids (SS) were found to decrease in both effluents. However, the decrease was very pronounced after the modification. Table 5.2 indicates a decrease in SS concentration from 39.2 to 9.4 mg/l. This represents about 76.4%.

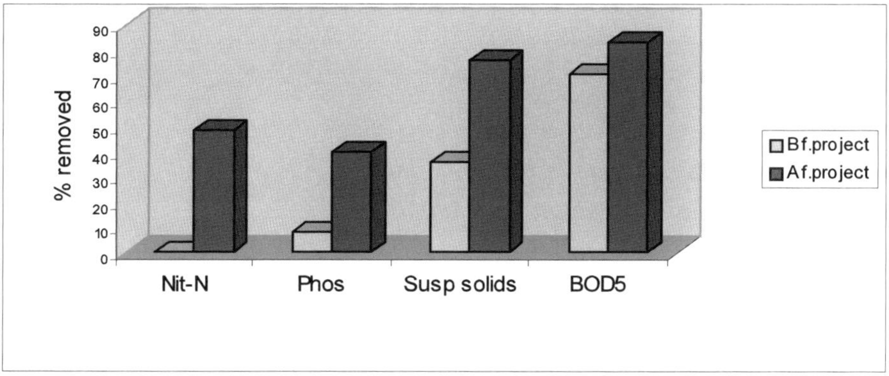

Fig. 5.2. Performance of the BioMax ATUs at the two different energy levels

On the whole, the general performance of the BioMaX ATUs (Fig. 5.2) was better after the modification in the aeration regime.

5.4.3 Argument for Energy Conservation

Figure 5.3 shows the energy distribution before and after modification of aeration period of the BioMax system. It was observed that 50% energy conservation was made when the system operated for 12 hours/day. This is also reflected in a 50% reduction in the operational cost. This means that 50% energy conservation reduced the operational cost also by 50%.

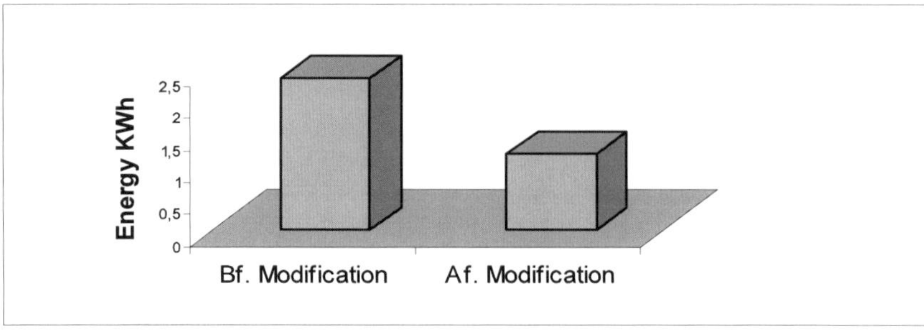

Fig. 5.3. Energy distribution in the BioMax ATUs before and after modification

5.4.4 Operational Cost of the BioMax C10 ATUs

The linear compressor of the BioMax C10 system that was used as an aeration device has the following specifications; power consumption of 0.099 kW, a rated voltage of 230 V.AC, rated airflow of 80 L/min, rated frequency of 50 Hz and a duty cycle that is continuous. Using a cost of electricity per unit of 13.94 cents. The cost of energy used per day if the compressor operates continuously for 24 hours to provide air for the suspended-growth chamber, can be calculated as:

- per day: 0.099 kW × 24 h × \$0.1394 per kW = \$0.3312 (5.2)
- per annum: \$ 0.3312 x 365 days = \$ 120.89 (5.3)

If the compressor operated for 12 hours a day (50% less energy used) then the cost of energy used can be calculated as:

- per day: 0.099 kW × 12 h × \$0.1394 per kW = \$ 0.1656 (5.4)
- per annum: \$0.1656 × 365 days = \$60.45 (5.5)

5.5 Discussion

As evident in Table 5.2, the modification experiment yielded better performance than the existed system. This could be attributed to a number of factors but the main one been the amount of air introduced into the system by the aeration regime. It could be said that perhaps the aeration period was just enough in the modification process to provide the necessary conditions for the various biological activities. Nitrogen removed was higher in the modification experiment than usual levels in the existed system. The higher percentage removal efficiency could perhaps be due to higher nitrification and denitrification rate in the aeration chamber. This is however clear, in support of a report by Wang et al. (2008), that nitrification and denitrification occur simultaneously when the dissolved oxygen (DO) in wastewater treatment plants drops in aeration tanks. It could also be due to the fact that under such an aeration regime as in the experiment, the periods between air-on and air-off was very short (1-hour), thus created post-aeration anoxic condition in the aeration chamber. According to Ouyang et al. (1999), denitrification, organic substrate oxidation and phosphorus uptake occur at the same time in an anoxic condition. Also, this is probably the reason for high phosphorus removal efficiency (40%) in the modification experiment. It is also believed that the aeration regime in the modification experiment allowed for an optimum mixing of fresh water sewage and recycled fluid from the aeration tank which according to Bathurst Regional Council (2002), is an environment that promotes the growth of phosphorus-hungry bacteria that in turn depend on the phosphorus for their food. Ouyang et al. (1999) also reported that phosphate-accumulating organisms in the aerobic chamber take up phosphorus that is released by the activated sludge in the anaerobic chamber.

However, no ammonia nitrogen removal was observed in the modification experiment (Table 5.2.). This might seem strange though it may possibly be linked to the high ammonia content of the wastewater which might have resulted in incomplete nitrification. In addition, it could be due to a low number of nitrifying bacteria probably because of the anoxic condition. This is because nitrifying bacteria require a higher amount of dissolve oxygen than the amount than exists in anoxic conditions. A research by Ouyang et al. (1999) also attributes such cases to two reasons, short sludge retention and hydraulic retention times. Not much can be argued on this line since no measurements of these parameters were made during the experiment.

There was a positive correlation between nutrient (nitrogen and phosphorus) removal efficiency, suspended solids and BOD. However, the significant differences in treatment performance characteristics in the various aeration regimes could be discussed in line with sludge retention times of the experiments. A report by Williams (1994), indicated that, variation of sludge retention time (SRT) will modify the entire process performance, including denitrification rates, sludge production and stability, mixed liquor concentration, oxygen uptake rates and the extent of nitrification. Improved efficiency of the BioMax system saved money, which means that by reducing the amount of aeration required, money is saved as less electricity is used to operate the electrical motors driving the aerators. Thus, it is observed from the experiment that simultaneous nitrification and denitrification is efficient and cost effective process for wastewater treatment.

5.6 Conclusions

It has long been thought that denitrification occurs only in the anaerobic chamber, and that a better wastewater treatment performance is usually associated with long period of aeration. From the results obtained during the two experimental studies, it was clear that the modification experimental design is feasible for removing nutrients from wastewater. This is an indication that sound aeration control of the aeration regime promotes simultaneous nitrification and denitrification in the aeration chamber. The most favourable nutrient (nitrogen and phosphorus) removal was between 1.7 and 48.5% at influent loading of 36.3 mg/L N, and between 23.7 and 40.0% at influent loading of 5.9 mg/L P. The results from the modification experiment showed significant improvement of the existed system. This means that, it is not worth operating the aerators for 24 hours per day. Instead, operating it for 12 hours per day is more efficient since there is an appreciable amount of energy saved.

To find out the performance characteristics of the BioMax ATU after cutting down its energy use, one could clearly observe that, in terms of energy conservation, the modification experiment was able to cut down the energy consumption by 50% of the original supply of 2.38 kW.h/day. Despite this energy reduction, there was also an appreciable increase in the nutrient removal performance efficiency of the BioMax ATUs. This however, achieved monetary savings of $0.1656 per day. This is a clear indication of an improvement to the existed system. Considering the differences in volume and quality of the wastewater flow into the BioMax C10 systems and the standard domestic installation type, one cannot generalise the above conclusion to be the same for all, hence the need to calculate the total flow to be able to estimate the effluent load depending on the flow rate of each size of the BioMax system. On the other hand the same experiment can be conducted for the different sizes of the BioMax Systems.

References

APHA – American Public Health Association (1998) Standard method for the examination of water and wastewater, 20th ed. APHA, American Water Works Association, and Water Pollution Control Federation, Washington, D.C.

BRC – Bathurst Regional Council (2002) Wastewater treatment works - The Process. Internet: http://www.bathurst.nsw.gov.au/environment/water-and-sewer/318-treatment-process.html, last accessed on 12.07.2010

Friedman D (2010) Alternative Septic System Design – Onsite Wastewater Treatment Methods for Difficult Sites. Internet: http://www.inspectapedia.com/septic/SepticTypes.htm, last accessed 12.07.2010

Lesikar B (1999) On-Site Wastewater Treatment Systems: Sand Filter. Texas Agricultural Extension Service, Fact Sheet Nr. L-5229, February 1999

NSFC – National Small Flows Clearinghouse (1996) Wastewater and onsite system. Internet: http://www.nesc.wvu.edu/wastewater.cfm, last accessed on 12.07.2010

Ouyang CF, Chuang SH, Su JL (1999) Nitrogen and Phosphorus Removal in a Combined Activated Sludge-RBC Process. In: Proceedings of the National Science Council, Republic of China, Part A: Physical Sciences and Engineering 23(2): 181-204

Wang J, Peng Y, Wang S, Gao Y (2008) Nitrogen removal by simultaneous nitrification and denitrification via nitrite in a sequence hybrid biological reactor. In: Chinese Journal of Chemical Engineering 16 (5): 778-784

William J (1994) Water reclamation facility, University of Florida: Controlling wastewater treatment. Internet: http://www.ufwrf.com/control1.html, last accessed on 12.07.2010

6 Technical and Economic Aspects of Grid-connected Solar Photovoltaics in Brazil

Jordi Cadilla

EC International Aid, Cooperation Officer for Infrastructures, EU Delegation in Kigali, Rwanda

6.1 Introduction

This first part of this chapter offers an overview of today's Brazilian energy sector, as well as a review of the government's development plan for the sector until 2030. In addition, the availability of solar resource in the country is portrayed. The central sections are the steps and results of a case study, consisting of the design of a grid-connected rooftop photovoltaic system for a hypothetical sports building in South Brazil using three solar module technologies (amorphous silicon, polycrystalline silicon, and copper indium diselenide). Finally, conclusions are drawn considering the economic and technical feasibility of the three configurations of the case study, the estimated environmental impacts associated with them, as derived from reviewed studies, and the current policy context in Brazil. These technical and economic aspects can be to some extent extrapolated to countries with similar climate conditions and problems to overcome barriers towards a larger deployment of the photovoltaic technology. The expansion of the use of renewable energies as a tool for avoiding the depletion of non-renewable resources; the analysis of environmental impacts as a tool for environmental protection; the study of problems and opportunities in developing countries as part of the environmental planning, as well as sustainability appraisals, are widely discussed within the context of Environmental and Resource Management (BTU 2009).

The main goal of this study was to analyse the potential and feasibility (technical and economic) of a renewable energy technology in a developing country. The case study was based on the solar PV (photovoltaics) directly connected to the public grid in Brazil. Since the current plans of the Brazilian government do not envision a significant role for the photovoltaic technology, the research question of this chapter was to find out whether this decision has good fundament from a technical, economic or environmental point of view. The chosen method consisted of the performance of a technical-economic study for a specific grid-connected PV facility in the Brazilian state with the lowest available solar irradiation (Santa Catarina). To provide context and background, a review of the main features of the country's energy sector, the assessment of the country's potential for PV deployment, and the results of relevant studies evaluating the environmental impacts associated to it, are subsequently presented.

6.2 The Energy Sector of Brazil: Composition of Brazil's Primary Energy Matrix

The summary published yearly by the Brazilian Ministry of Mines and Energy (MME, Ministério de Minas e Energia) called "Brazilian Energy Balance" showed in its 2007 issue that the Domestic Energy Supply (DES) of Brazil had grown from about 67 Mtoe (million tons of oil equivalent) in 1970 to 226.1 Mtoe in 2006. Since 1991, the evolution from 144.9 Mtoe means an average annual growth rate of approx. 3.0%, which in the same period surpassed the average annual economic growth (in terms of GDP) of approx. 2.75%, and the population growth rate of approx. 1.5% (MME 2007). This situated Brazil, according to UNEP Risoe Centre (UNEP 2007), as the 10th largest energy consumer in the world (about 2% of the global demand), and the 3rd largest in the Western hemisphere (behind United States and Canada). According to the data of MME, in 2006 fossil fuels provided 53.3% of Brazil's DES, split into 37.7% from oil and oil by-products, 9.6% from natural gas, and 6.0% from coal. Renewables accounted for more than 45% of the DES, consisting of 30.2% biomass (around half of it from sugarcane products, the rest from fuelwood and charcoal), about 13.3% hydropower (1.2% corresponding to imports), and an estimated 1.5% of other renewable sources. The contribution of energy from nuclear plants was 1.6% (MME 2007). Regarding the evolution of the fuel shares in the DES during the 1970-2006 period, the main observations are a strong decrease in the use of traditional biomass (firewood and charcoal), a significant increase of the weight of sugarcane products, and the maintenance of importance of fossil fuels. As for the Final Energy Consumption, in 2006 it amounted to 202.9 Mtoe, corresponding to 89.7% of the DES (i.e. losses amounted to 10.3%), around 3.3 times the 1970 level. The industrial, transport and residential sectors, with 38%, 26% and 11% respectively, accounted for 75% of the total (MME 2007). The high share attributed to the industrial sector is mainly due to the existence of energy-intensive industries in the country (e.g. steel, ferro-alloys, aluminium, non-ferrous metals, pelletization, and pulp and paper sectors) (IAEA 2006).

As for dependency on overall energy imports, Brazil managed to reduce them from about 45% in 1979 to a mere 8% in 2006. The remarkable expansion of Brazil's domestic oil production allowed a dramatic decrease of oil imports over the past two decades, falling from 80% in 1980 to 45% in 1990, 25% in 2000, and 0% (self-sufficiency) since 2005 (MME 2007).

6.2.1 Electricity Generation in Brazil

According to the balance published by MME in 2007, the electricity consumption in Brazil more than tripled in 2006 (about 380 TWh (Terawatt-hours)) when compared with 1980 levels (about 120 TWh), meaning an average annual growth rate of about 4.5%. Whereas since 1970 the residential sector has never exceeded a share of 25% (peak reached by the end of the 1990s), the industrial sector represented the highest demand during the whole period (around 50% of the total) (MME 2007). In 2006, hydropower was still the predominant generating technology (74.1% of total generation from large reservoir and 1.7% from small hydropower plants), the next significant ones being the thermal power plants representing a 12.3% (fired with coal, natural gas or biomass), and nuclear power plants contributing a 3.0%, apart from net imports of electricity which amounted to a 8.9% (which include purchases to Paraguay's large hydropower, and to self-producers). With respect to installed electricity capacity, of a total of 96.6 GW in 2006 (including public utilities and self-generators), the share of hydropower was about 76% (73.4 GW), and that of natural gas was about 9.5% (9.3 GW) (MME 2007). The reasons for the progressive reduction of the share of hydropower in recent years, in spite of its increasing contribution in absolute terms, lie in the government's plan to build in a short time several thermal power plants that could avoid a repetition of the events in 2001, when electricity shortages (caused by low water levels in dams) led to a rationing period with mandatory savings that lasted for almost one year (IAEA 2006).

6.2.2 Environmental Profile of Brazil's Energy Sector

The Brazilian fossil-fuel atmospheric carbon emissions level, in spite of having increased steadily since 1983, is relatively low in comparison with the worldwide standard. In 2004, it was estimated at 86.8 million metric tons of carbon (approx. 318.3 million metric tons of CO_2-equivalent). With this, in 2004 Brazil occupied the place of 18th biggest emitter in absolute value, but its per capita emission rate of 0.50 metric tons of carbon was well below the global average rate, estimated at 1.19 metric tons of carbon / capita (Marland et al. 2007). Regarding emissions per unit of energy used, the Brazilian government stated (MME 2007) that in 2006 the Brazilian economy emitted only 1.57 tCO_2-eq/toe, in comparison with a world average of 2.37 tCO_2-eq/toe. In terms of economic carbon efficiency, despite its economy's size, Brazil ranked very low at worldwide level in the year 2004 with a value of 0.54 $kgCO_2$-eq / $US\$_{GDP}$, the weighted global average being about 1.5 $kgCO_2$-eq / $US\$_{GDP}$ (Marland et al. 2007). As for carbon emissions attributable to Brazil's electricity mix, the official data (EPE 2007) indicate a value of about 22 $MtCO_2$-eq for the 370 TWh generated in 2005, which means a rate of about 60 gCO_2-eq/kWh. This is lower than the result of a life-cycle assessment study by Coltro et al. (2007), according to which 1 GJ (about 278 kWh) of delivered electricity in Brazil in 2000 would be responsible for the emission of 17.83 kg of non-renewable CO_2, 54.8 g of non-renewable CH_4, and 10.99 g of N_2O. Applying the

IPCC factors of Global Warming Potential at 100 years horizon (1 for CO_2, 21 for CH_4, 310 for N_2O), the corresponding GWP of that 1 GJ would sum up to 22.39 kgCO_2-eq. Thus the resulting rate (dividing by 278 kWh) would be about 80.5 gCO_2-eq/kWh.

6.2.3 The Brazilian Government's Strategic Energy Plan

In June 2007, the Brazilian Energy Research Corporation (EPE Empresa de Pesquisa Energética, a governmental agency subsidiary of the Brazilian Ministry of Mines and Energy) made public the final report of the "Plano Nacional de Energia 2030" (National Energy Plan 2030). This was claimed to be the first study of integrated energy resource planning undertaken by the Brazilian government. In the report of the strategic plan it is explained how the expected demand, in each of four scenarios considered, could be covered using different energy sources split into the following categories: Oil and oil-derived, Natural gas, Mineral coal, Wood and Vegetal coal, Sugarcane products, Biodiesel, Electricity, and others; and the possible contribution of each of them to the final consumption in the years 2010, 2020, and 2030 is determined for each scenario (EPE 2007). But the scenario that is finally accredited as more probable is Scenario B1 (corresponding to an expected average annual growth rate of Brazil's GDP of 4.1%), therefore the final recommended energy strategy is based on it. From that point on, the report goes into describing the situation in 2005 and justifying the demand evolution expected for each main energy source considered for the future supply. If all predictions were accomplished, the resulting energy mix in 2030 would be: 29% oil and derived; 16% natural gas; 7% coal and derived; 3% nuclear; 14% hydroelectricity and electricity imports; 6% wood and vegetal coal; 16% sugarcane derived; and 7% other renewables. Regarding electricity, the increase in supply capacity would rely mainly on new hydroelectric and gas power plants, together with increases in coal, nuclear, small hydro, biomass combustion and wind; and as big infrastructural advances unfold, the West of Brazil should be connected to the main electric grid (EPE 2007).

6.2.4 Solar Photovoltaic Potential in Brazil

Over the last decade there has been an effort, originally headed by technical experts associated with the U.S. National Renewable Energy Laboratory (NREL) and later joined by several other national and international institutions, to "map" the power generation potential of solar and wind resources in the LAC (Latin America and the Caribbean) nations considered likely to offer good potential. NREL produced geo-referenced solar and wind power potential maps, which were later used in the SWERA project ("Solar and Wind Energy Resource Assessment") sponsored by the United Nations Environment Programme (UNEP) and the Global Environment Facility (GEF) (Ripley 2006). In recent years, the European Photovoltaic Industry Association (EPIA) and Greenpeace have published joint annual reports on the development of solar photovoltaics. In the 2006 edition they forecasted the growth of the global photovoltaic market up to 110,000 million € (investments) and 60,000 MW/year (shipments) by 2025. And from that volume they estimated the share corresponding to Latin America as 18%. In a section devoted specifically to Brazil the report noted that, despite its poor participation in the PV market at the time (9 MW installed capacity according to Brazil's Energy Ministry estimates), the country has huge potential and with the right policy mix could become one of the PV market drivers in Latin America, achieving installed capacities of 150 MW by 2010 and over 11,000 MW by 2025. This could lead in the period 2006-2025 to the creation of about 100,000 related jobs, and a reduction of about 61 million tonnes of CO_2, thanks to an amount of electricity generated by photovoltaics estimated at 23.7 GWh (EPIA and Greenpeace 2009).

Also in 2006, a bilingual joint report of the actors that took part in the SWERA project in Brazil (UNEP, GEF, the SWERA team, and the Brazilian scientific institutions INPE, CPTEC, SONDA and LABSOLAR) was published under the title "Atlas Brasileiro de Energia Solar / Brazilian Atlas of Solar Energy" (Bueno et al. 2006). The main results (available for public access free of charge) brought about were: high resolution solar radiation digital and printed maps; generation of hourly temporal series; and scenarios for the utilization of solar energy by using GIS tools. In the main general map of the third section of that report, showing the annual average of daily global solar irradiation that reaches the Brazilian territory, one can observe that in spite of the climate diversity the global irradiation is fairly uniform, and the annual mean of daily horizontal global solar irradiation in any region of Brazil (1550-2350 kWh/m^2*year) is much greater than those for most European countries. The maximum solar irradiation value (6.5 kWh/m^2*day) occurs in the northern part of the Bahia state close to the border with the Piauí state, an area of semi-arid climate with low rainfall and the lowest average amount of clouds. Other maximum solar irradiation values are observed in the western area of the Northeast region, including a portion of northern Minas Gerais, the Northeast of Goiás and the South of Tocantins, all of them semi-arid regions with stable condition of low nebulosity. The lower global solar irradiation levels (4.25 kWh/m^2*day the lowest) are found on the northern coast of the Santa Catarina state, and on the shores of Paraná and São Paulo, all of them regions of temperate climate. The average global solar irradiation levels calculated by macroregion are: 5.9 kWh/m^2*day for the North-East; 5.5 kWh/m^2*day for the North; 5.7 kWh/m^2*day for the Center-West; 5.6 kWh/m^2*day for the South-East; and 5.2 kWh/m^2*day for the South. Regarding seasonal variability, it is lower than 40% throughout all the country, although the variation between winter and summer is smaller in the North region and greater in the South (the one with largest variation) and Southeast regions (Bueno et al. 2006).

In the section detailing application scenarios, the potential for deployment of photovoltaics is considered huge, and two main applications are proposed:

- Coupling PV generation capacity to about 286 existing diesel power plants in the Amazon region, which are not linked to the Brazilian interconnected system of electricity distribution (and whose operators currently make use of a fuel subsidy), constituting hybrid systems. The potential for using PV can be estimated in tens to hundreds of MWp in the Amazon region alone, whereas the wind resource distribution there is one of the worst in the country.

- Installing grid-connected PV system in urban areas. Commercial regions with high midday air conditioning loads have normally a demand curve in good synchronism with the solar irradiance. This is the typical picture of most capital cities in Brazil, thus adding a small amount of PV can have a peak-shaving effect and assist in reducing load requirements for the electricity feeders.

6.3 Case Study: Roof-mounted Grid-connected PV System for a Sports Hall in South Brazil

The building for which the system is to be dimensioned is a sports hall with a playing ground of 54 x 33 meters and a height of 10 meters. Integrated to the same structure, but divided by an internal wall, the facility would count with a service area of 13 x 33 meters (also 10 meters high). The described building is a virtual one, proposed for some of the currently unused areas of the district of Florianópolis called Pantanal, close to the university campus of the Universidade Federal de Santa Catarina (district Trindade). As the building is not yet in existence, the electricity supply needed was estimated using simulation software; the chosen application was the "EnergyPlus version 2.0" software, offered free of charge by the United States Department of Energy (DOE 2007).

6.3.1 Initial Data

After introducing all the data required by EnergyPlus in terms of geometry, materials, electrical and heat load features, and use schedules, the run of the simulation for an entire year delivered the following results for the monthly electricity consumption.

In our case we establish the target to adjust the dimensioning of the PV system to just cover the overall annual consumption, even if there are months when the generation is inferior to the consumption. Therefore we will adopt, as the reference level, the average daily consumption, which is obtained as the average of the average daily consumption of each month. From Table 6.1 this value is E = 91.1 kWh/day. The second basic input needed to determine the photovoltaic power to be installed is the solar irradiation in the area where the building is situated. In order to do that, the software "Radiasol" was used, developed by the Solar Energy Laboratory of the UFRGS, Universidade Federal do Rio Grande do Sul (UFRGS 2001). This application can provide for each target location an estimate of the average incident solar hours (1 solar hour = radiation of 1000 W/m^2 during 1 hour) in every month. Once the location is selected in the initial screen, the application opens a new screen offering the possibility to change the variables of tilt angle and azimuth angle (both set 0° as default).

Table 6.1. Simulated electric consumption needs for the proposed sports hall building. Results obtained using the EnergyPlus software

	Total electric energy demand in kWh	Nr. of days	Daily average in kWh/day
January	4529	31	146.1
February	3867	28	138.1
March	3898	31	125.7
April	2763	30	92.1
May	1999	31	64.5
June	2258	30	75.3
July	2388	31	77.0
August	2410	31	77.7
September	1789	30	59.6
October	2192	31	70.7
November	2328	30	77.6
December	2835	31	91.5
Annual Sum	33255	365	-
Average	2771	-	91.1

The lower buttons of this second screen allow the results of solar radiation throughout the year to be obtained, either graphically (only the monthly day averages) or in a table format (monthly day and hour average values). In practice, PV panels are always tilted a minimum angle towards the Equator (usually > 5º), to improve efficiency and to allow that the rain cleans their surface. Unless the solar modules are integrated or mounted directly on the roof, it is recommendable to consider the tilting of the modules to achieve their maximum output: the theoretical optimal tilt angle is one corresponding to the latitude of the absolute geographical coordinates of the design location, with an approximate variation of ±15º for winter and summer optimization; in our case Florianópolis has a latitude position 27º S (below the Tropic of Capricorn), therefore we should incline the solar modules an angle between 12º and 42º towards North. Using the software Radiasol, we find that the tilt angle for which the average annual solar irradiation on the plane of array is maximized is either 18º or 19º; as the higher the angle the more interspacing will be required to avoid shading, we will choose 18º. To summarise, the monthly values of average radiation to be used for Florianópolis with a panel inclination of 18º to the North are as shown in Table 6.2.

Table 6.2. Average daily irradiation (in kWh/m^2*day) by month according to Radiasol (Florianópolis, tilt 18ºN)

Jan	Feb	Mar	Apr	May	Jun	Jul	Aug	Sep	Oct	Nov	Dec	Aver.
5.79	5.32	5.21	4.64	4.08	3.59	3.69	4.37	4.24	4.83	5.37	6.02	4.76

The values shown above are the estimated daily averages of daily irradiation for every month of the year at the geographical location and panel orientation indicated. We can observe that the variation around the mean (4.76 kWh/m^2*day)

does not exceed 27% throughout the year. Multiplying these values by the actual panel surface installed, the panel efficiency and the overall system efficiency, we will be able to estimate the electricity production of the solar facility.

Regarding the available photovoltaic solar module technologies, in general PV cells can be classified as either crystalline (single crystal or multicrystalline) or thin film. According to EPIA-Greenpeace (2008), the most commercialized technologies in 2007 were polycrystalline Silicon (pc-Si) with module efficiencies 12-14%, monocrystalline Silicon (mc-Si) with module efficiencies 13-15%, amorphous silicon (a-Si) with module efficiencies 5-7%, and cadmium telluride (CdTe) with module efficiencies about 10%. Less relevant technologies in terms of market share but with promising technological aspects were copper indium diselenide (CIS) and copper indium gallium diselenide (CIGS) with module efficiencies 7-11%. For the configuration proposals of this case study the comparison between the results using CIS, pc-Si, and a-Si was considered.

6.3.2 Sequence for the Dimensioning of the PV System

Once the electrical power needs and available solar irradiation have been determined, a standard procedure is followed to estimate the size, power and layout of each intended photovoltaic arrangement First, the minimum (nominal) design power to be installed to cover the annual electricity consumption is calculated. The formula includes the average daily demand level, the average daily solar incident power on the plane of array chosen, and a factor for the overall system efficiency called PR (Performance Rate), with values between 0 and 1. In this case a mean value of 0.75 will be adopted, as no progressive loss of performance of the solar modules throughout their lifetime will be considered. The value obtained from the calculation is that 25.5 kWp of nominal power are needed. The area covered by the PV arrays to be installed can be calculated by dividing the nominal power by the generation efficiency of the PV panels. An additional consideration is the spacing between modules to avoid shading, which on occurance (even only partially) causes significant losses of power generation. With a tilt angle of 18º, the distance to avoid shading will mean an additional 54% (of the module side length) in the North to South direction.

In the next step it will be necessary to calculate the minimal cable section to be used in the DC (continuous current) section, that is between the photovoltaic arrays and the current inverters, to assure the losses by heat dissipation do not exceed a certain tolerated value. This can be an important cost factor for the installation. For that there is a formula relating all physical parameters of the installation. Additionally, the minimum section established by the normative of the country (for low voltage electrical installations of buildings) to avoid overheating due to the amperage of the transmitted current will have to be considered.

The final choice of section will be the minimum values indicated by the norms and the calculation. Afterwards the selection of the current inverter has to be done. For that, one should try to keep the quantity of inverters as low as possible and optimize their use by choosing an operation range where their efficiency is high.

Thanks to the wide range of products offered and their competitive prices, the "SunnyBoy" line produced by the company SMA (SMA Solar Technology AG, Niestetal, Germany) was deemed the best option in this case. In a comparison of technical data for the most used SunnyBoy inverters (with AC output voltage 240V and 60Hz frequency, suitable for Brazil's electric grid), in terms of efficiency and flexibility as well as specific cost, the best options are the ones of higher capacity, that is 6000 W and 7000 W (Affordable Solar 2008).

Finally one type of solar module has to be chosen and the minimum number required to cover the established supply level determined. Then, taking into account the type of preferred inverter, the optimal choice of: modules connected in series in one array, the number of arrays, arrays connected in parallel to each inverter, and total number of inverters, can be determined. Some commercial applications (such as "GenAu" from SMA) to do this task exist in the market, but it is also possible with the assistance of a simple spreadsheet software, for example Microsoft Excel.

6.3.3 Configuration Results

The first technology alternative considered was thin-film CIS (copper indium diselenide) solar modules, specifically the model WS11007/75 manufactured by Würth Solar, with 75 Wp of power per unit and an efficiency of about 10%. Assuming that the inverter SB7000US (by SMA) could be used, and following the steps outlined above, it was found that (from a theoretical minimum of 340) with 352 panels two good configurations could be obtained using four inverters. The chosen one, in view of the layout on the roof, was connecting 11 units in series to each array (disposed transversally) and 8 arrays in parallel (eight rows) to each inverter. The resulting configuration, with 352 solar modules and 4 inverters would have an installed capacity of 26.4 kWp, requiring a total roof surface of 395 m^2 (about 18% of the roof's total), of which 257 m^2 for the panels and the rest for spacing to avoid shading. The annual amount of electricity generated, considering a global performance ratio of 75%, would be 34,415 kWh, meaning a surplus of 1,161 kWh above the building's needs, in spite of falling short in some months (from January to March, and in June and July).

The second technology alternative considered was pc-Si (polycrystalline silicon) solar modules, specifically the model KC200GT manufactured by Kyocera, with 200 Wp of power per unit and a theoretical 14.2% efficiency. Assuming again the possibility of using the inverters SB7000US, and after all the dimensioning steps, it was found that already with 128 panels an optimal configuration could be obtained using four inverters, connecting 16 units in series to each array (disposed transversally) and two arrays in parallel (two rows) to each inverter. The resulting configuration, with 128 solar modules and 4 inverters would have an installed capacity of 25.6 kWp, meaning a total roof surface of 278 m^2 required (about 13% of the roof's total), of which 181 m^2 for the panels and the rest for spacing to avoid shading. The annual amount of electricity generated, considering a global performance ratio of 75%, would be 33,372 kWh, meaning only a surplus of 118 kWh above the building's needs and falling short in the months from January to April, June and July.

The third technology alternative considered was thin-film a-Si (amorphous silicon) solar modules, specifically the model GSA60 manufactured by Kaneka (60 Wp of power per unit), with a theoretical 6.3% efficiency. Again using the inverters SB7000US, an optimal configuration is obtainable with 456 panels and four inverters, connecting 6 units in series to each array (disposed transversally) and 19 arrays in parallel (as rows) to each inverter. The resulting configuration, with 456 solar modules and 4 inverters would have an installed capacity of 27.36 kWp, requiring a total roof surface of 667 m^2 (about 30% of the roof's total), of which 433 m^2 for the panels and the rest for spacing to avoid shading. The annual amount of electricity generated, considering a global performance ratio of 75%, would be 35,667 kWh, meaning a surplus of 2,412 kWh above the building's needs and falling short significantly only in the months from January to March.

6.3.4 System Assembly and other Technical Aspects

In the three configurations studied, the frame-mounted solar panels would be installed on the sport hall's roof area inclined towards the North at the angle that optimizes the annual average solar radiation, i.e. 18° for the region of Florianópolis. To make the installation easier in cases where the solar panels have one side longer than the other, it seems more convenient to place the longer side along the longest axis of the roof (in our building coincident with the E-W axis), minimizing the length of the frame supports as well as the spacing between rows to avoid shading.

The transformation of the generated direct current (DC) into alternating current (AC) to be able to feed in the public electric grid would be done by state-of-the-art inverters, with control microprocessors and a communications interface, which guaranteeing a sine wave with minimal distortion are able to inject into the grid all the power that the photovoltaic system is able to deliver at any time as well as to avoid losses during stand-by periods. Regarding safety, control and measurement systems, the grid-connected PV system should be fitted with all elements necessary for its correct operation according to regulations and specifications. The connection to ground of the main PV circuit and any metal part that could be subject to high voltage values is essential. Besides, the facility will have to be compliant with the applicable regulation for low-voltage electrical facilities (NBR 5410 in the case of Brazil), as well as any particular requirements that the local electricity distribution company to which the system will be connected establishes (Rüther 2004). Finally, the deployment will be subject to the country's legal and regulatory aspects. In this sense, two essential legal provisions are the law 8987/95 regulating the concession regime and public service permit, and the decree 2003/96, which regulates the production of electric energy by independent producers (Produtores Independentes de Energia - PIE) and self-producers (Auto Produtores - AP), under which the grid-connected PV systems are characterized (Rüther 2004).

6.3.5 Cost Considerations for the Reference Case

The economic indicators chosen to evaluate the convenience of the solar roof configurations proposed in this study are: the Net Present Value, NPV (that is today's value of the annual cash flows during the projected lifetime of the facility); the Investment Payback Time (that is how long it will take to recover the initial capital investment); and the Internal Rate of Return, IRR (that is the rate of interest that a bank should pay for the amount of the investment to equal the total cash flow resulting from the project over the facility's lifetime). The expected project lifetime used was 30 years, although most manufacturers offer a 20- or 25-year warranty. In order to do this evaluation, one must carry out the cost breakdown of every proposal and make the calculation of those three indicators by means of an electronic spreadsheet. The acquisition prices found for the solar modules and the inverters were: approx. 750 US$/unit (converted from 520€/unit) for the Würth Solar WS11007/75 modules (Catálogo Solar 2008); 920 US$/unit for the Kyocera 200GT modules and 225 US$/unit for the Kaneka GSA60 modules (Aten Solar 2008); and 4108 US$/unit for the SunnyBoy SB7000US inverter (Affordable Solar 2008). These prices were augmented by 22% due to the concepts of sale taxes (VAT or similar) and freight, and an additional 31.25% due to the concept of import taxes to Brazil, as indicated on the website of the country's Ministry of Finances (Ministério da Fazenda 2008). The cost of the remaining balance-of-system (BOS) components (mounting frames, fusing, cabling etc.) was estimated at about 1% of the sum of modules and inverters. The engineering and installation cost was estimated at 6000 US$ for all cases. As for outcomes influencing the annual cash-flow, an annual payment for maintenance was estimated at 0.2% of the initial PV system cost, which eventually should cover repairs or substitution of components; and the retail price for the electricity supplied by the utility to customers (in the case of Net Metering equal to the price that will be received for the electricity fed by the PV system to the utility) was assumed as 0.20 US$/kWh in the initial year. Finally, the country's annual monetary depreciation rate (inflation) was assumed at an average of 5%.

The formulae used for the calculation of the above mentioned indicators are:

$$\text{NPV} = \left[{}_1\Sigma^n \left((\text{Annual Cash flow}) / (1+i)^t \right) \right] - \text{Investment}, \tag{6.1}$$

where i = (Money depreciation rate / 100) and t = 1 ÷ Project lifetime (years), using if necessary the mathematical identity (6.2)

$$ {}_1\Sigma^n \left((\text{Annual Cash flow}) / (1+i)^t \right) = \text{Annual Cash flow} * \left[\frac{(1+i)^n - 1}{(1+i)^n * i} \right]; \tag{6.2}$$

Payback Time = value of 't' (in years) for which NPV = 0; (6.3)

IRR = value of 'i' (in %) for which NPV = 0 when t = project lifetime. (6.4)

The results obtained are as summarized in Table 6.3.

Table 6.3. Results of the calculation of investment indicators (base case, Florianópolis, 18ºN)

Concept / Configuration	1	2	3
Solar module make and model	Würth Solar WS11007/75	Kyocera KC200GT	Kaneka GSA60
Nominal power installed (Wp)	26400	25600	27360
Total initial investment (US$)	334054	223052	198368
Initial investment / installed nominal power (US$/Wp)	12.65	8.71	7.25
Initial investment / expected electricity generation (US$/kWh)	0.324	0.223	0.185
Total annual cash-flow (US$)	+6215	+6228	+6737
Net present value (US$)	-147604	-36212	+3712
Payback time (years)	53.7	35.8	27.9
Internal rate of return (%)	-3.41%	-1.11%	+0.12%

It can be noted that the level of investment required for the solar facilities designed (between about 200.000 and about 330.000 US$) is quite high. The two ratios below the absolute value of investment (investment over installed power and investment over expected generated electricity) give us an idea of how far away from investments in other electricity generation technologies this lies, knowing that the average values for those ratios are between 750 and 2200 US$/kW and 0.022 to 0.090 US$/kWh (EPE 2007). In view of the results of Table 6.3 for the main indicators proposed (last three rows), one can conclude that in this reference case none of these investments would be financially sound, as almost all of them obtain a negative (or almost zero) net present value, and their financial payback time is longer or practically equal that of the expected system lifetime. Besides, an IRR negative or close to zero means that the invested capital would give a better profit in any bank account that gives some interest. However, if one of them were to be chosen, the preferred configuration (as less disadvantageous in economic terms according to these indicators) would be number 3, corresponding to the a-Si module technology. An additional interesting result that can be easily obtained using the electronic spreadsheet is the equilibrium point in terms of cost per installed power under which the NPV of the designs in 30 years lifetime would be positive: this threshold lies at 7.38 US$/Wp of investment ratio.

6.3.6 Sensitivity Analysis of the Cost Calculations

To evaluate the extent to which the constraining factors implied by the location chosen and cost elements considered influenced the results, the calculation of the indicators under variation of some of them was undertaken. The factors considered were the following:

- *Solar irradiation level (use of the PV system in other climatic zones of Brazil with higher values as Santa Catarina)*: as an example in Natal (capital of Rio Grande do Norte, latitude 5.77 S, longitude 35.20 W), where the average solar radiation throughout the year on a horizontal plane amounts 5.66 kWh/(m^2*day) and there is little seasonal variation (minimum 4.53 in June, maximum 6.67 in November); the average value at the optimum 3ºN of tilt amounts 5.86 kWh/(m^2*day) (UFRGS 2001).
- *Assumption of an incentive purchase price system (feed-in tariff)*: under this system well established in Europe, all the electricity generated must be bought by the distribution company at a premium price (typically 2 to 4 times the retail sale price for regular customers), whereas the electricity consumed in the building is charged at the normal price. As an example, the calculations of the proposed economic indicators have been repeated for a modified version of the three configurations proposed, assuming that the electricity generation fed in the public grid is paid at triple price (0.60 US$/kWh at today's value) than the price of consumed electricity (0.20 US$/kWh at today's value).
- *Increase of the electricity cost above the inflation rate*: in many projects of renewable energies nowadays, the possibility of an increase of the energy prices above inflation rates is considered verisimilar; in that case, the future cash flows derived from electricity payments or savings must be calculated using this higher rate, but for the rest of money flows the normal inflation rate will be used. As an example, the calculations were repeated for the three configurations proposed, without any technical modifications but assuming an average annual percentage difference of 1% between the electricity cost increase and the inflation rate.
- *Partial subsidy or tax relief on the initial investment*: one could consider the factor that plans to promote the implementation of PV systems in the country include measures to relieve a fixed percentage of the initial investment, being a direct subsidy or an exemption of taxes. As example for this exercise, a reduction of 30% of the initial capital disbursement was assumed.

With all these considerations, a summarized table was prepared for each configuration with the results of the economic indicators proposed (NPV at 30 years in US$; Investment Payback time in years; IRR at 30 years in %), considering all possible combinations. The order of influence of the variables that can be observed is the following: firstly the greatest influence would come from the introduction of a feed-in tariff of 3 times the retail sale price, secondly from situating the building in a site with an average annual irradiation 23% higher; thirdly from a capital or tax subsidy of 30%, and finally from the hypothetical 1% annual increase of electricity prices above the inflation rate. For all cases, the investment can be seen as acceptable when the payback time is lower than the expected lifetime (in this case 30 years) and the NPV is positive; this has been marked with the numbers in italics. Besides, if the IRR is above the inflation rate considered (in this case 5%) the investment would be lucrative and therefore advisable for any potential investor; this circumstance has been marked additionally with bold case numbers. The results obtained are shown in the Tables 6.4, 6.5, and 6.6 below.

Table 6.4. Summary of economic indicator values for the PV system of configuration 1 (26.4 kWp of CIS modules with 18ºN tilt) in two sites, considering various scenarios

Indicator values (NPV; Payback; IRR)	Reference case [4.763 kWh/(m^2*day), 18ºN]	Higher irradiation site [5.863 kWh/(m^2*day), 3ºN]
No additional condition	-147604; 53.7; -3.41%	-99805; 42.8; -2.15%
A = Feed-in tariff (3 times the retail price)	+65843; 25.1; +1.20%	+209249; 18.4; +3.48%
B = Electr. price incr. 1% above inflation	-116836; 42.9; -2.46%	-61356; 35.7; -1.21%
C = 30% initial capital subsidy or tax relief	-47391; 37.6; -1.40%	+411; 29.9; +0.01%
A + B	+129338; 22.5; +2.14%	+294427; 17.0; +4.42%
A + C	+166059; 17.5; +3.88%	**+309465; 12.9; +6.61**
B + C	-16170; 31.9; -0.44%	+38860; 26.2; +0.97%
A + B + C	**+229554; 16.2; +4.84%**	**+394643; 12.2; +7.56%**

From the results in Table 6.4 can be derived that, for the first configuration and in the site initially planned, the investment would obtain a positive return only in the case of introducing the feed-in tariff (or that combined with any of the other improved conditions). An IRR above 5% could only be obtained in the original site with the confluence of the three conditions, or in the site with higher irradiation with at least the feed-in tariff and the initial capital subsidy.

From the results in Table 6.5 can be derived that, for the second configuration and in the site initially planned, the investment could obtain a positive return either introducing the feed-in tariff or the initial capital subsidy, in the higher irradiation site that would be attained under any of the three conditions or their combinations. An IRR above 5% could be obtained in the higher irradiation site with the introduction of the feed-in tariff, or in both sites with any combination of more than one condition including the feed-in tariff. Especially worth mentioning are the results in the scenario A+B (a feed-in tariff and an increase of the electricity retail prices an annual 1% above the inflation rate), as this can be considered a quite possible situation and the values obtained for NPV (equal or higher than the initial investment) and Payback time (close to or below half the expected lifetime) would be quite satisfactory.

Table 6.5. Summary of economic indicator values for the PV system of configuration 2 (25.6 kWp of pc-Si modules with 18ºN tilt) in two sites, considering various scenarios

Indicator values (NPV; Payback; IRR)	Reference case [4.763 kWh/(m^2*day), 18ºN]	Higher irradiation site [5.863 kWh/(m^2*day), 3ºN]
No additional condition	-36212; 35.8; -1.11%	+10153; 28.7; +0.29%
A = Feed-in tariff (3 times retail price)	+164731; 17.3; +4.02%	**+303799; 12.7; +6.77%**
B = Electr. price incr. 1% above inflation	-5928; 30.7; -0.16%	+47437; 25.3; +1.23%
C = 30% initial capital subsidy or tax relief	+30712; 25.1; +1.20%	+77068; 20.1; +2.81%
A + B	**+225387; 16.0; +4.96%**	**+385482; 12.0; +7.72%**
A + C	**+231646; 12.1; +7.27%**	**+370714; 8.9; +10.72%**
B + C	+60988; 22.4; +2.16%	+114353; 18.4; +3.77%
A + B + C	**+292303; 11.5; +8.23%**	**+452398; 8.6; +11.67%**

Table 6.6. Summary of economic indicator values for the PV system of configuration 3 (27.4 kWp of a-Si modules with 18ºN tilt) in two sites, considering various scenarios

Indicator values (NPV; Payback; IRR)	Reference case [4.763 kWh/(m^2*day), 18ºN]	Higher irradiation site [5.863 kWh/(m^2*day), 3ºN]
No additional condition	+3712; 27.9; +0.12%	+53268; 23.7; +1.61%
A = Feed-in tariff (3 times retail price)	**+232206; 13.8; +5.96%**	**+380814; 10.3; +9.00%**
B = Electr. price incr. 1% above inflation	+36089; 25.9; +1.06%	+93115; 21.3; +2.55%
C = 30% initial capital subsidy or tax relief	+63242; 20.6; +2.62%	+112778; 16.6; +4.36%
A + B	**+299108; 13.0; +6.91%**	**+470186; 9.8; +9.95%**
A + C	**+291716; 9.7; +9.69%**	**+440324; 7.2; +13.60**
B + C	+95599; 18.8; +3.57%	**+152625; 15.4; +5.32%**
A + B + C	**+358619; 9.3; +10.65%**	**+529696; 7.0; +14.56%**

From the results in Table 6.6 can be derived that, for the third configuration and in the site initially planned, the investment would obtain a significant positive return in case any of the modified conditions stands, and in the higher irradiation site that result would be attained even without any changes. An IRR above 5% could be obtained in both sites with the introduction of the feed-in tariff or any combination of more than one condition including the feed-in tariff. As in the previous case, it is worth mentioning the results in the scenario A+B, as this can be considered a quite possible situation and the values obtained for NPV (equal or higher than the initial investment) and Payback time (close to or below half the expected lifetime) would already be quite satisfactory.

6.3.7 Environmental Considerations

To evaluate the three technologies proposed in terms of environmental performance, several relevant published studies were reviewed (Frankl et al. 2004, Jungbluth et al. 2008, Ecoinvent 2007). Emissions of air pollutants of PV systems are due to energy use in the life-cycle stages previous to operation. In the final report of a project called ECLIPSE (Frankl et al. 2004) there is a table comparing the air emissions (in terms of CO_2, NMVOC, CH_4, NOx, Particulates, and SOx) attributable to the life cycle of four different PV families (mc-Si, pc-Si, a-Si and CIGS); the last three are the ones assumed for our case study configurations. According to that assessment, the mc-Si rankings are the worst in four of the five cases (except for Particulates); a-Si and CIGS show almost the same value of CO_2 and NMVOC emissions; CIGS shows a slightly higher value in CH_4, but ranks better in Particulates and SOx. So the best choice would be either a-Si or CIGS depending on what level of importance were set on each emission type (a-Si is better in terms of greenhouse gases for example).

In a specific comparison of life-cycle carbon emissions, a figure in the same report (Frankl et al. 2004) displays the levels corresponding to the three technologies used in this case study, under irradiation levels of South Europe (similar to Brazil's average): these are about 44 gCO_2eq/kWh for CIS, about 43 gCO_2eq/kWh for a-Si, and about 49 gCO_2eq/kWh for pc-Si. In this case the preference would be for a-Si, but this is practically equal to CIS. Using these values one can calculate the savings in terms of CO_2 emissions that the implementation of each of these technologies in our building would bring about (in the base case), taking as emissions average value for Brazil's electricity mix the one derived from the study of Coltro et al. (2003), that is 80.5 gCO_2eq/kWh. Using the values of expected annual electricity generation for each configuration, the results for a 30-year lifetime are: 37.68 tCO_2eq for CIS, 31.24 tCO_2eq for pc-Si, and 40.12 tCO_2eq for a-Si.

In a recent article by Jungbluth et al. (2008), one of its comparative bar graphs illustrates the non-renewable CED (Cumulative Energy Demand) estimated for the manufacturing and installation of slanted-roof PV systems of nine different technologies, among which are the three considered in this case study. The values from that publication are: 27.2 MJeq/Wp for CIS, 27.6 MJeq/Wp for pc-Si, and 29.0 MJeq/Wp for a-Si. If one multiplies them with the required installed capacity determined for each case (i.e. 26.40 kWp of CIS modules, 25.60 kWp of pc-Si modules, 27.36 kWp of a-Si modules), the resulting total energy requirement is: $7.181*10^5$ MJeq for CIS, $7.066*10^5$ MJeq for pc-Si, and $7.394*10^5$ MJeq for a-Si.

Therefore, if this were the factor to be considered, the preferred option would be pc-Si closely followed by CIS.

In addition, with the above values one can calculate the EPBT (Energy Payback Time) associated with each technology: considering a rate of conversion efficiency from primary energy to electricity of 42% (typical for EU countries), the calculation for the reference case leads us to the following results: 2.43 years for CIS, 2.47 years for pc-Si, and 2.60 years for a-Si.

Finally, in the same report (Jungbluth et al. 2008) the normalized LCA (Life Cycle Assessment) scores of seven module technologies for slanted-roof mounted-panel application, including the three types detailed in the case study, were compared, . A bar graph shows the final value obtained after a full LCA that considered ten impact categories (i.a. mineral extraction, fossil fuels, respiratory effects, climate change, carcinogenics, ecotoxicity, acidification and eutrophication), weighted in the final step using the method "Eco-Indicator 99" (in its hierarchist variant with an average weighting set). The values of interest for us are: approx. $3.8*10^{-3}$ points/kWhel for CIS, approx. $4.6*10^{-3}$ points/kWhel for pc-Si, approx. $4.9*10^{-3}$ points/kWhel for a-Si (the lower the better). Thus if the decision were to be taken based on this indicator the preferred technology would be CIS. For comparison, the value in the same scale corresponding to the Brazilian electricity supply mix in low-voltage grid (assuming 84% hydro, 11% conventional thermal, 3% biomass and 2% nuclear) would be 0.011 points/kWhel (Ecoinvent 2007), that is one order of magnitude higher than the results for PV.

The conclusion of this short review is that, in the reviewed LCA studies where the three technologies used in the case study were compared to one another (Frankl et al. 2004, Jungbluth et al. 2008, Ecoinvent 2007), the CIS (or CIGS) option obtains better results or is practically equal in all occasions, therefore one can state that from an environmental perspective it would be the most preferable option.

6.3.8 Conclusions of the Case Study

The conclusion that can be drawn after the realisation of this practical technical study is that, in this area of the state of Santa Catarina (and in most areas of Brazil), the building-integrated grid-connected photovoltaic systems proposed would be technically feasible but not financially attractive without any improvement of conditions, as explained in the cost considerations section (see 6.3.5). But the situation would become significantly advantageous if a feed-in tariff consisting of a remuneration of the generated electricity at three times the retail sale price, in line with the one enacted in Germany in 2004 (Stryi-Hipp 2004), were introduced. In that case even the most expensive alternative (the one with CIS solar modules) would become feasible in areas with higher irradiation like the states in the North-east of Brazil; the configuration with polycrystalline solar modules would become feasible and lucrative even in the areas with lower irradiation; and the configuration with a-Si solar modules would offer a very interesting remuneration (IRR above the inflation rate) in any location. These positive prospects would be further reinforced if it is assumed that the electricity costs might suffer an increase above the country's inflation rate. In the case of a 30% of initial capital subsidy or tax relief, as the effect is not so pronounced, only the pc-Si and a-Si solutions would become feasible, but not the CIS one; for the a-Si configuration, the investment would become close to lucrative in the areas of higher irradiation. Considering the environmental aspects, it has been shown that most comparative studies and calculations (including the EPBT) lead to results favourable to the CIS technology, but very closely followed by a-Si, which for example leads to bigger savings in CO_2 emissions. What seems clear is that among these three options pc-Si ranks the worst. On the other side, the comparisons with respect to the Brazilian electricity generation mix (in terms of CO_2 and LCA impact scores) confirm PV as preferable, despite the fact that Brazil has a relatively clean electric grid.

6.4 General Conclusions

This study examined and discussed arguments about the extent to which the conditions for further deployment of photovoltaic technology in Brazil could be unfavourable. It is assumed that the main factors against these systems could derive from their technical or economic non-feasibility or by a disadvantageous environmental balance. It has been shown in the overview of Brazil's energy sector that the governmental plan for the increase of energy supply in the next two decades is primarily based on the use of oil, sugarcane, natural gas, and hydropower. The increase in electricity consumption would give room for enlargement of all generation technologies, including renewables, especially wind and photovoltaics (both with large potential in the country); but the government envisages a very modest growth of wind power and for photovoltaics almost none. Fossil and nuclear technologies might be deemed preferable because of their maturity and lower specific investment and generation costs, but this ignores that today's PV technology is very advanced and progressing very rapidly, becoming an optimal solution for covering peak demand in areas of hot climate with lower transmission and distribution costs than using thermal power plants; and also disregards that the actual costs (especially in the case of fossil fuels) are a result of the market failure of not accounting for the real environmental costs. Regarding the environmental aspects of photovoltaics, there are numerous scientific studies proving the benefits of switching from fossil and nuclear electricity generation technologies to photovoltaics (particularly grid-connected) considering a life-cycle perspective, even when the benefits of solar module recycling in many cases are not considered. Also worth taking into account are the numerous non-monetary values associated to a renewable energy source like photovoltaics: e.g. improvement of the atmospheric quality (thus human health), supply security, decentralization and diversification, modularity, industry development, job creation, education on sustainability, and green image.

The case study presented demonstrates the technical viability of supplying a non-residential building with a rooftop photovoltaic system in one of the Brazilian regions with lowest irradiation; but also it shows that, although under the base case conditions the needed investment might not be considered profitable for certain technologies, the introduction of some incentive mechanism like a capital subsidy, a tax relief, or a feed-in tariff, would be enough to reverse the situation. The introduction of such measures at national policy level could make market conditions favourable for the large-scale deployment of the photovoltaic technology in Brazil, making it a viable alternative to contribute significantly to the expansion of the country's electricity supply capacity.

Further research is recommended into comparisons of "full" life-cycle assessments (including all impact categories that are actually involved) between the various PV technologies, between PV and other renewables, and between PV and the electricity mix of targeted receiving countries (in this case Brazil), to allow for better estimation of the potential benefits of substitution. Besides, there is need to follow up the assessment in similar terms of the alternatives to PV in the market of "clean energies".

References

Affordable Solar (2008) Technical data and price of the photovoltaic panels Kyocera KC200GT and prices of SMA Sunny Boy inverters. Internet address: www.affordable-solar.com, last accessed on 19.10.2010

Aten Solar (2008) Technical data and price of the photovoltaic panels Kaneka GSA60. Internet address: www.atensolar.com, last accessed on 19.10.2010

BTU – Brandenburgische Technische Universität Cottbus (2009) ERM graduate profile. Internet address: www.tu-cottbus.de/environment, last accessed on 19.10.2010

Bueno E, Ramos F, Luna S, Rüther R (2006) Atlas Brasileiro de Energia Solar - Brazilian Atlas of Solar Energy. DMA-CPTEC-INPE-MCT under SWERA-UNEP-GEF auspices. São José dos Campos

Catálogo Solar - Solar Home (2008) Technical data and price of the photovoltaic panels Würth Solar WS11007/75. Internet address: www.catalogosolar.com, last accessed on 19.10.2010

Coltro L, Garcia E, Queiroz G (2003) Life Cycle Inventory for electric energy system in Brazil. In: International Journal of LCA 8(5): 290-296

DOE – United States Department of Energy (2007) EnergyPlus version 2.0 application and documentation. Internet address: http://apps1.eere.energy.gov/buildings/energyplus, last accessed on 19.10.2010

Ecoinvent (2007) Ecoinvent database v2.01. Swiss Centre for Life Cycle Inventories, Duebendorf

EPE Empresa de Pesquisa Energética (2007) Plano Nacional de Energia 2030. Internet address: http://epe.gov.br/Estudos/Paginas/default.aspx?CategoriaID=346, last accessed on 19.10.2010

EPIA European Photovoltaic Industry Association, Greenpeace (2006) Solar Generation - Solar Electricity for over 1 billion people and two million jobs by 2020. Internet address: www2.epia.org/05Publications/Solargeneration.htm, last accessed on 19.10.2010

EPIA European Photovoltaic Industry Association, Greenpeace (2008) Solar Generation V. Internet address: www.epia.org/publications/epia-publications.html, last accessed on 19.10.2010

Frankl P, Corrado A, Lombardelli S (2004) Environmental and Ecological Life Cycle Inventories for present and future Power Systems in Europe (final report of the project ECLIPSE)

IAEA International Atomic Energy Agency, COPPE School of Engineering of the Federal University of Rio de Janeiro, CENBIO Brazilian Reference Centre on Biomass, UNDESA United Nations Department of Economic and Social Affairs (2006) A country profile on sustainable energy development. IAEA, Vienna

Jungbluth N, Tuchschmid M, Wild-Scholten M de (2008) Life Cycle Assessment of Photovoltaics: update of Ecoinvent data v2.0. ESU-services Ltd., Uster

Marland G, Boden TA., Andres RJ (2007) Global, Regional, and National CO2 Emissions. In Carbon Dioxide Information Analysis Center (2007) Trends: A Compendium of Data on Global Change. United States Department of Energy National Laboratory, Oak Ridge

Ministério da Fazenda (2008) Simulação do tratamento tributário e administrativo das importações. Internet address: www4.receita.fazenda.gov.br, consultation made on 16.09.2008

MME – Ministério de Minas e Energia (2007) Brazilian Energy Balance, year 2006. Internet address: www.mme.gov.br/mme, last accessed on 20.09.2008

Ripley K (2006) Mapping LAC's Solar and Wind Power Potential. Internet address: www.temasactuales.com/temasblog, last accessed on 15.09.2008

Rüther R (2004) Edificios Solares Fotovoltaicos - O Potencial da Geração Solar Fotovoltaica integrada a Edificações Urbanas e Interligada à Rede Elétrica Pública. LabSolar (UFSC), Florianópolis

Stryi-Hipp G (2004) The effects of the German Renewable Energy Sources Act (EEG) on market, technical and industrial development. In: publications of the 19th European Photovoltaic Solar Energy Conference, Paris, 7-11 June 2004

UFRGS – Universidade Federal do Rio Grande do Sul - Laboratório de Energia Solar (2001) Radiasol version 2.1 application. Internet address: www.solar.ufrgs.br, last accessed on 01.09.2008

UNEP Risoe Centre on Energy Climate and Sustainable Development (2007) Development first: linking energy and emission policies with sustainable development for Brazil. Roskilde

7 Wind Power Projects in India and Clean Development Mechanism (CDM) Approach

Shrinivas Tukdeo[1] and Satyanarayana Narra[2]

1 Ecolution India Pvt Ltd
2 Chair of Mineral Processing, Brandenburg University of Technology (BTU), Cottbus, Germany

7.1 Introduction

This chapter aims to discuss the necessity of increasing wind power plants with respect to the increasing power demand and the availability of the wind resource in India. The maximum available wind potential for power production is higher than the present installed capacities. This creates a chance for further sustainable development. This chapter is an original research work carried out by the company Ecolution India Pvt Ltd.

This chapter first gives a basic idea on the wind energy potential in India and continues with the Clean Development Mechanism approach with a case study of a 15 MW wind power project in the state of Karnataka, India. The case study deals with the registration of VERs by following the standards defined by UNFCCC for obtaining CERs. Further, the carbon emission reduction (CER) certificates and the present trend of the market will also be discussed. The present market trend shows a decline in the registration of wind power projects at the "United Nations Framework Convention on Climate Change (UNFCCC)" in obtaining CERs. This declining market trend has lead to the development of the voluntary market (voluntary emission reductions (VER)). This chapter aims to display how the market shifts from CER to VER due to a high rejection rate for wind power projects by UNFCCC. This study concludes that the development of VER projects is helpful for many investors due to the minimum security of these schemes.

7.2 Wind Energy in India

Renewable energy from the wind has been used for centuries to power windmills to mill wheat or pump water (Demirbas 2006). Nowadays, large wind turbines are used to generate electricity. Wind energy is one of the most viable technologies among the available options of renewable electricity generation where input fuel is in abundance and without any cost. The development of wind power in India began in the 1990s, and has increased significantly in the last few years (MNRE, 2009). Grid-connected wind based power generation has been one of the main growing power sectors in India. Exponential increase in wind potential has been observed from the year 2003 where the energy produced was only 2100 MW (MNRE 2009). In figure 7.1 it can also be observed that there was a decrease in the installed wind capacity in 2006 due to the damages caused by Tsunami. The Indian Carbon market started maturing in 2006 (IGES 2010) and the significant increase in installed wind capacity from year 2006 can be regarded as a result of additional benefits provided by the Clean Development Mechanism (CDM) market (Baumert et al. 2000) towards wind power project (Figure 7.1).

India has a total wind potential of 45,000 MW (MNRE 2009). Even though exponential growth in the wind power production has been observed (Figure 7.1), the wind power production is only about 19% of its total potential (MNRE 2009). Table 7.1 gives the detailed information of the present wind power production in comparison with the total wind power which can be achieved from different states in India. Table 7.1 gives the percentage of untapped wind energy potential from different states. The states West Bengal, Kerala, Andhra Pradesh, Madhya Pradesh and Rajasthan show a huge potential, which can be explored. The state Tamilnadu which is utilizing almost all of its wind energy potential can be an example for the other states in India.

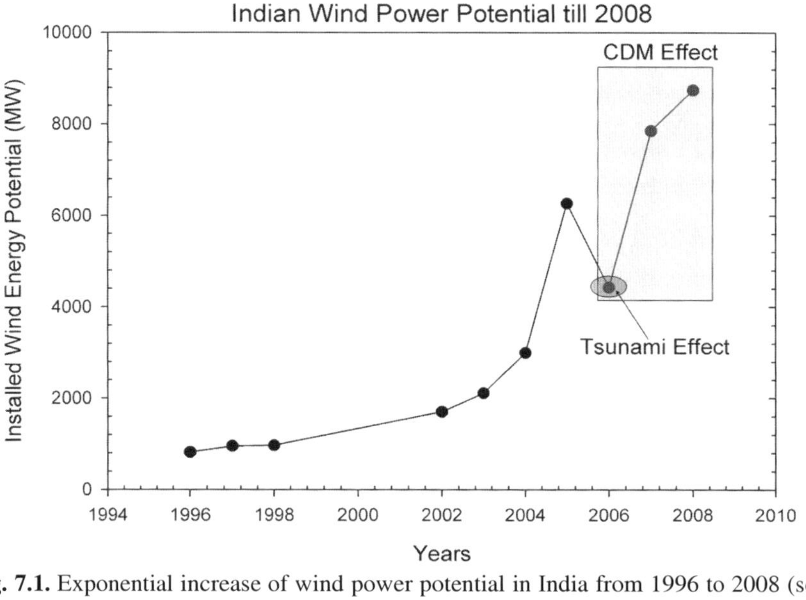

Fig. 7.1. Exponential increase of wind power potential in India from 1996 to 2008 (source: MNRE 2009)

Table 7.1. Information about the wind power in India giving the maximum potential in each state with the amount of present potential (source: MNRE 2009)

State in India	Present Potential (MW)	Maximum Potential (MW)	Installable (%)
Andhra Pradesh	122.5	8275	98.5
Gujarat	1252.9	9675	87
Karnataka	1011.4	6620	84.7
Kerala	10.5	875	98.8
Madhya Pradesh	187.7	5500	96.5
Maharashtra	1755.9	3650	51.9
Rajasthan	538.8	5400	90.0
Tamilnadu	3020	3050	0.9
West Bengal	1.2	450	99.7
Others	3.2	2990	99.8
Total	8757.2	45,195	80.6

7.3 CDM Approach

Wind projects in India were the major early movers in Indian Clean Development Mechanism projects with considerable success. The total number of Indian wind power projects registered is currently 54, and these registered projects are expected to generate 2 million CERs annually (Kalpagam 2007). As of June 2008, 86% of the wind projects that initiated the CDM process in 2005 have been registered. This success rate has been declining steadily thereafter in years 2006 (36%), 2007 (10%) and 2008 (none) (UNFCCC 2010). This decline in the success of CDM registration is due to the stringent rules of the Executive Board (EB) (Guest et al. 2003). The decline in registration of CDM wind projects has evolved a Voluntary Emission Reduction (VER) market in India (Bellassen and Lequet 2007; Bird and Lokey 2007). The difficulty in registering the already commissioned projects at the CDM – EB has resulted in the progress of VER market. The Chicago Climate Exchange (CCX) and Voluntary Carbon Standard (VCS-07) are the most preferred VER standards in India (Kalpagam 2007; Bellassen and Lequet 2007). The advantage of VER is that, it reduces the processing time and the risk of rejection is reduced. The other notable advantage of VER is that the project proponents can claim the emission reductions from past vintages (Bellassen and Lequet 2007; Bird and Lokey 2007) which is not possible with the CER. The disadvantage of this VER is the lower Emission Reduction prices per unit (1 VER = 1$ to 5 $) compared to Carbon Emission Reduction (1 CER = 20 $) (Capoor and Ambrosi 2007; Bird and Lokey 2007; CarbonFinance 2009).

7.4 Case-study: 15 MW Wind Power Project in the State of Karnataka is Presented to Analyze the VER Market

The case study presented here is a project by Ecolution India Pvt Ltd. The Project was not submitted to the UNFCCC for registration to obtain CERs as it was an ongoing project. The UNFCCC will not accept any ongoing projects for registration, due to this the project applied for registration and acquisition of VERs to Chicago Climate Exchange and Voluntary Carbon Standards. These two standards are the most prominent VER standards in India.

The projects activity is to generate electricity through sustainable means using wind power resources and to utilize the generated output by selling it to the Hubli Electricity Supply Company (HESCOM). The project supplies electricity to the grid, which is already suffering from deficiency due to a low demand to supply ratio. The project activity is located in the districts of Davangare and Gadag in the state of Karnataka, India (Table 7.2). The wind technology is provided by company RRB Energy Ltd. The project is a bundled project combining three different wind power mills in two different districts of the state together (Table 7.2).

Table 7.2. Description of location of the project

	Windmill Type	State	District	Town/Village
1.	Vestas RRB	Karnataka	Davangere	Horosagara, Daginkatte and Hosakere – 4.2 MW
2.	Vestas RRB	Karnataka	Gadag	Unachagere, Rajur, Vadegola and Kuntoji – 5.4 MW
3.	Vestas RRB	Karnataka	Gadag	Unachagere, Rajur, Vadegola and Kuntoji – 5.4 MW

7.4.1 Methodology

To register this project activity under CCX – VER, the methodology followed was for a UNFCCC approved small scale CDM project (UNFCCC 2010), which is a small scale grid connected renewable electricity production methodology. The methodology applies to renewable energy generation units, such as photovoltaic, hydro, tidal/wave, wind, geothermal and renewable biomass that supply electricity to and/or displace electricity from an electricity distribution system, that is or would have been supplied by at least one fossil fuel fired generating unit. If the unit added has both renewable and non-renewable components (e.g. a wind/diesel unit), the eligibility limit of 15MW for a small- scale CDM project activity applies only to the Renewable component. If the unit added co-fires fossil fuel, the capacity of the entire unit shall not exceed the limit of 15 MW (CDM rulebook 2010; EcoSecurities 2002 and 2003). The project activity produces renewable energy from the wind mills and it falls within the small scale rating as the total generation capacity is only 15 MW, which complies with the methodology.

7.4.2 Calculation of Emission Reductions

The project activity is about producing electricity using wind energy and exporting it to the southern grid system in India, which is also fed by other fuel sources such as fossil and non-fossil types. Emission reductions due to the project activity are considered to be equivalent to the emissions avoided in the baseline scenario by displacing the grid electricity. Emission reductions are related to the electricity exported by the project and the actual generation mix in the grid system (UNFCCC 2010).

7.4.3 Baseline Emissions

As the project activity consists of installation of Wind Turbine Generator (WTG) for fuel free power generation and does not modify or retrofit an existing electricity generation facility. The baseline scenario is electricity delivered to the grid by the project that would have otherwise been generated by the operation of grid-connected fossil fuel fired thermal power plants and by the addition of new generation sources. Further as per CCX rule book – The baseline emissions are calculated based on the net energy (MWh/year) provided to the grid and an emission factor (t CO_2 /MWh) for the displaced grid electricity provided by CCX for Indian Wind / Solar projects.

$$BE_y = EG_y \text{ x } EF_y \tag{7.1}$$

Where:

BE_y =	Baseline emissions in year y (t CO_2)
EG_y =	Net electricity generated by the project activity (MWh)
EF_y =	Baseline emission factor for the project grid (t CO_2/MWh)

This project activity is commissioned in southern part of India having a grid factor of 0.9, indicating 90% of the energy supplied from the grid is dependent on Fossil fuels.

7.4.4 Emission Reductions

The emission reductions from the project activity are equal to the baseline emissions minus sum of project emissions and leakage. Since the project activity generates electricity from wind, which is a zero emission source, there are no associated project emissions. As per AMS – I D (UNFCCC 2010), the leakage need not be considered since there is no transfer of energy generating equipment from another activity or transfer of existing equipment to another activity. Therefore, project emissions and leakage from the project activity are zero and thus emission reductions from the project activity are directly equal to the baseline emissions:

$$ERy = BEy - (PEy + Ly) \tag{7.2}$$

Where:
PEy = Project Emissions in year y (zero in this case)
Ly = Leakage in y (zero in this case)

Implying that there are no project emissions and leakages, the equation transforms into:

$$ERy = BEy \tag{7.3}$$

7.5 Results and Discussion

India has both an immediate energy need to sustain its economic growth and a great potential in wind energy. Presently wind energy only accounts for about 5% of the total energy generation. 63% of the India's electricity is produced using fossil fuels, therefore the development of the renewable energy sector, which currently accounts for around 8% of the total energy, will play an important role in Indian's fight against climate change in the near future. Wind energy already demonstrates its domination in the renewable energy sector of the country. The wind energy sector is attracting many investors nationally and this is mainly due to the additional benefits which can be availed of the CDM and VER markets. The project was submitted directly to the CCX instead of submitting it to UNFCCC as it was already a commissioned project. The project document (PD) was submitted to the CCX for approval by Ecolutions Carbon India Pvt Ltd. and was approved in 2008 by CCX board for Voluntary Emission Reductions. The amount of VERs generated is around 30,000 t of CO_2 equivalent.

7.6 Conclusions

Wind energy in India has a potential of 45,000 MW (MNRE 2009), this attracts increasing attention to the sector. Presently the installed wind power contribution is only 19% of the total potential of energy supply. Wind energy, being one of the cleanest sources of energy, will play an important role in combating global climate change problems. It is difficult to register Indian wind CDM projects at the UNFCCC due to the additionality challenges in obtaining CERs. This has resulted in the emergence of VER market in India. The VER market is a realistic option for investors to avail of additional benefits, thus encouraging the development of new wind power parks.

Acknowledgements

The authors would like to thank Mr. Kiran Patil, Managing Director, Ecolutions India for sharing his experience and providing guidance in the CCX approval process.

References

Baumert K, Kete N, Figueres C (2000) Designing the clean development mechanism to meet the needs of a broad range of interests. Climate Notes, WRI

Bellassen V, Leguet B (2007) The emergence of voluntary carbon offsetting. Research Report No.11, September 2007

Bird L, Lokey E (2007) Interaction of Compliance and Voluntary Renewable Energy Markets. Technical report. National Renewable Energy Laboratory. Internet address: http://www.eere.energy.gov/greenpower/pdfs/42096.pdf, last accessed on 15.10.2010

Capoor K, Ambrosi P (2007) State and Trends of the Carbon Market 2007. World Bank Institute

Carbon Finance (2009) The World Bank Carbon Finance Web Site. Internet address: http://carbonfinance.org, last accessed on 15.10.2010

CDM Rulebook (2010) Small-Scale, What is the CDM-SSC-PDD? Internet address: http://cdmrulebook.org/pageid/459, last accessed on 15.10.2010

Chicago Climate Exchange (CCX) (2008) CCX registry. Internet address: http://www.chicagoclimatex.com/content.jsf?id=501, last accessed on 15.10.2010

Demirbas A (2006) Global Renewable Energy Resources. In: Energy Sources, Part A: Recovery, Utilization, and Environmental Effects 28(8): 779-792

EcoSecurities (2002). Clean Development Mechanism (CDM): Simplified Modalities and Procedures for Small-Scale Projects. Internet address: http://www.ecosecurities.com/Asets/23529/Pubs_Clean%20Development%20Mechanism%20(CDM)%20Simplified%20modalities%20and%20procedures%20for%20small%20-%20scale%20projects.pdf, last accessed on 15.10.2010

EcoSecurities (2003) The Role of Emissions Trading in Asian Clean Energy Finance. Internet address: http://www.ecosecurities.com/Assets/23545/Pubs_The%20role%20of%20emissions%20trading%20in%20Asian%20clean%20energy%20finance.pdf, last accessed on 15.10.2010

Guest J, Stuart M, Wellington F (2003) The Role of Emissions Trading in Asian clean energy finance, JASSA, issue 4. Internet address: http://www.ecosecurities.com/Assets/23545/Pubs_The%20role%20of%20emissions%20trading%20in%20Asian%20clean%20energy%20finance.pdf, last accessed on 15.10.2010

Jagadeesh A (2000) Wind energy development in Tamil Nadu and Andhra Pradesh, India Institutional dynamics and barriers-A case study. In: Energy Policy 28(3): 157-168

Johnson GL (1985) Wind Energy Systems. Dissertation, Manhattan, 419 pp

Kalpagam U (2007) India's Business Prospects in the Global Emissions Market. In: Global Business Review 8(2): 237-250

MNRE – Ministry of New and Renewable Energy (2009) http://www.mnre.gov.in/, last accessed on 15.10.2010

IGES – The Institute for Global Environmental Strategies (2008) Climate Change Policies in the Asia-Pacific. ISBN/ISSN: 978-4-88788-048-1

IGES – The Institute for Global Environmental Strategies (2010) CDM in CHARTS Version 10. Internet address: http://www.iges.or.jp/en/cdm/report.html, last accessed on 15.10.2010

UNFCCC – United Nations Framework Convention on Climate Change (2010) Indicative simplified baseline and monitoring methodologies for selected small-scale CDM project activity categories. Internet address: http://cdm.unfccc.int/UserManagement/FileStorage/SJI52M6QXGKFNOZABTHDYPU789EV3C, last accessed on 15.10.2010

8 The Clean Development Mechanism Worldwide and in Brazil

Sören Noack

Brandenburg University of Technology (BTU), Cottbus, Germany

8.1 Introduction

Global warming has received increasing public attention during the past years. The Clean Development Mechanism (CDM) is one of the three flexible mechanisms established by the Kyoto Protocol to the United Nations Framework Convention on Climate Change. Similar to Emission Trading and Joint Implementation, CDM is a market-based approach (Michaelowa 2004), but obtains a special position in integrating developing countries into combating climate change. Although in theory effectively designed in ecological and economic terms (Pohlmann 2004), in reality problems arise from certain project criteria related to aspects of additionality and sustainability. Furthermore, CDM projects are inequitably distributed (Jung 2005) among potential host countries. Therefore many debates arise as to whether activities under the CDM actually lead to sustainable development and contribute to climate change mitigation. This chapter briefly outlines the theoretical concept of the CDM and critical aspects of criteria such as additionality, sustainability and the distribution of projects. Special attention is given to implications for Brazil, since the country is one of the most important hosts for activities under the Clean Development Mechanism. The case of Brazil shows that inequitable distribution of CMD projects is not only a phenomenon on global scale, but also occurs within host countries. Activities tend to concentrate in the rather well developed parts, while the number of projects in less developed region is very limited.

The chapter starts with an overview on the flexible mechanisms established by the Kyoto Protocol to mitigate climate change. Section 8.2 provides the theoretical conception of the CDM as one of the three flexible mechanisms. Section 8.3 highlights potential problems related to the main criteria for CDM projects such as additionality, sustainability and global distribution of the activities. In this context, Section 8.4 analyzes the Brazilian CDM market regarding the country's mitigation options and regional distribution of activities within the country. Section 8.5 discusses a case study on a project in the South-eastern part of Brazil involving eucalyptus plantations to provide the local steel industry with charcoal. The chapter ends with conclusions provided in Section 8.6 highlighting the inequitable distribution of activities under the CDM, both on a global and regional scale. Furthermore, the case study on a specific project suggests that an impact assessment on the project level might be insufficient in case of projects with a high potential of replication.

8.2 Flexible Mechanisms of the Kyoto Protocol

In 1992, the UN Framework Convention on Climate Change has been adopted to achieve *"stabilization of greenhouse gas concentrations in the atmosphere at a level that would prevent dangerous anthropogenic interference with the climate system"* (Article 2, UNFCCC, UN 1994). During the following years, there have been several conferences of the parties on how to implement the convention in reality. At the third conference in Kyoto 1997, the participants agreed on a protocol on the emission reduction of greenhouse gases by industrialized countries and countries in transition. The so-called Kyoto Protocol includes regulations and guidelines on how to fulfil these goals. At the follow-up conferences 2001 in Bonn and Marrakesh, the contracting nations could agree on open questions and exact definition of the flexible mechanisms (Betz et al. 2005).

According to their agreement, industrialized and transitional countries have to reduce their emissions of the six "Kyoto greenhouse gases", i.e. carbon dioxide, methane, dinitrogen oxide, hydrofluorocarbons, perfluorcarbons and sulfur hexafluoride. All gases are transferred into CO_2-equivalents according to their global warming potential. The obligation to reduce emissions of these greenhouse gases differs from country to country. The European Union for example, committed itself to a reduction by 8% during the first commitment period from 2008 to 2012. However, within the EU a burden-sharing agreement regulates the individual reduction targets for each member state.

Within the frame of the Kyoto Protocol, three so-called "flexible mechanisms" have been developed to assure cost-efficient ways of fulfilling the emission reduction obligations set in the Kyoto Protocol. The basic principle is to implement emission reduction measures where it is most economic, based on the assumption that climate change is a global problem and therefore it does not make a difference where these measures are carried out. The first important differentiation is where emission reductions are realized. For domestic emission reductions, the Kyoto Protocol establishes the "International Emission Trade" in article 17. This allows the trade between countries with emission rights granted in the Kyoto Protocol that are not needed as consequence of emission reduction measures. For example, if country A has more than enough emission rights, so called "Assigned Amount Units" (AAUs), it can sell them to country B which needs more emission rights. This approach has also been taken over by the European Commission for the EU-wide emission trade of more than 10,000 instalments (Betz et al. 2005). For projects undertaken in other countries, it is important to differentiate between countries listed in Annex-I to the UNFCCC and the so-called Non-Annex-I countries. Both CDM and Joint Implementation (JI) are project based mechanisms. That means that an Annex-I country or a company of an Annex-I country supports a project in the other country in order to obtain tradable emission grants. In the case of Joint Implementation (Article 6 of the Kyoto Protocol), the project takes place in another Annex-I country, i.e. in a host country with emission limitations. The investor earns so-called "Emission Reduction Units" (ERUs), that can be used to fulfil own national obligations or traded on the emission allowance market.

On the other hand, Clean Development Mechanism projects take place in developing countries or countries in transition, which have no obligation to reduce their emissions and are therefore not mentioned in Annex-I of the Kyoto Protocol. In this case, the investor obtains "Certified Emission Reductions" (CERs) that be traded or used to fulfil national obligations, similar to the ERUs derived from Joint Implementation projects. The main difference is that ERUs are subtracted from the assigned emission permits of the host country of JI projects as they also have obligations to reduce their emissions, while this is not the case in CDM projects as these host countries have no obligation. Compared with the other two flexible mechanisms, the CDM offers several advantages for investments mainly due to the incorporation of projects in industrializing countries which go along with attractive emission avoidance costs and the "prompt start". Emission reductions are accredited from January 2000 onwards, while emission permits obtained by Emission Trading and Joint Implementation are accredited only from 2008 onwards. One of the disadvantages is the higher transaction costs due to more complex verification procedures (Pohlmann 2004). In general, the project cycle of the Clean Development Mechanism can be considered as ecologically and economically effective. Rigid mutual control mechanisms between the involved parties and public control assure that emission reductions in the form of CERs fulfill the necessary requirements. At the same time, CDMs offer the chance of participation to a wide range of potential investors (Pohlmann 2004).

8.3 Problems of the Clean Development Mechanism

However, problems may arise from certain requirements related to additionality and sustainability. Both criteria are characterized by a lack of clear and international-wide accepted definitions. Furthermore, CDM activities are inequitable distributed.

8.3.1 Additionality

Additionality is an important criterion for the certification of CDM projects in order to assure that only emission reductions beyond the business-as-usual scenarios are considered. This implies that the baseline scenario is the weak point for the exact calculation of generated emission reductions. Even though the baseline scenarios undergo rigid examinations by the Executive Board (Betz et al. 2005), Pohlmann (2004) distinguishes four different types of additionality of which only two have been accepted in the Bonn Agreement and the Marrakesh Accords: Environmental and financial additionality. In other words, a CDM project has to include processes and practices that are superior to the current standards and that go beyond existing laws and regulations. Furthermore such activities may not be funded by public finances on an existing regular basis. On the other hand, there has been consent neither for criteria regarding investment additionality, referring to private financing, nor for criteria dealing with technological additionality.

8.3.2. Sustainability and Distribution

While sustainable development is one of CDM's aims, no precise sustainability criteria for projects have been agreed so far. The decision on the sustainability of a project is in the hands of the host country, who are not required to state a reason for the decision. Such imprecise criteria for projects may bear the risk of a "race to bottom" between host countries in order to attract more projects (Sutter and Parreño 2005). Inequitable global distribution of CDM activities is likely to increase this risk. While more than 95% of the projects are located in Latin America and the Asian-Pacific region, only a few are located on the African continent. The four leading countries (Table 8.1) China, India, Brazil and Mexico host more than 75% of all projects, responsible for 78% of emission reductions. India attracts 30% of the CDM projects, followed by China (24% of projects). Furthermore, China alone is responsible for 53% of all emission reductions achieved by projects under the Clean Development Mechanism, as it hosts several projects aimed at the reduction of methane and other Kyoto greenhouse gases with higher CO_2-equivalents.

The attractiveness of host countries is strongly related to the market for traditional foreign direct investments. This following of pathways traditional for foreign direct investments might lead to the impression that some of these FDIs are "green washed" by the help of the Clean Development Mechanism. Therefore, particularly in countries with a rather low attractiveness, the risk of lowering sustainability criteria seems to be potentially high. Jung (2005) highlights that even a further CDM capacity building in less attractive countries might only be a short term response. Due to the market based strategy, Jung (2005) raises the question of whether it would be more appropriate to distribute the opportunities under the Clean Development Mechanism more equally.

Table 8.1. Global distribution of CDM activities (Source: UNEP Risoe Centre 2008)

Country	Amount of Projects	Emission Reductions
China	24.1%	53.0%
India	30.1%	13.6%
Brazil	12.2%	8.5%
Mexico	8.9%	3.3%
Others	24.6%	21.7%

Consequently, this leads to the issue of including sink projects in the CDM. Sink projects are characterized by reforestation or afforestation activities in order to create carbon sinks. Approximately one fifth of the global anthropogenic carbon dioxide emissions are caused by unregulated land use and might be reduced by forestry projects (Böswald et al. 2001). Despite this their inclusion in the CDM is controversial. The United States and sympathizing nations, as well as a majority of Latin American and African countries have been in favour of including forest projects, while particularly the European Union, China and India have opposed such measures. One reason for the disagreement has been the fear of hindrances to the transfer of superior and innovative alternative energy saving technologies (Sutter and Parreño 2005) due to cheap carbon credits generated from sink projects. Another issue includes uncertainties regarding the perdurability of carbon fixation by forest activities (Van Vliet et al. 2003). Indeed, if these problematic aspects are not properly addressed, the final result might be counterproductive to significant reductions of greenhouse gases in the atmosphere.

8.4 The Clean Development Mechanism in Brazil

A review of CDM activities in Brazil reveals that the above mentioned issues are also relevant within the country. Brazil is not only one of the world's most unequal countries in terms of economic and social equity (Serroa da Motta 2002), but also made major contribution towards the establishment of the Clean Development Mechanism (Michaelowa 2004).

8.4.1 Spatial Distribution of CDM Activities within Brazil

Comparable to the global situation, CDM projects in Brazil are concentrated in the more developed regions. Only a few CDM projects can be found in less developed North and Northeast. More than two-thirds of the activities take place in the South (25%) and Southeast (43%) which is the economic centre of Brazil. The Central-west hosts 20% of all projects (UNEP Risoe Centre 2008).

Table 8.2. Distribution of CDM activities within Brazil (sources: UN Risoe Centre 2008; UNDP 2003)

Federal State	Share on CDM projects	HDI (2000)
São Paulo	22.76%	0.820
Minas Gerais	14.32%	0.773
Rio Grande do Sul	10.74%	0.814
Santa Catarina	8.18%	0.822
Mato Grosso	7.93%	0.773
Others	36.06%	0.723

Analyzing the distribution of CDM activities by federal states (Table 8.2) reveals that the top-three states of São Paulo, Minas Gerais and Rio Grande do Sul host 48% of all projects in Brazil. Together with Santa Catarina and Mato Grosso, 64% of the activities are located in five out of 26 Brazilian federal units. At the same time, these units are among the most developed, as indicated by the Human Development Index (HDI). Therefore the CDM in Brazil seems to be not an appropriate measure contributing to reduction of inequalities, as it rather partakes in exacerbating the existing situation.

8.4.2 Opportunities for Brazil under the CDM

The main opportunities for CDM activities in Brazil lie in the energy sector and in sink projects. Though the Brazilian electricity structure is mainly based on hydropower (Hirschle 2006), the available hydroelectric potential near the consumption centres is almost fully occupied. Consequently, CDM provides the opportunity to create incentives for renewable energy options in order to *"revert, at least partially, the damaging consequences of large-scale adoption of fossil fuel thermoelectricity"* (Seroa da Motta 2002). Considering current CDM activities, the majority of projects belong to the biomass sectors. Power generation from bagasse as well as the waste management sector and reductions of emissions from animal waste and manure by livestock farming activities are of interest (Hirschle 2006).

Table 8.3. Sectoral Distribution of Brazilian CDM projects (source: Brazilian Ministry of Science and Technology 2008)

Sector	Number of Projects (%)	Contribution to Annual Emission Reductions (%)
Renewable Energies	47	39
Livestock Farming	17	6
Waste Management	12	27
Fossil Fuel Change	12	7
Energy Efficiency	7	4
Reforestation	0	1
Other	4	17

Regarding present CDM activities (Table 8.3), renewable energies (47%) including cogeneration with biomass is the most frequent project type. However, their share of annual emission reductions is limited to 39%. In case of activities related to the reduction of emissions from livestock, the situation is similar. In contrast, waste management projects account for 12% of the CDM projects, but contribute to 27% of the annual emission reductions, as these measures reduce methane. In the industrial sector for example, steel companies developed measures to increase energy efficiency (7% of all projects), but currently their contribution to annual emission reductions is limited to a share of 4%.

The opportunities in the forestry sector for carbon sequestration and enhancement sinks is considered to be more promising, even though at the current state it is not playing a major role. According to Seroa da Motta (2002) large areas of degraded land, unsuitable for further agricultural activities, are ideal for forest plantations aiming at the production of pulp, timber and biomass for energy. Silvicultural plantations are seen as an important option to sequester carbon. However, there are social and environmental risks associated with monoculture plantations, further, the impacts of climate change might lower the benefits of silviculture plantations (Fearnside 1998). Therefore, the avoidance of deforestation might be the first best solution and more efficient than any other sequestration form (Fearnside 2001, Seroa da Motta 2002), as Brazil's major source of carbon dioxide emissions is related to deforestation of the Amazon Rainforest. In this context, Fearnside's (2001) proposed that Brazil could accept emission limitations in order to benefit from the preservation of the Amazon rainforest with its high biological diversity as a natural carbon sink under the International Emission Trade regime. This also has to be taken into account on the global level, given the extent of the Amazon Rainforest's influence on the Earth's climate system and the conservation of biodiversity.

Since the Bali conference at the end of 2007, the discussion about avoiding deforestation, as a further option for climate change mitigation, again received higher public attention. Referred to as Reduced Emissions from Deforestation and Degradation (REDD), the actual design of such a mechanism is not yet decided. However, REDD could play an important role in integrating developing countries into measures for climate change mitigation after 2012, especially those that currently are not considered attractive for activities under the CDM.

8.5 Case Study: The Plantar Project

Central activities of the Plantar project in Minas Gerais (Brazil) are the continuation of using charcoal as a reducing agent in pig-iron plants and the reforestation with eucalyptus as a sustainable source of charcoal production. The main objective is to generate carbon credits that can be commercialized in form of Certified Emission Reductions under the Clean Development Mechanism. As one of the projects in World Bank's Prototype Carbon Fund, it is controversial due to possible environmental risks and socioeconomic consequences. The project consists of three main components. The first constituent deals with the carbon storage in eucalyptus plantations, while the second part addresses the avoidance of a fuel switch from charcoal to coke. Improvements of kilns for charcoal production are the subject of the third component. In total, the project aims to reduce emissions of greenhouse gases by approximately 12,8 Mio tons of CO_2-equivalents.

Involving new eucalyptus plantations of 23,100 ha, the first component is a carbon sink project. During the first seven years of the project, every year 3,300 ha are planted. After a seven years growing period, the eucalyptus fields are harvested. The timber is then converted into charcoal, corresponding to the companies' annual demand. Because this cycle can be repeated twice more, this component aims to guarantee a sustainable charcoal supply over a period of 21 years. According to the baseline methodology, it is assumed that without financial support resulting from the consideration as carbon project, Plantar could not continue its reforestation activities. The land would be converted into pasture area for cattle. All in all, this component is expected to generate 4.5 Mio CERs. The baseline for the avoided fuel switch component is based on the tendency in Brazil's pig iron industry to convert from charcoal to coke due to lower prices for imported coke and shortages of fuel wood from native forests.

Another trend in the iron industry is to concentrate in large-scale coke-based iron mills, because the usage of coke allows for operation of bigger blast furnaces. Therefore, it is assumed that without incentives in form of carbon credits, Plantar would cease its iron production. Plantar's market share would be conquered by companies using coke, which unlike charcoal, is not considered as carbon neutral. The company claims this activity avoids emissions of ca. 7.9 million tons of CO_2-equivalents. Currently, the carbonization process of converting timber into charcoal is done in simple kilns causing the creation of methane as an undesired by-product. Due to improvements of the process, Plantar expects to reduce methane emissions by at least 70% and to generate further 437,326 tons of CO_2-equivalents (May et al. 2004).

However, the baseline scenarios for the components regarding the carbon storage and avoided fuel switch are doubtful. Critical NGOs started to campaign against the project, because they are also concerned about the negative impact on biodiversity and high water consumption of eucalyptus monocultures, as well as the risk of contamination of water bodies by fertilizers and pesticides. Furthermore they criticize bad working conditions and the concentration of land property and power in the region (Lohmann 2006). This argument is however not restricted to the actual Plantar project, but mainly linked to impacts resulting from the history of eucalyptus plantations in the region since their establishment in the 1960s.

On the other hand, proponents of the project stress that the project supports the attraction of foreign investments and technology, creates jobs in a region that is in economic recession and will reduce pressure on native forests as source for charcoal production. Plantar claims to aim for an improvement of working conditions and social benefits (May et al. 2004). With proper risk management, existing environmental risks appear to be tolerable. However both groups address the impacts on different levels. Therefore an impact assessment on a higher level than the project level, comparable to the strategic environmental assessment, would be desirable to more adequately deal with the concerns. Due to doubts about the additionality of two components, the future of the Plantar projects is rather unsure. So far, only the methane reduction received registration by the CDM Executive Board.

8.6 Conclusions

The Clean Development Mechanism is a first approach to integrate developing countries in climate change mitigation with a combination of climate protection, emission trading and promotion of sustainable development. While CDM is In theory ecologically and economically effective, in reality problems exist due to imprecise criteria for sustainability and additionality. Currently, activities under the CDM are inequitably distributed, with the result that only the most developed regions, those which already receive a considerable share of traditional foreign direct investments, may profit.

A more detailed view of CDM activities in Brazil as one of the favoured host countries reveals that the above mentioned issues are also relevant within the country. Brazil is not only one of the world's most unequal countries in terms of economic and social equity, but also made major contribution towards the establishment of the Clean Developing Mechanism with its proposal of a Clean Development Fund. Comparable to the global situation, CDM projects in Brazil concentrate in the more developed regions, most notably the federal state of São Paulo, Brazil's economic centre. Particularly the poorly developed Northeast and the Amazon region host only a few projects. Therefore, the CDM in Brazil seems to be not an appropriate measure contributing to reduction of inequalities, as it rather partakes in worsening the existing situation. Despite its controversies, the Plantar case furthermore suggests that an impact assessment on the project level alone might be insufficient to address all impacts, especially those of projects with a high potential of replication.

Further, the major source of Brazilian greenhouse gas emissions is related to the deforestation of the Amazon rain forest, which is currently not tackled at all by the project based Clean Development Mechanism, but measures to reduce emissions by avoiding deforestation are already under discussion and might be an option available for the time after 2012.

References

Betz R, Rogge K, Schleich J (2005) Flexible Instrumente im Klimaschutz: Emissionsrechtehandel, Clean Development Mechanism, Joint Implementation [Flexible Mechanisms for Climate Protection: Emission Trading, Clean Development Mechanism, Joint Implementation]. Umweltministerium Baden-Württemberg, Stuttgart

Böswald K, Martini S, Rumberg M, Schulte A (2001) Das Kyoto-Protokoll und die möglichen Folgen für die Weltforst- und -holzwirtschaft [The Kyoto Protocol and possible Impacts on Forestry worldwide]. In: Schulte A, Böswald K, Joosten R (eds) Weltforstwirtschaft nach Kyoto: Wald und Holz als Kohlenstoffspeicher und regenerativer Energieträger. Shaker Verlag, Aachen, pp. 34-47

Brazilian Ministry of Science and Technology (2008) Current status of the project activities under the Clean Development Mechanism in Brazil and the world. Internet address: http://www.mct.gov.br/upd_blob/0026/26986.pdf, last accessed on 15.10.2010

Fearnside PM (1998) Plantation forestry in Brazil: Projections to 2050. In: Biomass and Bioenergy 15(6): 437-450

Fearnside PM (2001) The potential of Brazil's forest sector for mitigating global warming under the Kyoto Protocol. In: Mitigation and Adaption Strategies for Global Change 6: 355-372

Hirschle A (2006) CDM Market brief: Brazil, 2nd edition. German Office for Foreign Trade (bfai), Cologne, 2006

Jung M (2005) Host country attractiveness for CDM non-sink projects. HWWA Working Paper, Hamburg Institute of International Economics (HWWA), Hamburg, 2005

Lohmann L (2006) Carbon Trading. Dag Hammerskjöld Foundation. Uppsala, 2006

May PH, Boyd E, Veiga F, Chang M (2004) Local Sustainable Development effects of forest carbon projects in Brazil and Bolivia. IIED, 2004

Michaelowa A (2004) Clean Development and Joint Implementation. In: Lucht M, Spangard G (eds) Emissionshandel: Ökonomische Prinzipien, rechtliche Regelungen und technische Lösungen für den Klimaschutz. Springer Verlag, Berlin, pp. 137-151

Pohlmann M (2004) Kyoto Protokoll: Erwerb von Emissionsrechten durch Projekte in Entwicklungsländern [Kyoto Protocol: Acquiring Emission Allowances by Projects in Developing Countries]. Duncker & Humblot, Berlin

Seroa da Motta R (2002) Social and economic aspects of CDM options in Brazil. In: International Journal of Global Environmental Issues 2(3-4): 310-321

Sutter C, Parreño JC (2005) Does the current Clean Development Mechanism deliver its sustainable development claim? International conference: Climate or development? October 28-29, 2005. Hamburg Institute of International Economics (HWWA), Hamburg

UNDP – United Nations Development Program (2003) Atlas do Desenvolvimento Humano do Brasil [Atlas of Human Development of Brazil]. Internet address: http://www.pnud.org.br/atlas/dl/unico/AtlasIDH2000.exe, last accessed on 15.10.2010

UNEP Risoe Centre (2008) UNEP Risoe CDM/JI Pipeline Analysis and Database, November 1st 2008

UN – United Nations (1994) United Nations Framework Convention on Climate Change

Van Vliet OPR, Faaj APC, Dieperink C (2003) Forestry Projects under the Clean Development Mechanism? In: Climatic Change 64: 123-156

9 Cleaner Production in Jeans Laundries in Northeast Brazil

Sören Noack

Brandenburg University of Technology (BTU), Cottbus, Germany

9.1 Introduction

Fast economic growth is often given higher importance than a more sustainable development. The textile cluster around Caruaru in Northeast Brazil serves as an example. For this rather poor region the textile industry is of high economic importance. However, jeans production goes along with severe environmental impacts. For years, a 'devil's deal' between authorities and entrepreneurs (Tendler 2002) fortified the situation and inhibited any improvements of working conditions and environmental impacts. During the past years however, the situation has started to change. While aspects of high water consumption and pollution have already received attention (Almeida 2005), the field of energy efficiency in jeans laundries has been left aside. There is a huge potential to reduce the consumption of firewood, which is in most cases of illegal origin, by several measures such as improved insulation, reclamation of heat energy and solar heating.

This chapter presents the environmental impacts of the jeans industry, in the case of 'jeans laundries', in Northeast Brazil and discusses possible solutions under the given socio-economic constraints of this region. Special attention is given to aspects of energy efficiency and use of renewable energies to reduce the emissions of greenhouse gases and deforestation. Section 9.2 provides socio-economic background information about the economic development and importance of the textile industry for Northeast Brazil. Section 9.3 describes the associated environmental impacts due to high water consumption and pollution in the local jeans laundries. Also the applied treatment technology is briefly introduced. Section 9.4 highlights the potential methods of optimizing the energy consumption. First, fuel costs for the use of wood and several alternatives are compared. Since the illegal cut firewood is the cheapest option, the reduction of energy losses is an important aspect. In this context, the three most promising opportunities to increase energy efficiency are analyzed - proper insulation, heat reclamation and solar thermal power. Section 9.5 discusses the future of the local jeans industry given the possible construction of an industrial area. The introduction of an adequate environmental and quality management scheme may provide additional economic benefits. The chapter ends with a summary and conclusions in Section 9.6 highlighting that improved environmental and quality management provides better market chances. In addition to advances in technology, environmental education for producers as well as consumers is equally important in achieving this long-term goal.

9.2 Socioeconomic Background

Compared to other developing countries, indicators of living standards for Brazil are relatively good, though the country still faces problems common to the developing world. Brazil is still one of the most unequal countries, particularly in terms of income distribution and land possession which are both highly concentrated (Seroa da Motta 2002). Furthermore, differences in development between the regions can be observed. Pernambuco is one of the nine federal states in Northeast Brazil and belongs to the least developed parts of the country. Besides the touristic areas along the coastline, in people's perception the countryside is associated with poverty and droughts. Regarding the poverty level, the region can be compared with Central African countries. Approximately 75% of the inhabitants, and respectively 60% of the urban population, are living at or even below the poverty line (Meier and Wahl 2005).

Bearing this in mind, the importance of strengthening environmental awareness and education becomes evident, since the acceptance of lowering environmental quality in return for economic growth can be high, especially among the lower income-classes. Many companies are lacking knowledge concerning the main initiatives on global environmental issues, though a great majority already recognize the relevance to their business activities. Even the current political agenda concentrates rather on economic growth and reduction of social gaps. Environmental concerns have to be balanced against development and equity issues (Seroa da Motta 2002). Consequently, authorities may refrain from pursuing environmental policies, as pointed out in the following.

Providing around 140,000 jobs, the garment industry is the second most important economic sector. The major cluster of clothing industry emerged in the municipalities of Caruaru (289,086 inhabitants), Toritama (29,907 inhabitants) and Santa Cruz do Capibaribe (73,667 inhabitants). Located ca. 130 km from the capital, Recife, this area comprises a population of almost 400,000 inhabitants (IBGE 2007). Supplying ca. 18% of the country's jeans production, this area became Brazil's major jeans manufacturing centre. This industrial sector is furthermore characterized by a high fraction of small and medium sized family enterprises (see Figure 9.1). In several cases, one member of a family owns the dressmaking company, while another family member takes responsibility for the laundering activities. Ongoing market liberalization puts pressure on the local textile industry due to cheap imports of mass products from Asian countries like China.

Fig. 9.1. Typical scenery of a small laundry (source: photo taken by the author)

During the first half of the 1990s, more than 90% of firms in the sector were informal (Meier and Wahl 2005). But for years the government of Pernambuco also accepted the unspoken agreement in form of a 'devil's deal' (Tendler 2002). Government officials freed entrepreneurs from compliance with labour, environmental and tax regulations in turn for votes at elections. Due to the absence of tax payments however, the government did not feel obliged to invest in improving the infrastructure. Another outcome of informality was the inability to access bank credits and support from governmental agencies for vocational training, as well as joining business associations. This situation started to change with the election of a new board of the business association of textile industry, Sindivest, in 1997. The new board of Sindivest started to take care of the interests of local businesses and successfully lobbied for tax reductions (Almeida 2005). Regularization of enterprises enabled firms to obtain support in order to improve product quality and diversity. Clothes produced in the region were known to be cheap and of low quality. Only a few companies were able to sell their products in other important markets in Brazil. This situation improved already, but urgently needs further efforts to defend its market share in the face of the ongoing liberalization of the Brazilian market and also to conquer other markets to ensure that this sector can survive.

9.3 Environmental Impact of Jeans Laundries

Compared to the production of other clothes, denim has a strong impact on the environment. First of all, a huge amount of water is required during the whole production cycle from planting the cotton to the end product. In total, Chapagain et al. (2006) estimated an average water consumption of 10,850 litres per pair of jeans. Since most of the amount of water is related to cotton growing, for jeans production in Caruaru and Toritama the main impact is caused by the washing process. In this last step of production, detergents, conditioners and other chemical substances are applied to obtain jeans with the desired look. The exact amount of water needed varies depending on the individual washing process which is mainly influenced by the different design of jeans. Values for water consumption range between 60 and 100 litres per pair of jeans (Almeida 2005). A total output of one million jeans every month by all companies therefore, implies not only the consumption of up to 60-100 million litres of water, but also that the same amount of wastewater needs to be treated in order to avoid environmental damages and risk to health. Furthermore, water and wastewater treatment are considerable cost factors.

One of the first steps towards environmental improvements was taken more or less by chance after the droughts in 1999. The price for water increased dramatically and laundries had to organize the transport of water by trucks from nearby cities. Interested in an economical solution to reduce the high costs for water, the owner of the largest laundry in Toritama got in contact with BFZ (Training and Development Centers of the Bavarian Employers' Association) from Germany. BFZ developed a technology to recycle water and control water pollution. This low-cost solution was 70% less expensive than already existing methods, since it used only material available in the region. The other important factor was the nomination of a new public attorney in Toritama in 2001. At the same time, CPRH, the state agency for environment and water resources, started their investigations on environmental pollution by jeans laundries (Almeida 2005). Since the low-cost solution of BFZ was available, the laundries were obliged to implement a wastewater treatment system. Most of the treatment facilities have been planned and implemented by ITEP, the Technological Institute of Pernambuco. At present, all laundries possess their own wastewater treatment system. Furthermore, workers benefit from increased security, even though there is still need for better protection. Nevertheless, all efforts undertaken so far have to be considered as first steps only. Further improvements are necessary to increase the removal efficiency of the wastewater treatment plants. The resulting sludge from the treatment has to be adequately disposed.

9.4 Aspects of Energy Efficiency in Jeans Laundries

Jeans laundries are using steam at three stages during the laundering. Usually, inside the washing machines hot steam with a temperature of about 200°C is mixed with water of ambient temperature to obtain the required temperature. The temperature depends on the specific washing process applied and ranges from 40°C to 95°C. Additionally, steam is required to dry the textiles after laundering and during ironing of jeans. During all stages, including the steam production, energy is lost. This is not only a financial issue, but also leads to significant environmental impacts.

9.4.1 Steam Production

The vast majority of companies use wood in their boilers. Since control mechanisms are lacking, illegal cut wood is the most attractive option. Most of the owners reported paying about 25 Brazilian Real (R$)[1] or even less per m³ of firewood. Licensed wood of better quality costs ca. 40 R$/m³. Alternative options include natural gas, bagasse and the use of solar energy to preheat the water before entering into the boiler. Bagasse could be an especially promising alternative, as it can be considered as a residue derived from processing sugar cane to alcohol and sugar. In theory, one ton of bagasse could replace up to seven cubic meters of wood (Cabral 2007). However, there are already several other applications for bagasse, for instance as animal feed. Research is also being done into the production of alcohol from bagasse. Thus, the available amount would not meet demand of all laundries of the textile cluster.

Table 9.1. Fuel costs of a laundry in Toritama (source: Personal communication with a laundry's owner in Toritama)

Fuel	Specific Fuel Costs (R$/piece)	Fuel costs per month (R$)
Wood	0.0770	7700
Bagasse	0.1706	17060
Babassu	0.2367	23670
Petcoke	0.1763	17630

For one of the biggest companies, five fuel options have been analyzed (Table 9.1), such as firewood, bagasse briquettes, babassu (a palm tree) and petcoke. Petcoke is a residual from the petroleum industry and represents the only viable fossil fuel option, since natural gas by pipeline is still not available in the region. The nuts of the babassu tree can be used to produce oil, which is a promising renewable fuel source. It is not surprising however that in the comparison of the considered fuel types, wood is the most competitive possibility. The analysis of specific fuel costs per pair of jeans clearly shows that bagasse (0.17 R$ per pair of jeans), considered as most attractive alternative to firewood, is more than twice as expen-

[1] 1 Brazilian Real is equivalent to 0.582 United States Dollar (exchange rate as of 12.11.2010, source: Yahoo! Finance)

sive as the use of fire wood (less than 0.08 R$ per pair of jeans). Even though a difference of 0.09-0.10 R$ in specific costs might be not that huge, given a monthly output of 100,000 jeans, it amounts in an increase of fuel costs of approximately 9,360 R$ compared to the use of wood.

One of the medium sized laundries in Caruaru switched from fuel wood to bagasse pellets. It was possible to observe their laundering process for one day. In total, 241 pieces of jeans were washed, resulting in the consumption of 240 kg of bagasse and 13,000 litres of water. For this company, specific fuel costs amount to 0.21 R$ per pair of jeans. It is however difficult to say in how far this represents a typical average value. Nevertheless, this laundry serves as example that the use of bagasse seems to be economically feasible.

9.4.2 Energy Flows and Losses in Laundries

Based on an analysis of one of the biggest laundries, typical examples for energy losses will be presented. It has to be noted that the situation in many of the smaller, less-organized laundries is often worse. Besides the lack of knowledge, for many owners it seems to be simply not attractive to invest in measures to improve energy efficiency. Firewood is quite cheap in absence of control by authorities. Especially in smaller laundries, old boilers with combustion efficiencies of 60% or even below are still in use. More advances steam boilers typically have combustion efficiencies of 70-80%. The main problem is excess of air during the combustion process (Baudach 2007). Furthermore, the overcapacity of many boilers in use contributes to lower efficiency. The above mentioned boiler systems consist of a furnace and the actual boiler part (see Figure 9.2). In latest-developed devices available on market both functional parts are combined, reducing additional heat losses. Therefore, replacement of the older boiler by models of the newest generation with an adequate capacity might improve energy efficiency considerably.

Furthermore, in many laundries steam tubes from boilers to washing machines and driers are either incompletely or not at all insulated, which leads to significant and unnecessary losses of energy. In cases where tubes are insulated, very often valves and connections lack insulation. Particularly in smaller and less-organized companies, tubes are unnecessarily long and not insulated at all. Proper insulation is neither complicated nor requires high investment costs. It contributes significantly to the improvement of efficiency and thereby offers benefits for the entrepreneurs as well as for the environment. Due to insufficient awareness and cost controlling by the owners, this point often receives no attention at all.

Additionally, Baudach (2007) mentions the potential for reducing the amount of steam and electric energy used for the driers by avoiding too long drying processes. Installing control technology with sensors for temperature and humidity allows the stopping of the drying process automatically once threshold values have been reached. Further, employing heat exchangers allows for the use of heat energy contained in exit air in order to preheat air entering the machines.

Fig. 9.2. Old steam boiler and furnace (source: photo taken by the author)

Given the high water consumption, more advanced strategies for increasing energy efficiency have to consider measures to reduce the amount of fuel used to produce steam. An analysis of the distribution of required water temperatures reveals that 54% of the total water consumption refers to 'cold water', i.e. water of ambient temperature. A further 31% describes water with temperatures in the range of 40 to 60°C. Under these conditions, two very promising options exist. First, heat exchangers could be used to preheat water entering the machines by the remaining heat of the effluent. The second option includes the application of solar energy to produce hot water.

Regarding the first option, Baudach (2007) refers to a theoretical potential to reduce energy consumption of up to 40% by installing heat exchangers. The main obstacle lies in the complexity of applied washing processes, which complicates the separation of the used water. Another low-cost possibility could be using heat energy of the gas leaving through the furnace chimneys in order to preheat water before entering the boiler. In any case, the area of reusing heat energy deserves more research.

The second option, using solar collectors, might be even more promising and also a visible sign of a more 'ecologically correct laundry', at least in terms of energy issues. However, solar energy would require high investment costs, given the high demand for hot water. According to experts from the federal university UFPE, a 100% generation of hot water (up to 60°C) by solar collectors for a big laundry needs an initial investment of approximately 400,000 R$ (Costa, 2007). Bearing in mind only the average annual fuel costs for wood, the minimum pay off time corresponds to five years and four months. Consequently, the vast majority of laundries are unable to apply this technology, even though rising fuel prices have to be expected. A pay off after five years or even more is simply to long for many laundries due to unsure future projections.

Nevertheless, one of the laundries shows high interest in solar power and currently plans to generate up to 50% of its demand on hot water by solar collectors. Main objective of the owner is to present an 'ecologically correct' way of laundering jeans in order to become certified after important worldwide accepted quality (ISO 9000 series) and environmental (ISO 14000 series) management standards (Costa 2007). With regard to the company's role in promoting low-cost wastewater treatment technology in the region, this company might be again motivating other laundries to develop similar concepts. Furthermore, these improvements in the field of energy efficiency might be a chance for all stakeholders to exit this 'devil's cycle' regarding the use of unsustainable and often illegal cut firewood and offer a win-win situation for the benefit of the whole region. Textiles of high quality, produced in an environmentally correct way, may have a higher market potential and allow this regionally extremely important industry to continue, without harming the environment.

9.5 Future of Jeans Laundering in Caruaru and Toritama

So far, several first steps to minimize the environmental impact have been developed. In particular the treatment of wastewater and solid waste residues has already received attention. But still there is need for further improvements, mainly in the area of energy efficiency. To address these issues properly, the optimal solution might be the establishment of an industrial area for jeans laundries outside the centres of Caruaru and Toritama. This idea has already been under discussion for several years and is lately receiving more attention. The main ideas include a central utility providing steam, hot water and the treatment of produced wastewater.

Such an approach offers several advantages. Due to scale effects, solutions can be more cost-efficient and thus allow the implementation of better technology in the wastewater treatment station, as well as using renewable energies for the heating of water and steam. Competition between the involved companies could no longer be used as excuse for not fulfilling environmental standards, since steam and wastewater are provided centrally with the same costs for all, but rather set further incentives to invest in more efficient devices. Clustering these activities in an industrial area, would also allow small enterprises to work together and possibly to join in cooperatives.

Additionally, the efforts of involved authorities would be reduced, because they would not need to inspect dozens of laundries, each having separate boilers and wastewater treatment systems. In case the centralized services violated environmental regulations, e.g. by using illegal cut wood or improper treatment of wastewater, this would also draw much more attention of the public, and therefore all stakeholders involved have interest to avoid such scandals. Last but not least, if laundries move away from cities and neighbourhoods, impact on local population will be reduced, such as smoke and dust from furnaces, odours caused by wastewater etc.

Unfortunately, there are also several problems connected with the establishment of an industrial area. Doubts on general feasibility also shared among experts of ITEP. Most important issues seem to be financial aspects. The enterprises alone are unable to take responsibility for initial investment costs. Consequently, this leads to the question of whether smaller laundries should be allowed to remain in towns, and only the medium-sized and large-scale companies, with all negative consequences this may have for the local population would be moved. The size of enterprises correlates with possibilities to invest in treatment technology. Smaller laundries have more financial limitations to upgrade technology than bigger companies.

One option to obtain financial support could be a carbon project under an emission trading regime, such as the Clean Development Mechanism (CDM) established by the Kyoto Protocol. Entities from countries with obligations to reduce greenhouse gas emissions have the opportunity to invest in projects in developing countries, which have no reduction obligations. Resulting emission reductions can be traded and used by those that have to reduce their emissions. In such a way, a carbon project could for example contribute financing the use of renewable energy resources and measures to increase energy efficiency in the jeans laundries.

Another concern is the availability of data in order to provide sufficient capacity for steam generation and wastewater treatment. Again, this counts especially for small-sized laundries that often have no exact information on water and steam consumption. Therefore, it seems to be sometimes surprising how they can maintain their activities. Furthermore, precise data are needed to develop a reasonable methodology for any climate change mitigation project.

Aside from the question of whether the industrial area will finally be built, one of the biggest laundries has started activities to reduce the environmental impacts along with increasing product quality. So far, the vast majority of produced jeans are sold within the region. Producing textiles of higher quality improves the chances of reaching further markets. If the company succeeds, it could demonstrate that upgrading technology reduces not only the environmental impacts, but also offers economic benefits. Given the potential for replication, most environmental improvements could be adopted by the other laundries.

In future, textile imports from Asian countries are expected to increase. Part of a successful strategy for continuation of the local textile industry is to conquer new markets. Entrepreneurs try to establish export routes to several African countries, but 'ecologically correct produced jeans' of high quality may open opportunities to export to Europe or North America as well. This however also implies that consumers are willing to accept slightly higher prices.

9.6 Summary and Conclusions

Fast economic growth is often given higher importance than sustainable development, as in the case of the textile cluster around Caruaru in Northeast Brazil. For years, a 'devil's deal' between local authorities and entrepreneurs fortified the situation. During the last years however, the situation started to change. Aspects of water consumption and pollution have already received attention, but the field of energy efficiency in jeans laundries has been left aside. A huge potential exists to reduce the consumption of firewood by increasing energy efficiency and use of solar thermal systems. But as long as illegal cut wood is available for a low price, entrepreneurs will be tempted to continue illegal practices.

On the other hand, some companies have already switched to alternative fuels and show interest in applying solar heaters. The motivation behind this is to become certified by environmental and quality management systems. Textiles of high quality, produced in an ecologically correct manner, may have a higher market potential. Thus, this important industry can continue operating while reducing harm to the environment.

Concluding, these examples demonstrate that companies can be convinced to invest in cleaner production most effectively by the help of economic arguments, when a clear link between economic benefits and environmental improvements can be presented. Difficulties arise from the interest in short-term profits, though costs related to environmental degradation in the long run might be much higher. Therefore, rather than simply presenting some technical solution for the problems, this case study stresses the importance of environmental education in the field of development assistance,

Finally, the aspect of environmental awareness also leads back to the responsibilities of consumers, especially those in developed nations, given the clear link between consumption behaviour and environmental degradation, which often rather affects the poor more than the rich.

References

Almeida M (2005) Understanding Incentives for Clustered Firms in Brazil to Control Pollution: The Case of Toritama. IPEA - Discussion Paper, April 2005

Baudach (2007) Analysis of energy fluxes in the laundry Mamute, Toritama (Unpublished)

Cabral S (2007) Logística reversa estimula reaproveitamento de materiais [Reverse logistics stimulates reuse of materials]. In: Journal da Industria, Number 47, p. 5, FIEPE, Recife, July 2007

Chapagain AK, Hoekstra AY, Savenije HHG, Gautam R (2006) The water footprint of cotton consumption: An assessment of the impact of worldwide consumption of cotton products on the water resources in the cotton producing countries. In: Ecological Economics 60(1): 186-203

Costa E (2007) Lavandaria ecologicamente correta [The environmentally friendly laundry]. In: Diário de Pernambuco, Recife, September 24th 2007

IBGE – Instituto Brasileiro de Geografia e Estatística (2007) Contagem da População 2007 [Census of population 2007]. Internet address: http://www.ibge.gov.br/home/estatistica/populacao/contagem2007/PE.pdf, last accessed on 15.10.2010

Meier R, Wahl M (2005) How a business membership organization can contribute to improving the business environment. Paper presented to the International Conference on Reforming the Business Environment, Cairo, 2005

Seroa da Motta R (2002) Social and economic aspects of CDM options in Brazil. In: International Journal of Global Environmental Issues 2(3-4): 310-321

Tendler J (2002) Small Firms, the Informal Sector, and the Devil's Deal. IDS Bullentin, Volume 33, No. 3, July 2002

10 Future of Alternative Energy in Thailand

Angkarn Wongdeethai

Science, Technology and Innovation Policy Research Department, National Science and Technology Development Agency, Thailand

10.1 Introduction

The objective of this paper is to identify the major opportunities and barriers of alternative energy production activities in Thailand, working towards a sustainable future. The paper analyses the historic and current energy consumption patterns and identifies the major energy intensive activities in each sector. Thailand's recent energy strategies, policies and oil prices have been studied and discussed based on the potential of alternative energy production and technology. The paper describes the key government programs and policies relating to the promotion of alternative energies and presents their major successes and failures. Thailand's average energy consumption grew at a rate of 5.5 percent per year from 1999 to 2006 and the domestic energy production cannot accommodate the increasing demand of the country (EPPO 2008a). Thailand's energy production depends largely on imported fossil fuel which represents a considerable financial cost.

The world depends largely on conventional fossil fuel resources and will continue to do so for several decades before the coming era of oil depletion. Before this critical point is reached and because of concerns about rising oil prices Thailand is seeking alternative energies and promising technologies. At the moment, conventional fossil fuels are cheaper than several alternative energies. All sizes of industries as well as businesses which have already installed or switched to an increased consumption ratio of renewable energy may have to reconsider their current situation. It is hard to tell how long the oil prices will remain stabile and how long fossil fuel emissions will continue to adversely impact the environment, e.g., CO_2 emissions. First, people tend to consume energy more because it is inexpensive. Second, the renewable energy sources are relatively less cost-effective; and their relatively smaller profit margins have prompted potential big commercial dealers of energy to tighten their budgets for sustainable energy programs. Third, the Governments confronting financial and economic crises will tend to limit their expenditures, especially on research and incentive packages. Moreover, the rising cost of capital is making it harder for both consumer and suppliers of alternative energy equipment and services to finance new projects. Funding from banks in many countries has dried up as firms move to conserve capital. However, the government of Thailand continues to subsidize long term alternative energy programs.

Despite the rapid growth of energy demand, Thailand's per capita commercial energy consumption is still very low in comparison with other industrialized countries at an average of 1.27 tons of crude oil equivalent (toe). As a result, the greenhouse gases emission per capita is estimated to be about 5.5 tons of CO_2 (Amranand 2008).

10.2 Thailand's Energy Status

In 2007, the total Energy Demand of Thailand was 64,686 kilotons of crude oil equivalent (ktoe), a rise of 2.3% from the previous year, whilst Thailand's economy grew at an annual rate of 4.8%. Modern or Commercial Energy shared 53,110 ktoe or 82.1% of the total Energy Demand whereas the Renewable Energy consumed was 11,576 ktoe or 17.9% (DEDE 2007). The total commercial primary energy consumption amounted to 80,019 ktoe (Amranand 2008), of which oil constituted 42%, natural gas 38%, coal 15%, hydro 2%, and others 3%. This consumption came from 4 major sectors, i.e. industry (38.2%), transportation (36%), residential and commercial (20.5%) and agriculture (5.3%) (see Figure 10.1). Thailand's primary energy consumption expenditure accounted for 17.7% of the Gross Domestic Product (GDP), and the value of primary energy imported was 10.4% of GDP. This illustrates the high dependency on energy import, which amounted to 59% of the primary energy consumption (EPPO 2008a). In 2004, Thailand's energy intensity was 20,993 kilojoules commercial energy consumed for each dollar of GDP, and ranked 48th out of 55 countries, whereby most developed countries such as USA, Japan, and Germany have lower energy intensity, between 4,000-7,000 kilojoules (IMD 2008).

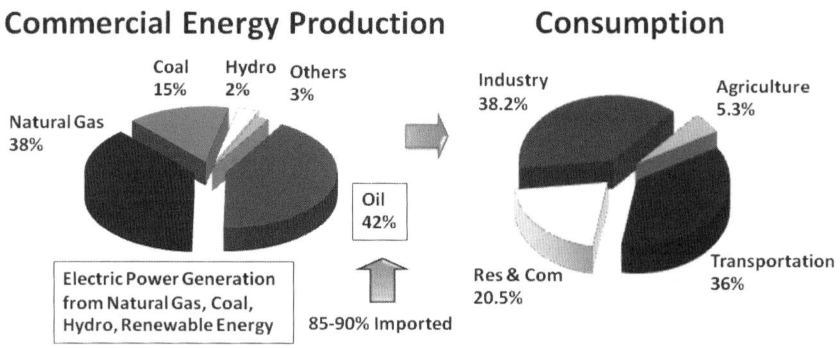

Fig. 10.1. Thailand's Commercial Energy Production and Consumption in 2007 (adapted from: DEDE 2008)

For electric power generation in 2007, the peak demand was 22,586 MW. The electric power was generated from 5 major supply resources: natural gas (65%), coal (19.8%), renewable energy (5.5%), hydro-electricity (5%), and purchase from other countries (2.8%). The total electricity production amounted to 160,062 Gigawatt hours (GWh) (DEDE 2008). For transportation, almost 80% of energy consumption was used in land transportation, whilst 78.6% of the energy was used by cars and light/heavy trucks, and only 0.5% by rail; transportation by waterway accounted for only 4.6%, and the remaining 16.3% was for air transportation (EPPO 2008b).

The number of newly registered vehicles in Thailand had been increasing steadily; in 2007, the number of vehicles reached 25.6 million, a 3% increasing from 24.5 million in 2006 (DLT 2008). The Ministry of Energy reported that the country consumed about 730,000 barrels of oil equivalent per day (116 Million litres per day). Bangkok alone consumed 44% while Thailand's remaining 75 provinces accounted for 56% of total oil consumption. If Bangkok is able to reduce its oil consumption and use more alternative energy, the country can save significant money from reduced oil imports (Chatkaew 2008). Currently, 85-90% of oil is imported and this high dependency on imported energy, aside from causing a susbtancial loss of foreign currency, puts Thailand at risk of energy supply disruption and volatility of energy prices and threatens its competitiveness.

This together with quadrupling of the world oil price during the past 5 years has pushed the cost of Thailand's net energy import to $19.5 billion in 2007, equivalent to 7.9% of GDP (Amranand 2008). In 2001, due to the growing number of cars, passengers using the mass transportation in Bangkok and its vicinities decreased from 1,224 million in 1997 to 938 million. In addition, passengers using inter-province buses reduced from 12.6 million in 1997 to 10.8 million in 2001. Likewise within the same period, passengers using rail transport dropped from 64.9 million to 56.7 million (EPPO 2008b). In comparison, the main transportation system in urban cities in developed countries, for example Germany and Japan, is the rail system, which is promoted by the governments due to its energy efficiency.

In 2003, Thailand faced such a risk of oil supply disruption and price volatility that the government had to introduce an oil price stabilization measure in order to alleviate the impacts of oil price hikes on the economic development as well as domestic consumers. The country's push to strengthen the national energy security and competitiveness comprised development strategies focused very much on efficient energy management and promotion of renewable energy. This was coupled with strategies to extend the availability of indigenous energy reserves for as long as possible. Thailand has limited indigenous fossil fuel reserves and at the rate of consumption as of 31 December 2009, it was estimated that the country's crude oil resources would dry up within the next 3-15 years; condensate within 8-22 years; natural gas within 10-27 years, and; lignite within 67-114 years (EPPO 2009) (see Table 10.1). Several efforts and initiatives have been implemented to make the country energy self-reliant. The balance between the energy consumption, energy production, and energy intensity are key determinant factors in enhancing Thailand's national energy security and economic development.

Table 10.1. Energy Reserves as of 31 December 2009 (Source: EPPO 2009)

Energy type (original unit)	Reserves*			Production in 2009	Available for use (years)		
	P1	P1+P2	P1+P2+P3		P1	P1+P2	P1+P2+P3
Petroleum							
Crude Oil (MMbbl)**	180	652	821	56	3	12	15
Condensate (MMbbl)	255	591	677	31	8	19	22
Natural Gas (BCF)***	11,026	23,692	29,862	1,092	10	22	27
Lignite (m. Tons)	1,181	2,007	2,007	18	67	114	114

Note: P1 = Proven reserves, P2 = Probation reserves, P3 = Possible reserves
* source of data: Department of Mineral Fuels
** The abbreviation 1 MMbbl has historically meant one million barrels, 1 oil barrel = 158.9873 litres
*** BCF = billion cubic feet, 1 $feet^3 = 0.0283\ m^3$

In October 2008, Minister of Energy, Mr. Wannarat Channukul announced Thailand's Energy Policy to deal with the energy problems (see Box 10.1)

Box 10.1. Imperatives of the Thailand's Energy Policy (source: Channukul 2008)

1. Enhance energy security to ensure sufficient energy supply for the country's development and to increase energy self-reliance for the people's well-being.
2. Monitor energy prices to be appropriate, stable and in line with the economic and investment situations.
3. Promote research and development of all forms of alternative energy on a continuous basis.
4. Emphasize the creation of energy saving discipline as a national culture and encourage the Local Administration Organizations to be focal points for disseminating 'Energy Saving Culture'.
5. Protect the environment from impact of energy industry, generated by both energy production and consumption processes, as well as promote the tackling of global warming and support the Clean Development Mechanism (CDM).

Within the energy policy the priority was set to 'increase energy self-reliance', by promoting specific measures for renewable energy to enhance people's well-being and improve the community. Imperative 1 in Box 10.1. was particularly significant, especially for large numbers of farmers in rural areas. Only after energy production exceeded their energy needs would commercialization of energy be considered. In the long run, with this self-reliance approach/model together with other effective promotion policies and appropriate government investments in renewable energy, Thailand expect to develop a well-built and strong sustainable energy structure, adequate to overcome the country's outstanding energy problems.

10.3 Thailand's Alternative Energy Development

At the national level, Thailand possesses abundant biomass and solar resources, with good potential for wind and hydro-electricity development. There are several alternative energy measures and incentives given by the government within the energy sectors of: solar, wind, mini-hydro electricity facilities, biomass, biogas, municipal solid waste (MSW), ethanol, biodiesel, and natural gas vehicles (NGV)[1].

10.3.1 Electricity and Thermal Energy

It is estimated that the potential for renewable resource use for electric power production is 4,400 MW - from biomass such as bargasse, paddy husk, woodchips, and municipal wastes. Furthermore, there is potential to generate another 1,100 MW from biogas received from pig farms and other types of agro-industry such as corn cob and wastes from palm oil factories. The potential also exists for another 50,000 MW from solar, 1,600 MW from wind, 2,600 ktoe from biofuels (1,500 ktoe from ethanol and 1,100 ktoe from biodiesel), and 8,000 ktoe of thermal energy production from solar, biomas, biogas, and MSW to be harvested (DEDE 2008). Targets for renewable energy utilization have been set at 8%; and for alternative energy utilization at 11.5% by 2011. The target for renewable energy utilization has been further set at 11.6% in 2016 and 12.2% in 2022. The future target for alternative energy utilization is 19.9% in 2016, and 20.4% in 2022 (Pongpirodom 2008) (Table 10.2).

In 2007, the Surayud Chulanond government issued a number of sweeping changes to the policy to promote energy efficiency and renewable energy, in quick reaction to rising oil prices and the problem of global warming. There were amendments for supporting measures for small power projects (SPP) and very small power projects (VSPP) by putting a higher incentive, namely an 'adder' on top of the normal tariff for 7-10 years from the Commercial Operation Date (COD) for proposals submitted before the end of 2008 (Amranand 2008). The total SPP's purchasing target was set at 1,600 MW, and the first programme was for 1,030 MW, which consisted of a cogeneration programme (500 MW) and a renewable programme (530 MW).

[1] NGV (natural gas vehicle) is a vehicle that runs on a mix of clean alternative fuel, particularly compressed natural gas (CNG).

Table 10.2. 15-Years Alternative Energy Plan (2008-2022) (Source: DEDE 2008, Pongpirodom 2008)

Energy Type	Potential	Existing 2008	Target 2011	Target 2011	Target 2016	Target 2016	Target 2022	Target 2022
Electricity	**MW**	**MW**	**MW**	**ktoe**	**MW**	**ktoe**	**MW**	**ktoe**
Solar	50,000	32	45	4	95	11	500	56
Wind	1,600	1	115	13	400	45	700	78
Mini-Hydro	700	50	156	16	281	73	324	85
Biomass	4,400	1,597	2,800	942	3,235	1,682	3,700	1,933
Biogas	190	29	60	27	90	40	120	54
MSW	320	5	100	45	130	87	160	96
Hydrogen			0	0	0	0	3.5	1
Total		**1,714**	**3,276**	**1,047**	**4,231**	**1,938**	**5,508**	**2,303**
Thermal	**ktoe**	**ktoe**		**ktoe**		**ktoe**		**ktoe**
Solar	100	0.3		5		17		34
Biomass	7,400	2,345		3,660		4,915		6,725
Biogas	470	79		370		540		600
MSW	78					25		35
Total	**8,048**	**2,424**		**4,035**		**5,497**		**7,394**
Biofuels	**Ml/d**	**Ml/d**	**Ml/d**	**ktoe**	**Ml/d**	**ktoe**	**Ml/d**	**ktoe**
Ethanol	5.4*	1.2	2.4	653	6.2	1,686	9.0	2,447
Biodiesel	3.3*	1.3	3.0	953	3.6	1,145	4.5	1,416
Hydrogen			0.0	0	0.0	0	0.1MKg	124
Total		**2.4**	**5.4**	**1,606**	**9.8**	**2,831**	**13.5**	**3,987**
Total Energy Demand (ktoe)		**65,420**		**79,811**		**88,389**		**112,046**
Renewable Energy Demand (ktoe)		**3,412**		**6,688**		**10,266**		**13,684**
Ratio of RE Utilisation		**5.2%**		**8.0%**		**11.6%**		**12.2%**
Gas NGV (MMSCFD)**		**91.5**	**345.0**		**826**		**1,035**	
Total Alternative Energy Demand (ktoe)				**9,204**		**17,556**		**22,819**
Ratio of Alternative Energy Utilisation				**11.5%**		**19.9%**		**20.4%**

* Potential for ethanol and biodiesel production is calculated from material residues (production, national consumption and exporting)
** MMSCFD = million standard cubic feet per day, a unit of measurement for liquids and gases that is predominantly used in the United States. 1 feet^3 = 0.0283 m^3

The renewable programme, provided an extra incentive through the ‘adder’, and announced the initial targets for renewable energy capacity being solicited from various types of renewable energy sources (Table 10.3). The ‘adder’ costs for MSW, wind, and solar energy was fixed. Apart from these ‘adder’ costs, e.g., for biomass, the SPP’s ‘adder’ was determined through a competitive bidding system where the government issued a solicitation for 300 MW on 1 May 2007. There is also an extra ‘adder’ for SPPs/VSPPs in the three Southern most provinces (Yala, Pattani and Narathivath), with an additional 1.50 baht/kWh for wind and solar energy[2], and 1.00 baht/kWh for other types of renewable energy to compensate for risk from any political unrests (Amranand 2008). Incentives were also given through financial soft loans and investment subsidies for energy production from biogas and mini-hydro. Biogas can be produced from various wastes such as pig farms, municipal wastes, and factory wastes (e.g., production of tapioca starch, palm oil, rubber sheet, ethanol and other types of agro-industry).

Some renewable projects are not SPPs or VSPPs, but simply produce energy for their own use or off-grid village-based projects in remote areas. Moreover, government agencies were supported with a budget in order to implement mini and micro hydro projects. As in most cases, obtaining the various permits would be extremely difficult for the private sector. A financial support provision to the private sector was made for assist in the acquisition of technical assistance for pilot projects and also for aid in the venture into new or unfamiliar technologies. Private investment is being encouraged through Energy Service Companies (ESCO) and the ESCO Venture Capital Fund which is being established. Concerning global warming reduction efforts, the trading of carbon credit through CDM scheme has given an enormous boost to a number of marginal projects, particularly biogas and municipal waste projects.

Table 10.3. SPP and VSPP Adder Costs (adapted from: DEDE 2008)

SPP (10 MW< SPP ≤ 90 MW)	Adder Costs (baht/kWh)	Initial Target (MW)	**VSPP (VSPP ≤ 10 MW)**	Adder Costs (baht /kWh)	
Type of Energy	General		Type of Energy	General	3 Southern Provinces
MSW	2.5 (fixed)	100	MSW	2.5	3.5
Wind Energy	3.5 (fixed)	115	Wind Energy	3.5	5
Solar Energy	8.0 (fixed)	14	Solar Energy	8	9.5
Other Alternative	0.3 (bidding)	300	Mini-Hydro (50-200 kW)	0.4	1.4
	Total	**530**	Mini-Hydro (< 50 kW)	0.8	1.8
			Biomass	0.3	1.3
			Biogas	0.3	1.3

10.3.1 Responses from SPP, VSPP Incentives

Feedbacks from policy changes in 2007 have been remarkable. As of 31 August 2007, 31 new cogeneration SPP projects have submitted applications for sale of 2,416 MW of electricity to Electricity Generating Authority of Thailand (EGAT), which exceeded the target of 1,600 MW by 51%. The main hindrance to new SPPs is probably the availability of natural gas supply. As a result, EGAT had to tempo-

[2] Baht (THB) is the Thai currency, 1 THB is equivalent to $0.029 (exchange rate, Dec 2008)

rarily stop the purchase of power from cogeneration SPPs from 31 August 2007. At the end of 2007, 16 cogeneration facilities under SPP program were selected with total generating capacity of 1,663 MW and total sale of electricity into the grid of 1,314 MW (Amranand 2008). This reflected the policy loopholes, which allowed more cogeneration power projects using conventional fossil fuel, mainly natural gas, instead of increasing the use of renewable fuels. This was repeated in 2008 when the electricity coming from conventional fuel amounted to 1,670 MW, or 73% of total SPP sold into the grid. 382 MW or 17% of the electricity sold to the grid came from renewable resources, mainly from bagasse and paddy husk; another 10% came from combined mixture of bio-resources and conventional fossil resources (Table 10.4).

Table 10.4. SPP Power purchasing project (adapted from: Amranand 2008)

Fuel Type (SPP)	New Projects			Projects In Operations		
	Number	Generation Capacity (MW)	Sale to Grid (MW)	Number	Generation Capacity (MW)	Sale to Grid (MW)
Non-conventional Fuel						
Biomass						
Paddy Husk	5	39.8	33.5	5	57.3	46.8
Bagasse	-	-	4	11	273.6	81.5
Black Liquor	-	-	-	1	32.9	25
Waste & Flared Gas	-	-	6	2	21	7.7
Mixed Biomass/others	4	189.6	110	11	333.8	220.3
MSW	-	-	-	1	2.5	1
Sub-total	9	229	154	31	721	382
Conventional Fuel						
Fuel Oil	-	-	-	1	10.4	9
Coal	-	-	-	4	392.2	196
Natural Gas	20	2,952.1	1,704	21	2,277.6	1,465
Sub-total	20	2,952	1,704	26	2,680	1,670
Combined						
Waste Gas/Coal	-	-	-	1	108	45
Black Liquor/Coal	-	-	-	1	40	8
Eucalyptus Bark/Coal	-	-	-	2	328	180
Sub-total	-	-	-	4	476	233
Grand Total	**29**	**3,182**	**1,858**	**61**	**3,877**	**2,286**

As of June 2008, 441 very small power plants (VSPPs) had submitted applications to sell 1,853 MW of electricity into the grid. Among these, 434 projects are renewable energy with total sale into the grid of 1,819 MW (93% of total new VSPP projects) while the other 7 projects are cogeneration projects (Amranand 2008).

The main resources for VSPP projects are renewables. This is due to the VSPP's criteria of not selling more than 10 MW to the grid; therefore, bigger projects such as cogenerations are not applicable. The VSPP program has provided a great opportunity to establish small renewable energy projects, such as solar, wind, biogas, biomass, biodiesel, MSW, and mini-hydro (Table 10.5).

Table 10.5. VSPP Power purchasing project (adapted from: Amranand 2008)

Fuel Type (VSPP)	Applications			Projects In Operations		
	Number	Generation Capacity (MW)	Sale to Grid (MW)	Number	Generation Capacity (MW)	Sale to Grid (MW)
Non-conventional Fuel						
Solar						
Solar PV Roof Top	64	0.72	0.71	35	0.148	0.148
Solar PV Farm	60	320.3	288.2	2	1.57	1.54
Solar Thermal/CSP	95	607.3	603.8	-	-	-
Wind	6	20.6	20.6	-	-	-
Biogas						
Animal Wastes	14	3.17	2.77	8	1.6	1.33
Industrial Waste Water	35	58.8	49.3	8	15	9.2
Biomass						
Paddy Husk	45	406.5	319.1	9	49.3	41.1
Bagasse	31	602.8	175.8	24	423.3	135.3
Woodchips	23	145.6	123.2	-	-	-
Palm Wastes	16	89.9	65.4	4	23	12.9
Rice Straw	8	3.09	2.9	3	1.64	1.46
Corn Cob	4	26	21.5	1	0.16	0.135
Coconut Fibre	4	25.5	21.2	-	-	-
Other Biomass	3	31	22.2	1	12	6.2
Biodiesel	1	0.025	0.025	-	-	-
MSW	19	109.9	97.1	3	3.22	2.45
Mini Hydro	4	5.16	5.13	1	0.04	0.03
Wind	2	0.33	0.33	0	0	0
Sub-total	434	2,457	1,819	99	531	212
Conventional Fuel						
Coal	4	124	21	1	9.5	3
Natural Gas	3	26.7	12.4	-	-	-
Sub-total	7	151	33	1	10	3
Grand Total	**441**	**2,607**	**1,853**	**100**	**540**	**215**

10.3.2 Biofuels and Natural Gas for Vehicles (NGV)

In 2003, oil companies began to market E10 premium gasoline (gasohol blended from 10% ethanol and 90% gasoline with a research octane number of 95). In November 2007, the lower ex-factory price of ethanol together with the lower level of oil funds increased the price differential between the normal gasoline and E10 from 1.50 baht per litre to 4.00 baht per litre, making E10 very popular. With the aim of increasing biofuel use, discussion between the government, ethanol producers, oil companies and automobile manufactures resulted in the introduction of NGV E85. Thailand should have enough agricultural raw materials for all gasoline vehicles to run on E85, but a sufficient amount of time is required for the automobile and oil industries to adjust. In 2005, Biodiesel B5, which is a blend of 5% methyl ester (B100) and 95% normal diesel, was on sale. Besides good quality B100, Thailand also allowed the sale of 'community' biodiesel, which is lower quality B100 made from a number of feedstocks, particularly used cooking oil. In 2007, the government issued a policy requiring all diesel fuel to be B2 and in 2008; clearer and stricter standards were issued for B100, B2 and B5, and the automobile manufactures also agreed that all diesel vehicles in Thailand could run on B5. Mandating B5 as the normal grade for diesel would require 2.5 million litres per day of B100, and there is insufficient amount of raw palm oil or other feedstock, to achieve this. The government, therefore, provided soft loans for the expansion of oil palm plantation for mandating B5 by 2011 (Amranand 2008). For more details of the potential capacity and production targets of biofuels see Table 10.2.

In 2007, Thailand consumed 3,421 million cubic feet per day[3] (MMCFD) of natural gas with 26% being imported from Myanmar (Amranand 2008). Various incentives on NGV provided by the government ranged from the provision of soft loans and direct subsidy for conversion, to the exemption of excise tax on natural gas used in vehicles. This was coupled with ambitious targets for the establishment of NGV filling stations all over the country. There were 247 NGV stations in October 2008, which led to a rapid conversion of various vehicles to natural gas, particularly taxis, buses and trucks. A total of 117,146 vehicles were converted, of which 97,678 vehicles or 84% were passenger cars, and the other 18,800 vehicles or 16% were trucks. Although the number of NGV trucks amounted to only 16% of all vehicles, they shared around 55% of total NGV consumption (PTT 2008a). The period between 2005 and 2007 saw a fast growth in NGV consumption, rising from 7 million cubic feet per day in 2005 to 37 million cubic feet per day in December 2007. It further rose to 60 million cubic feet per day during the first 7 months of 2008, equivalent to 1.68 million litres per day of crude oil equivalent or 2.4% of gasoline and diesel demand (Amranand 2008). However, the fixed selling price of NGV may increase from 8.5 baht/kg to 12-13 baht/kg in the near future (possibly in 2009-2010), after which the NGV may be sold at the real market price (PTT 2008a).

---

[3] 1 feet^3 = 0.0283 m^3

Before the economic slowdown in 2008, there were significant pricing gaps between different types of gasoline and biofuels, which gave motorists the chance to compare and choose. In December 2008, with gasoline prices getting cheaper, the effect brought biofuels prices down, and made the pricing gaps among fuels very narrow. The price of the newest biofuel introduced into the market (gasohol E85) was much cheaper than gasohol E20 or the diesel palm (PTT 2008b). At the time of authorship of this paper, gasohol E85 had become more expensive. In such circumstance, it would be difficult to encourage motorists to change their habits of using conventional fossil fuels to a greener alternative fuels as gasohol, biodiesels and NGV.

10.4 Conclusions and Recommendations

A review of the Thailand experience in terms of the future of alternative energy leads to a number of conclusions. It is important to secure and stabilize the energy situation, in order to generate a healthy and competitive environment. Looking at a holistic view of the energy sector, there are several problems that have to be resolved, such as: dependence on imported oils, inefficient logistics, and lack of energy-saving behaviour from the consumer. All in all, the problem at the end-of-pipe is that the country's energy consumption is greater than the production of alternative energy. This problem can be alleviated by 1) reducing the energy consumption 2) enhancing the energy efficiency 3) using more alternative energy.

1. To reduce energy consumption, the concept of energy conservation has been introduced to both public and private sectors, in order to reduce the energy consumption in industrial, transportation, residential, commercial, and agricultural sectors. In 1992, the Energy Conservation Promotion Act (ECP Act) was introduced (B.E. 2535) as a tool to promote energy conservation activities, particularly in the private sector. It was reported that the electricity consumption from 1993 to 1995 increased by 0.3%, but the oil consumption reduced by 25%, in spite of the real GDP growth increasing from 8% to 9.3% (EPPO 2008c). The relationship between the relevant factors of economic growth, oil prices, energy consumption, and energy saving shows varying, non-linear and dynamic behaviour. Thus successful renewable energy projects should be closely related to the appropriate mix of these factors. Nevertheless, cutting the energy demand through promoting the energy-saving policy is one of the indispensable strategic tools that must be employed at all levels of energy management, as it would help to reduce future problems at the beginning of the pipe.

2. To enhance the energy efficiency, the focus issues are mainly on the improvement of energy efficiency across all sectors. One sector which has high potential for improving energy efficiency is transportation. Thailand's logistics rely mainly on road transportation. Efficient logistics rely on rail and water transportation which can load/serve more goods/passengers than road transportation. An urban decentralization is highly recommended in order to distribute growth to neighborhood areas, which can alleviate the congestion in the big city. Existing

rail and water transportation infrastructure should be improved and upgraded to provide better networking as well as more access and connection points. In Bangkok, mass rapid transport (electric train) should expand its service areas to allow passengers to change their mode of transportation to public ones. Nevertheless, the mass transportation option could fail if the citizens still favor the use of their own vehicles.

3. To use more alternative energy is one of the key strategies for reducing the consumption of imported crude oil. In order to achieve renewable energy target goal of 8% in 2011, particularly at current economic downturn, one important factor must be overcome: how to make alternative energy competitive in an era of low-priced conventional fuels? One solution could be - finding an opportunity in crisis periods, when the transition to renewables is easier. In Germany and China the governments support generation projects for renewable power, which will sustain the long-term energy demand and help to reach their CO_2 emission targets. Adaptation to the market conditions, cost control, resilience capacity and appropriate alternative energy technologies are essential. Short-term and long-term support measures in adition to new initiatives from the Thai government for proper pricing strategies are needed, and should go hand in hand.

The historic tendency to look at Thailand's energy consumption collectively, and in particular mainly through the perspective of the government, is especially inappropriate as one looks to the future. As the global environment is continually changing, the economy, companies and industries have their own adaptability and resilience. Shifting the focus of problem/question may provide not only a new perspective but also the most effective solution. For example changing the focus from "how much energy do we need?" to "how much energy do we have?" may start an investigation into how to appropriately match and configure future energy resources in Thailand.

References

Amranand P (2008) Alternative Energy, Cogeneration and Distributed Generation: Crucial Strategy for Sustainability of Thailand's Energy Sector. Special Report. Energy Policy and Planning Office, Ministry of Energy, Thailand. Internet address: http://www.eppo.go.th/doc/Piya-RE-in-Thailand.pdf, last accessed on 09.11.2010

Channukul W (2008) Thailand's Energy Policy. Ministry of Energy, Thailand. Internet address: http://www.eppo.go.th/doc/policy-wannarat-E.html, last accessed on 09.11.2010

Chatkaew Y (2008) Mass Rapid Transit and the used of energy efficiency in transportation sector, Mass Rapid Transit Authority of Thailand (MRTA), National Science and Technology Congress, Bangkok, 17 Sept. 2008, Congress Report (in Thai)

DEDE – Department of Alternative Energy Development and Efficiency (2007) Thailand Energy Situation. Ministry of Energy. ISSN 0857-8494

DEDE – Department of Alternative Energy Development and Efficiency (2008) Proceedings of Alternative Energy Workshop, 21 April 2008, Prince Palace Hotel, Bangkok (in Thai). Ministry of Energy. Internet address:

http://www.dede.go.th/dede/fileadmin/usr/os/pr/alternative%20energyplan%2015%20year.pdf, last accessed on 15.10.2010

DLT – Department of Land Transport (2008) Land Transport Management Bureau, Technical and Planning Group, Statistics Sub-Division (in Thai). Internet address: http://apps.dlt.go.th/statistics_web/brochure07/cumcar07.xls, last accessed on 15.10.2010

EPPO – Energy Policy and Planning Office (2008a) Energy Statistics: Economic Data and Analysis. Internet address: http://www.eppo.go.th/info/7economic_stat.htm, last accessed on 09.11.2010

EPPO – Energy Policy and Planning Office (2008b) Energy Strategy: Energy for Thailand's Competitiveness. Internet address: http://www.eppo.go.th/doc/strategy2546/strategy.html, last accessed on 09.11.2010

EPPO – Energy Policy and Planning Office (2008c) Energy Conservation in Public Sector: Summary of Energy Conservation. Internet address: http://www.e-report.energy.go.th/ (in Thai), last accessed on 09.11.2010

EPPO – Energy Policy and Planning Office (2009) Energy Statistics: Energy Reserves. Internet address: http://www.eppo.go.th/info/stat/T01_03_01.xls, last accessed on 09.11.2010

IMD – International Institute for Management Development (2008) Energy Intensity (2004), Commercial energy consumed for each dollar of GDP in kilojoules. In: IMD World Competitiveness Yearbook 2008, p. 456

Pongpirodom P (2008) Draft of Alternative Energy - 15 Years Plan, Workshop Report (in Thai)

PTT – PTT Public Company Limited (2008a) Draft of 15-Years Alternative Energy Plan: NGV. PTT Pubilc Co., Ltd., Thailand (in Thai)

PTT – PTT Public Company Limited (2008b) Thai Fuel Price (THB) (2005-2008). Internet address: http://www.pttplc.com/en/news-energy-fact-oil-price-bangkok.aspx, last accessed on 09.11.2010

11 Energy Challenges, Problems and Strategies in China

Shouke Wei

Department of Ecosystem and Environmental Informatics, Brandenburg University of Technology, Cottbus, Germany

11.1 Introduction

Energy is vital to the survival and development of human beings. The increasing demand for energy and the related environmental problems have become an extremely important issue. China takes the first place in energy production and the second in consumption in the world. It is playing and will continue to play an important international role in energy production and consumption, energy configuration, as well as related environmental and ecological challenges. This study aims to investigate China's energy situation, and the related challenges and problems through an analysis based on environment and fundamental resource-economy statistics. To address China's energy challenges and problems, five important strategies were proposed. The results of this study are expected to help energy scholars, planners, strategists and organizations to further investigate China's energy problems and to make energy policy decisions.

Energy is one of the essential factors constraining the socio-economic development and life-style of a nation. Humans have experienced many energy evolutions, from firewood to coal, and to petroleum oil, nuclear, and biofuels (Jiang 2008). Every energy evolution caused a great leap in productivity, which greatly promoted the socio-economic development (Jiang 2008). However, in the past decades, increasing energy consumption and its related environmental problems have gained greater attention, the world over. According to a BP Statistical Review of World Energy (BP 2008), in 2007 world primary energy consumption increased by 2.4%, global oil consumption by 1.1%, gas consumption by 3.1%, and coal consumption by 4.5% (Fig. 11.1a). Limited energy can also bring about socio-economic instability. In 1970s, the two world oil crises resulted in the economic deceleration of some developed countries, and the fluctuation of the world economy. Similarly, in this century, the continuous oil price increase has caused social instability in some countries. Figure 11.1b demonstrates the changes of crude oil prices in both nominal US$ prices and 2007 US$ price from 1861 to 2007. From this figure, the two price peaks and constant price are clearly visible, as well as the projected increasing trend in the few years to follow.

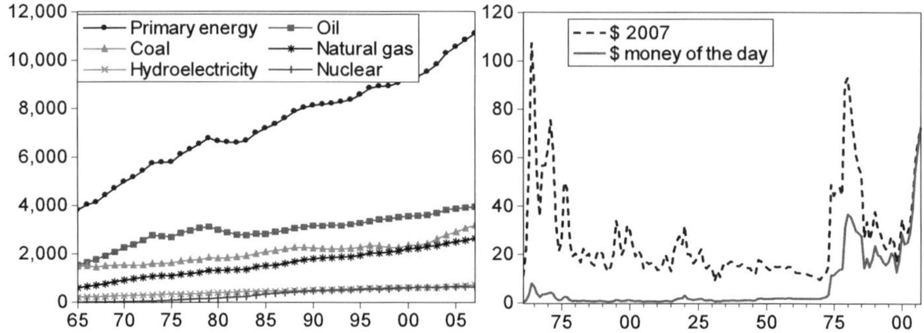

(a) (b)

Fig. 11.1(a). World energy consumption (Mtoe) since 1968; **Fig. 11.1(b).** Changes of crude oil price (US$/barrel) since 1961 (data sources: BP 2008; EIA 2010)

With the increase of energy consumption, severe environmental and ecological problems have arisen (Ni 2007). In this context, the consumption of fossil fuels is a main source of green house gas (GHG) emissions (CO_2, CH_4 and N_2O. etc.). With Carbon dioxide (CO_2) being the most important GHG, the Intergovernmental Panel on Climate Change (IPCC 2007) illustrated that annual CO_2 emissions have increased between 1970 and 2004 by about 80%, from 21 to 38 gigatonnes (Gt), contributing 77% of total anthropogenic GHG emissions in 2004. The global warming trend over the 50 years from 1956 to 2005 is nearly twice that for the 100 years from 1906 to 2005. In 2006, world CO_2 emissions from the consumption and flaring of fossil fuel reached 12064.64 Million Metric Tonnes (Fig.11.2a). Figure 11.2b illustrates the linear relationship between annual atmospheric Mauna Loa CO_2 concentration and average global temperature from 1959 to 2007. This linear trend demonstrates a strong correlation between CO_2 concentration and temperature. The linear equation reveals that average global temperature would increase an average 0.01°C if the CO_2 concentration increases by 1 ppm.

Internationally, China takes the first place in energy production and the second in consumption. However, in this century, China is facing even more serious problems and challenges in energy fields due to its shortage of energy reserves per capita, limited environmental capacity, the fragile ecology, inefficient energy consumption, large population as well as unstable international energy markets. Regarding these challenges and problems, the questions are: How can the tremendous energy supply required in order to meet the huge demand be ensured? Does China have adequate environmental carrying capacity to accept such consumption? From which sources can such high quantities of energy be sustainably obtained? The following section starts by presenting China's energy status in the world. This is followed by an exploration of the challenges and problems related to China's energy production, supply and consumption in section 11.3. In section 11.4, strategies for sustainable energy development are proposed, followed by conclusions in section 11.5.

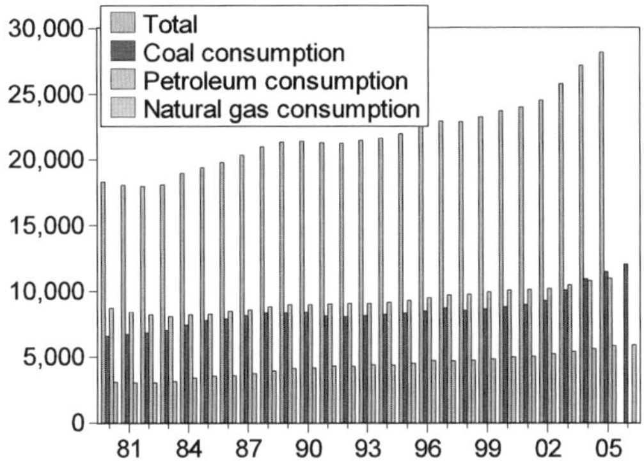

(a)

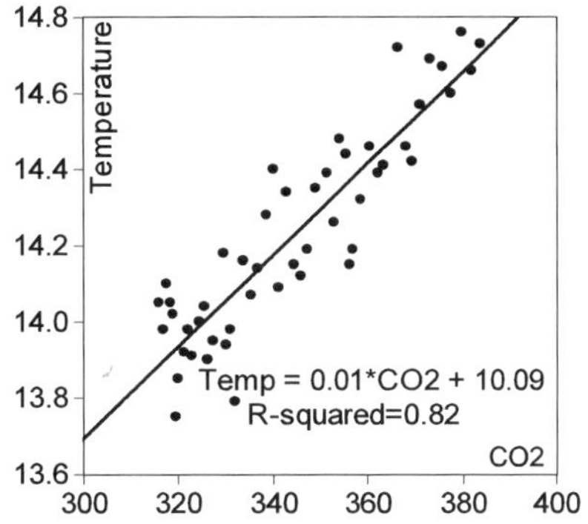

(b)

Fig. 11.2(a). World Carbon Dioxide Emissions (Million Tonnes) from the consumption of fossil fuels; **Fig. 11.2(b).** Increasing trend of average global temperature (°C) and atmospheric CO_2 concentration (ppm) and from 1957 to 2007 (data sources: EIA 2008; GISS 2008; ESRL 2010; EPI 2009)

11.2 International Status of China's Energy

China has been the world's largest energy producer since 2005 and the second largest energy consumer (RGCEDS 2007). At the end of 2007, it was estimated that China had proven oil reserves of 2.1 billion tonnes oil equivalent (toe), natural gas reserves of 1.88 trillion m^3, coal reserves of 114,500 million toe; this equates to 1.3%, 1.1% and 13.5% of world total in those three energy types, respectively. World primary energy consumption increased by 2.4% in 2007, which is less than growth rate of 2.7% in 2006. As China's economy grows, so does its energy consumption. In 2007, China's economic growth was 7.7%, the weakest since 2002, and it again accounted for half of global energy consumption growth half of global energy consumption growth (BP 2008).

Based on data from the China Energy Statistic Yearbook (DITSSSB and EBNDRC 2007), China produced 1640.94 million toe of Primary Energy, and consumed energy of 890.34 million toe in total in 2005, which ranked 14.31% and 12.92% of the world amounts, respectively, in that year. According to Statistical Review of World Energy (BP 2008), China shared 4.8% of world oil, 2.4% of world natural gas and 41.1% of the world coal in production (Fig. 11.3a). In the world consumption, China imported oil 9.3%, natural gas 2.3%, coal 41.2% and hydroelectricity 15.4%. China's international share of nuclear energy consumption was 0.08% in 1993, but stood at 2.3% in 2007. Tables 11.1 and 11.2 compare energy production and consumption of the top five countries, from 2002 to 2005.

Table 11.1. The top five countries in total energy production (million toe) (data source: DITSSSB and EBNDRC 2007)

Country or Area	2002	2003	2004	2005	% of World in 2005
World	10294.74	10611.98	11130.25	11467.75	100.00
China	1202.31	1331.34	1509.41	1640.94	14.31
United States	1666.04	1634.52	1647.02	1630.68	14.22
Russia	1034.48	1106.87	1158.44	1184.86	10.33
Saudi Arabia	474.78	530.53	548.71	576.70	5.03
India	436.45	394.22	408.40	419.04	3.65

Table 11.2. The top five countries in total final energy consumption (million toe) (data source: DITSSSB and EBNDRC 2007)

Country or Area	2002	2003	2004	2005	% of World in 2005
World	6110.96	6426.07	6725.50	6892.65	100.00
United States	1549.47	1570.93	1599.74	1598.10	23.19
China	619.13	683.55	802.33	890.34	12.92
Russia	409.62	419.47	422.22	417.29	6.05
Japan	352.48	346.68	350.65	350.85	5.09
Germany	239.48	250.59	252.56	261.01	3.79

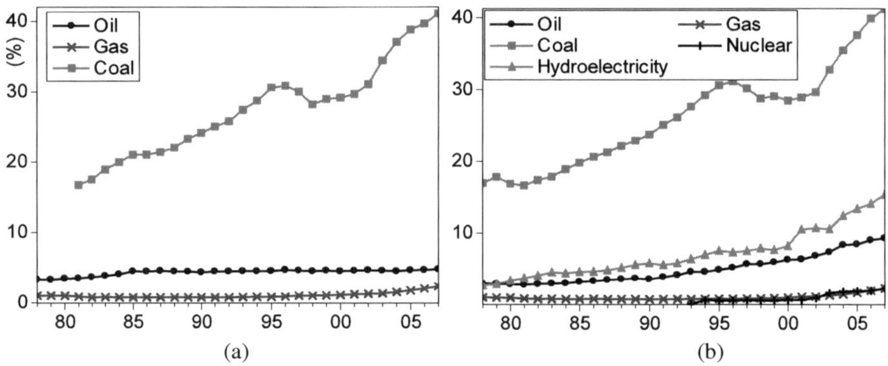

Fig. 11.3. Proportion of China's energy in the world since 1978: Fig. 11.3(a) presents production, whilst 11.3(b) presents consumption

11.3 Energy Challenges and Problems in China

Having analyzed China's international energy status from a macro perspective, this section will evaluate China's energy issues from its national and the micro points of view. Among the challenges faced by China are extreme shortage of energy, poor energy production and consumption structure, inefficient energy consumption, low energy technology, tremendous need for energy supply for rural areas, severe energy-related pollution and so on.

11.3.1 Three big challenges

For a deeper discussion, this section focuses on investigating three key energy challenges, i.e. extreme shortage of energy, severe energy-related pollution and tremendous energy supply for rural area.

a) Extremely Insufficient Energy Production

China's Energy Consumption Elasticity Coefficient (ECEC)[1] has decreased from 13.5 in 1985 to 0.66 in 2007, but it still reflects the fast consumption growth rate. What is ECE? With continuous population increase and economic growth, huge energy demand will give greater pressure on energy supply. Table 11.3 displays how large the average daily energy consumption of China in the recent four years has been. Energy supply and demand has already gone above the present estimated energy amount. Figure 11.4 shows a comparison of total energy production and consumption from 1978 to 2007. From the figure, it can be seen that the total energy consumption has surpassed the total energy production since 1991, and the differences seem to be becoming larger. In the past two decades, international Reserve-to-Production (R/P) ratios of oil and natural gas remain around 40 and 60 (Jiang 2007). Compared to the world average, China R/P ratios of oil is low at only 11.1 in 2006. Currently, China's shortage of liquid fuels is much more serious, and the dependence on imported oil was already 57.7% in 2007. With further increases in economic and population growth, China will import more oil from other countries. Facing continuing increasing international oil price, what should China do?

Energy supply per capita is also an indictor reflecting energy insufficiency. According to China Energy Statistics (DITSSSB and EBNDRC 2007), in 2005 China's energy supply per capita was 1.32 toe, which is lower than the 1.78 toe of the world and far lower than 7.89 toe of United states. Another indicator is energy supply in relation to GDP, which reflects the average energy supplied to produce one unit GDP. China's energy requirement per unit of GDP has increased from 0.86 toe per thousand (2000 US$) in 2002 to 0.91 toe per thousand (2000 US$).

---

[1] Energy Consumption Elasticity Coefficient (ECEC) is used to reflect the relations between economic growth and energy consumption, and the calculation expression is: ECEC= annual energy consumption growth rate/ annual economic growth rate.

China is entering the so called 'heavy-chemical' stage, in which a rapid boost of energy demand is obvious (Ni 2007). Facing insufficient supply, how can China supply such huge amounts of energy to ensure the consumption in the future? Does China have sufficient environmental carrying capacity to accept such consumption?

Table 11.3. Average daily energy consumption by energy type (data source: NBSC 2008a)

Type of Energy	2000	2003	2004	2005	2006	2007
Coal (10,000 tonnes)	361.6	463.6	530.4	593.8	655.4	708.6
Coke (10,000 tonnes)	28.6	39.7	47.3	64.7	75.6	83.1
Crude Oil (10,000 tonnes)	58.2	68.3	78.8	82.4	88.3	93.2
Fuel Oil (10,000 tonnes)	10.6	11.6	13.1	11.6	12.0	11.2
Gasoline (10,000 tonnes)	9.6	11.2	12.9	13.3	14.4	15.1
Kerosene (10,000 tonnes)	2.4	2.5	2.9	3.0	3.1	3.4
Diesel Oil (10,000 tonnes)	18.6	23.0	27.1	30.1	32.4	34.2
Natural Gas (100 million m^3)	0.7	0.9	1.1	1.3	1.5	1.9
Electricity (100 million kWh)	36.9	52.1	60.2	68.3	78.3	89.6

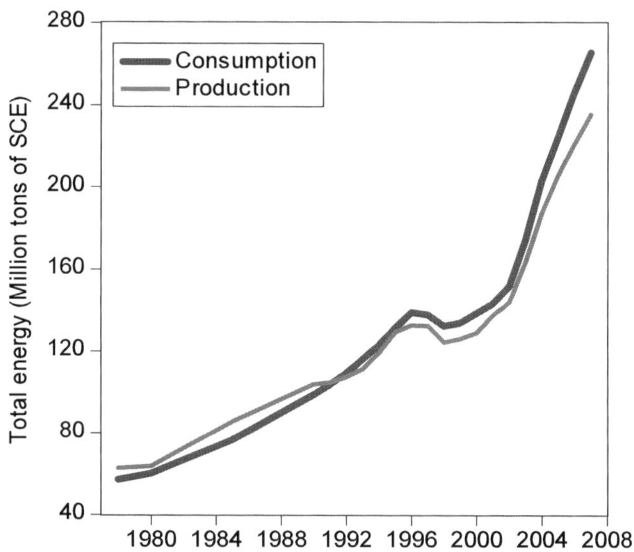

Fig. 11.4. Comparison of total energy supply and total energy consumption in China since 1978 (data source: CSSB 2008)

b) Severe Pollution

Since 2003, the average annual GDP growth rate, calculated at constant prices, was more than 10%. However, this rapid increase in economy was aided by the consumption of large amounts of fossil energy and the emission of great amounts of GHGs, which degraded environmental and ecological systems (Ni 2007). In 2005, China's CO_2 emission from the consumption and flaring of fossil fuels reached 5322.69 million metric tonnes, sharing 18.9% of the world. Figure 11.5 illustrates the comparison of the emissions from China and the US, and the proportion of China's emission in the world total.

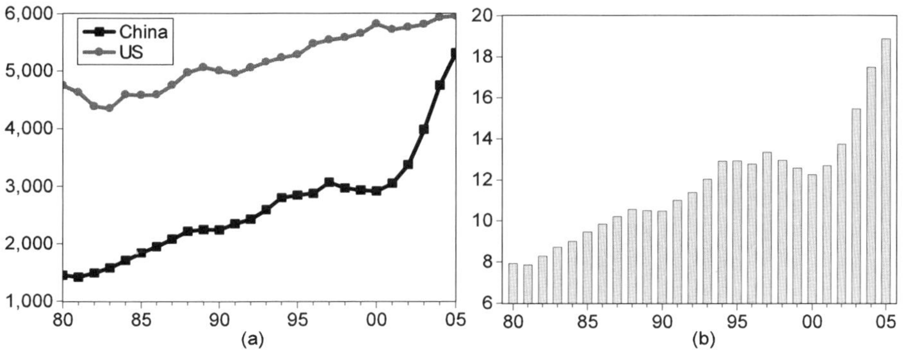

Fig.11.5(a). Carbon Dioxide Emissions (Million Metric tonnes) from the consumption and flaring of fossil fuels in China and US (1980-2005); **Fig. 11.5(b).** Proportion China's Carbon Dioxide Emissions (%) in the world emission (data source: EIA 2008)

China's per capita CO_2 emissions from the consumption and flaring of fossil fuels, was 4.07 metric tonnes in 2005, lower than the world average of 4.37 metric tonnes; and far less than the US per capita emissions of 20.14 metric tonnes,. However, compared with the emissions of 1.48 metric tonnes in 1980, China's per capita emission has increased almost 3 times (Figure 11.6). Imagine what the world GHGs emission would be if China's per capita emission was similar to that of the USA. China signed the Kyoto Protocol in 2002, and is trying its best to reduce its CO_2 emission (Ni 2007). As a developing country, China's emission per capita will likely increase further, due to economic development and population. How can China mitigate its emission greatly?

c) Rural Energy

in 2007, China's rural population was 727.5 million, sharing 55.06% of the total population (NBSC 2008a). It is a daunting task to supply sustainable and affordable energy to 700 million rural residents. More than 10 million rural residents did not have electricity (NDRC 2007) and a lot of rural residents were still relying on firewood, stalks and grass (Ni 2007). It was estimated that in 2006 Chinese non-commercial firewood energy consumption in rural residences was 189.9 million tonnes or about 96.8 million tonnes Coal Equivalent (tce), and the stalks consumption was 378.5 million tonnes or ca. 177.9 tce. Yet it has been stated that firewood consumption directly causes air pollution (DITSSSB and EBNDRC 2007). Another big challenge is to balance the rural energy development between Eastern China and Western China. In the rural area of western China, residences are widely lacking energy provision. Comparatively speaking, the eastern and middle parts of China are better off, but still in need of improvement, especially in the rural and poor areas.

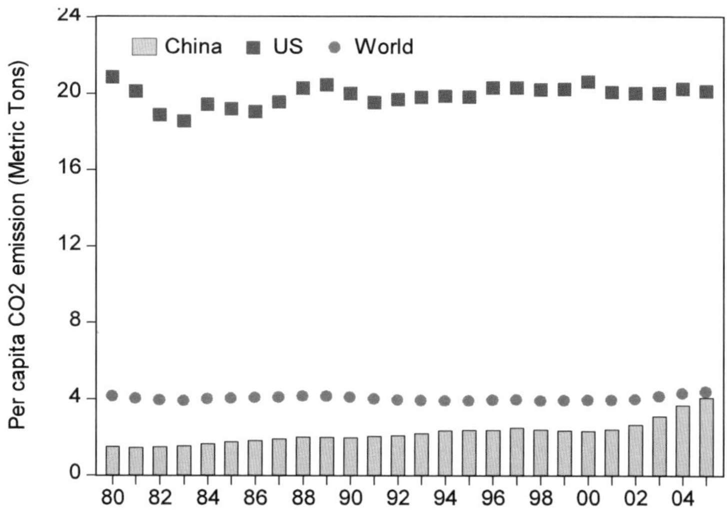

Fig. 11.6. Per capita CO_2 emissions from the consumption and flaring of fossil fuels of China, US and the World (Data source: EIA 2008)

11.3.2 Main Problems

China is also facing a lot of problems related to energy production and consumption (DICC 2007). In general, the main problems can be summarized as an outdated energy structure, inefficient energy consumption, poor energy policy system, imperfect market system, low energy technology, as well as low energy saving awareness. These are subsequently discussed in detail.

a) Outdated Energy Structure

Energy structure herein refers to the configurations of energy supply and consumption among different socio-economic sectors. With respect to energy composition, coal is the main source, sharing more than 70% of the total annual average from 1978 to 2007. In developed countries, coal accounts for around 21% of energy consumed. Figure 11.7 displays energy supply and consumption composition in 2007. Coal consumption is a main source of air pollution (IOSCC 2007). It was estimated that direct combustion of coal has caused emission of 70%-80% or more SO_2, NOx, Hg, particulates and CO_2 (Ni 2007). During the period of China's 10th Five Year Plan (2000-2004), the energy structure was adjusted and many small and middle coal companies in poor condition were closed by government. However, it is far from enough.

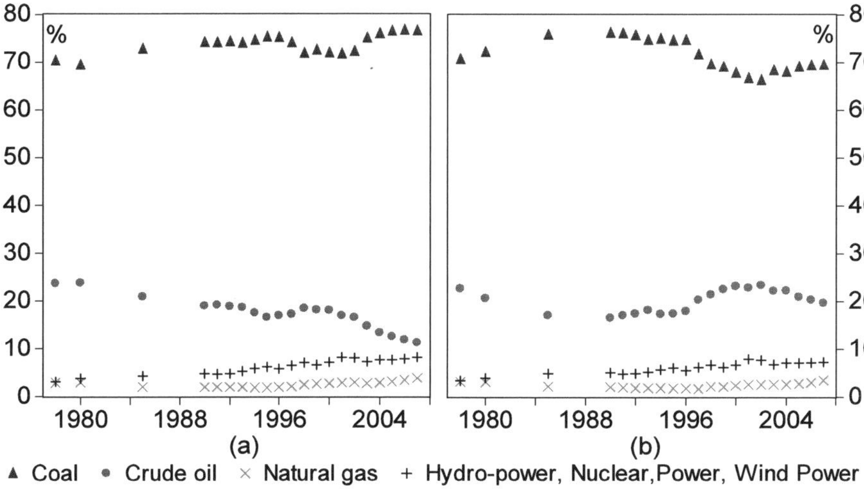

Fig.11.7. China energy composition structure: (a) supply, (b) consumption

With reference to the energy consumption structure among different socio-economic sectors, industrial energy consumption accounted for 71% of the total consumption in 2007 (Fig.11.8). A large portion of industries, especially manufacturing, exhibited relatively high energy consumption per unit value of output (Rosen and Houser 2007). This consumption structure has caused energy wastage and also caused energy shortage for households and the agriculture sector (Jin 2003).

b) Inefficient Energy Consumption

One widely used factor of energy efficiency is energy consumption per unit of GDP. This indicator reflects how much energy is used to produce one unit of GDP. The data reveals that energy consumption per unit of GDP was 8.33 toe per 10 000 US$ in 2004 (NBSC 2008a). However, the world average was 2.65 toe per 10 000 US$, and the United States 1.99 toe per 10 000 US$ (see Table 11.4). This shows that energy consumption in China is still not efficient, although it has already achieved a great improvement in energy saving.

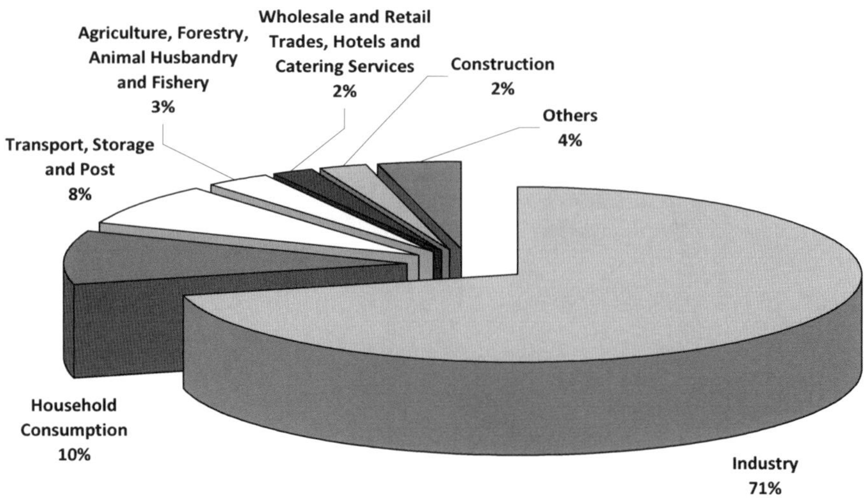

Fig.11.8. China energy consumption structure among different socio-economic sectors

Table 11.4. Comparison of energy consumption per GDP in China with some other selected developed countries (ton of oil equivalent per 10,000 US$) (source: NBSC 2008b)

Country or Area	1990	2000	2001	2002	2003	2004
China	**24.43**	**9.37**	**8.46**	**8.34**	**8.42**	**8.33**
Australia	2.74	2.76	2.85	2.63	2.08	1.77
Canada	3.65	3.50	3.49	3.45	3.07	2.75
France	1.83	1.94	1.99	1.83	1.51	1.34
Germany	2.09	1.81	1.87	1.71	1.42	1.27
Japan	1.48	1.14	1.27	1.34	1.22	1.16
New Zealand	3.13	3.29	3.32	2.93	2.14	1.79
United Kingdom	2.14	1.61	1.63	1.45	1.29	1.10
United States	3.35	2.36	2.24	2.20	2.09	1.99
World	**3.95**	**3.12**	**3.16**	**3.10**	**2.85**	**2.65**

c) Others

Within the Policy context, economic policies and economic successes are considered key evaluation criteria by most Chinese political and administrative officials. Under this policy paradigm, GDP growth is the most important factor; but energy consumption efficiency and environmental protection are usually neglected in many regions. Light punishment for infringement of law; and inadequate regulatory frameworks, have also contributed to people, companies, organization failing to save on energy.

Within the Market context, China has established an energy market, but it is still not perfect. The market energy price did not reflect the energy scarcity, relations between demand and supply, benefits of different users and stakeholders. Therefore, nobody had incentive to consume energy efficiently.

Within the Technology context, China's productivity was 398 tonnes per year per person, and mechanization level only 45% in 2005 (Jiang 2008). Comparing this techno-economic index, for example, USA's productivity was 13,849 tonnes per year per person, and mechanization level was 100%, in 2004. However, as for energy efficiency, cement, fertilizers, iron and steel, and aluminium industries in China consume per product unit about 20%-30% more energy than in developed countries (Ni 2007).

11.4 Energy Strategies for Amendment

Faced with these challenges and problems, which strategies China should adopt? Energy industry comprises a large, complex and interconnected system, which is related to different socio-economic aspects: population, resources, environment, culture, industry, agriculture, household life, technology, transportation, military, politics etc. Therefore, energy strategies should be comprehensive and consider all the interconnected aspects. In this part, five important macro strategies are proposed, which can be expressed as embodying reasonable structure, high efficiency, diversified development and less pollution, functioning market and friendly international cooperation. These proposals remain open to empirical confirmation, and at this stage, are intended to ignite debate.

11.4.1 Adjusting the Current Energy Structure

The outdated and unsuitable energy supply and consumption structure is one of the main subjective reasons for insufficient energy supply and pollution. Therefore, it is vital to adjust the current energy structure in China. Firstly, China should invest more in hydro-power, nuclear power and wind power, and develop new energy sources. Secondly, it should limit industrial energy consumption by increasing industrial energy price, taxing the energy-wasting industries, and subsidizing the energy-efficient ones.

11.4.2 Improving the Energy Consumption Efficiency

Facing huge energy demand in the future, China should not copy the historical energy-wasting development styles of developed countries. It should consider energy saving as the first important strategy. In doing so, the following important goals should be taken into account:

- To develop new energy-saving methods and styles;
- To provide information regarding new energy-saving technologies;
- To raise the energy-saving awareness among the society;
- To strengthen energy-saving in the sectors of industry, transportation and architecture, and in the developed regions;
- To change the traditional achievement evaluation standard, i.e. economic growth rate;
- To improve the energy laws and increase enforcement and their punitive forces.

11.4.3 Developing Diversified Energy

In order to change the coal dominated energy production and consumption structure, China has to develop diversified energy, such as hydro-power, nuclear power, wind power and solar power, and other new energies. The key points are:

- Reducing the proportion of coal consumption, and;
- Raising consumption proportion of hydro-power, nuclear power, wind power and solar power;
- Increasing investment to develop other new environment-friendly energy and related technology.

11.4.4 Improving Energy Market System

A reasonable energy market system should include two important aspects: a powerful regulating system and a practical price system. A powerful regulating system should have strict laws and regulations, and firmly control organizations. A practical energy price system means that energy price should reflect energy scarcity, situation of energy supply and demand, cost to environmental and ecological protection, and the cost and benefits of different users and stakeholders. Only when energy price sends correct signals to energy users, producers, managers and policy-makers; and energy-related controlling systems protect the benefits of different energy stakeholders, only then, will the market effectively guide different energy users to consume energy efficiently.

11.4.5 Amplifying International Cooperation

The worlds need China, and China also relies on the world. Development of international cooperation is therefore, another vital strategy for China to solve its energy supply shortage, and environmental and ecological degradation problems. In the future, China's increasing dependence on imported oil is set to remain. China should enhance international cooperation from the following main points:

- To increase energy-related technology exchange;
- To enlarge international investment in energy development;
- To actively communicate with other countries in the international energy market in order to get a friendly international environment and stable energy prices;
- To obtain more international investment and advanced technology for energy saving and pollution mitigation.

11.5 Conclusions

With its significant economic development and internationalisation, China has become a global player in the energy aspects. From macro and micro points of view, this study investigated energy supply and consumption; the challenges and problems in China, using available data and environmental economic principles. It illustrated three big energy challenges in China: insufficient energy supply to meet demand, severe energy related pollution and rural energy shortage. It also explored China's main problems in energy structure, energy consumption efficiency, energy policy, energy market, technology and energy saving awareness. Based on those challenges and problems, the study proposed five important strategies from aspects of reasonable structure, high efficiency, diversified development, less pollution, functioning market, as well as friendly international cooperation. It is concluded that these proposals can form a basis for comprehensively considering and addressing the looming energy, and related, challenges facing China, now and in the future.

References

BP – British Petroleum (2008) Statistical Review of World Energy June 2008. BP, London

CDIAC – Carbon Dioxide Information Analysis Center (2008) Global Fossil Fuel Carbon Emissions. Internet address: http://cdiac.ornl.gov/trends/emis/meth_reg.html, last accessed on 09.11.2010

DICC – Development and Innovation Committee of China (2007) National Strategies of China to Climate Changing. DICC, Beijing (in Chinese)

DITSSSB and EBNDRC – Department of Industrial and Transport Statistics of State Statistics Bureau and the Energy Bureau of National Development and Reform Commission (2007) Chinese energy statistical yearbook (1997-2007). China Statistics Press, Beijing

EIA – Energy Information Administration (2008) International Energy Outlook 2008. Energy Information Administration, Office of Integrated Analysis and Forecasting, U.S. Department of Energy Washington, DC 20585

EIA – Energy Information Administration (2010) World Crude Oil Prices. Internet address: http://tonto.eia.doe.gov/dnav/pet/pet_pri_wco_k_w.htm, last accessed on 09.11.2010

EPI – Earth Policy Institute (2009) EPI Data Center: Climate, Energy, and Transportation. Internet address: http://www.earth-policy.org/data_center/C23, last accessed on 09.11.2010

ESRL – Earth System Research Laboratory (2010) Trends in Atmospheric Carbon Dioxide at Mauna Loa. Internet address: http://www.esrl.noaa.gov/gmd/ccgg/trends/index.html, last accessed on 09.11.2010

GISS – Goddard Institute for Space Studies (2008) Global Temperature Anomalies in 0.01 degrees Celsius. Sciences and Exploration Directorate, Earth Sciences Division. Internet address: http://data.giss.nasa.gov/gistemp/tabledata/GLB.Ts.txt, last accessed on 09.11.2010

IOSCC – Information Office of the State Council of China (2007) China's Energy Conditions and Polices. IOSCC, Beijing

IPCC – Intergovernmental Panel on Climate Change (2007) Climate Change 2007: Synthesis Report. Internet address: http://www.ipcc.ch/pdf/assessment-report/ar4/syr/ar4_syr.pdf, last accessed on 09.11.2010

Jiang ZM (2008) Reflection on energy issues in China. Journal of Shanghai Jiaotong University 42(3): 345-359 (in Chinese)

Jin J (2003) World and China energy structures. In: Energy Research and Information 19(1): 20-26 (in Chinese)

NBSC – National Bureau of Statistics of China (2008a) China Statistical Yearbook 2008. China Statistics Press, Beijing.

NBSC – National Bureau of Statistics of China (2008b) International Statistical Yearbook 2008. China Statistics Press, Beijing

NDRC – National Development and Reform Commission (2007) The Eleventh Five Year Energy Plan. NDRC, Beijing

Ni W (2007) China's energy-challenges and strategies. In: Frontiers of Energy and Power Engineering in China 1(1): 1-8

RGCEDS – Researching Group of China's Energy Demand and Supply (2007) Analysis on China's Energy Demand and Supply. In: Statistical Research 24(10): 3-8 (in Chinese)

Rosen DH, Houser T (2007) China Energy - A Guide for the Perplexed. Peterson Institute for International Economics, Washington, D.C

12 Review of Future Energy Supply and Targets for Climate Change: The Idea of Ecosystem Services

Ernest Fongwa[1], Vincent Onyango[2] and Albrecht Gnauck[1]

1 Department of Ecosystems and Environmental Informatics, Brandenburg University of Technology (BTU), Cottbus, Germany
2 Department of Environmental Planning, Brandenburg University of Technology (BTU), Cottbus, Germany

12.1 Introduction

Climate change is considered as one of the biggest challenges for decades to come (BP 2008; CDIAC 2008; Reddy and Hodges 2000; IEA 2007). This is unless significant investments are diverted towards development of natural capital that regulates the environment (World Bank 2008). Although energy supply from renewable energy sources and renewable technologies are growing rapidly, their capacity will still not be enough to significantly offset fossil fuel demand (BP 2008; CDIAC 2008; Grunwald 2008; IEA 2007). This means energy supply from non-renewable sources will still contribute to the release of large emissions of GHGs that cause climate change (EPI 2010; ESRL 2010). Even though there are policies and strategies on emission control to fight climate change, it is argued here that these efforts should not only focus on emission reductions, but also on mitigation measures. An analysis of future energy projections (see World Bank 2010; EIA 2008; ESRL 2010; IEA 2007) reveals a need to explore other avenues for mitigating emissions from this energy trend.

This paper argues that to achieve targets for climate change, more focus and financial investment should be diverted to the development and maintenance of ecosystem services; alongside the policy targets for renewable energy, emissions control and reductions, and demand and supply side management programs for efficient energy use. The concept of ecosystem services has received significant attention since the appearance of the Millennium Ecosystem Assessment (MEA 2005a). This is because of the agreement reached that ecosystem services are critical to sustainable development and that they ought to be preserved, if not enhanced (Slootweg and Beukering 2008; MEA 2005b).

Furthermore, it was suggested that tools for promoting sustainable development, such as impact assessments, appraisals and planning tools, should integrate and consider the value of ecosystem services (Slootweg and Beukering 2008).

This follows from the observation that ecosystem services, as an integral part of sustainable development have rarely been incorporated into planning and policy formulation (Slootweg and Beukering 2008; MEA 2005b).

Ecosystem services are the benefits people obtain from ecosystems and an overview of relevant literature can be found at the MEA (2005a). Ecosystem services can be understood as the benefits provided by the ecosystem in terms of goods and services (MEA 2005b). That is the natural environment provides multiple resources and processes that provide benefits to human beings; and these resources and processes, which are linked to the physiochemical processes of the natural environment (Albrechts 2008; Ranganathan et al. 2008), are collectively known as ecosystem services (MEA 2005b). Examples of ecosystem services evaluations are found in MEA (2005b). To date, ecosystem services have rarely been used to translate the environment into social benefits (Slootweg and Beukering 2008).

In this paper, a conceptual argument for the potential of ecosystem services to fight climate change and how their value can be harnessed and incorporated into efforts for fighting climate change, is presented. This is possible if appropriate value is given to them. The potential for ecosystem services shall be elucidated by developing and presenting the linkage between climate change and ecosystem services. Furthermore, how business developments based on ecosystem services can provide a more sustainable approach to climate change mitigation is clarified. This approach can be both financially and environmentally beneficial in ecosystems with high natural potential for carbon sequestration, for example tropical rainforests, peat bogs, marshlands, permafrost forests (Slootweg and Beukering 2008; Schulze and Freibauer 2005). Direct valuation of ecosystem services has been suggested as a means of facilitating the formulation of sustainable plans, polices and projects within the context of well-informed strategic decisions-making (MEA 2005b). This is because decision-makers will explicitly recognize the value of ecosystem services and make more transparent the trade-offs between competing economic, social, political and cultural interests. The already existing trade in carbon finance is such an example where a price is being set to capture the costs of carbon clean-up by our ecosystem services (see World Bank 2010). This paper has mainly relied on the projections indicated in the 2008 World Energy Outlook (IEA 2008).

The current world market energy supply trends show that the highest capacity is coming from non-renewable sources (CDIAC 2008; IEA 2007). Non-renewable energy sources cause carbon emissions to the atmosphere leading to global warming and climate change (EPI 2010; ESRL 2010). Worldwide, fossil fuels such as oil, gas and coal continue to dominate the energy mix, in which the use of coal is set to grow most rapidly, driven largely by demand in the power-sectors (EIA 2008; IEA 2007). These trends lead to an expected continuous growth in global energy-related emission of carbon- dioxide (CO_2) equivalent from about 27 billion tonnes in 2005 to an estimated 42 billion tonnes by the year 2030, representing a rise of about 57% (IEA 2008). At the same time, the use of renewable energy and cleaner energy technologies is currently growing rapidly. This is accompanied by falling costs as renewables and clean technologies mature; and carries an inherent assumption of higher relative prices for fossil-fuel (EIA 2010). Plans, policies and programs to provide opportunities for the development of the renewable energy industry seem to be on the increase (Grunewald 2008). The reliance of the renewable energy sector on subsidies to bring their technologies into mainstream shows that their capacity will be limited for a long time and that non-renewables will still be leading the energy industry (IEA 2008). Figure 12.1 below shows the trend of energy capacity supplied in the world market by various energy sources in the industry.

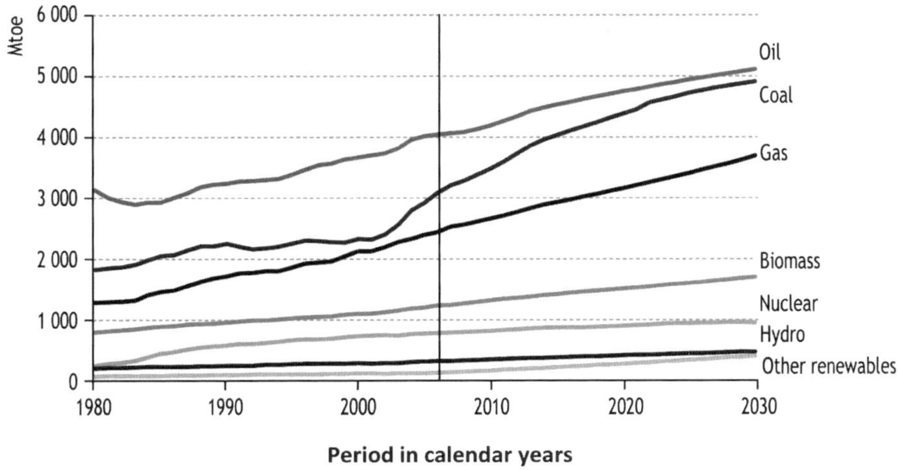

Fig. 12.1. Trend of world energy demand (source: IEA 2008)

The figure provides a scenario of world primary energy demand projected from the year 2008 up to 2030. Increasing energy supplies from oil and coal was dominating from 1980 to 2008 and will continue over the projected scenario. The total capacity of renewable energy supplies are growing, but will not reach that of non renewable energy. World demand for coal will increase, and its share in global energy demand will climb from 26% in 2006 to 29% in the 2030 scenario. About 85% of the rise in the global coal consumption will come from increasing construction of power plants in China and India (IEA 2008).

The share of nuclear power in primary energy demand edges down over the outlook period (1980 to 2030). That is from the growth rate of 6% in 2008 to a projected 5% in 2030 and its share of electricity output will drop from the growth rate of 15% to 10% in the same projected period, reflecting the consistency of the anticipated changes in the energy world. This is due to the high increasing supply of non- renewable energy like oil, coal and gas indicated in the projection to meet the growing capacity of energy demand. Excluding biomass and traditional hydropower, renewable energy sources such as wind, solar, geothermal and tide wave energy together are growing faster than any other source worldwide at an average rate of 7.5% per year over the projection period of 2030. Nevertheless, their total energy supply in the world market will remain relatively insignificant as this share of non-hydro-renewable energy supplies is only expected to grow from 1% in

2006 to 4% in 2030. Hydropower output will slightly increase, though its share of electricity production in the global market will drop to 14%. Therefore the projected outlook demonstrates that, at least until 2030, the capacity of fossil fuel will come first in the merit order of world energy supply.

It has been stated that energy management programs that focus on demand and supply (i.e. measures to improve energy efficiency) are the cheapest and fastest ways to curb energy related emissions in the near future (Stringer 2002). That is management schemes for energy saving both on the demand and supply sides. This has given an opportunity for the development of nano-technologies for the production of energy materials with high efficiency and possible reduction of energy losses. They have also given rise to energy saving equipments, which together with other energy management efforts on both demand and supply sides are used to solve energy challenges. These efforts can make a greater contribution to the energy challenges over longer time periods (Ibid.). Whilst these management and technological approaches could make major contributions to control the energy demand and supply, as well as the related emission saving, it is far from clear whether they would be able to alter the energy scenarios outlook (Fig. 12.1).

In the future one could expect efforts towards emission reductions, which could come from several sources such as improved efficiency in industry, building and transport; switching to nuclear power (but problems of handling nuclear waste and material which need special facilities) and renewable energy supply, and world wide spread deployment of emission capture and storage. To achieve emission savings, several approaches could be applied such as quick and vigorous policy actions by all countries and development of technological advances that entail low cost. Therefore, to contribute to the achievement of national and global goals to reduce emissions and fight climate change, this paper proposes that the focus needs to be put on natural mitigation measures that are potentially viable and more sustainable such as the development and maintenance of ecosystem services. In addition to the current focus on emission policies, consideration should be given to the development of ecosystem services and those activities that promote them. This is because without these services (ecosystem services) of the natural ecosystems acting as regulators of the environment, then it is possible without preserving them to reach scenarios with extreme high temperatures. This has been justified from the synthesis of desertification in the MEA (2005a). For example greenhouse gas emissions in the atmosphere are sequestrated by forest, green plants, soil, water bodies and others, which are the services of the natural ecosystems (Kasting 1998). That is without these services, it will be possible that the rate of ozone level depletion causing climate change would increased drastically due to the rapid rate of increased in those gases that are justified from the emission scenarios (Wall 2008; IEA 2008). This is because the available capacity of ecosystem services cannot capture the huge amount of emissions. Therefore ecosystem services need to be developed and maintained in order to reduce the potentials of climate change from gases through sequestration services from the natural ecosystems. This means efforts and investments on climate change should be diverted on their development, while still considering the other measures.

12.2 Global Climate Change Projections

According to the World Energy Outlook, future scenarios project that the rise in the concentration of greenhouse gasses will double in the atmosphere by the end of the century (IEA 2008). This is expected to entail an eventual global average temperature increase of up to 6 degree Celsius (IEA 2008). The trend points to a continuing growth in emission of CO_2 and other greenhouse gases that greatly contribute to global climate change. Global energy-related CO_2 equivalent emission is projected to rise from 28 billion tonnes in 2006 to 41 billion tonnes in 2030 projections, showing an increase of 45%. This 2030 projection is only 1billion tonne lower than that projected in the 2007 Outlook (IEA 2008), even though the 2007 Outlook assumed a scenario with higher relative energy prices and slightly lower growth in world GDP.

World greenhouse gas emissions, including non-energy CO_2 and all other gases are projected to grow from 44 billion tonnes CO_2 equivalent in 2005 to 60 billion tonnes CO_2 equivalent in 2030, an increase of 35% over 2005 (Wall 2008). However, in a growth scenario with a slightly faster growing global GDP, it is predicted that energy demand will rise by 6% and CO_2 emission by 7% (Ibid.). Also, the trend predicts a continued growth in global energy-related emission equivalents from 27 billion tonnes in 2005 to 42 billions tonnes in 2030, a rise of 57% (IEA 2008). Therefore new policy instruments need to promote mitigation measures like the development of ecosystem services such as conservation banking for restoration of ecosystems. The concept of conservation banking was introduced in the United States (Shwartz 2000) and a similar approach should be adapted and scaled-up where possible. Conservation banking is concept of giving monetary value and creating a trade system for ecosystem service, which should be applied more widely to include areas beyond wetlands, as applied in the US. This could target any ecosystem restoration activities to maintain, and safeguard and secure ecosystem services that regulate and control the environment. But however, preserving and conserving ecosystem services requires that their role as protecting the environment have to be understood and appropriate values be given to them (Slootweg and Beukering 2008; Farber et al. 2002), although it is considered that nature offers them free of charge. For instance they play an importance role in the reduction of emission gases to fight climate change. Plants and forest function as regulatory service of climate through sequestration of emission gases through the process of photosynthesis, where photosynthetic organisms convert emission gases and water into sugar and other organic compounds using solar energy (Kasting 1998). But these uptakes of emission are not constant throughout the lifespan of trees, which mean they have to be constantly maintained and developed. Therefore afforestation and reforestation are essential for maintaining and developing regulatory ecosystem services.

12.3 Ecosystems Services as Targets for Climate Change

The topic of ecosystem services can attract the scientific community through its strategic importance for sustainable development and the fight against climate change. This is not only because ecosystem services are currently threatened and their importance is being undermined (MEA 2005b; Vitousek 1997), but because they offer opportunities for financial gain. This is important as it promotes conservation of natural ecosystems through economic incentives. Therefore, an understanding of the role of ecosystem services and encouraging incentives to invest in them could play a vital role in the fight against climate change. For instance, the Millennium Ecosystem Assessment (MEA) research (reports from about a thousand international environmental experts) has compiled results of the benefits from ecosystem services from global, regional to local scales (MEA 2005b). Therein, is explained how an understanding of these benefits and preservation of these services could play a vital role in mitigating climate change and reducing the cost of the huge technology expenditures on efforts to fight climate change. The report found that 60% of global ecosystem services are being degraded or used unsustainably. This is mainly a consequence of over-utilization of natural resources to satisfy growing consumption of goods and services, primarily in the private sector. This means that if ecosystem services are not developed, restored, maintained and preserved, no matter the technological improvement on emission reductions, climate change will remain a big problem for a long time. This assumes that cost of technological solutions have opportunity costs and cost-benefit thresholds, beyond which humanity cannot afford. Since our natural environment provides services that regulate, control and maintain beneficial environmental functions (ecosystem services), more effort is justified to support their development. Ecosystem services could be subdivided into five categories (Ranthanathan et al. 2008; Albrechts 2008; MEA 2005b), which are summarized in Figure 12.2:

- provisions, such as the production of food and water
- regulating, such as the control of climate and disease
- supporting, such as nutrient cycles and crop pollination
- cultural, such as spiritual and recreational benefits; and
- preserving, which include guarding against uncertainty through the maintenance of diversity

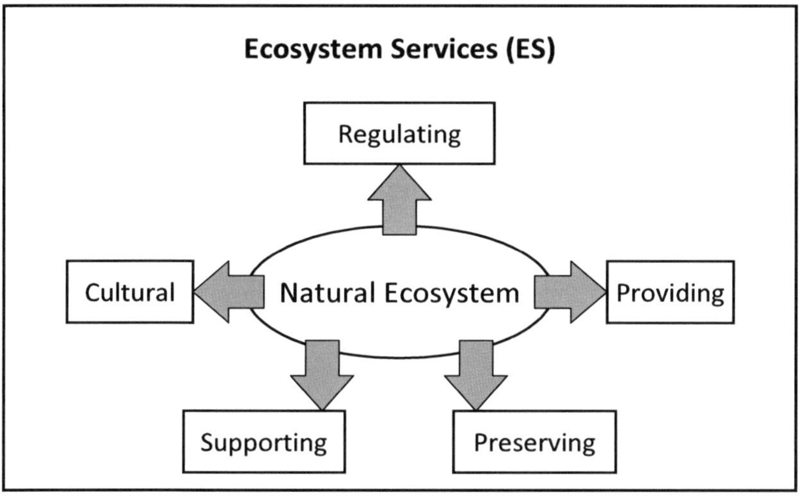

Fig. 12.2. Ecosystem Services and their linkage to the natural ecosystem

ES can be seen as an anthropogenic and anthropocentric concept based on the understanding that it provides society with various benefits. For example, they provide humans with valuable resources such as minerals (source functions); and act as a sink for wastes released by industrial processes through metabolism (sink functions) (Albrechts 2008). It is easy to grasp the importance of tangible services produced by ecosystems like timber from woodland, food from agricultural land (tangible ES). However, the importance of those services, which are less tangible, such as climate control, the nitrogen cycle, and the pollination of plants are not easy to discern. The following is a list of them produced by Hawken (1999), though the list is itself not exhaustive:

- Fixation of solar energy and conversion of material
- Production of oxygen
- Biological and genetic diversity
- Purification of water and air
- Storage, cycling and distribution of fresh water
- Regulation of the atmosphere
- Migration and nursery of habitats for wildlife
- Decomposition, sequestration and detoxification of human and industrial waste
- Genetic library for human application
- Natural pest and disease control
- Management of erosion and sediment runoff
- Flood prevention and regulation of runoff
- Protection against cosmic radiation
- Regulation of chemical composition of the oceans
- Regulation of climate
- Formation of topsoil and maintenance of fertility

- Production of grasslands, fertilizers and food
- Storage and recycling of nutrients
- Crop pollination

12.4 Understanding our Environment

Everything we do within the environment, whether consumption or production or exchange of processes, commodities and services can be traced to constituents provided by nature (Dasgupta 1996). For example the atmosphere is a swirl of biological, chemical and physical dynamic processes and keeping them balanced is one of the most indispensable services that one may receive from an ecosystem (Wall 2000). If ecosystem services are not maintained and developed, one could think of how hard it will be to re-create them. Temperature control could be a good example to show the relation between change in temperature and the effect on the environment. For example human beings can only survive within a certain range of optimum temperatures. All warming and cooling devices (which are themselves based on a network of natural systems) might not be able to maintain these optimum ranges of temperature, should ecosystem services collapse or fail to function adequately (Wall 2000). Without them regulating the global climate and temperatures year round, it is possible that the Earth's temperature would fall outside the range that is necessary for human survival; or liquid water would become scarce (Ibid.). This means human survival in such scenarios would be a big problem that could cost a lot of money on technologies for heating or cooling the environment, which those technologies themselves would also need to relay on ecosystem services (Farber et al. 2002; Daily and Ellison 2002). When these ecosystem services do not function as we understand them today, it is for example possible to envisage other scenarios in which there will be no air or no water; no food because the species that pollinate our crops do not exist any more. It is only when the role and value of ecosystem services is understood that humanity will invest in preserving ES within levels requisite for sustaining quality human life (Farber et al. 2002).

12.5 Valuation of Ecosystem Services

It is recognised that valuing ecosystem services directly facilitates the achievement of sustainability; and their values can be useful within the context of well-informed strategic decision-making to facilitate a better representation of the three pillars of sustainability i.e. (Slootweg and Beukering 2008):

- Financial sustainability of environmental and resource management;
- Social sustainability by facilitating participation of stakeholders and by highlighting and addressing equity issues;

- Environmental sustainability by providing better insight in the long and short term trade offs of investment decisions.

If ecosystem services are considered inexhaustible, indestructible and are known as free goods, especially the less tangible services, then it follows that giving them a value would be very challenging. This is because their values would be under-estimated since they would be considered free of charge. Nevertheless, based on an argument that it is urgent to develop them in order to fight climate change and mitigate the increasing associated environmental problems, appropriate values need to be given to them (Farber et al. 2002; Daily 2000). These values need not only attach importance on the survival of human life, but also on all other functions that underlie modern civilization (Balvanera et al. 2001; Chan et al. 2006). However, the idea of ecosystem services has already been recognised among scientists, as reflected by the emergence - between economics and ecology - of the discipline ecological economics that begins to describe what potential value could be attach to a particular ecosystem services (Slootweg and Beukering 2008; Freeman 1993; Franz 2006).

The monetary value of ecosystem services might be assumed to be zero, but this is incorrect and misses an opportunity to harness this value for a viable and profitable incentive-disincentive system that will guarantee ecosystem services and natural ecosystem longevity. Without an appropriate market for ecosystem services, their degradation may continue unabated and the lost services may have to be artificially replaced with expensive technology and at high collateral costs. Today, there are a lot of ongoing debates within the scientific community on the valuation of ecosystem services (MEA 2005b; Albrechts 2008). Furthermore, political, economic and environmental models that could better explain the need for their valuation are being presented (Fongwa and Gnauck 2009; Farber et al. 2002). Also government and businesses are recognizing the latent value of many ecosystem services (World Bank 2010), and these actors are willing to pay for the protection of these services and provide opportunities for business development within ecosystem services. But there is also the problem of free rider syndrome which leads to the requirement of huge subsidies for ecosystem service maintenance. Therefore, governments should not subsidise or encourage those activities which lead to overuse of resources and land degradation. Instead, an opportunity exists in which businesses can be encouraged to leverage real financial incentives to, for example, keep trees in the ground, maintain a mangrove forest, conserve water catchments, and thereby protect ecosystem services. However, some people may argue that market-based approaches could not solve ecosystem degradation problems, especially as the poor depend more on natural ecosystems for their livelihood (World Bank 2010; MEA 2005b). This has led some to believe that it will be difficult to determine appropriate market-based arguments for business development for the preservation of ES. Nevertheless, it has been established that of all the jobs in the world, the majority have either a direct or an indirect relation to ecosystem services. This means that even the poor who are mostly in rural areas that ecosystem services are highly distributed with resilience to such areas has the potential to benefits them with the development of a good market system. Therefore, the possibility of targeting valuation for ecosystem services without appropriate incentive and policy instruments to allow investment in them would not hold a potentially viable business model that can guarantee their preservation. This is because the poor would not have the appropriate finance to invest in their development.

Since it is a basic human right that everybody should have access to a healthy environment and by extension the derived ecosystem services, it is imperative that they should be preserved. This has already led to the introduction of incentive programmes such as market-based schemes for the development and conservation of the natural services offered by the environment. Such market-based schemes could be appropriately encouraged as an avenue for the development and promotion of ecosystem services. Notably, payment and trading schemes for ecosystem services are emerging as world-wide small-scale solutions, where one can acquire credits for activities such as sponsoring the development of carbon sequestration sources or the restoration of ecosystem services providers (World Bank 2010; Daily 2006). For instance the Kyoto Protocol establish role for carbon trading scheme (Lauterbach, 2007), which protected existing forests are not accepted as carbon sequestration source for credit but afforestation and reforestation projects. This is because as already mention the uptake of plants reduces through their lifespan (Kasting 1998). Therefore, businesses can gain a new prospective for judging their own environmental impact and estimating their consumption of ecosystem services by investing in their preservation at a level that would upset the dangers.

12.6 Potential Markets for Ecosystem Services

Since examples of ecosystem service-related markets already exists (World Bank 2008; Hawken 1999) there is a foundation for widening and mainstreaming the potential for businesses based on them. Credit can be given to developers of such services to sell to individuals who create damage to the environment through their developmental activities, or better still, to those whose activities meet a threshold at which their treatment of the ecosystem services as a common good of low value would be deemed detrimental to human welfare. Such a determination would involve setting of standards of environmental protection, sustainable development and equity, especially in relation to consumption of global and national ‘public goods’ from ecosystem services. These types of business development have already been growing among ecosystem developers like landscape, biodiversity and forest managers. Even some re-insurance companies are now creating risk policies on assets that are critical to environmental damage such Muichre re-insurance company (MunichRE 2010). They are developing proactive environmental policies, such as lobbying for increase in global climate change research and the development of ecosystem services. This underscores the business risks and opportunities perceived by the insurance industries, especially if the pay-outs for environmental disasters related to climate change become significant. Also, these re-insurance companies have begun to look at how degraded ecosystem services are going to affect their bottom line (MunichRE 2010).

In this context, emission trading schemes give credits for emission reduction to be sold to companies who exceed their emission targets, as an effort towards the fight against climate change. Such trading schemes could be extended to ecosystem services for developmental activities and modelled on an improved version of the Clean Development Mechanism (CDM) as a method of fighting climate change. Projects towards CDM can provide tradable credit certificates that could be sold in the market to encourage development of ecosystem services. There are numerous emerging markets that can be considered as potential targets, including:

- Credit market for carbon sequestration e.g. for forest or crop development;
- Water quality credit market for interested purchasers to buy water quality credits e.g. on the basis of promotion of forest watershed protection or development; development of water supply watershed or as compensation for landowners who maintaining watershed cover on their property,
- Wetlands and species conservation banking, i.e. projects that create and enhance wetlands or habitats for endangered species. The credits then become saleable to developers to satisfy their permit requirements.
- Also there are many other derivative markets that could be drawn from ecosystem services development and preservation.

Unlike carbon markets which can be global, most of the markets for ecosystem services are regionally limited because they are locally or regionally driven by specific operations which require the determination of a Total Maximum Daily Load (TMDL), except for the cultural services that depend on personal value judgement. For example water quality markets are usually driven by local or regional issues such as the needs of a wastewater treatment operating in a specific watershed and are impaired when they exceed their determined TMDL. The room for potential combinations of various ecosystem service markets may also be considered under defined circumstances, for example TMDL plans for some pollutants may allow forest practices to mitigate and address the impairment caused by pollutants. This shows how the market for ecosystem services could be interlinked. Therefore, these markets need to be organized as a one basket market, where it is easy to inter-trade for permits for type of ecosystem services with another. But while built on a regional scale, they could be scaled-up and vertically integrated to involve a continental or global scale. This offers the advantage that other regions which do not have the financial means to develop ecosystem services, especially poorer countries might benefit from funds that might be diverted to their countries by richer nations to invest in ecosystem restoration activities in need of acquiring credit certificates. It also allows for reductions in areas of lower costs. This will provide a global market for less tangible ecosystem services and spearhead the maintenance of them within a win-win situation. The investors in ecosystem services will get financial reward; the consumers of ecosystem services will be assured of services; and the natural ecosystem will be conserved; and an added approach to global fight against climate change in a way that will bring income for a majority of poor developing but ecosystems-rich countries to provide ecosystem services (equity distribution of wealth).

12.7 Justifications for Developing Ecosystem Services

This paper has given a review of world energy outlook scenarios and the trends to climate change until 2030. Also, it projects that non-renewable energy supply in the world market will continue to exist for the next 50 years, and projects that the potential concentration of greenhouse emission gases in the atmosphere will continue to increase. In addition, non-renewable energy has an apparent inverse relationship with ecosystem services. Therefore, an increase in non-renewable energy supply in the world market will reduce ecosystem services, and conversely, adequate development of them will reduce climate change. Since future scenarios predict that climate change will continue, there is room for ecosystem services to play a role in mitigating climate change. Therefore, strategies, policies, programs, projects, and investment in climate change mitigation measures should strongly favour the development of ecosystem services and provide markets for them. These markets should give ecosystem services an appropriate value, and ensure that investments in them enjoy direct economic return. Furthermore, the Kyoto Protocol mechanisms are inadequate to address the emissions challenge (Schulze 2008). However, caution is needed over investment motives that might favour artificial projects for clean-up activities at the expense of the benefits that could be realised from the development of less expensive ecosystem services. Therefore market-based motive should not be used to justify investment in projects to fight climate change, but the cost of fighting climate change should be taken into consideration.

12.8 Conclusions

Since emissions from fossil fuels are likely to continue, there is need to analyse future scenarios in order to effectively develop strategies and measures to meet desired future climate change targets. The future energy trends may still exist, but the climate could remain stable if efficient efforts are made in the development and preservation of ecosystem services. These ecosystem services would then contribute in maintaining the balance in environmental parameters that sustain our livelihoods. This is because they do not only mitigate emission problems, but also provide a raft of other services necessary for quality human life e.g. food and drinking water. Therefore, to live in a future scenario that is sustainable, efforts towards stable climatic conditions have to be the main priority in adapting a multi-solution approach to fight climate change. To achieve this, this paper has argued that the development of ecosystem services, in addition to other responses, is a worthy and justifiable approach. More so, ecosystem services can play a vital role in fighting climate change, but the challenge remains how it could be market-based whilst avoiding the free rider problem and "the tragedy of the commons" involved in the consumption of public goods.

References

Albrechts C (2008) Ecosystem services: Solution for problems or a problem that needs solutions? Workshop on Ecosystem Services, Salzau Castle Germany. Ecology Center University of Kiel-Germany

BP – British Petroleum (2008) Statistical review of world energy June 2008. BP, London

CDIAC – Carbon Dioxide Information Analysis Center (2008) Global fossil fuel carbon emissions. Internet address: http://cdiac.ornl.gov/trends/emis/glo.html, last accessed on 19.11.2010

Daily GC (2000) Management objectives for the protection of ecosystem services. In: Environmental Science & Policy 3: 333- 339

Daily GC (2006) Conservation planning for ecosystem services: In: Public Library of Science 4: 2138- 2152

Dasgupta P (1996) The economics of the environment: Proceeding of the British Academy 90: 165- 221

EIA – Energy Information Administration (2008) International Energy Outlook 2008. Energy Information Administration, Office of Integrated Analysis and Forecasting, U.S. Department of Energy Washington, DC 20585

EIA – Energy Information Administration (2010) World crude oil prices. Internet address: http://tonto.eia.doe.gov/dnav/pet/pet_pri_wco_k_w.htm, last accessed on 19.11.2010

EPI – Earth Policy Institute (2010) Eco-economy indicators: Carbon emissions. Internet address: http://www.earth-policy.org/index.php?/indicators/C52/, last accessed on 19.11.2010

ESRL – Earth System Research Laboratory (2010) Trends in atmospheric carbon dioxide - Mauna Loa. Internet address: http://www.esrl.noaa.gov/gmd/ccgg/trends/index.html, last accessed on 19.11.2010

Farber SC, Costanza R, Wilson MA (2002) Economic and ecological concepts for valuing ecosystem services. In: Ecological Economics 41: 375-392

Fongwa E, Gnauck A (2009) Value creation from ecosystem services for business development. In: Gnauck A (ed) Modeling and Simulation of Ecosystems, Kölpinsee Workshop 2008. Shaker Verlag, Aachen, pp. 43- 56

Franz W (2006) Organizing a public ecosystem service economy for sustaining biodiversity. In: Ecological Economics 59(3):296- 304

Freeman AM (1993) The measurement of environmental and resource values: theory and methods. Resources for the Future, Washington DC

Grunwald M (2008) The clean energy scam. TIME Magazine, March 27, 2008, Time Warner Publishing, Amsterdam

Hawken P, Lovins A, Lovins L (1999) Natural capitalism: What are the services we get from the Ecosystem? Little, Brown & Co., New York (NY)

IEA – International Energy Agency (2007) World Energy Outlook 2007. Organisation of Economic Cooperation and Development (OECD)/ International Energy Agency, Paris

IEA – International Energy Agency (2008) World Energy Outlook 2008. Organisation of Economic Cooperation and Development (OECD)/ International Energy Agency, Paris

Kasting J (1998) The carbon cycle, climate and the long-term effect of fossil fuel burning. In: Consequences: The Nature and Implications of Environmental Change 4(1):15-27

MEA – Millennium Ecosystem Assessment (2005a) Guide to the Millennium Assessment Reports. Internet address: http://www.maweb.org, last accessed on 19.11.2010

MEA – Millennium Ecosystem Assessment (2005b) Ecosystems and human well-being: Synthesis. Washington, Island Press

MunichRE (2010) Changing values: A risk of change. Internet address: http://www.munichre.com/publications/302-06506_en.pdf, last accessed on 19.11.2010

Ranganathan J, Munasinghe M, Irwin F (eds) (2008) Policies for sustainable governance of global ecosystem services. Edwarg Elgar Publishing Ltd, Cheletenham

Reddy KR, Hodges HF (eds) (2000) Climate Change and global Crop Productivity. CABI Publishing, New York

Schulze ED, Freibauer A (2005) Carbon unlocked from soils. In: Nature 437(8): 205- 205

Shwartz M (2000) Find a market for ecosystem services: How much is an ecosystem worth? The New York City experience. Press release by Stanford University 29.11.2000

Slootweg R, van Beukering P (2008) Valuation of ecosystem services and strategic environmental assessment: Lessons from Influential Cases. Netherlands Commission for Environmental Assessment, Utrecht

Stringer J (2002) Basic research needs to assure a secure energy future: Energy Bioscience Follow-up workshop, October 21-25, 2002

Vitousek P (1997) Human domination of earth's ecosystems. In: Science 277: 494-499

Wall P (2000) Know your environment: The value of ecosystem services. A publication by the Environmental Association

World Bank (2010) Environment: Carbon finance. Internet address: http://web.worldbank.org/WBSITE/EXTERNAL/TOPICS/ENVIRONMENT/EXTCARBONFINANCE/0,,menuPK:4125909~pagePK:64168427~piPK:64168435~theSitePK:4125853,00.html, last accessed on 19.11.2010

Part II - Planning and Decision-making

Michael Schmidt, Dmytro Palekhov

Department of Environmental Planning, Brandenburg University of Technology (BTU), Cottbus, Germany

Part II of this volume presents various research results and opinions on how decision-making and planning can contribute to sustainability in the energy sector. In Chapter 13 the requirements of and issues with implementation of Strategic Environmental Assessment (SEA) as a tool for promoting Sustainable Development in Ukraine, are presented. A variety of internal and external factors determine the necessity of implementing the principles of sustainable development in Ukraine. It is argued that the Ukrainian system lacks a process for integrating environmental concerns into development policies, plans and programmes, hence the need for an additional law that would provide for efficient implementation of SEA as a sustainable development instrument. The national SEA procedure must consolidate transparency, accountability and justice in the work of administrative institutions and public authorities.

Chapter 14 shows how planning for efficient electricity in Turkey can benefit from spatial analysis. The chapter presents decision-making criteria for planning for effective energy management and policy-making. The study revealed that population distribution, industrialization level of provinces and type of the industries, factories holdings and service sectors comprise the main determinants affecting the observed consumption patterns. Therefore, projection of future generation and consumption figures should be done using a model that uses consumption and generation data as well as population and GDP of provinces, life-time of current facilities and consideration of the facilities planned and under-construction. If such a projection could be developed then the result of this study would be very effective tool for energy management and decision-making on energy policies in Turkey.

In Chapter 15, research results from a US case study show How Risk Based Decision Making improves energy efficiency in Oil and Gas industry. Reducing the risk to personnel, assets and environment to As Low as Reasonably Practicable (ALARP) in Oil and Gas Safety studies resulted in energy efficiency based on a Cost-Benefit analysis. In Chapter 16 a critical appraisal of government forestry polices from a sustainability standpoint in Cameroon, is presented. It concludes that conservation and sustainable management of forest resources will be more feasible if government policies and especially the forestry laws are more rational, equitable, transparent and streamlined, improving monitoring and information gathering, strengthening capacities to enforce compliance and ensuring that policies take account of the economy and social dynamics that underlie illegal logging. This chapter is relevant to the energy focus because forests in Cameroon provide a significant proportion of energy, in terms of fuel-wood, firewood and charcoal, to local communities. Finally, in Chapter 17, criteria for evidence-based decision-making in the agrofuel industry of Sub-Saharan Africa are presented. This is at a time when agrofuel crops are experiencing increasing interest globally, and recently, in sub-Saharan Africa. The extent of land-use, investments, scientific research, media coverage and political interest dedicated to agrofuels has increased rapidly. Yet, decision-making principles and criteria for policy and planning agrofuel production are not adequately established.

13 Requirements and Issues with Implementing SEA as a Sustainable Development Instrument in Ukraine

Dmytro Palekhov and Michael Schmidt

Department of Environmental Planning, Brandenburg University of Technology (BTU), Cottbus, Germany

13.1 Introduction

This chapter aims to discuss the requirements and issues associated with the implementation of Strategic Environmental Assessment (SEA) as an instrument for sustainable development in Ukraine.

Having signed the UNECE SEA Protocol in 2003 (UNECE 2003), Ukraine actually recognised the necessity of using, at the national level, the European mechanisms for preventive environmental regulation. Implementation of SEA procedure into the practice of public administration in Ukraine, similar to other countries with economies in transition, is of principal importance for the balanced social and economic development, while preserving natural resources and securing quality of the environment. Furthermore, the practical application of SEA as an instrument for devising strategies promoting sustainable development requires special studies on adaptation of SEA procedure for national practice. It is important to critically evaluate the status and potential of SEA procedure, while taking into account the specific conditions, institutional realities and political circumstances in the country.

The main focus of this chapter is therefore to reflect on the main reasons for, and benefits from, implementation of SEA as an instrument aiding sustainable development in Ukraine. With this view, the chapter has the following objectives:

- to analyse the main principles of sustainable development and distinctive features of the Ukrainian approach towards their realisation;
- to analyse the characteristics of Ukrainian environmental assessment system and potential place for SEA within it; and
- to define the criteria reflecting the effectiveness of applying SEA as an instrument aiding sustainable development.

In this context, this chapter supplements and continues the studies on potential of SEA as a planning and decision-making tool in Ukraine. The chapter starts by exploring the concept of sustainable development and discussing its significance for Ukraine. Section 13.2 describes how instruments of sustainable development were formed and analyses the main factors for realisation of the new development model in Ukraine. Section 13.3 highlights that the Ukrainian system of environmental assessment inherited from the Soviet Union differs significantly from the 'western-type' assessment system in both framework and procedure. It is illustrated that the development and implementation of SEA procedure is a necessary step towards realisation of sustainability principles in Ukraine. The primary purpose of SEA is to provide adequate consideration of environmental concerns in all elements of socio-economic system. On this line, Section 13.4 discusses the system of criteria or indicators that display the reaction of the socio-economic structure to the administrative influences, as well as changes in its sustainability.

The chapter ends with conclusions and recommendations in Section 13.5 highlighting which reforms could contribute to implementation of SEA as a sustainable development instrument in Ukraine.

13.2 Concept of Sustainable Development in Ukraine

Transition to sustainable development is a long-term process that involves binding efforts, collective commitments and responsibility for guaranteeing a high quality of life on a global scale. At the same time, the selection of the methodology for sustainable development has to reflect the specific conditions and priorities on a country level, to be voluntary and to conform to the immediate needs of a country. The following sections consider the basic principles of sustainable development and the peculiarities of a national approach towards their realisation in Ukraine.

13.2.1 Principles of Sustainable Development and Aiding Instruments

The idea of sustainable development and the principles surrounding its realisation have been evolving in both scientific communities and numerous international forums over the course of many decades. The Stockholm Declaration of the United Nations Conference on the Human Environment (1972) agreed that there is an urgent need to take measures against environmental degradation (UN 1973); a report for the Club of Rome (1972) focused attention on the 'limits to growth' and necessity that civilisation switches to the balanced economy model, working on the principles of the global dynamic equilibrium (Meadows et al. 1972).

According to the definition provided by the World Commission on Environment and Development, also known as the Brundtland Commission, sustainable development is "development that meets the needs of the present without compromising the ability of future generations to meet their own needs" (WCED 1987, p. 43). This definition refers to development without exceeding the limits of environmental capacity, and which does not have an irreversible impact on the environment nor does it jeopardize the future of humanity.

The concept of sustainable development achieved its moral, political and legal status at the United Nations Conference on Environment and Development in Rio de Janeiro (1992). At the Conference it was declared that there is a direct interdependence between the level of social and economic development of society and the state of the environment, and the means for providing sustainable development were defined as: complementary and mutually supportive integration of three components – economic growth, social development and protection of the environment (UN 1993, pp. 3-8). Without dwelling on the analysis of numerous interpretations of this approach, we understand it as a balanced management of social and economic development, which, at the same time preserves natural resources and secures quality of the environment for current and future generations.

The politics of sustainable development aims to solve a number of issues by facilitating the implementation of methods for: poverty reduction, achieving sustainable patterns of consumption and production, enhancing efficiency in environmental protection and the rational use of natural resources. These tasks are complex and long-term and they can, in addition, cause conflicts of interests between different social groups. Therefore, as is stated in chapter 40 of the Agenda 21, development management requires appropriate information, assessment tools and indicators (UN 1993, pp. 473-479).

Instruments aiding sustainable development aim to influence the system of social relations with the purpose of keeping and increasing the potential of social and economic development, while at the same time, maintaining and improving the quality of the environment.

The application of instruments aiding sustainable development presupposes that there are certain assessment criteria or *indicators* available: "Indicators of sustainable development need to be developed to provide a solid basis for decision-making at all levels and to contribute to a self-regulating sustainability of integrated environment and development systems" (UN 1993, p. 473).

Resolution 2 of the World Summit on Sustainable Development in Johannesburg emphasises that each country has: the primary responsibility for its own sustainable development, makes its own decisions about instruments and methods for achieving it and ensures efficiency of legislation and availability of the necessary infrastructure (UN 2002). Moreover, countries with transitional economies (such as Ukraine) can have objective difficulties and peculiarities in their approaches to realisation of the new social model (i.e. sustainable development). Past experience and practice reveals that traditional methods of development are ineffective in achieving sustainability, especially in terms of long-term effect (Costanza et al. 1991).

As is well known, only at the end of the seventies did most counties begin to outline the transition from the policy of mitigating the consequences of environmental damage to the policy of precaution and prevention of adverse impacts. A number of countries started to test and evaluate the economic instruments of environmental governance, some of them proved to be very effective (e.g. taxes for pollution of water bodies in the Netherlands or the experience of the US in regulating emissions to the atmosphere). Currently, the whole spectrum of economic, legal, institutional and administrative instruments aiding sustainability is well developed and widely used – environmental certification of products, production and control systems, environmental audits, environmental monitoring, spatial planning etc. And among all instruments aiding sustainable development a principal place can be given to the institution of environmental assessment.

13.2.2 Main Factors for Sustainable Development in Ukraine

A variety of internal and external factors determine the necessity to implement principles of sustainable development in Ukraine. The external factors include both the Ukraine's aspiration for European integration and requirements to comply with its international obligations.

It should be noted that the system of environmental and resource management that was formed in Ukraine is highly inefficient. This resulted in the distressing dynamics of a raising level of environmental pollution and general deterioration of environment. Ukraine has the highest proportion of ploughed land in Europe, its economy is characterised by extensive use of water resources and the rapid rate of deforestation. Anthropogenic and industrial pressure on the Ukrainian environment is more then three times higher when compared with the relevant indices in the EU member states (MEP 2008).

A considerable majority of the industrial facilities were built in the 1950s-1970s and now do not comply with current environmental requirements and recent achievements in scientific and technical progress. The share of the most environmentally polluting industries – mining and quarrying, energy and chemical – constitutes approximately 60% of the national GDP. Forty years ago the majority of adverse environmental impacts were of local character and could have been alleviated by individual environmental actions. At present, the crisis situations are not localised; they affect whole industrial agglomerations and adjacent territories – for instance, the Krivoi Rog iron-ore basin, the West-Donbass coal basin, and the Dnepropetrovsk-Dneprodzerzhinsk-Novomoskovsk agglomeration etc. The unsatisfactory quality of the environment has a significant impact on human health and welfare (Palekhov et al. 2008). All these factors heighten the necessity to develop environmentally sound development strategies.

Building the eco-social market economy became a strategic target for Ukraine after the country gained independence in 1991. The Ukrainian Constitution of 1996 provided in Art. 16 that the state is obliged to "ensure ecological safety and to maintain the ecological balance on the territory of Ukraine". As a result an advanced system of environmental legislation was developed. It is hierarchical and governs various social relations in the field of environmental protection, rational use of natural resources and sustainable development. A variety of framework documents specify the targets set by Ukrainian environmental policy according to the principles of sustainable development. These include the: "Main directions of the national policy of Ukraine for environmental protection, natural resource use and environmental safety"; "Concept of improving health of the population of Ukraine"; "Programme for the formation of national ecological network for 2000-

2015" and "Complex programme for implementing at the national level decisions of the World Summit on Sustainable Development for 2003-2015".
Figure 13.1 shows the three main constituent parts of the national strategy on sustainable development in Ukraine, which can be summarized as:

1. Environmental safety: conservation and restoration of natural ecosystems, stabilising and improving quality of the environment
2. Economic stability: building a socially effective and competitive economy with adequate incorporation of environmental considerations
3. Social welfare: life expectancy of populations, family planning and rationalisation of personal consumption, improvement of the human environment, development of social activity, provision for equal access to health care, social protection of vulnerable groups

Internationally Ukraine declared its will to transition to sustainable development at the Conference in Rio de Janeiro in 1992, where the Rio Declaration was signed, and confirmed its intention to reach sustainability at the following conferences "Rio+5" in New York and "Rio+10" in Johannesburg. In May 2003 Ukraine signed the international Protocol on Strategic Environmental Assessment to the Convention on Environmental Impact Assessment in a Transboundary Context (UNECE 2003). The issue of development of the national procedure for strategic environmental assessment (SEA) was postponed for many years. This was due to a variety of reasons; however the main reason was the inert attitude of officials towards the legal status of environmental assessment (Palekhov 2007). The new "Concept of the national environmental policy of Ukraine for the time period up to 2020" (2007) adopted by the Cabinet of Ministers Order No. 880-p for the first time officially sets the target to implement SEA into practice for regional planning, sectoral and spatial planning and for management of natural resources.

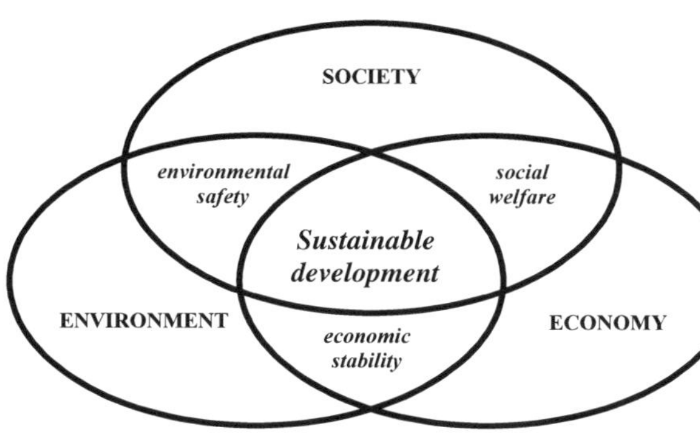

Fig. 13.1. Concept of sustainable development in Ukraine (adapted from: IUCN 2006, p. 2)

13.3 Issues with Implementing SEA as a Sustainable Development Instrument in Ukraine

It is necessary to note the Ukrainian system of environmental assessment inherited from the Soviet Union differs significantly from the 'western-type' assessment system in both framework and procedure. For better understanding of issues related to the implementation of sustainability principles within Ukraine the following sections will consider how each of these systems was developed.

13.3.1 SEA as a Sustainable Development Instrument

The modern practice of environmental assessment in the European Union includes two fully developed processes: project-level environmental impact assessment (EIA) and strategic environmental assessment (SEA). It is important to mention that originally the purpose of environmental assessment was solely to prevent local environmental problems. The United Nations Economic Commission for Europe defined EIA as "an assessment of the impact of a planned activity on the environment" (UNECE 1991, p. 1). And its purpose is to prevent environmental degradation by providing decision-makers with relevant information about environmental implications of a proposed activity to allow for a rational decision on whether or not to authorise the development.

For the first time on a regular basis the EIA process was applied in the USA after the US National Environmental Policy Act – NEPA was released in 1969. After adoption of NEPA the new process quickly gained a wide acceptance and EIA systems have been established throughout the world, for instance Canada in 1973, Australia in 1974, West Germany in 1975, France in 1976 and others (Glasson et al. 2005). The Council Directive 85/337/ EEC on the assessment of the effects of certain public and private projects on the environment (often referred to as EIA Directive) unified the EIA procedure and made it mandatory for all member states of the then European Communities (now European Union).

It is worth noting that the process of environmental assessment of development projects is in constant development. The Espoo Convention (1991) set forth the requirements for EIA procedure that reflected the new views on objectives of regulation of social and economic development. These are: 1) impacts on the natural environment should be studied on a par with other elements of the environment – social factors and population health; 2) public participation is an obligatory element of the procedure; 3) adequate and effective information must be made available to public about the nature of the proposed activity and its potential impacts on the environment, including human health.

In response to ideas of sustainable development, it was eventually realised that it is necessary to incorporate environmental considerations at a more strategic level, at an earlier stage in the decision-making process, when the major decisions concerning development activities are not yet taken. SEA was identified as a tool able to fulfil this task. The purpose of SEA is to integrate environmental considerations into the process of making policies, plans and programmes for a wide range of actions and development sectors to provide for social progress with a minimal harm to the environment while taking into account concerns of the future generations (Therivel and Partidario 1996).

Figure 13.2 shows how SEA procedure contributes to pursuing sustainability as fundamental objectives of strategic decision-making.

Currently a vast number of countries worldwide have established SEA and SEA-type systems that introduced SEA as a separate process from project-EIA (Dalal-Clayton and Sadler 2005). In 2001 the European Parliament and the Council jointly adopted the Directive 2001/42/EC on the assessment of the effects of certain plans and programmes on the environment (commonly known as the European SEA Directive), which was published on 21 July 2001. The SEA Directive came into force on 21 July 2004, the deadline for implementation by member states, either instead of - or in addition to - any existing state SEA systems, and provided a unified legal format for the SEA process in the EU member states (Therivel 2004). By mid-2006, the SEA Directive had been integrated by most of the EU member states, with only three states having no SEA legislation in force – Portugal, Greece and Luxemburg (Fischer 2006). Objectives of the SEA Directive (Art. 1) are closely related to the targets of environmental policy of the European Union and include integration of environmental considerations into the preparation and adoption of development strategies with a view to promoting sustainable development.

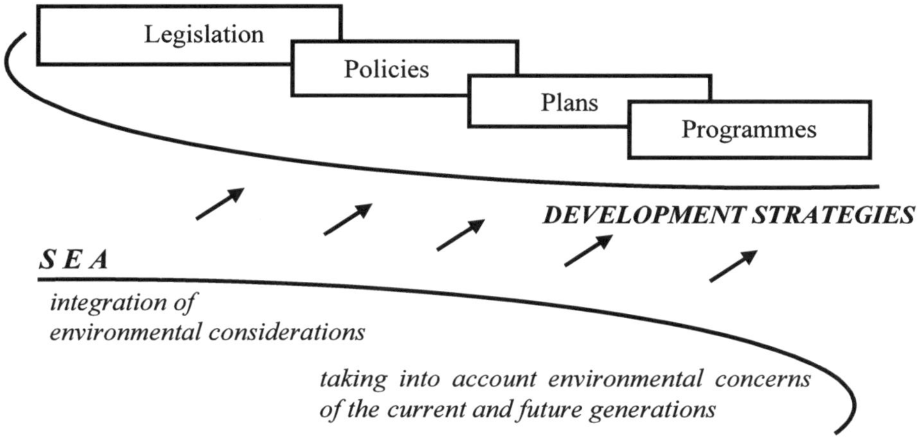

Fig. 13.2. Purpose of SEA as an instrument for sustainable development

13.3.2 Evolution of Environmental Assessment System in Ukraine

The foundations of the environmental assessment system that is currently in place in Ukraine were laid in the former Soviet Union. In practice this system covers almost only assessments at a project level and has the form of Environmental Expertise (in Ukrainian: *Ekologichna Expertysa*)[1] or State Environmental Expertise (SEE). The SEE procedure is compulsory for all development proposals and "serves not only as an element in the environmental assessment process, but also as a universal environmental-permit and pollution-control procedure" (Cherp 2001a, pp. 344-345). This type of environmental assessment system was determined by the distinctive features of the soviet planning system.

Since the beginning of the 1970s the soviet planning system included coordination of project and planning documentation with the numerous expert committees – expert reviews or *expertizas*. Expert committees were part of the *Gosstroy of the USSR* and *Gosplan of the USSR*[2], other ministries and regional authorities. Each of the committees carried out assessments of project and planning documentation in a specific field. Projects for construction and reconstruction of industrial facilities and enterprises, high-level planning decisions (allocation schemes for productive forces, spatial development plans etc.) could only be implemented after the appropriate expert committee gave its consent. For most of the development proposals, conforming to the planning and design rules and norms was the precondition for such consent. Only for some of the large-scale projects were potential impacts on the environment estimated. As a consequence, three decision alternatives were possible: 1) a project was authorised; 2) a project was rejected; 3) a project proposal was sent for revision to identify additional measures for environmental protection.

Cherp and Lee (1997) highlighted that the process of environmental assessment by expert committees was facilitated by the requirement, introduced in the 1970s, to include in the majority of planning documentation a section entitled "The protection of the natural environment". Its purpose was to describe the proposed measures for protection of the natural environment.

Worsening of environmental problems in the 1980s brought the realisation that the current methods of administration were inadequate for the conservation and effective protection of the environment. To combat this, the Soviet government made the decision to further develop the expert review procedures, while at the same time searching for new instruments for the prevention of environmental problems. In 1985 the *Gosstroy of the USSR* adopted the "Instruction on development of project documentation for constructing industrial enterprises, residential

---

1 The term *Ekologichna Expertysa* is translated typically as 'Environmental Expertise' (e.g. Dalal-Clayton and Sadler (1998), Grachev (2007), et al.). Other commonly used translations are 'Ecological Expertise', 'Ecological Examination', 'Environmental Examination' or 'Environmental Expert Review' (e.g. Cherp (2001a), Cherp (2001b), Cherp and Laevskaya (2009), et al.).

2 Gosstroy of the USSR – State committee of the USSR for construction; Gosplan of the USSR – State committee of the USSR for planning.

buildings and facilities". This instruction laid down the foundations of the *OVOS*[3] procedure.

At that time the Soviet government established the inter-ministerial scientific and technical Council for complex problems of environmental protection and rational use of natural resources (MNTS)[4]. The main task of this council was to study the contemporary instruments for preventing environmental problems and to develop fundamentals for the environmental assessment system in the USSR. As a result, the system of the State Environmental Expertise was developed, which was fit into the existing vertical planning system.

At the beginning of 1988 the government adopted a Decree "On the radical reform of nature protection". This decree provided for the creation of the State committee for nature protection (later on it was reorganised into the Ministry of Environment). The committee affiliated special Departments for the state environmental expertise that functioned in all regions and conducted SEEs of projects, plans, programmes, new materials and technologies.

Soviet-type environmental expertise systems, which were either retained or reformed, are operated in most post-Soviet countries – Ukraine, Russia, Belarus, Moldova, Kazakhstan etc. (Dalal-Clayton and Sadler 2005).

After Ukraine gained independence, a number of legal acts and regulations providing for environmental assessment had been adopted, in particular the Laws of Ukraine "On environmental protection" (1991), "On environmental expertise" (1995). The latter included many progressive provisions for the environmental assessment of projects, which were adopted from the European legislation of that time. The SEE procedure became more flexible and transparent; with the establishment of the procedure for public environmental expertise.

At the same time the current system of environmental assessment is not fully developed, as it lacks a process for integrating environmental concerns into strategic decision-making, i.e. into development policies, plans and programmers.

13.3.3 Limitations of Ukrainian Environmental Assessment at Strategic Level

As discussed in the previous subsection, the Ukrainian environmental assessment system has the form of environmental expertise (EE) which is also applied in many other post-Soviet countries.

Ukrainian legislation provides for various types of environmental expertise:

- state environmental expertise (SEE),
- public environmental expertise (PEE), and

[3] OVOS is the anglicised Russian acronym for the procedure similar to EIA called 'assessment of impacts on the environment' (*Otsenka Vozdejstviya na Okruzhayushchuyu Sredu*).

[4] Cherp and Lee (1997) provided a shorter translation of the Council's title – Interministerial Council on Environmental Science and Technology (p. 180).

- other types of environmental expertise (specialised environmental expertises).

Moreover, environmental expertise can be carried out at the national, regional and local levels, including state-level environmental assessment and environmental reviews as part of public inquiries. However, only actions upon the conclusions of SEE are compulsory, unlike the conclusions of PEE and other types of environmental expertise, which have the form of recommendations only and are not binding, i.e. may or may not be taken into consideration during decision-making (Art. 12 of the Law of Ukraine "On environmental expertise"; Art. 28, 30 of the Law of Ukraine "On environmental protection").

The structure of state environmental expertise (SEE) includes two interrelated stages: 1) OVNS[5] – assessment of impacts on the environment, and 2) expert review of the project documentation, including impact assessment report.

Under the Ukrainian legislation, SEE is a prerequisite for initiation of any projects or strategic actions[6]. According to the Laws of Ukraine "On environmental protection" (Art. 27) and "On environmental expertise" (Art. 7), SEE applies to draft strategic decisions and any project documentation, economic systems and facilities, normative acts and documents regulating economic activity; documentation for the introduction of new equipment, technologies, materials and substances; and implementation or production thereof, which could lead to violation of environmental safety standards and cause negative environmental impacts. Under Ukrainian legislation, all investment programmes and projects are subject to the Complex State Expertise, which includes SEE and other sectoral expertises.

Therefore, from this broad perspective, the SEE process includes the assessment of development policies, plans and programmes that have spatial and physical relevance (including urban and regional plans, regional programmes, etc.), i.e. assessment of strategic actions should be carried out within the SEE. In practice, however, SEE applies mainly to project documentation; it is a prerequisite for initiating any industrial project (e.g. capital construction and renovation projects; development of a new equipment, technologies, etc.). Application of SEE for strategic actions, i.e. policies, plans and programmes is very limited.

The main problem of Ukrainian environmental assessment system is that it has no relevant procedure adjusted for the assessment of strategic decisions. Legislation provides for the application of a common procedure for proposals at all deci-

---

[5] OVNS is the anglicised Ukrainian acronym for the procedure of 'assessment of impacts on the environment' (in Ukrainian: *Otsinka Vplyvu na Navkolyshne Seredovyshe*).

[6] In most post-Soviet countries legislation makes no distinction between environmental assessment at the project and programme level. For instance, according to Art. 14 of the Law of Ukraine "On environmental expertise" (1995), the state environmental expertise applies to a broad spectrum of development actions, including state investment programmes; plans and programmes for territorial and sectoral development; draft settlement master plans; project documentation for construction, expansion and renovation of enterprises and other facilities that may have negative environmental impacts; draft legislation and other regulatory acts that may have negative environmental impacts; documentation for the introduction of new equipment, technologies, materials and substances that potentially pose environmental risks; etc.

sion-making levels, both project and strategic. In this context, there are a number of doubts about suitability and applicability of the SEE procedure for preparing development strategies:

- *Firstly,* SEE evaluates, in general, the likely impacts of development projects and activities in terms of compliance with environmental legislation and normative requirements; SEE procedure should also examine if a project involves the rational use of natural resources. Thus, SEE is not a proactive instrument for preparing development proposals; rather it is used as a tool in the state permit system (i.e. as a part of the state licensing process).
- *Secondly,* according to Ukrainian legislation, the SEE process does not include requirements to assess impacts on human health, nor obligations to conduct consultations with health authorities. Impacts on the natural environment are not studied on a par with other elements of the environment – social factors and population health; issues of the protection of human health are addressed in the framework of the sanitary and hygiene control. Therefore, there is a need in appropriate assessment procedure that would address the environmental risks of development proposals, as well as the associated threats to public health and safety.
- *Thirdly,* none of the legal documents (Law of Ukraine "On environmental protection" (1991), Law of Ukraine "On environmental expertise" (1995), State construction norms (DBN), official guidelines, etc.) clearly define the roles and responsibilities of various actors involved in the assessment process, or any procedural requirements for using SEE at the stage of preparing strategic actions.

Therefore, following the analysis above it is possible to draw the following conclusions. The Ukrainian environmental assessment system, in the form of environmental expertise, is a systematic process for evaluating the environmental implications of development projects in order to ensure that these projects comply with environmental legislation, meet relevant environmental requirements and involve rational use of natural resources. Moreover, Ukrainian legislation provides for various types of environmental expertise, including state environmental expertise, public environmental expertise and other types of environmental expertise (i.e. specialised environmental expertises). Currently, only actions on the decisions of the state environmental expertise are compulsory and this procedure remains the basis of the environmental assessment system in Ukraine.

It is possible to argue that Ukrainian environmental assessment system is not fully developed, as it lacks clearly defined rules and procedure for integrating environmental concerns into development policies, plans and programs. A number of procedural elements for assessing the environmental impact of strategic actions are missing and those available are not up to the standard of 'western-type' SEA procedures. Furthermore, in the framework of the SEE process it is not necessary to assess impacts on human health or conduct consultations with health authorities; none of the legal documents regulating SEE clearly define the roles of actors involved in the assessment process at the stage of preparing development strategies.

Therefore, currently there is a need to establish key principles and rules for carrying out environmental assessment in strategic decision-making. Furthermore, development and implementation of SEA procedure which is compatible with international practice is a necessary step towards realisation of sustainability principles in Ukraine.

13.4 Indicators of Sustainable Development in Ukraine

The purpose of SEA, as a sustainable development instrument, is to ensure the environmental consistency of all components of the socio-economic system. The efficiency of applying SEA as a sustainable development instrument can be measured with the help of special criteria or indicators that display the reaction of a socio-economic system to administrative influences, as well as changes in its sustainability (see Figure 13.3). Sustainable development indicators are widely used in strategic decision-making practice in the USA, Great Britain, Denmark, Finland etc. As discussed by Palekhov and Schmidt (2006), such indicators have not, so far, been used in Ukrainian planning practice. Moreover, studies on problems of developing environmental assessment in the post-Soviet countries usually do not consider this issue; example cases include "Pilot Study to Assess the Capacity of Russia's Environmental Assessment System", see von Ritter and Tsirkunov (2003); "National Strategy for Introduction of SEA and Implementation of the UNECE SEA Protocol requirements: Ukraine", see UNECE (2006).

Sustainable development indicators (SDI) are indicators that measure progress made in sustainable growth and development (EEA 2008). They are various statistical values that collectively measure the capacity to meet present and future needs. SDI can provide an early warning, raising the alarm in time to prevent economic, social and environmental damage. They are also important tools to assist decision-makers and policy-makers at all levels and to increase focus on sustainable development. Hence, the SDI must, on the one hand, reflect integration of social, economic and environmental development parameters into a single complex and, on the other hand, characterise the level of sustainability of the environment, its ability to self-restore when development parameters are changed.

It is necessary to note that cooperation of different authorities, administrations and scientific institutions is essential for development of SDI. As an example, in Finland almost 20 ministries and research institutes participated in development of the national SDI and the so-called indicator network which has been created. Therefore, the chosen indicators were able to reflect many points of view and were developed according to the needs of their users.

In most cases SDI are arranged in four groups based on sustainable development themes: social, economic, environmental and institutional (Schmidt et al. 2005). There are also other frameworks providing means for structuring SDI sets. For example, framework developed by the OECD[7] groups the SDI into state indi-

[7] Organisation for Economic Cooperation and Development

cators – population density, resources reserves, access to information etc.; response indicators – environmental protection expenditures as a percent of GDP, waste recycling and reuse etc.; driving force indicators – annual energy consumption, unemployment rate, land use change etc. (Segnestam 2002).

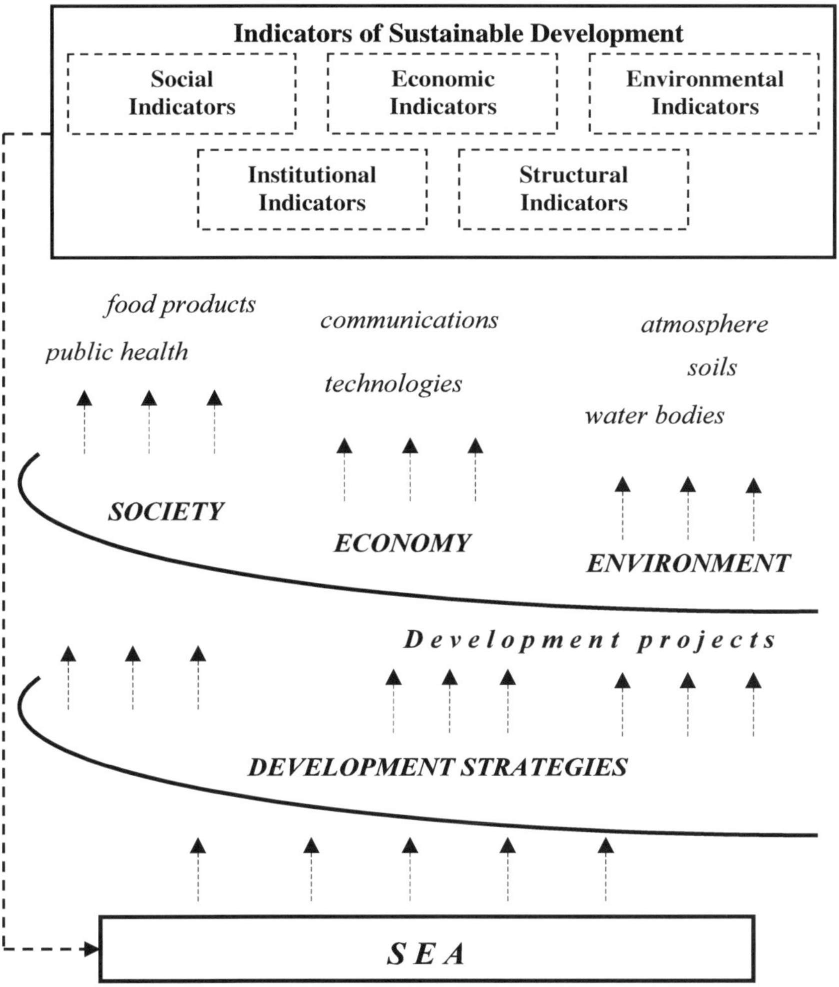

Fig. 13.3. Reaction of socio-economic system to strategic actions

Considering the main development priorities of Ukraine set forth in the "EU – Ukraine Action Plan", which was endorsed in the framework of the European Neighbourhood Policy (EC 2005), in the context of SEA, it is possible to apply the following groups of SDI:

1. ***Social indicators:*** human health and demographic dynamics (fertility, morbidity, mortality etc.); environmental properties of food products; life sustaining infrastructure (such as drinking water, level of sanitation); opportunities for recreation; environmental awareness and legal consciousness; share of public involved in making of environmentally significant decisions etc.
2. ***Economic indicators:*** competitiveness of environmentally friendly products and technologies; investments into upgrading and modernisation of production and into environmental protection systems; reduction of materials and energy consumption, development of recycling technologies; production and consumption of renewable resources etc.
3. ***Environmental indicators:*** quality level of different environmental components (quality of atmospheric air, biodiversity, proportion of ploughed land, sealed land, quantity and quality of water etc.); environmental stresses (pollution of atmospheric air, water, soil, contamination with solid wastes and toxic substances, land degradation, emissions of greenhouse gases, environmental disasters etc.); development state of the instruments for environmental protection (e.g. setting standards and thresholds, environmental taxes, licensing, subsidies, planning, environmental assessment – EIA and SEA, environmental audit, environmental liability etc.); the degree of integration of environmental concerns into development policies, plans and programmes; transboundary environmental impacts etc.
4. ***Institutional indicators:*** ability of public authorities to address environmental issues; transparency and accountability of public authorities; informing public about development strategies and related environmental problems; presence and efficiency of relevant environmental institutions on all tiers of planning and administration (international, national, regional, sectoral) etc.
5. ***Structural indicators:*** mutual consistency of policies, plans and programmes in addressing environmental issues; cooperation of public authorities and NGOs in addressing environmental issues etc.

The proposed system of indicators would require specification and elaboration at every level of planning and administration – national, regional, municipal.

13.5 Conclusions and Recommendations

As illustrated in this chapter, a variety of internal and external factors determine the necessity of implementing the principles of sustainable development in Ukraine. The system of environmental and resource management that has been formed is highly inefficient. Building the eco-social market economy, while providing for the three main constituent parts of sustainable development – environmental safety, economic stability and social welfare, became a strategic target for Ukraine following independence. In support of a sustainable development policy, Ukraine signed the Protocol on Strategic Environmental Assessment to the Convention on Environmental Impact Assessment in a Transboundary Context. At the same time, however, the implementation of SEA in Ukraine remains a difficult issue. The Ukrainian system of environmental assessment covers almost only assessments at a project level and has the form of state environmental expertise. It lacks a process for integrating environmental concerns into development policies, plans and programmers.

There is a need for an additional law that would provide for efficient implementation of SEA as a sustainable development instrument. The national SEA procedure must consolidate transparency, accountability and justice in the work of administrative institutions and public authorities. This will require the further development of the methodology for making official decisions in the context of sustainable development at national, regional and local (municipal) level. Specifying the set of criteria (indicators) that would reveal efficiency of SEA as a sustainable development instrument is also of great importance. Such a set must include social indicators, economic indicators, environmental indicators, institutional indicators and structural indicators.

References

Cabinet of Ministers Order No. 880-p of 17.10.2007 "On approval of Concept of the national environmental policy of Ukraine for the time period up to 2020". In: Official gazette of Ukraine (Ofitsiyny visnyk Ukrainy) No. 79 of 29.10.2007, p. 170, st. 2961

Cherp A (2001a) EA legislation and practice in Central and Eastern Europe and the former USSR. A comparative analysis. In: Environmental Impact Assessment Review 21(4): 335-361

Cherp A (2001b) Environmental assessment in countries in transition: Evolution in a changing context. In: Journal of Environmental Management 62(4): 357-374

Cherp A, Lee N (1997) Evolution of SER and OVOS in the Soviet Union and Russia (1985-1996). Environmental Impact Assessment Review 17(3): 177-204

Cherp A, Laevskaya E (2009) Independent review of Ukraine's legal, administrative and other measures to implement the provisions of the Convention. Report by consultants. United Nations Economic Commission for Europe, Meeting of the Parties to the Convention on Environmental Impact Assessment in a Transboundary Context, Implementation Committee. U.N. Doc. ECE/MP.EIA/IC/2009/5 Internet: http://www.unece.org/env/documents/2009/eia/ic/ece.mp.eia.ic.2009.5.e.pdf, last accessed on 16.11.2010

Constitution of Ukraine, adopted at the 5th session of the Verkhovna Rada of Ukraine on 28 June 1996. In: Bulletin of Verkhovna Rada (Vidomosti Verkhovnoi Rady), 1996, No. 30, st. 141, amended according to the Law of Ukraine No. 2222-IV on 08.12.2004, Bulletin of Verkhovna Rada, 2005, No. 2, st. 44

Costanza R, Daly HE, Bartholomew JA (1991) Goals, agenda, and policy recommendations for ecological economics. In: Costanza R. (ed) Ecological economics: The science and management of sustainability. Columbia University Press, New York, pp. 1-20

Council Directive 85/337/EEC of 27 June 1985 on the assessment of the effects of certain public and private projects on the environment. In: Official Journal (OJ) L175 of 05.07.1985, pp. 40-48

Dalal-Clayton B, Sadler B (1998) Strategic Environmental Assessment: A Rapidly Evolving Approach. In: Donnelly A, Dalal-Clayton B, Hughes R (eds) A Directory of Im-

pact Assessment Guidelines: 2nd Edition. International Institute for Environment and Development, London, pp. 31-42
Dalal-Clayton B, Sadler B (2005) Strategic environmental assessment: A sourcebook and reference guide to international experience. Earthscan, London
Decree of the Central Committee of the Communist Party of the Soviet Union and the Council of Ministers "On the radical reform of nature protection" No. 32 of 07.01.1988. In: Collection of Decrees of the Government of the USSR (Sobranie postanovlenii Pravitelstva SSSR), 1988, No. 6, st. 14
Directive 2001/42/EC of the European Parliament and of the Council of 27 June 2001 on the assessment of the effects of certain plans and programmes on the environment. In: Official Journal of the European Communities (OJ) L 197 of 21.07.2001, Vol. 44, pp. 30-37
EC – European Commission (2005) EU-Ukraine Action Plan, UE-UA 1051/05. DGE VI. Internet: http://ec.europa.eu/world/enp/pdf/action_plans/ukraine_enp_ap_final_en.pdf, last access on 16.11.2010
EEA – European Environment Agency (2008) Multilingual environmental glossary. Internet address: http://glossary.eea.eu.int/EEAGlossary, last access on 16.11.2010
Fischer TB (2006) SEA in spatial/land use planning in the 25 EU member states – a July 2006 update. In: UVP-report 20(3): 127-131
Glasson J, Therivel R, Chadwick A (2005) Introduction to environmental impact assessment: 3rd Edition. Routledge, London
Grachev VA (2007) Draft Federal Law No. 401845-4 "On Amendments to the Federal Law "On Environmental Expertise" and to the Urban Development Code of the Russian Federation". In: Environmental Expertise and Environmental Impact Assessment 1(65): 58-62
IUCN – International Union for Conservation of Nature (2006) The future of sustainability: Re-thinking environment and development in the twenty-first century. Report of the IUCN Renowned Thinkers Meeting, 29-31 January 2006. Internet address: http://cmsdata.iucn.org/downloads/iucn_future_of_sustanability.pdf, last accessed on 16.11.2010
Law of Ukraine "On environmental expertise" No. 45/95-VR of 09.02.1995. Bulletin of Verkhovna Rada (Vidomosti Verkhovnoi Rady), 1995, No. 8, st. 54, last amendment on 19.03.2009, Official gazette of Ukraine (Ofitsiyny visnyk Ukrainy) No. 26 of 17.04.2009, p. 32, st. 856
Law of Ukraine "On environmental protection" No. 1264-XII of 25.06.1991. Bulletin of Verkhovna Rada (Vidomosti Verkhovnoi Rady), 1991, No. 41, st. 546, last amendment on 19.03.2009, Official gazette of Ukraine (Ofitsiyny visnyk Ukrainy) No. 26 of 17.04.2009, p. 32, st. 856
Meadows DH, Meadows DL, Randers J, Behrens WW (1972) The limits to growth: A report for the Club of Rome's project on the predicament of mankind. Universe Books, New York
MEP – Ministry for Environmental Protection of Ukraine (2008) Annual reports of the Ministry on state of the environment in Ukraine (in Ukrainian). Internet address: http://www.menr.gov.ua/cgi-bin/go?node=NAC%20dop%20p%20NPS, last accessed on 16.11.2010
Palekhov D (2007) Consideration of the legal instruments for sustainable development of industrial regions (in Ukrainian). In: Zhurlov AM et al. (eds) Collected scientific and

methodological papers: Forming the modern strategy for development of entrepreneurship. Kherson State University Publishing House, Kherson, pp. 235-243

Palekhov D, Schmidt M (2006) Implementing SEA as an instrument for devising regional sustainable development strategies. In: Sustainable Development at the National, Regional and Local Level – Polish Experiences and their Possible Implementation in Ukraine. Publishing House of Catholic University of Lublin, Lublin, pp. 96-104

Palekhov D, Schmidt M, Pivnyak G (2008) Standards and Thresholds for EA in Highly Polluted Areas – The Approach of Ukraine. In: Schmidt M, Glasson J, Emmelin L, Helbron H (eds) Standards and Thresholds for Impact Assessment. Springer Verlag, Heidelberg, pp. 33-48

von Ritter K, Tsirkunov V (2003) How Well is Russia's EA System Working? Pilot Study to Assess the Capacity of Russia's EA System (in Russian). Alex Publishing House, Moscow. Internet address: http://www.alexpublishers.ru/envassess.pdf, last accessed on 16.11.2010

Segnestam L (2002) Indicators of Environment and Sustainable Development. Theories and Practical Experience. Environmental Economics Series, Paper No. 89. The World Bank Environment Department, Washington, D.C.

Schmidt M, Palekhov D, Shapar A (2005) Criteria and requirements for the implementation of sustainable development policy in Ukraine. In: Ecology and nature management: Collected scientific papers of the Institute of Nature Management and Ecology Problems by the NAS of Ukraine, Dnepropetrovsk, Issue 8, pp. 18-22

Therivel R (2004) Strategic environmental assessment in action. Earthscan, London

Therivel R, Partidario MR (1996) The practice of strategic environmental assessment. Earthscan, London

UN – United Nations (1973) Report of United Nations Conference on the Human Environment, Stockholm, 5-16 June 1972. U.N. Doc. A/CONF.48/14/Rev.1. New York

UN – United Nations (1993) Report of the United Nations Conference on Environment and Development, Rio de Janeiro, 3-14 June 1992. Volume I: Resolutions adopted by the conference. U.N. Doc. A/CONF.151/26/Rev.1 (Vol.1). New York

UN – United Nations (2002) Report of the World Summit on Sustainable Development, Johannesburg, South Africa, 26 August-4 September 2002. U.N. Doc. A/CONF.199/20 & A/CONF.199/20/Corr.1. New York

UNECE – United Nations Economic Commission for Europe (1991) Policies and Systems of Environmental Impact Assessment. Environmental Series 4. United Nations, New York

UNECE – United Nations Economic Commission for Europe (2003) Protocol on Strategic Environmental Assessment to the Convention on Environmental Impact Assessment in a Transboundary Context. 21st of May 2003, Kiev, Ukraine. Internet address: http://www.unece.org/env/eia/sea_protocol/contents.htm, last accessed on 16.11.2010

UNECE – United Nations Economic Commission for Europe (2006) National Strategy for Introduction of SEA and Implementation of the UNECE SEA Protocol requirements: Ukraine, May 2006 (official version 1). Internet address: http://www.unece.org/env/eia/documents/SEA_CBNA/Ukraine_strategy_en.pdf, last accessed on 16.11.2010

WCED – World Commission on Environment and Development (1987) Our common future. Oxford University Press, Oxford

14 Spatial Analyses of Electricity Supply and Consumption in Turkey for Effective Energy Management and Policy-making

Evren Deniz Yaylacı[1,3], Abdurrahman Belel Ismaila[2], Onur Uşkay[2] and Şebnem Düzgün[3]

1 KCM Project and Consulting Co. Ltd., Turkey
2 Department of Geodetic & Geographic Information Technologies, Middle East Technical University, Ankara, Turkey
3 Department of Mining Engineering, Middle East Technical University, Ankara, Turkey

14.1 Introduction

Over the past decades, both public and private institutions have extensively analyzed energy supply and demand on national and international bases (WEC-TNC 2004; Munasinghe and Meier 1993). The main focus of these analyses has mainly been the security of the energy supply and the determination of income and price elasticity of energy consumption (Zachariadis and Pashourtidou 2006). In addition, concerns about climate change are considered as another motivation for these analyses (Kuik 2003). This kind of information is useful for making inferences about energy policy implications. Moreover, energy plays a vital role in the economic, social and political development of any nation (Surrey 1996; Varian 2002; ECN 2006). Therefore, no modern society can seriously address development issues if the consideration is not based on a foundation of an adequate, sustainable, and affordable energy supply (Akinbami and Lawal 2009).

An efficient, resilient energy infrastructure to reliably supply sufficient, affordable energy to meet increasing demand is crucial for achieving these goals. Like other nations, Turkey faces an ever-increasing demand for electricity. Between 1980 and 2000, the average growth rate of total electricity consumption in Turkey was 8.1% per annum, while the real GDP grew an average of 4.4% annually during the same period. Electricity consumption per capita also steadily grew from 459 kWh in 1980 to 1457 kWh in 2000. This was still low compared to other countries in the Organisation of Economic Developing Countries (OECD). Turkey faced electricity shortages during the early 1980s and the 1990s, and the same period was also marked by economic crises. Insufficient public funds and the poor performance of state-owned electricity monopolies led to a reform in the electricity sector following the economic crisis in 2001, aiming to create a competitive energy market, (Özkývrak 2005; Altınay and Karagöl 2005).

Therefore, Turkey must have sufficient capacity and secure energy sources to be able to supply affordable electricity constantly to compete in world markets. To achieve this, effective and measurable decision-making tools and approaches for energy management and policymaking must be in place. Thus, this study aims to investigate the spatial distribution of electricity generation and consumption in Turkey using Geographical Information System (GIS) and spatial data analysis methods. This can provide information that will guide decision and policymaking on energy management in Turkey.

The chapter is organised as follows: section 14.1 starts with a discussion of the importance of energy management and possible uses of spatial analysis in energy sector management and policymaking. Section 14.2 describes data collection and processing. Section 14.3 shows visualisation results of electricity generation capacity and consumption data, and section 14.4 presents exploration results. This section also describes the methods employed in the study and the reasoning behind their usage. The chapter ends with a conclusion and recommendation for further studies in section 14.5.

14.2 Data Collection and Processing

Spatial analysis of electricity generation capacity and consumption first requires the collection of relevant data based on certain geographical units. In this study, the Nomenclature of Territorial Units for Statistics level 3 (NUTS level 3), a standard designed for European countries to aid in the referencing of administrative divisions for statistical purposes, is adopted as the main geographical representation of the data. NUTS level 3 divides Turkey into 81 provinces (see Figure 14.1).

Fig.14.1. Map of Turkey showing the 81 provinces based on NUTS level 3 (source: digitised from Başarsoft 2010)

The data used in this study are divided into three basic categories: electricity power plants, consumption, and supply. The power plants data includes information on hydro, thermal, wind, geothermal, gas, fuel oil, and hydro autoproducers. These data come from Turkish Electricity Generation Inc. (EÜAŞ), Turkish Electricity Distribution Inc. (TEDAŞ), State Water Works (DSİ), Energy Market Regulatory Authority (EPDK), Internet sources, journals and other relevant literature. The data were in various formats, including excel files, shape files, Jpeg etc. The attributes of the data include: the name of the power plant, the location (province and town), installed capacity, annual generation capacity, operation commencement date, and present operational status. The electricity consumption and supply data for all 81 provinces in the years 1997 to 2006 was obtained from the Turkish Directorate of Statistics (TÜİK) in excel format.

This study utilised ArcMap and MapInfo, two major GIS software packages. Therefore, all the data were transformed to a GIS data format, specifically the shape file format (used by ArcMap). Using the master/slave registration method, the Jpeg files were registered, and the necessary information was digitised into different layers. The excel data files containing the attribute information were linked to the spatial data (i.e., power plants and provinces) as a database. Conversion from a shape file to the TAB file format (used by MapInfo) was performed as needed.

14.3 Visualisation

Once the data is prepared for spatial analysis, the next step is to visualise it to determine appropriate spatial data analysis methods. Visualisation is a simple and useful spatial data analysis tool for data containing geographical information. It provides researchers and decision-makers an idea of the situation in different locations with easily understandable colours or graphs. In short, visualisation can be described as the visual summary of data sets containing geographical information. In this study, thematic maps are used to visualise the installed capacities of the electricity generation facilities, consumption, and supply for all of the provinces.

14.3.1 Installed Capacities of Electricity Generation Facilities

Based on the data collected in this study, the installed electricity generation capacity of Turkey in December 2007 was calculated as 40,392.63 MW. Table 14.1 shows the distribution of the electricity according to the different energy sources.

The hydro and thermal power plants are grouped into two categories: autoproducers and non-autoproducers, where autoproducers are allowed to generate electricity for their own use in their facilities and may sell up to 40% to the main grid (EPDK 2008).

Table 14.1. The total installed capacity in Turkey at the end of 2007 (source: calculations based on the data obtained during this study)

Type of plant	Installed cap. (MW)	Installed cap. (%)
Hydro autoproducers	559.70	1.39
Thermal autoproducers	2,831.59	7.01
Fuel oil	197.90	0.49
Geothermal	27.90	0.07
Thermal	13,293.60	32.91
Wind	146.30	0.36
Natural gas	10,518.79	26.04
Hydro	12,816.85	31.73
Total	**40,392.63**	**100.00**

14.3.2 Existing Electricity Generation Capacities of the Provinces

The generation capacity of each province was calculated by determining the geographic location for each available electricity generation facility. Using graduated symbols, these facilities were mapped (Figure 14.2). It is observed that hydro power plants are located mostly in the south-eastern provinces which comprises of Adana, Osmaniye, Şanlıufa, Diyarbakır, and along the eastern Black Sea Costal Region from Samsun to Artvin. Autoproducer thermal plants are located in the northwest provinces, especially around Istanbul, because of the large concentration of industries in these regions. This is shown in Figure 14.3.

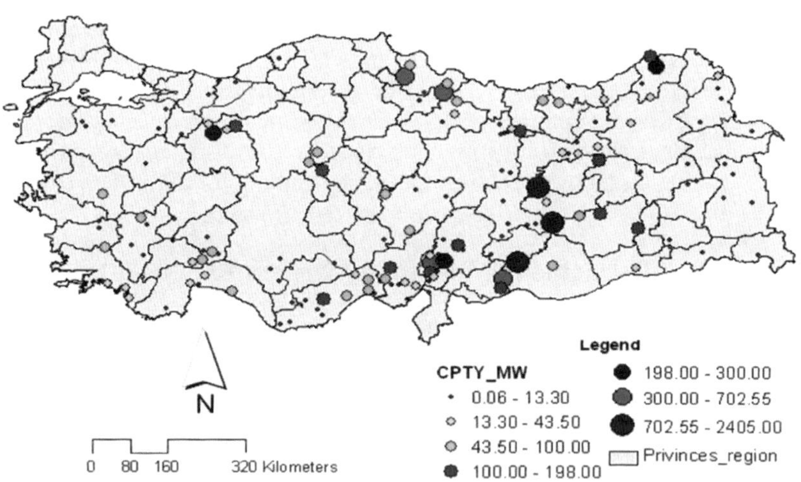

Fig. 14.2. Existing hydro plants

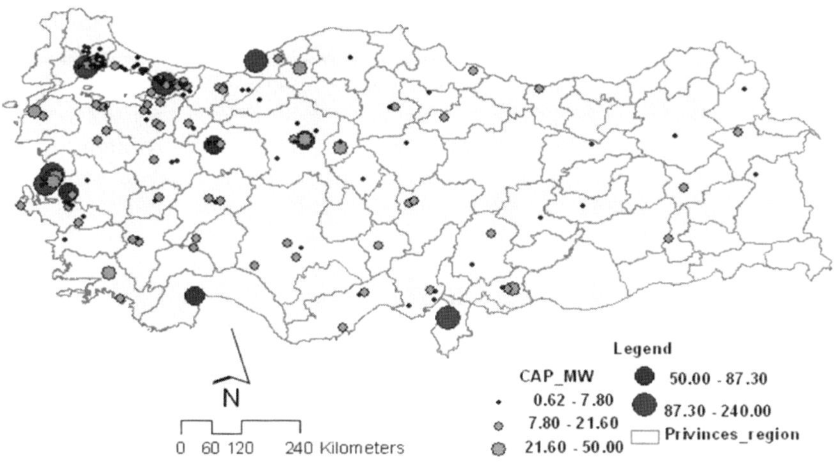

Fig. 14.3. Autoproducer thermal plants

In addition to the capacity and locations of the different types of power plants mentioned above, the generation facilities from other sources were also determined. This information was then used to determine the total generation capacity of each province, which is shown in Figure 14.4.

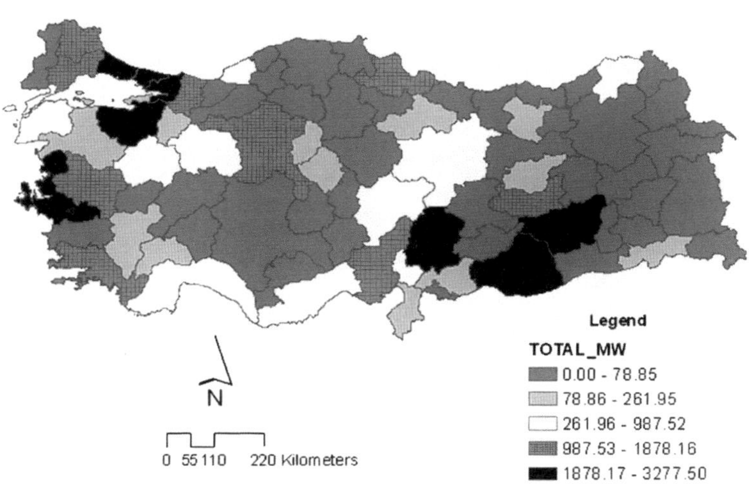

Fig. 14.4. The electricity generation capacities of each province in Turkey in 2007

Seven provinces have the highest generation capacities. Three of these provinces (Istanbul, Kocaeli, and Bursa) are in the northwest and are highly industrialised provinces, Izmir in southwest, and the others (Diyarbakır, Şanlıurfa, and Kahramamaraş) are in the southeast and are less industrialised provinces (compared to those in the northeast). Based on the information shown in these maps, it can be concluded that the installed capacities of electricity generation plants are clustered according to two factors: 1) industry, which is seen in the case of the northwest provinces, and 2) the availability of natural resources, which is seen in the southeast provinces. In fact, when the lower levels of electricity generation capacity are considered, such as 3rd level (shown in yellow), the main determining factor is also attributed to availability of natural resources as in the case of some central and the south coast provinces.

14.3.3 Electricity Consumption in Turkey

Visualisation of electricity consumption of all sectors was performed for the data between 1997 and 2006. Although the study comprises 10 years of data, only those from 2006 (Figure 14.5) are presented here. The difference between eastern and western provinces is clearly seen. The pattern shows an artificial separating line between the northwest and the southeast that crosses the central Anatolia diagonally. To the left of this line, five high-consumption clusters are observed. These clusters are located in the northwest, the west, central, southern coast, and the environs of the southeast coast. These provinces have high population densities and harbour energy intensive industries such as iron and steel, and cement. In fact, more than 70% of the country's total population lives in these regions clustered to the left of the artificial separating line. These provinces also produce about 86% of Turkey's GDP and they account for 86% of the total electricity consumed in Turkey (TÜİK 2008 and TEDAŞ 2009).

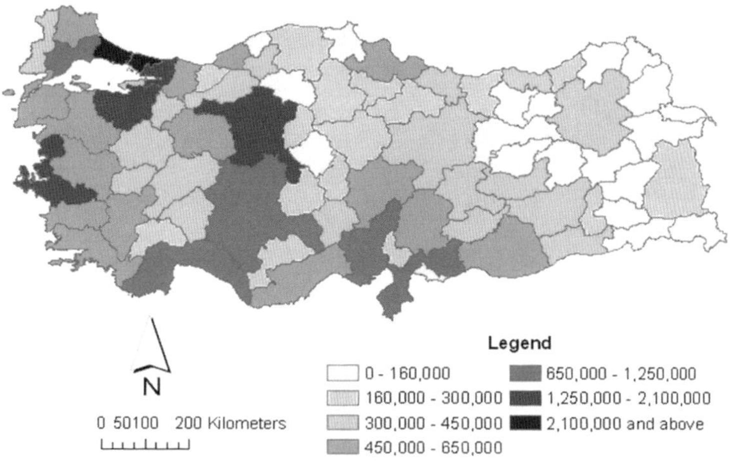

Fig. 14.5. Electricity consumption (kWh) in 2006

On the right of this line, there are two clustering groups that belong to the low electricity consuming provinces. Most of these provinces have a lower population and less industrialization. For all of the provinces in this group, the main industries are agriculture alongside basic commercial activities. It should also be noted that a few provinces in this group have a higher population than those with similar provincial economic characteristics in the west; however, their consumption figure is considerably different. This result is mainly due to the very high electricity leakages in these provinces (e.g., Diyarbakır, see TÜİK 2008).

14.3.4 Sectoral Electricity Consumption in Turkey

Based on available consumption data, the sectoral electricity consumption was also visualised for the 10-year period from 1997 to 2006. Only two of the years (1997 and 2006), however, are presented here (Figures 14.6 and 14.7, respectively). The pie charts on these figures display data only from those provinces that have consumption greater than 900,000 kWh for 1997 and 1,500,000 kWh for 2006. Additionally, the line mentioned above, which divides the country into two segments based on consumption (see subsection 14.3.3), is also seen in these figures. The size of the pie chart reflects the amount of electricity being consumed; larger pie charts represent larger consumption. These maps are useful because they provide information regarding the changes in sector size during the 10-year period. For example, the industrial sector electricity consumption in Istanbul, which is represented by the largest pie chart in the northwest (Figure 14.6), is almost half of the total consumption in 1997, whereas in 2006 it represented only 1/3 (Figure 14.7). This change may be due to the switch in Istanbul's economic activity as the focus changed from an energy intensive industry to the service sector.

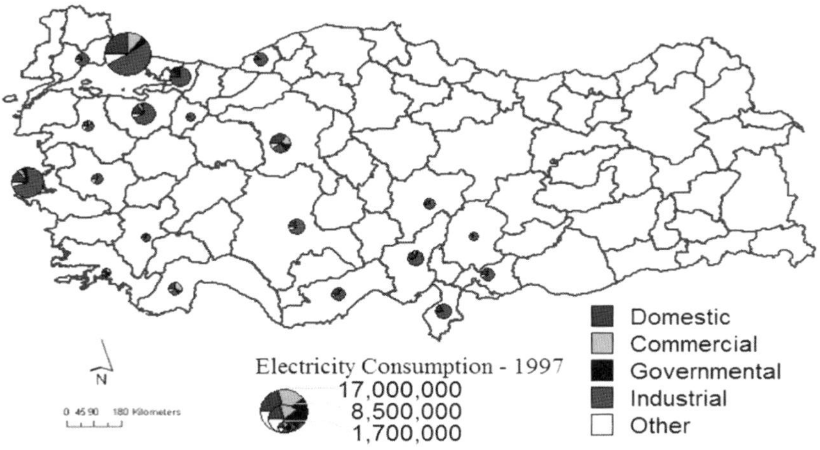

Fig.14.6. Sectoral electricity consumption (kWh) in 1997

Examining the consumption in Ankara, the capital city of Turkey, it is clear that neither the industrial nor the domestic sector has changed significantly during the same 10-year period. On the other hand, Figure 14.6 and Figure 14.7 show that industrial activities can be considered to be the main factor affecting electricity consumption in the central-southern portion of the country.

There is a distinct contrast between the clusters of high electricity consuming provinces in the west and the low electricity consuming provinces in the east. This contrast is marked by the artificial dividing line discussed in subsection 14.3.3. It might be concluded, therefore, that the nature of the spatial pattern of electricity consumption is a clustering directly related to industry type (energy intensive, high scale or services) and population. In other words, the determinants of the observed spatial pattern in Turkey are the type of commercial activity and the population size (see subsection 14.3.3).

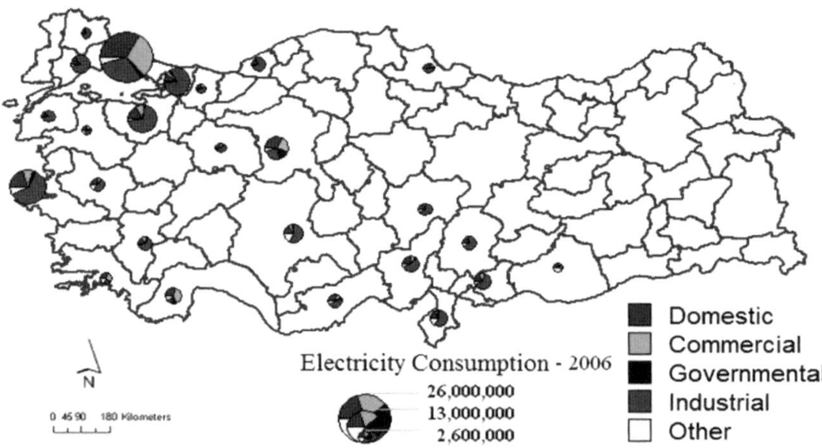

Fig.14.7. Sectoral electricity consumption (kWh) in 2006

14.4 Exploration

Visualisation allows decision makers to grasp the spatial nature of the phenomena under investigation. Exploring spatial data, though, provides better insight into the data for identifying spatial patterns and relationships. Exploratory spatial data analysis methods were implemented to provide an in depth investigation of the spatial patterns of, and correlations between, electricity consumption and supply. These methods are also useful to check the validity of the conclusions derived from the visualisations shown in section 14.3. Using exploration techniques provides increased objectivity in the analyses, which can then generally be used with higher confidence as a support tool for decision making during policymaking and management processes. Exploration of spatial data has two basic components: exploration of first order effects and exploration of second order effects. The first order effects relate to global trends in the data, while second order effects refer to spatial correlations. In this study, Kernel Density Estimation, which is detailed in subsection 14.4.1, is used for the first order exploration. As an alternative to Kernel Density Estimation, quadrat analysis can be used. With this method, the study area is divided into certain sized quadrats and the number of events (i.e., the amount of electricity consumption, the number of power plants) in each quadrat is mapped. However, in this approach it can be difficult to define an appropriate quadrat size. For the second order analysis, the Local Moran's I, which was developed by Luc Anselin (subsection 14.4.2), and Hotspot Analysis (Getis-Ord Gi* statistics) (subsection 14.4.3) are used to provide local scale correlations. The second order effects can also be explored by the Moran's I and Geary's C correlation measures. These measures provide the spatial correlation throughout the whole study area. Unfortunately, this is inappropriate for a country scale because it does not reflect local spatial correlations. For this reason, local spatial correlation measures were selected as the second order exploration methods.

14.4.1 Kernel Density Estimation

The Kernel Density Estimation (KDE) method has received considerable attention in the field of nonparametric estimation of probability densities (Wu and Mielniczuk 2002) and is a popular technique for analysing one- and two-dimensional data (see Scott 1992 and Simono 1996 for examples). There are two types of KDE functions: fixed and adaptive kernels. The fixed kernel function is usually less computationally intensive and uses an optimal spatial kernel (bandwidth) over the study space. Nevertheless, in sparse data seen areas fixed kernel function can produce large local estimation variance. Contrary to this, if data are dense then it may mask subtle local variations (Fotheringham et al. 2002; Páez et al. 2002a,b given in Luo and Wei 2009, p. 57). On the other hand, the adaptive kernel function represents the spatial heterogeneity degree better than fixed kernel and it ensures certain number of nearest neighbours as local samples (Luo and Wei 2009, p. 57). In this study, the adaptive kernel function was used. The general form of KDE is shown in equation (14.1) and is performed using the Spatial Analyst Tool in ArcMap 9.3.

$$\hat{\lambda}_\tau(s) = \sum_{i=1}^{n} \frac{1}{\tau^2} k\left(\frac{s - s_i}{\tau}\right) \tag{14.1}$$

where $k(\,)$ is the kernel, τ is the bandwidth, and the adaptive bandwidth is taken as:

$$\tau(s_i) = \tau_0 \left(\frac{\hat{\lambda}_g}{\tau(s_i)}\right)^{\alpha} \tag{14.2}$$

where $0 \leq \alpha \leq 1$ is the sensitivity parameter, and $\hat{\lambda}_g$ is the geometric mean of the pilot estimates $\hat{\lambda}(s_i)$ at each s_i.

KDE is used as the first exploration approach to analyse 2008 electricity generation and 2006 electricity consumption data from the 81 provinces in this study. Four different kernel bandwidths were selected based on trial and error. Only the result from a 225 km bandwidth map (see Figures 14.8 and 14.9) gives a realistic result.

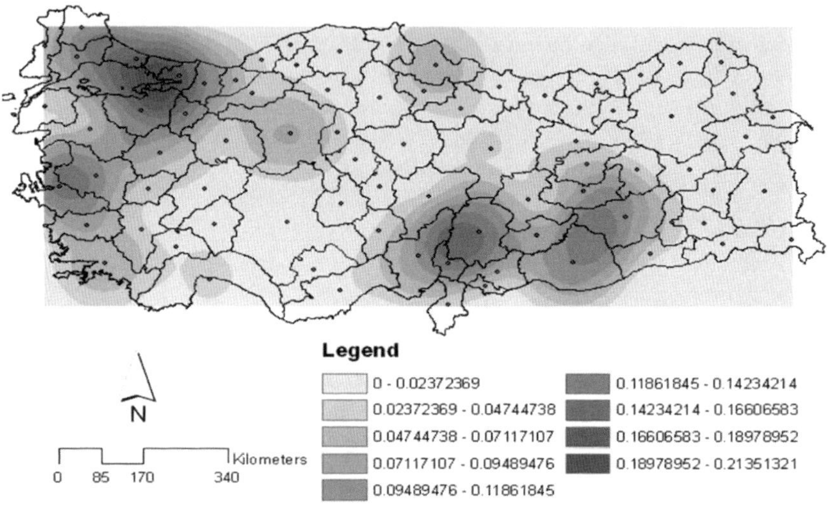

Fig.14.8. Electricity generation capacity in 2008 (units in the legend are km, bandwidth: 225 km)

Since KDE is used to find the intensity values of a given pattern, it does not require any statistical inferences, and a significance level cannot be assessed. As seen in Figure 14.8, four clusters comprising the electricity generation capacities of the Marmara Region can be clearly seen. Istanbul is at the centre, the central Aegean Region and the area around Izmir, and the western part of the southeast Anatolian Region, covering Diyarbakır, Şanlıurfa, Kahramanmaraş, Adana, and Osmaniye are also seen. Figure 14.9 shows the Kernel function result for electricity consumption in 2006. There are four clusters throughout Turkey. The first and most prominent cluster is located in the northwest region of the map, while the second cluster is in the west on the Aegean coast. The third cluster is observed in the western part of the South East Anatolia, and the fourth cluster is in Central Anatolia around Ankara.

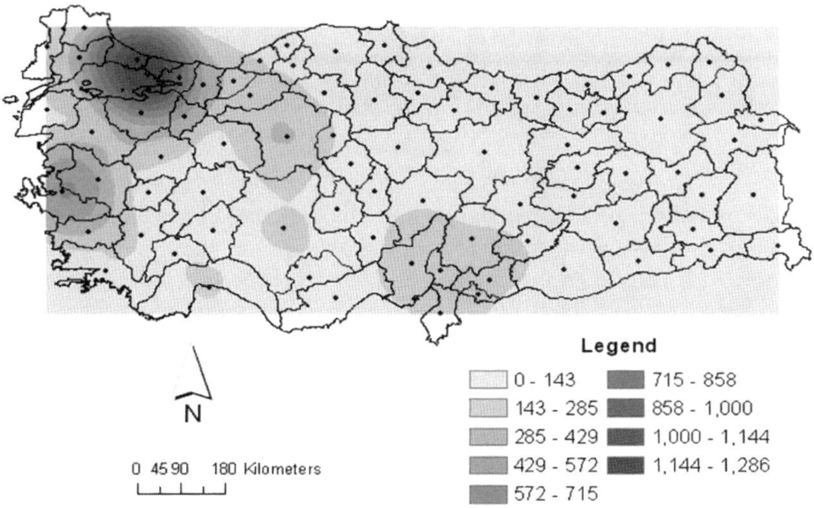

Fig. 14.9. Electricity Consumption in 2006 (units in the legend are km, bandwidth: 225 km)

14.4.2 Anselin Local Moran's I

Anselin Local Moran's I is used to analyse the autocorrelation of provinces based on electricity consumption. A positive value for I indicates that the given feature is surrounded by features of similar values. In its most basic form, Anselin Local Moran's I uses the following equation (Bailey and Gatrell 1995; Anselin 1995; Mitchell 2005):

$$I_i = \frac{x_i - \overline{X}}{S_i^2} \sum_{j=1, j \neq i}^{n} w_{i,j} \left(x_i - \overline{X} \right) \tag{14.3}$$

where x_i is an attribute for feature i, $\overline{X}$ is the mean of the corresponding attribute, $w_{i,j}$ is the spatial weight between feature i and j, and

$$S_i^2 = \frac{\sum_{j=1, j \neq i}^{n} w_{ij}}{n-1} - \overline{X}^2 \tag{14.4}$$

where n is the total number of features.

The z_{I_i} - score for the statistics is computed as:

$$z_{I_i} = \frac{I_i - E[I_i]}{\sqrt{V[I_i]}} \tag{14.5}$$

$$E[I_i] = -\frac{\sum_{j=1, j \neq i}^{n}}{n-1} \tag{14.6}$$

$$[I_i] = E[I_i^2] - E[I_i]^2 \tag{14.7}$$

This analysis is performed using the Spatial Statistics Tool in ArcMap 9.3. Figure 14.10 shows the positive and negative autocorrelation for the provinces and their neighbours with respect to the amount of electricity consumed. The darkest colours represent a higher positive autocorrelation between a province and its neighbours and vice-versa.

Figure 14.10 shows four positive autocorrelation clusters. The most obvious of these clusters is in the northwest part of the country, including Istanbul. This is followed by a cluster on the west coast around Izmir. These provinces are characterised by a developed industrial sector and high population densities. Therefore, the positive autocorrelation in these clusters means higher electricity consumption in the provinces and their neighbouring provinces. This is also concluded in previous analyses (see Figure 14.9). In fact, the other two positively autocorrelated clusters that are located in the northern and north-eastern part of the country are observed due to low electricity consumption in these provinces and their neighbours.

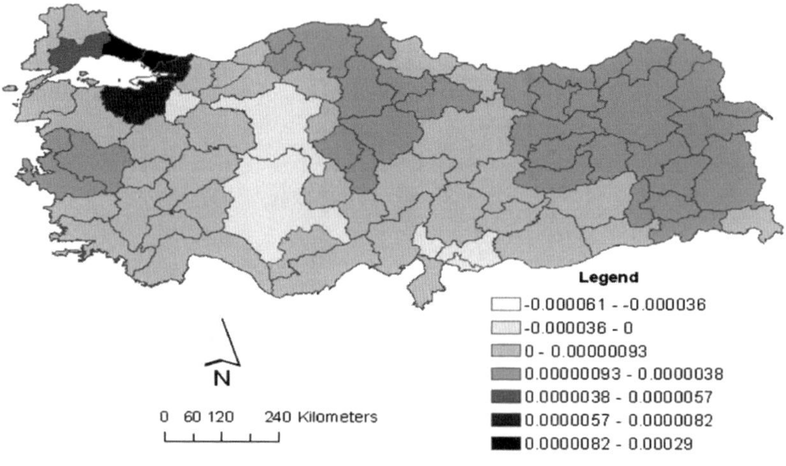

Fig. 14.10. Anselin Local Moran's I analysis for electricity consumption in 2006

In contrast, two clusters with negative autocorrelation values (the lighter coloured groups) are observed, one around the central part of the country, including Ankara, and one around the southeast portion of the country, around Osmaniye and Gaziantep, as a result of higher electricity consumption in these province clusters than their neighbouring provinces. For instance, since Ankara, seen in the central part of the country, has higher electricity consumption than its neighbouring provinces, a clear negative autocorrelation with a light colour is seen in this part of the figure.

14.4.3 Hot Spot Analysis (Getis-Ord Gi*)

Gi(d) and Gi*(d) statistics are described by Ord and Getis (1995) for the study of local patterns in spatial data. Ord and Getis indicate the extent to which a location is surrounded by a cluster of either high or low values. In other words, these statistics show areas where higher-than-average or lower-than-average values tend to be found near each other. Positive values indicate clustering of high attribute value locations and negative values indicate clustering of low attribute value locations. The more positive or negative the value, the more significant the results are. Equation 8 shows the usual form for Getis-Ord Gi* (Bailey and Gatrell 1995; Mitchell 2005; Scott and Warmerdam 2005). The analysis is carried out using Spatial Statistics Tool in ArcMap 9.3.

$$G_i^* = \frac{\sum_{j=1}^{n} w_{i,j} x_j - \overline{X} \sum_{j=1}^{n} w_{i,j}}{S \sqrt{\frac{\left[n \sum_{j=1}^{n} w_{i,j}^2 - \left(\sum_{j=1}^{n} w_{i,j} \right)^2 \right]}{n-1}}} \tag{14.8}$$

where x_j is the attribute value for feature j, $w_{i,j}$ is the spatial weight between feature i and j, n is equal to the total number of features and:

$$\overline{X} = \frac{\sum_{j=1}^{n} x_j}{n} \tag{14.9}$$

$$S = \sqrt{\frac{\sum_{j=1}^{n} x_j^2}{n} - \left(\overline{X}\right)^2} \tag{14.10}$$

As the most recent data should be enough to determine the most recent hot spot locations of high electricity consumption, data for 2006 is used for this analysis (Figure 14.11). The map shows that Istanbul, in the northwest corner of the country, was the most significant location of electricity consumption in 2006, with more than 99% confidence. This indicates that there is a high chance that the area can be considered a 'hot-spot'. Four provinces have the second biggest circles. These are: Kocaeli, Bursa, Izmir and Ankara. These provinces create the second significant hot-spot group with a confidence level of more than 95%. The common features related to the electricity consumption of these provinces include a high degree of industrial activity, especially high energy-intensive and high capacity industries, and high population densities. These were discussed previously in the visualisation section (section 14.3).

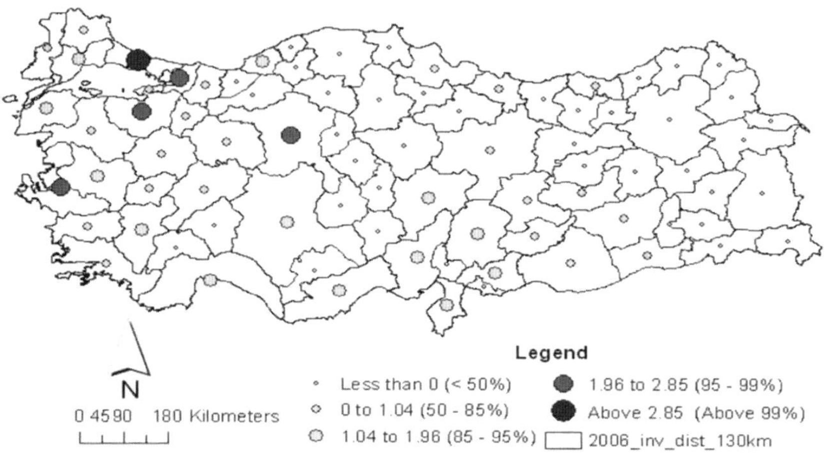

Fig.14.11. Getis-Ord Gi* Analysis of Electricity Consumption in 2006

14.5 Conclusions and the Outlook for Further Study

This study revealed that thermal, hydro and natural gas power plants are the three main types of installed electricity generation in Turkey. In comparison, geothermal and wind sources have the smallest contribution and they are yet to be fully exploited. The main factors affecting the nature of the observed consumption pattern are the industrialisation level of the provinces and the types of industries that are present, including: small and medium sized enterprises or high energy-intensive and high capacity factories owned by multi-national or national holdings. In addition, the considerable impact of population on electricity consumption was also observed by analysing total sectoral consumption amounts in the available 10 years of data.

The present evolution in energy use patterns indicates a considerable difference in electricity consumption patterns between eastern and western regions. Hence, high-demand clusters are located mainly in the northwest region, Marmara Region, and few other big cities, i.e., Izmir, Ankara, in the western and central parts of the country respectively. Low-demand clusters, in contrast, are seen in the East Anatolian and northeast provinces on the Black Sea coast.

A brief summary of the extended study on electricity generation and consumption data between 1997 and 2008 was given here. Unfortunately, even this extended study is not enough for well developed, effective energy management and decision making because the outcomes do not give any information regarding possible changes in coming years.

Therefore, projection of future generation and consumption figures should be done using a model that should use consumption and generation data and data about the population and GDP of the provinces. Projections should also include information about the lifetime of current facilities and consideration of the facilities that are planned and under construction. If such a projection could be developed, then the results of this study combined with results of the projection would be a very effective tool for energy management and decision making on energy policies in Turkey.

Acknowledgement

One of the co-authors wishes to express his profound gratitude to The Scientific and Technological Research Council of Turkey (TUBİTAK) for the support of his PhD programme.

References

Akinbami JF, Lawal A (2009) Opportunities and Challenges to Electrical Energy Conservation and CO_2 Emissions Reduction in Nigeria's Building Sector. Internet address: http://siteresources.worldbank.org/INTURBANDEVELOPMENT/Resources/336387-1256566800920/6505269-1268260567624/Akinbami.pdf, last accessed on 09.12.2010

Altınay G, Karagöl E (2005) Electricity consumption and economic growth: Evidence from Turkey. In: Energy Economics 27(6): 849-856

Anselin L (1995) Local Indicators of Spatial Association – LISA. In: Geographical Analysis 27(2): 93-115

Bailey TC, Gatrell AC (1995) Interactive Spatial Data Analysis. Pearson Education Limited, Edinburg, UK

Başarsoft (2010) Website: http://www.basarsoft.com.tr/assets/images/map3.jpg, last accessed 20/01/2010

DSİ - Devlet Su İşleri (State Water Works of Turkish Republic) (2008). Website: http://www.dsi.gov.tr/, last accessed on 09.12.2010

ECN – Energy Commission of Nigeria (2006) Federal Republic of Nigeria: Renewable Electricity Policy Guidelines. Internet address: http://www.iceednigeria.org/Policy_Guidelines_postconference.pdf, last accessed on 09.12.2010

EPDK – Enerji Piyasası Düzenleme Kurulu (Energy Market Regulatory Authority of Turkish Republic) (2008) Website: http://www.epdk.org.tr/, last accessed 09.12.2010

EÜAŞ – Elektik Üretim AŞ (Electricty Generation Inc.) (2008) Website: http://www.euas.gov.tr, last aaccessed on 09.12.2010

Fotheringham AS, Brunsdon C, Charlton, ME (2002) Geographically Weighted Regression: The Analysis of Spatially Varying Relationships. John Wiley & Sons Ltd., Chichester, UK

Kuik O (2003) Climate change policies, energy security and carbon dependency: Trade-offs for European Union in the longer term. In: International Environmental agreements: Politics, Law and Economics 3(3):221-242

Luo J, Wei DY (2009) Modeling spatial variations of urban growth patterns in Chinese cities: The case of Nanjing. In: Landscape and Urban Planning 91(2): 51-64
Mitchell A (2005) The ESRI Guide to GIS Analysis, Volume 2. ESRI Press
Munasinghe M, Meier P (1993) Integrated national energy planning (INEP). In: Munasinghe M, Meier P (ed) Energy policy analysis and modelling, 1st edition. Cambridge University Press, Cambridge, pp. 12-19
Ord JK, Getis A (1995) Local Spatial Autocorrelation statistics: Distribution issues and an application. In: Geographical Analysis 27(4):286-306
Özkývrak Ö (2005) Electricity restructuring in Turkey. In: Energy Policy 33(10):1339-1350
Páez A, Uchida T, Miyamoto K (2002a) A general framework for estimation and inference of geographically weighted regression models: 2. Spatial association and model specification tests. In: Environment and Planning A 34(5):883-904
Páez A, Uchida T, Miyamoto K, (2002b) A general framework for estimation and inference of geographically weighted regression models: 1. Location-specific kernel bandwidths and a test for locational heterogeneity. In: Environment and Planning A 34(4):733-754
Scott DW (1992) Multivariate Density Estimation: Theory, Practice, and Visualization. John Wiley & Sons Inc., New York
Scott L, Warmerdam N (2005) Extend Crime Analysis with ArcGIS Spatial Statistics Tools in ArcUser Online, April-June 2005
Simono JS (1996) Smoothing Methods in Statistics. Springer-Verlag, New York
Surrey J (1996) From public to private ownership: Introduction. In: Surrey J (ed) The British Electricity Experiment. Privatization: The Record, the Issues, the Lessons. Earthscan, London, pp. 3-13
TEDAŞ – Türkiye Elektrik Dağıtım AŞ (Electricity Distribution Inc. of Turkey) (2009) Website: http://www.tedas.gov.tr/29,Istatistiki_Bilgiler.html, last accessed on 09.12.2010
TÜİK – Türkiye İstatistik Kurumu (Turkish Directorate of Statistics) (2008) Website: http://www.tuik.gov.tr/Start.do, last accessed on 09.12.2010
Varian HR (2002) Intermediate Microeconomics: A Modern Approach. WW Norton & Company, 6th revised edition
WEC-TNC – World Energy Council Turkish National Committee (2004) Elektrik Enerjisi Sektörü. World Energy Council Turkish National Committee Publications, Ankara, Turkey
Wu WB, Mielniczuk J (2002) Kernel Density Estimation for Linear Processes. In: The Annals of statistics 30(5): 1441-1459
Zachariadis T, Pashourtidou N (2006) An empirical analysis of electricity consumption in Cyprus. Internet address: http://papers.econ.ucy.ac.cy/RePEc/papers/4-2006.pdf, last accessed on 09.12.2010

15 How Risk Based Decision Making improves Energy Efficiency in Oil and Gas Industry

Bibek Das[1] and Robert Atkinson[2]

1 Bureau Veritas North America, Houston, Texas, USA
2 Department of Environmental Planning, Brandenburg University of Technology (BTU), Cottbus, Germany

15.1 Introduction

Quantified Risk Assessment studies are carried out with the objective of reducing the risk to personnel, assets and environment to As Low As Reasonably Practicable (ALARP). With the increasing use of this principle in oil and gas safety studies to reduce the tolerable risks to ALARP level, Risk Based Decision Making (RBDM) has witnessed improved energy efficiency as a bi-product. This paper proposes a method to set energy efficiency as an objective of such analyses, rather than just a bi-product, in Capex and Opex projects. The ALARP decision is based on a Cost-Benefit analysis methodology, and the related benefits include not only the obvious risk reduction potential and improvement in reliability and availability, but also improvements in energy efficiency. Thus, setting energy efficiency as a goal and combining it with the ALARP method will be beneficial for the operating companies.

This paper explains the methodology of Risk Based Decision Making (RBDM) and ALARP principles. With an example case, the possibility of using this process to form the very basis of decision making when comparing energy source efficiency, is demonstrated. The paper also discusses how the benefits of risk management can be extended to efficient energy decisions in every stage of a project, from conceptual front-end engineering design (FEED) through engineering procurement and construction (EPC) up to and including operation and decommissioning. The paper also explains why the Oil and Gas sector is chosen as an example. Thus, the paper proposes a holistic approach using Risk Based Decision Making to optimise safety, reliability, environmental impact mitigation and 'uptimize' energy efficiency over the entire lifecycle of a project.

Energy efficiency improvements in the Oil and Gas industry can be achieved in a number of ways, two of which are directly relevant to this paper. The first of these is the replacement of existing energy sources with a completely new, more efficient and cleaner source. Hence, efficiency here can be considered to be an inherent property. The second is the improvement of reliability and operability of existing systems or of new systems during the design stage itself. Examples are included for both the techniques with lessons learned from real-world experiences. It should be noted that the project scope included risk analysis and ALARP and the idea of energy efficiency as an objective is proposed as an extension to the studies performed. RBDM is a promising tool for application to rationalise and optimise new projects or changes and improvements to old ones; however this is presently under-utilised in this context and instead used primarily to aid decision making on safety and environmental issues. This paper presents the RBDM approach as a tool that can be employed to optimise safety, reliability, environmental impact mitigation and to 'uptimize' energy efficiency, thus providing a holistic approach to decision making. The example cases cited in this paper are intended to support the proposed framework. Due to confidentiality agreements, the actual results and names of operating companies are not presented nor are the tools and methodology detailed in this paper of a prescriptive nature. This paper focuses on:

1. Introducing RBDM process;
2. Using RBDM to improve energy efficiency in the Oil and Gas industry.

15.2 Why Oil and Gas?

The first thing that comes to mind when we talk about oil and gas sector are the inherent environmental pollution and safety hazards associated with the attendant operations and usage. However, oil and gas are the largest sources of energy today and will continue to be, if speculations and statistics are to be believed, for 60 more years or so. It is also a large source of GDP for many developed and developing countries. For example Global Energy Usage in 2005 showed a dominant 60% contribution from the oil and gas sector (OPEC 2005). Figure 15.1 shows the global oil reserves forecasted in 2005 (OPEC 2005).

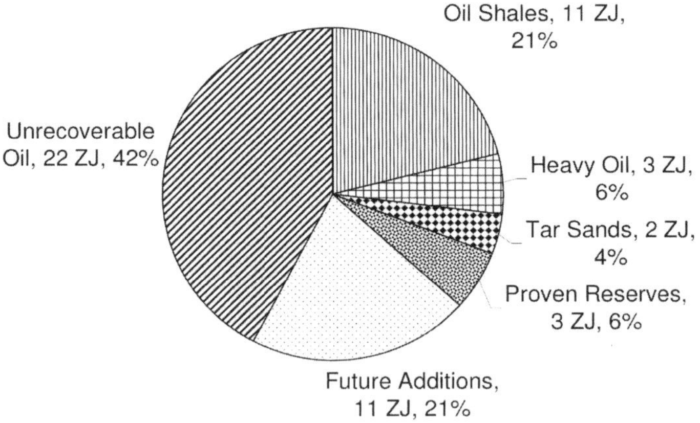

Fig. 15.1. World Oil Reserves 2005 (source: OPEC 2005 Annual Statistical Bulletin)

The current oil consumption is at the rate of 0.18 ZJ ($1x10^{21}$ J) per year and the USGS World Energy Assessment Team gave the forecast of global fossil fuel reserves in 2005 shown in table 15.1 (OPEC 2005).

Table 15.1. Fossil Fuel Reserves 2005 (source: OPEC 2005 Annual Statistical Bulletin)

Fuel	Energy Reserves in ZJ
Coal	290.0
Oil	18.4
Gas	15.7

These statistical data are based on:

1. Present technological capabilities of Oil and Gas exploration and forecasting
2. Present technological capabilities of Oil and Gas extraction, refining and transportation
3. Usage pattern forecasts

If the technological improvements in research and production are taken into consideration, along with a significant increase in efficient renewable energy sources, thus reducing the rate of depletion of fossil fuels, oil and gas reserves are expected to be sufficient for more than a century. This surely calls for more focus on the safety, environmental and energy efficiency issues commonly attributed to oil and gas projects and in fact significant financial investment is made to identify and manage such issues over the lifetime of processing and production facilities.

15.3 Risk Based Decision-Making Process

Figure 15.2 shows a graphical representation of the RBDM process. The first step is to qualitatively identify hazards in a hazard identification workshop. These qualitatively derived hazards are used to develop the hazard scenarios for the Quantitative Risk Analysis (QRA). There are many accepted methods for quantifying risk but in general the QRA determines, based on the physical, spatial and temporal effects of the potential incidents, the probability of negative effects. The effects which are considered are those which may impact: people, assets, environment as well as company reputation (OGP IPIECA 2006). The outcome of this analysis is the risk associated with each hazard expressed in terms of the relative potential magnitude of the impact multiplied by the probability of occurrence (OGP IPIECA 2006). These values are then reported in terms of risk to individuals and risk to society.

Individual risk criteria and societal risk criteria (Figure 15.3) give the measure of risk perception of society; these can be monetised by applying cost benefit analysis methods to give a value to each effected component. For example if an incident has a potential to cause environmental damage, then the cost of clean-up could be calculated to provide a comparison point. Again the calculated value of each component is then summed to provide a theoretical monetary cost of the incident. It should be noted however that in some societies this is not an acceptable method due to the necessity of applying a monetary value to human life.

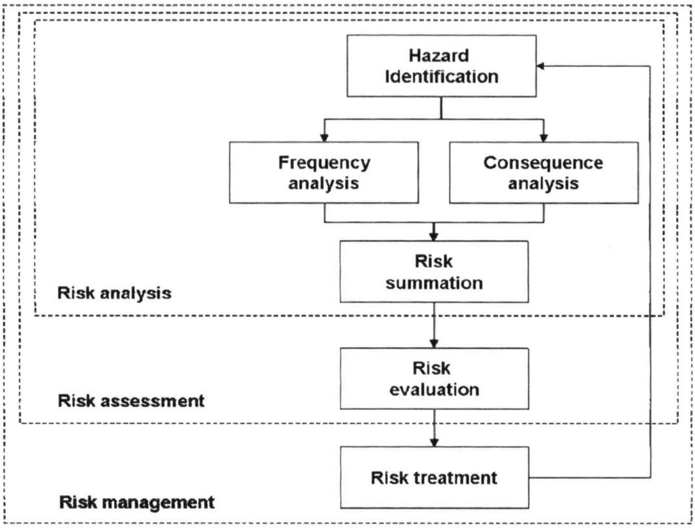

Fig 15.2. Risk Analysis, Assessment and Management Process

The example criteria shown in figure 15.3 are not taken from any particular company standard or procedure, but the numerical threshold levels presented here are followed widely in the industry. The comparison of risks with the criteria will determine whether risk reduction measures are either necessary or desired. A Risk Reduction Workshop is then carried out to identify and evaluate the potential risk reduction measures based on the inputs from the Risk Analysis. Whether or not the proposed reduction measures lead to ALARP risk levels, is then determined through iterative analysis.

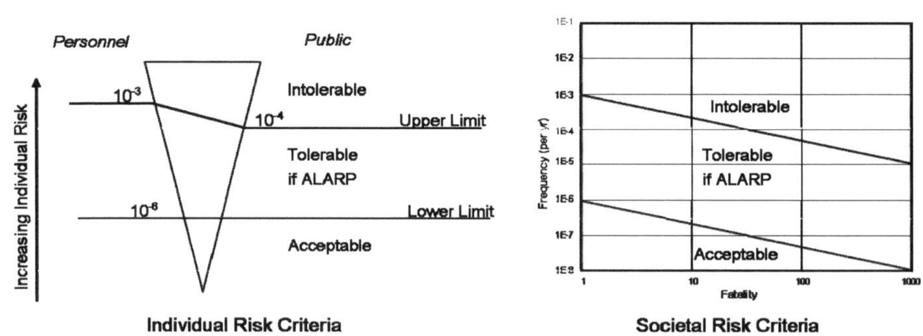

Fig. 15.3. Individual and Societal Risk Criteria (source: Bolsover 2006)

15.4 ALARP Principle

The first question to be asked is why use ALARP. The following two objectives of ALARP Demonstration help answer this question:

1. The hazards associated with a facility can be in large number. Not all the hazards would require a reduction in the risk associated with them as that would mean an excessive financial burden. Hence to avoid this, the hazards have to be classified according to the risks associated with them; only those hazards with a significant level of risk are then targeted. After identifying the risks to be reduced, all the measures that could reduce the likelihood of occurrence and/or severity will become the subject of study. A prerequisite for conducting an ALARP Demonstration is the identification of potential risk reduction measures. Figure 15.4 shows the usual order of effectiveness of the risk reduction strategies (Das 2007).
2. Using different tools for the appraisal of such measures will result in 'Reasonably Practicable' measure of risk reduction. It is possible that sometimes a combination of these strategies is required to achieve the desired risk reduction. A broader risk management program also ensures that existing controls are being correctly practiced to ensure acceptable risks remain in the tolerable zone.

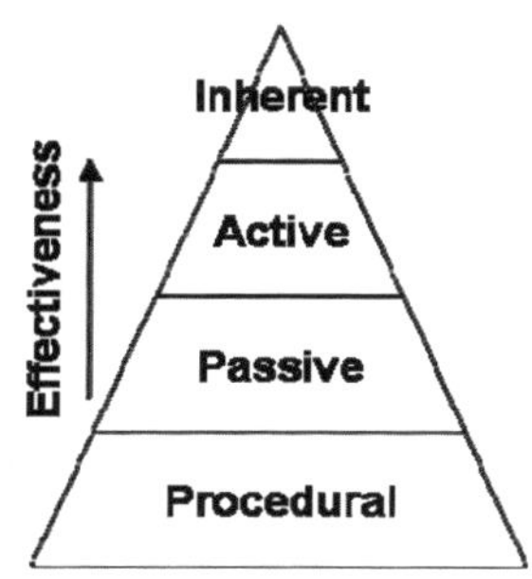

Fig. 15.4. Risk Management Strategies for risk reduction (source: Das 2007)

The ALARP principle is based on criteria which segregates the risk into intolerable, tolerable and acceptable zones (see Figure 15.3). The risks falling in the tolerable region are desired to be reduced to As Low As Reasonably Practicable based on company values. 'Reasonably Practicable' calls for all potential risk management strategies (inherent, active, passive and procedural) to be identified to reduce the risks and to weigh the risk reduction benefits against the cost of implementation, including the time and effort needed to achieve the level of risk reduction. This can be done by comparing the theoretical financial cost of a potential incident, calculated in the QRA, with the cost of implementation. Thus the result is the financial feasibility of risk reduction implementation based on the potential cost of the hazards associated with the process. The document R2P2, issued by

HSE UK (2001), states three principles for ALARP. These principles help to clarify the assumption prior to the ALARP demonstration. The assumption is that suitable controls are in place to address all the significant hazards. Additionally these principles stress the importance of considering both individual and societal risks for ALARP as well as a periodic review of risks to ensure that they continue to meet the ALARP criteria for the relevant, applicable time period.

15.5 Combined ALARP and Energy Efficiency

Figure 15.5 shows how combining ALARP principle with the goal of improving energy efficiency works to realise the 'uptimized' solution. The term 'uptimize' is coined to stress the objective of increasing energy efficiency as well as the goal of optimising safety, reliability etc. The common factor in ALARP and energy efficiency is cost. A Capex (Capital Expenditure) project would, upon implementation of this principle, receive the benefits of reduced operational costs as well as increased performance and profits from the very beginning. An efficient energy option would, based on this principle, be an inherent characteristic of such a plant or process. Ensuring an optimum reliability and availability from the beginning would also mean a sound operating strategy along with increased energy efficiency. However, it is never too late to implement the proposed framework. An Opex (Operational Expenditure) project would also benefit by ensuring minimisation of plant or process disruptions as well as mitigating the hazards related to an existing plant or process. It should be noted however that the process of carrying out multi-objective optimisation is beyond the scope of this paper.

The Risk Based Decision Making process can provide benefits over the entire life-cycle of a plant. The next section describes how each phase of a plant, from cradle to grave, benefits by implementation of the above framework.

15.6 RDBM – Life Cycle Approach

The RBDM process is employed for different purposes during different phases of a project. It is a useful to for complete asset integrity management over the entire lifecycle of the plant. Figure 15.6 outlines typical phases in the life of a plant and describes the purpose of RBDM tool for each. Expanding the benefits of risk management to optimise energy efficiency in the industry can be achieved in the two ways shown in Figure 15.6, with different goals applying to Capex and Opex stages.

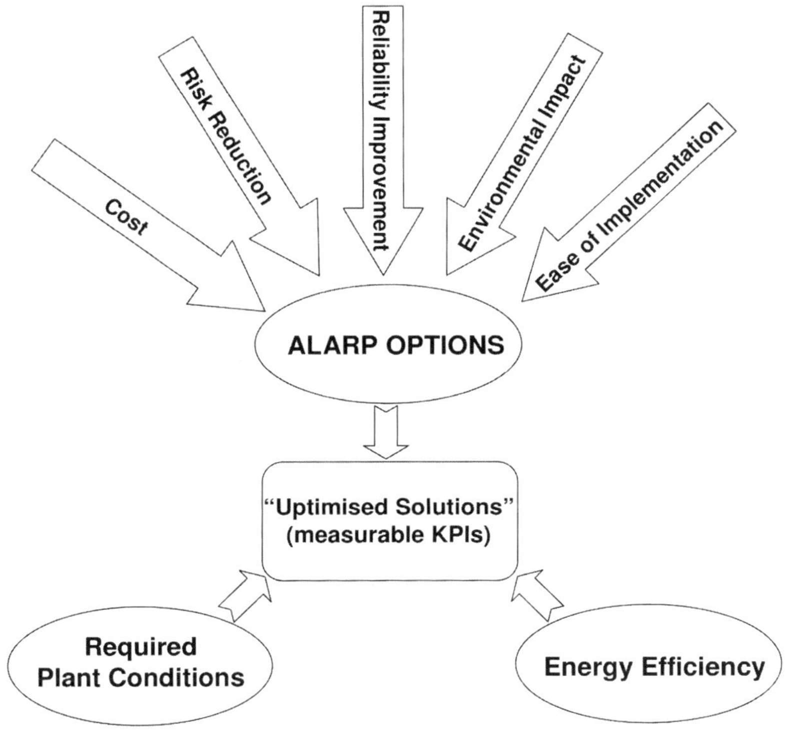

Fig. 15.5. 'Uptimized' Solution Framework

During the initial phases, improving energy efficiency should be a major goal when designing for increased reliability, operability and profitability. Although making major changes in order to realise these goals will be less of a cost burden if implemented at the beginning, it is never too late to improve energy utilisation during the operation stage. However, major improvements may not be a viable option; for example, complete change-out of power generation facilities is, in the operational stage, financially unfeasible due to the necessary investment in equipment and man-power as well as the likely extended period of shut-down. A major plant overhaul, on the other hand, may be undertaken based on utilisation of the RBDM tool if the 'uptimized' solution is economical and practical.

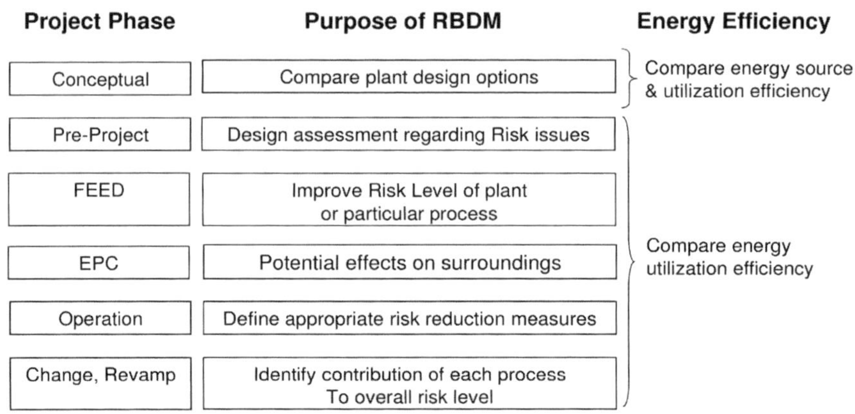

Fig. 15.6. Purpose of RBDM in each Project Phase

15.7 Role of Legislation and Directives

Many EU countries have legislation that makes RBDM a mandatory process in projects involving use of hydrocarbons and other dangerous chemicals. Some governmental agencies, which are given mandates to determine the acceptable risk level, have also adopted the ALARP principles. Thus to a certain extent, legal systems are also involved and help to ensure a fair, unilateral implementation of RBDM methodology. Risk management can also be seen as an investment for sustainable development. Bodies like the UK's Health and Safety Executive (HSE) and NORSOK of Norway have established Directives to facilitate and enhance the application of RBDM process. Unfortunately, countries involved in most of the import and export of Oil and Gas, like USA, Russia, China and India do not have a formal and mandatory legislation in place to address RBDM process. This can be seen as a barrier to successful implementation of the RBDM process and inclusion of energy efficiency goals, as proposed in this paper. Establishing good energy policies should follow energy risk management strategies as well. Here energy risk management refers to a different context from that which is discussed with respect to the RBDM process in this paper.

15.8 Case Study 1: CAPEX Project

As mentioned earlier, one of the possible methods of improving energy efficiency in the oil and gas industry is replacing an existing energy source with a new, efficient and cleaner source. The example cited here is a Capex project undertaken to replace LPG fuels with LNG. Natural Gas reserves are larger than the oil reserves, from which petroleum gas is usually obtained, and the need for cleaner energy has boosted the use of natural gas in particular as a fuel for power plants. The main drivers of the huge increase in consumption are: 1. LNG introduction in highly populated and developing countries like China and India; 2. The USA becoming an importing country and its gas deficit increasing sharply; and 3. Gas fired power plants becoming more popular in countries where nuclear plant programs have been stopped or cancelled (Cosmao and Mello 2005).

Both LNG and LPG are transported over long distances from the source to the distributor as a liquid. While petroleum gas is predominantly composed of propane with lesser amounts of butane and is transported under high pressure, natural gas is composed of methane which can be condensed at near to atmospheric pressure, albeit at extremely low temperatures. When in liquid form both are non-flammable, the biggest hazard related to them however comes with atmospheric release as both gasses are extremely flammable. The comparative physics of vapour cloud formation is however different as the components of petroleum gas are heavier than air and therefore tend to form a denser cloud than the lighter, more easily dispersed natural gas. This means that the risk of an explosion and/or fireball is higher for petroleum gas. In addition the auto-ignition temperature of natural gas is higher than that of petroleum gas, although the flammability range (the concentration range within which a gas/oxygen mixture will burn) of petroleum gas is narrower than that of natural gas. In terms of overall safety however it can be said that LNG is preferable to LPG. In terms of efficiency, while the heavier petroleum gas is more energy dense, combustion of natural gas is more efficient, with less production of CO_2.

The example given here is that of a Natural Gas Distribution (NGD) project in a city with a population of 1 million. Adhering to the Company codes of practice, a comprehensive Health, Safety and Environmental Impact Assessment (HSEIA) was carried out during the project's feasibility study phase. The Company had the objective of undertaking the design and construction of a natural gas distribution system within its supply areas in the city, which included both gas distribution systems and gas utilisation systems. The gas distribution system is comprised of a number of facilities, including primary and secondary pressure regulating stations (PRS), distribution pipelines and distribution mains.

The risk of the Company's natural gas distribution facilitics to surrounding population, environment and occupational health was analysed and assessed (due to confidentiality agreements the name of the Company and actual results are not discussed in this paper). A comparison was made for different aspects of existing LPG network and proposed NGD. The HSEIA concluded with the result that changing over to natural gas was a practical and cost-effective solution to provide cleaner and efficient source of fuel for domestic, commercial and industrial uses. However, since the pipeline ran through a populated area of the city, certain recommendations were proposed to reduce the risk to ALARP level. Thus an RBDM approach was employed to aid decision making on safety, environmental pollution and change over to more efficient energy with prioritisation of actions to be implemented.

Lessons Learned – Case Study 1

This project used RBDM as a rational decision-making tool to replace an existing energy source with a new, more efficient and cleaner source. By comparing the two situations, i.e. the status-quo and the proposed project, in terms of risk, the company was able to directly determine not only the relative incident potential, but also the comparative financial benefits. The outcome of this comparative study would, in this case perhaps have been made clearer by the inclusion of energy efficiency as a decision criterion. Regardless, the following conclusions can be drawn in favor of RBDM process based on the example above (due to confidentiality agreements some conclusions have been drawn based on aspects not mentioned in the case-study):

1. A risk-based decision making process provides a rational argument for prioritisation of areas of concern.
2. The decision maker has more economically viable options during the conceptual stage.
3. The risk-based decision making paves the way for more efficient and cleaner energy and provides sustainable development by identifying those risks to future generations that present generations would find unacceptable.

15.9 Case Study 2: OPEX Project

The second way of improving energy efficiency is by improving the reliability and operability of existing systems or of conceptual system designs. The example given here is that of an Opex project, which had the goal of improving an existing system. The operator of a petrochemical plant, in operation for more than four decades, with ageing equipment and structures, wished to operate for five more turnaround cycles. The high pressure systems dealing with toxic and flammable inventory as well as frequent shutdowns added to the complexity of the problem. Refurbishments had been undertaken from time to time, however reliability of instrumented protective functions along with failures involving rotating machinery remained concerns. A rational approach to problem solving was much needed to help decide when and on what to invest.

The RBDM process proved to be a useful tool in achieving the objectives. The process started with the identification of Key Performance Indicators (KPIs). The study involved many analyses of the 'as is' condition of the process, equipment, instruments and structures. In the end a list of actions were drafted that was prioritised based on the expected improvements in the KPIs and the criticality of the assets. The timeline and cost of implementation of actions were carried out by the operator.

KPI's in this case include such aspects levels of reliability and operability; health and safety; impacts to the environment; as well as financial considerations such as the financial investment, manpower and shut-down hours required for implementation. Once again this can be seen as a comparative study between a number of possible alternatives. In such studies the more independent comparison points available the more likely it is that a clear decision will be possible. Consider for example two alternative approaches judged solely on hazard potential and financial investment required. If these two approaches are similar then it may be difficult to decide, based on these parameters, which is more suitable. If, however, further decision criteria were to be included, such as environmental impact potential and energy efficiency, then the decision may well become clearer.

Lessons Learned – Case Study 2

This project further justified the use of RBDM approach to improve energy efficiency by improving the reliability and operability of existing systems. By extending the lifetime of the plant in question, the project allowed for significant energy savings. What is more, if energy efficiency were to be included as a KPI in the RBDM then the decision would likely have been made easier. The following conclusions can be drawn in favor of RBDM process based on the example above (due to confidentiality agreements conclusions have been drawn based on aspects not mentioned in the case-study):

1. The implementation of actions could be justified to the upper management of the operating company based on a sound assessment.
2. RBDM combines both the likelihood and consequence components to assess risks for both current and anticipated conditions, with the option of examining either specific events or an integration of those events over time.
3. It was realised that improvement in supply chain management could also be achieved by following this assessment framework.
4. The turnaround period was expected to remain unchanged thus giving a direct benefit in terms of energy efficiency.
5. A single framework addressed the multi-faceted problems and issues involving process, energy, static and rotating equipments and instrumented systems in an economic way and within a short time frame.

15.10 Barriers to Successful Application

With the experience of using the RBDM approach in many Oil & Gas and related Power Generation projects, the author realises that there are barriers to using the proposed methodology for improving energy efficiency. Some of the main barriers are listed below:

1. The biggest barrier to the successful application of RBDM is availability of adequate information. Since RBDM is a data intensive process, availability of process, economic, environmental and equipment data plays a significant role in the analyses.
2. It requires involvement of experts from multiple disciplines at the same time which requires a lot of commitment and motivation from the company.

3. Consensus building on the optimal targets for each key performance indicator (KPI) by all the stakeholders is another significant barrier. KPIs may include risk, reliability, cost, energy efficiency etc.
4. Lack of internationally consistent assessment methodologies and software is also another area of concern.
5. Though many EU countries, such as the UK and Norway have legislations on assessment techniques, no formal endorsements exist in the USA, Russia or in developing countries like China and India, which account for most of the import and export of crude oil and gas.

15.11 Impetus to Implementation

If the stakeholders realise the benefits of the RBDM approach at an early stage of the project, the barriers mentioned above may be overcome. The proposed methodology has numerous advantages which may provide an impetus for its implementation. Some of them are listed below:

1. Even with the absence of any legislative framework, since it is easy to understand the benefits of the strategy, the framework should be well-accepted by the operator. The benefits penetrate down to each division in a process plant while addressing the multi-objectives and thus should easily be approved by the concerned disciplines within the operating company.
2. It provides a framework for the whole lifecycle of the plant. A real time model can be developed with measurable KPIs to keep track of the performance periodically.
3. The approach incorporates knowledge sharing among multiple departments and increased understanding of the process, operations, maintenance and the management within the company.
4. A prioritisation of optimised actions addressing multiple objectives is certainly a method to improve the plant's performance over its lifecycle.

15.12 Conclusions and Recommendations

In a period characterised by financial difficulties, increased energy demand and continued dependence on oil and gas as an energy source, there is a need to understand the economic benefits of improving energy efficiency alongside safety, operability, reliability, availability and environmental performance in process plants. New technical solutions to realise these goals are continually being developed and adherence to ALARP criteria has become more important in the local and global contexts. The paper recommends identifying energy optimisation as a goal to the existing practice of ALARP framework. This can be carried out at different stages of the project as proposed in this paper. The Risk Based Decision Making process has its benefits over the entire life-cycle of a plant. The paper has also described how each phase of a plant, from cradle to grave, benefits by implementation of the proposed 'uptimized' framework. The identification of relevant goals and Key Performance Indicators (KPIs) before the employment of the RBDM process during different phases of a project is recognised in this paper as an important factor. The proposed framework and a systematic implementation plan for 'uptimized' solutions is certainly a challenging but promising strategy to achieve the required / desired results.

References

OPEC – Organization of the Petroleum Exporting Countries (2006) Annual Statistical Bulletin 2005. OPEC Data Services Department, Vienna

OGP-IPIECA (2006) Controlling Health Risk at Work: A Roadmap to Health and Safety Assessment in the Oil and Gas Industry. Internet address: http://www.ogp.org.uk/pubs/384.pdf, last accessed on 12.12.2010

BP – British Petroleum (2006) BP Statistical review of World Energy June 2006. British Petroleum, London

HSE UK – Health and Safety Executive (2001) ALARP Suite of Guidance; HSE UK. Internet address: http://www.hse.gov.uk/risk/theory/alarp.htm, last accessed on 12.12.2010

HSE UK – Health and Safety Executive (2001) Reducing Risks, Protecting People – HSE's decision making process - (R2P2). Crown

Bolsover A (2006) Internal document: Risk Acceptance Criteria and ALARP, Bureau Veritas

Bowles DS (2003) ALARP Evaluation – Using Cost Effectiveness and Disproportionality to Justify Risk Reduction. ANCOLD 2003 Conference on Dams

Das B (2007) ALARP Demonstration and Its Level of Intensification. International Petroleum Technology Conference IPTC 2007

Löfstedt RE (1997) Risk Evaluation in the United Kingdom: Legal Requirements, Conceptual Foundations, and Practical Experiences with Special Emphasis on Energy Systems. Centre for Environmental Strategy, University of Surrey Guildford

Todinov M (2006) Risk-Based Reliability Analysis and Generic Principles for Risk Reduc tion. Elsevier Science, Amsterdam

Tweeddale M (2003) Managing Risk and Reliability of Process Plants. Gulf Professional Publishing, Burlington

Cosmao T, Mello S (2005) Internal document: Introduction to Bureau Veritas Services for LNG Import Terminals, Bureau Veritas

16 A Critical Appraisal of Government Forestry Policy in View of Forest Sustainability in Cameroon

Victor N. Cheo[1], Balgah Sounders Nguh[2], Adeline A. Awemo[3] and Wolfgang Schluchter[1]

1 Chair of Environmental Issues in the Social Sciences, Brandenburg University of Technology (BTU), Cottbus, Germany
2 Department of Geography University of Buea, Cameroon
3 Chair of Environmental Geology, Brandenburg University of Technology (BTU), Cottbus, Germany

16.1 Introduction

The economic crises of the mid 1980s and 90s inflicted serious negative consequences on Cameroon's forest ecosystems and forest resources, as they became the target of intense exploitation for multiple purposes. A rapidly increasing population, coupled with poor economic performance exacerbated the over-exploitation of forests, imposing stresses on forest biological resources for agricultural lands, urbanization, fuelwood, food and shelter. Furthermore, the presence of timber companies and small local traders in timber products accelerated unsustainable forest management practices in Cameroon.

The contribution of forestry to Cameroon's national economy is significant. Timber alone accounted for 10% of the GNP, and generates about 6.4 million US dollars annually. Roughly 55,000 people are employed directly or indirectly in this sector (Ndenecho 2005). Forestry makes a major contribution to export receipts with timber accounting for about 28% of total export earnings, making it the second most important source of foreign exchange after petroleum (47%). This figure excludes the considerable revenue lost to illegal logging each year (DFID 2002). Cameroon's forests are a major source of the world's tropical timber. A forest policy reform in the early 90s, at the behest of the World Bank was intended to regulate forest exploitation in a sustainable way. This chapter, through a three-tier methodological approach of a survey, content analysis and observation, aims at appraising the potential of the current forest policy to significantly mitigate, on long term basis, non-sustainable forest exploitation. A breakdown of the chapter composition is as follows: section 16.2 presents the problem statement and main objective of the paper, while section 16.3 focuses on the methodological approach. Section 16.4 evokes the evolution of forest administration and policy in Cameroon and section 16.5 adumbrates the current forest policy framework. Section 16.6 espouses community forestry while sections 16.7, 16.8 and 16.9 describe the different legal and forest regulatory mechanisms in force in Cameroon. Section 16.10 examines the various sustainability initiatives at play and section 16.11 is dedicated to conclusions and recommendations.

16.2 Problem Statement and Study Objective

Cameroon's forests and great biodiversity potential are being degraded through exploitative logging, fuelwood demands, clearing for agricultural purposes, overgrazing and fire. An estimated 200,000 hectares of forest are lost annually to these activities, of which 75,000 to 95,000 hectares are taken up by shifting cultivation alone (Biwas 1992). In some areas of cleared forest, financially profitable foreign tree species introduced by man, such as rubber and oil palms, have replaced the original forest (Ndamukong 2001).

In the early 1990s, the administration initiated a policy reform process, in conjunction with a World Bank structural adjustment loan. Despite the enactment of a forest legislation and management policy, forests in Cameroon have continued to suffer degradation (DFID 2002; GFW 2000). Ndenecho (2005) attributes this perennial degradation to the fact that the indigenous people, in part, have not always respected forest legislation, especially, when their livelihood or interests are threatened. Meanwhile, protected area status has often been imposed, without prior consultation, thus ignoring the socio-economic and cultural situation of those whose survival depends on the forest. This approach has often provoked social tension and conflicts, which usually undermine the possibility of implementing and achieving basic conservation objectives. This paper, therefore, attempts an appraisal of government forest policy with the aim of highlighting significant challenges, which if properly addressed, will greatly enhance the sustainable management of the rich forest and biodiversity heritage in Cameroon.

16.3 Methodology

Three distinct methods were applied in order to elicit the data for this study, these were: content analysis, field observation and interview survey. The main objects of the analysis were the current forest legislation and forest policy framework enacted over a decade ago. In detail, the units of analysis were the articles under legislation as well as the different terms of reference in the policy framework. Using secondary sources, such as legislative and policy documents, books, journals, newspapers, and annual reports, provided a basis for evaluation. Content analysis was embarked upon with the aim of better understanding and appreciating the validity of the forest legislation and policy framework as instruments for enhancing forest sustainability. Field observation was carried out as a primary source of data.

A structured interview survey was used to gain further insight and clarification about certain substantive issues. These included among others, the difficulties between forest management transfer and actual community forest ownership; and approaches to sustainable forest practices and strategies. Thus, forest stakeholders, viz. officials in the ministry of forestry and wildlife, managerial staff of forest NGOs (local and international) as well as members of local forest communities were interviewed.

16.4 Evolution of Forest Administration and Policy Reforms in Cameroon

According to Fonyam (2001), of all the five-year Development Plans by the Cameroon government, beginning from 1961, only the fifth (1981/1986) and sixth (1986 - 1991) contained vague phrases alluding to the environment. In 1984 a decree on the organization of the government assigned an additional responsibility to the Ministry of Planning and Regional Development, namely, that of regional development policy and matters relating to the environment. A subsequent decree led to the organisation of the department of Regional Development and Environment. Section 51(1) of decree no. 84/797 entrusted a Sub-Department of Human Settlements and the Environment with the task of formulating a national environmental policy and drawing up periodic reports on the country's environmental situation. The Sub-department was also charged with proposing all the measures for rational management of natural resources, the protection of the environment, the prevention of natural disasters and the fight against pollution. But the department was handicapped by the lack of adequate human and financial resources.

Historically, Cameroon's forest sector has been hampered by weak institutions, lack of transparency and corruption. Legislation introduced by the Ministry of Agriculture and replaced by the Ministry of Environment and Forests in 1994, such as the 1981 Forestry Law and the subsequent 1983 Implementation Decree did not provide an adequate legal framework for land use planning and production activities. The prevailing land tenure regime assigned usufruct rights to anybody who cleared and cultivated the state owned land that make up most of the dense forest. This provided an incentive for deforestation (O'Halloran and Ferrer 1997). These legislative orders failed to address either the existing concession system that encouraged rent-seeking behaviour and inefficiency, or the distorted tax system, which was designed to protect an inefficient sector.

The logging concessions allocation system was not transparent and gave the industry incentives to unsustainably exploit the forest. In addition, the lack of transparency in the allocation mechanism fuelled rent-seeking behaviour. This was exacerbated by the fact that there was no prerequisite condition for the companies receiving the concessions to embark on sustainable forest exploitation methods. Concessions were awarded for a period of five years and based on mutual agreement between the timber companies and government authorities. Although these contracts were renewable, the preceding five-year period, considered to be short, undoubtedly acted as incentive for companies to over-log their concessions. Logging companies, reportedly, concentrated on a few very valuable species (Essama-Nssah et al. 2002). They dug roads inside the forest to access sought-after trees and thus opened forest areas to individual settlers and bush meat hunters. Although section 23 of the1981 law, and section 8 of the 1983 Decree clearly stipulated that the exploitation of any forest shall be subject to a prior inventory of the zone by the services in charge of forestry, this was to a large extent never respected. Worst still, government subsequently relied on inventory of private individuals or companies with vested interest in forest exploitation. Their results could not be trusted (Essama-Nssah et al. 2002).

There was also a policy requirement that 60% of all timber products be processed locally. Some stakeholders contend that the short period for which concessions were awarded and the high capital cost involved in sawmill investment created incentives for companies to use old and cheaper machinery, leading to inefficiency at a rate of about 75% wastage (Ndenecho 2005; O'Halloran and Ferrer 1997). Also, throughout the 1980s, the government paid no attention to community forest management or to fostering any sense of partnership as a mechanism to enhance protection and sustainability of its forest resources or to ensure that the local elite did not capture the benefits intended for the local communities. Furthermore, the Ministry of Agriculture lacked the administrative capacity to ensure that the receipts from taxes were shared with local communities. Worse still, forest sector policy was subservient to the development of the country's agricultural sector.

With respect to the forestry fiscal system, it could be said that although it was used to boost government revenues, it was equally an indirect instrument of regulation, albeit a weak one. Four major taxes were in force in Cameroon. These included a surface area tax at 98 CFA francs per hectare per year and a Stumpage tax fixed at 5% of the value of a cubic meter of wood. This value depended on the species and the origin of the log (to account for transport costs). The value of the log, however, was set administratively below market value. Besides, government relied on the loggers' declarations with respect to the volume and the origin. This information led to low revenues being collected. There was also an export tax, a flat tax at 20% of an administratively estimated value of the log. This source accounted for about 75% of the total tax amount collected from the forest sector. This tax created distortions to the extent that processed wood was exempted, thus reinforcing the inefficiencies of the sawmill sub-sector by providing it a high level of protection. Finally, there was a specific forest export tax set at 10%, aimed at discouraging log export (Essama-Nssah and Gockowski 2000). Generally, the situation prior to the current reform was characterized by lack of adequate legal and planning frameworks, a concession system that encouraged rent-seeking behaviours and inefficiency, and a tax system designed to protect an inefficient sector.

Table 16.1. Forest Taxes in Cameroon: 1994-99 (source: Essama-Nassah et al. 2002)

	Fiscal Law 1994-95	Fiscal Law 1995-96	Fiscal Law 1996-97	Fiscal Law 1997-98	Fiscal Law 1998-99
Area tax (CFA franc/ha/year	98	300	300	1,500-2,500	1,500-2,500
Stumpage (% mercurial)	5	7	2.5	2.5	2.5
Export tax on logs (%)	25	25	25	17.5	17.5
Export tax on processed wood (%)	15	15	15	12.5	3-4

16.5 Current Government Forest Policy Framework

The overall objective of the Cameroon forest reform is to improve practices of forest exploitation and management. The current forest policy, enshrined in the 1994 Forest, Wildlife and Fisheries Regulations and the 1996 Environmental Management Regulations, is set out to correct the past non-sustainable practices in natural resource management. It assigns a high priority to the protection of the rich and important biodiversity of the country. In April 1992, in a bid to attain this objective, the government created a full-blown Ministry in charge of the Environment and Forests (MINEF) with provincial, divisional and sub divisional delegations all over the country. This was as a result of the Cameroon government's commitment to enhance environmental sustainability as well as improve on the efficiency of policy and decision making. This new ministry whose appellation changed in 2005 to Ministry of Forest and Wildlife has the following responsibilities vis-à-vis the forestry sector in Cameroon:

- to manage and protect national forests and those belonging to communities and councils;
- to control exploitation of forestry resources,
- to implement the execution of programmes and the regeneration of trees and development of forests,
- to collaborate with the professional bodies in the forestry sector,
- to develop and manage botanic gardens, and
- to elaborate and put into effect, national policies on fauna and hunting.

In short, the Ministry of Forest and Wildlife implements the government's sustainable development policy, for which it has the responsibility to propose measures for a rational management of national resources in collaboration with other specialized ministries and organizations concerned with forestry. In 1994, a new forestry law No 94/01 of 20th January was enacted. Its decree of implementation was the outcome of Prime ministerial decree No.95-531 of 23rd August 1995. One highlight of this law, which among other things enhances forest sustainability, includes the introduction of a forest classification system based on ownership. Hence, the national forest estate falls under two broad categories; permanent and non-permanent forests. Permanent forests comprise lands that are used solely for forestry and/ or wildlife. Examples of permanent forests include; national parks, game reserves, hunting areas, game ranches belonging to the state, wildlife sanctuaries, buffer zones, state owned zoological gardens, integral ecological reserves, production forests, recreation forests, teaching and research forests, plant life sanctuaries, botanical gardens and forest plantations.

Any development of a permanent forest must be based on a plan which ensures the sustained production of forest products and services, without affecting the primitive value, compromising the future productivity of the forest or causing any damage to the physical and social environments. Meanwhile non-permanent forests comprise forest lands that may be used for purposes other than forestry and includes communal forests, community forests and forests belonging to private individuals. Communal forests are those, which do not belong to the state, local council or private individuals, and do not include orchards, agricultural plantations, fallow land, wooded land adjoining an agricultural farm, pastoral and agroforestry facilities. Although there is provision for communal forests in the law, what the local population can benefit most from such forests is a customary right, defined as "the right, which is recognized as being that of the local population to harvest all forests, wildlife and fisheries products freely for their personal use, except the protected species" (Fonyam 2001; GFW 2000).

16.6 The Concept of Community Forests in Cameroon

An innovation of the 1994 forest law is the provision allocated to community forestry. A community forest is defined in section 3(11) of the implementing decree as a forest forming part of the non-permanent forest, which is covered by a management agreement between a village community and the forestry administration. Management of such forests is the responsibility of the village community concerned, with the technical assistance of the forestry administration. Thus, in order to promote the management of forest resources by village communities who so desire, a management agreement is signed between the government and the community whereby the government transfers rights of management of its forests for the benefit of village communities. They must, in turn, manage it in accordance with a previously drawn up plan. Meanwhile all forest products resulting from the management of community forests belong wholly to the community concerned (Sections 37 and 38, 1994 Forest Law).

However, community participation cannot be restricted to ensuring that the local population shares in the benefits accruing from forestry activities, as the forestry law seems to suggest. Thus, although community forestry is one of the principal innovations of the new forestry law, the practical applications betray certain flaws and contradictions. For instance, the concept of community forest as conceived by the 1994 Forestry Law is not a wholesale transfer of property rights but simply a transfer of management, since the state is the de jure owner of the resources. Thus the appellation is a misnomer. According to Tumnde (2001), the wording of section 37(1) of the Forestry Law suggests that there will be a partnership between the forest service on the one hand and the local community on the other, in the management of the community forest. But this is not the case because the local community implements the management agreement under the supervision of the forestry service which can either suspend the activities in the management plan or annul the agreement. Also, the sale of standing volumes or authorization to cut poles falls within the prerogative of the state to be undertaken by it on behalf of the community. This gives the impression that the community forest is an ephemeral rather than a long-term project. Furthermore, it does not provide any long term assurance to the community as it is meant to perpetuate the firm grip of the state over forest resources. In the light of all these aspects, participation actually becomes a burden and is passively accepted. Since the exploitation of forest resources is the prerogative of the state, there is no equitable distribution of benefits, a cardinal principle of the community forest management system. Besides, despite legal provisions which stipulate that technical services will be provided free by the forestry administration to help the communities to prepare their applications, the cost remains high. This is a disincentive to the proliferation of community forests.

16.7 Legislation as an Instrument of Regulating Forest Exploitation

Fonyam (2001) posits that the law as an instrument of social control has a paramount role to play with regard to forest protection. The1994 forest legislation currently in force in Cameroon spells out prerequisites for the exploitation of forests. Section 25 of the forestry law states that "forest shall be exploited either under state management, or under license, by the sale of standing volume or under a felling permit or authorization granted to companies or individuals". A state forest may equally be granted for exploitation to a government corporation, or to a company in which the government has at least 51% of the capital. In reality however, most of the logging is done under license. Furthermore, the law restricts the maximum number of hectares that may be granted to any one logger to 2,500 hectares and forest exploitation contracts are renewable for a maximum period of fifteen years. The authority to grant exploitation licenses is predicated on the forest area. When the area to be exploited is less than 10,000 hectares, it is the minister's responsibility, while above that it is the prime minister's. Furthermore, the license or permit usually carries with it certain specifications like quantities and the zone of exploitation (Section 56(1)).

Regarding special products such as ebony, ivory, wild animal horns, as well as certain animals, plant and medicinal species of particular interest, there is provision for a special permit under section 56(2) for a maximum non-renewable period of one year. Equally, section 56(3) provides that for other special forest produce (ebony, ivory, wild animal horns, plant and medicinal species), firewood, and poles, desired by an individual for non-commercial use, exploitation permit can be granted by mutual agreement for a non-renewable period of three months. On the other hand, the law in section 40 provides that exploitation of any forest shall be subject to a prior inventory of the said forest in accordance with the rules fixed by the Ministry of Environment and forests.

16.8 Logging Ban on Rare Hardwoods

The government imposed a log export ban in 1999 on endangered hardwoods in *Clorophora excelsa* (iroko), *Erythrophleum ivorence* (maobi) and *Guibourtia demeusel* (bubinga), though not sapelli and ayous, the country's largest hardwood exports. This followed five years of intensive logging and government's failure to effectively implement a policy aimed at reducing raw-log exports and encouraging processed wood exports. This act helped to promote the exploitation of hitherto underutilize species. Also, the policy requirement that 60% of all timber products be processed locally was increased to 70% (Article 71 of law 94-1). The advantage here is that bi-products of the timber processing, such as saw dust used for cooking, would be beneficial to the local people thereby mitigating fuelwood demand and consequently, deforestation.

16.9 Sanctions

The 1994 Forestry Law upholds the legacy that fines and terms of imprisonment can be imposed for non-complience with the twin objectives of deterring would-be offenders on the one hand and compensating the damage done on the environment on the other hand. As a matter of fact, section 141(1) of the 1994 forestry law stipulates that:

> "Without prejudice to the prerogatives of the legal Department and the judicial police officers having general jurisdiction, sworn officials of the services in charge of forestry...shall, on behalf of the state, local councils, communities or private individuals, investigate, establish and prosecute offenses relating to forestry".

Section 154 of the same law levies a penalty as from 5,000 to 50,000 CFA francs (10 to 100 US dollars) or imprisonment for up to 10 days or both, on any person who carries out activities contrary to the law (sub-sections 6 and 25, 1994 forestry Law) with respect to forest ownership and exploitation. This also applies to anyone who contravenes the laws and regulations governing customary exploitation rights provided for in sections 8, 26 and 36. Also, according to provisions of section 42 of the 1994 forestry law, exploitation licenses are not transferable and its holder should not exploit products not mentioned in the license. A fine of 200,000 to 1,000,000 CFA francs or imprisonment from one to six months or both fines shall be applied for non-compliance. Meanwhile Section 14 of the law prohibits anyone from setting fire to state forest or lighting fire that may cause damage to the vegetation without prior authorization. Any offender risks a fine of 50,000 to 200,000 CFA francs or imprisonment of up to 20 days or both.

16.10 Other Forest Sustainability Initiatives

16.10.1 Zoning Plan Strategy

In the face of continuous strife in warding off major threats to the rich tropical forests, Cameroon is pursuing a zoning plan strategy. The strategy aims at bolstering an expected 30% of the national territory as permanent forest estate. This is a good idea because each year 75-95,000 hectares of forest are lost to agriculture alone. Also, fuelwood demand is expected to increase coupled with a population growth rate of about 3%. Targeted by this strategy are the production forests, the designated locations for active logging concessions. For example, the land use planning exercise which covers the 14 million hectares of the forested southern part of Cameroon of which inventory data are already available is a means of ensuring that enough forests are conserved and well managed. The area now under permanent forest estate is about 13% of the national territory (Ndenecho 2005; Essama-Nssah et al. 2002; Essama-Nassah and Gockowski 2000; Besong and Ngwasiri 1995), though Tesi (2004) contends that this is merely on paper.

16.10.2 Agricultural Research/ Personnel Training

Although the government took certain measures restricting some forest areas from the population, thanks to Global Environmental Facility (GEF) and Dutch (DGIS) grants obtained in 1995 to help in the protection of the country's biodiversity, it registered little success. Moreover, the government stepped up its agricultural research through a National Agricultural Research Project which was made possible by funds from donor agencies like the World Bank, GTZ and ODA. This project which involved some of the country's leading research institutes, like IRA and IRZV, aimed at increasing the productivity and incomes of small-scale agricultural producers through technology creation and transfer and ran effectively from 1988 to 1993.

Similarly, a national training and agricultural extension programme began in 1997. It employed 2,394 personnel. With the increased mobility of the extension agents following the distribution of motorcycles, a good number of farmers were reached. These measures enhanced crop productivity while at the same time reducing deforestation for agricultural purposes. A major setback of this project was organizational deficiencies such as lack of qualified technicians, especially women, to meet extension demands and the arbitrary relocation of extension agents (Essama-Nssah et al. 2002; Essam-Nssah and Gockowski 2000).

16.10.3 Partnership with International NGOs

To mitigate unsustainable forest practices in the country, the government entered into cooperation with international NGOs. NGOs like Birdlife International, World Wildlife Fund for Nature (WWF) and Living Earth etc, have been working with local forest dwellers, transferring technology and knowledge in the domains of agriculture, bee farming as well as other livelihood alternatives (Ngwa and Fonjong 2002). These activities were aimed at enhancing forest sustainability. However, attempts by the National Forest Development Authority (NFDA) to protect or rehabilitate the forest are at times contradicted by development measures of the ministries of agriculture, and animal husbandry (increasing expansion and market orientation of market gardening, food commodity production and livestock). These measures degrade the forest by promoting encroachment (Ndenecho 2005).

16.10.4 Environmental Education

Some strides are being made in the domain of environmental education aimed at sensitizing pupils, students and the general public. The training of primary and secondary school teachers in seminars and workshops on environmental issues and the introduction of environmental education and clubs at all levels is evident. It is also in recognition of, and an attempt to respond to the serious environmental problems and challenges that the government created the pioneer environmental science department in the University of Buea in 1996. The department is involved in public sensitization and various research programmes which help to create awareness as well as provide solutions to some of the environmental hazards.

Meanwhile to enhance public environmental education, both the government and other stakeholders, such as NGOs, are employing the traditional mass media and other forms of communication to disseminate environmental messages. As a matter of fact, virtually all of Cameroon's state own media have slots dedicated to environment. However, a major constraint to this conventional media use remains the fact that the national and regional stations do not transmit their broadcasts nationwide, especially to the remote areas. This imbalance and major disadvantage to the rural people necessitated the establishment of government rural radio stations in Kembong (Mamfe), Oku and other communities. Muluh (2002), posits that the main reasons behind the establishment of the rural radio stations were to reach out to the rural audiences and promote basic educational and technical skills, as well as to assist rural audiences in undertaking basic decision making at the community level.

16.10.5 Afforestation and Reforestation

The government of Cameroon meanwhile, launched a forest regeneration programme in 2009 aimed at planting about three million trees in the country with special priority given to ecologically fragile zones. The Minister of Forestry and Wildlife, Elvis Ngolle Ngolle said that the forest regeneration program is aimed at fighting climate change. According to this programme, which is sponsored by the governments of Cameroon, Chad and the United States of America, 13,000 trees will be planted across the North West Region, 60,000 trees in Mt. Bamboutos in the West Region and 90,000 trees along Lake Chad. But perhaps it is worthwhile mentioning here that tree planting is only part of the solution to the serious problem of deforestation and forest resources degradation. There is need for a twin approach of conservation and rural development.

16.11 Conclusions and Recommendations

On the whole, Cameroon could be said to have a fairly good environmental policy but for the fact that it lacks a suitable implementation strategy. Some principal constraints to policy implementation are bad governance, corruption, weak institutional capacity, limited enforcement and lack of monitoring capacity (Essama-Nssah and Gockowski 2000). Against a backdrop of the economic crisis, the size of the civil service has dwindled amid hiring freezes, early retirement and low wages. Consequently, inefficiency is a major hurdle to the strengthening of the institutions necessary for the sustainable development of forest and agricultural resources. Without additional support, the full potential of the current forest policy would not be realized. Furthermore, regarding the new dispensation of forestry management, the local people and communities should be given a direct and tangible interest in the sustainable management and conservation of forests. Communities cannot be effective at managing their forest resource unless their authority is clearly established and recognized. It is only by involving the local people as full partners with appropriate incentives that effective management can take place. Lastly, strong measures need to be taken against corruption in Cameroon's forestry sector.

To preserve its forests, Cameroon requires a system of sustainable management that guarantees a steady flow of socio-economic benefits. Sustainable strategies geared towards rural development would minimize damage and to some extent improve the environmental benefits of the forest ecosystem. Since smallholder agriculture is a major source of land degradation, any forward-looking multisectoral approach must start with agriculture and rural development. Furthermore, a policy-led effort to intensify perennial crop and food crop systems to deflect further encroachment on the forest margin is needed.

References

Awemo A (2006) Medicinal Plants and Intellectual Property Rights in Cameroon: The Case of Prunus Africana in Oku (Unpublished MSc. Thesis, Chair of General Ecology, BTU Cottbus, Germany)

Besong J, Ngwasiri CN (1995) The 1994 Forestry Law and Rational Natural Resources Management in Cameroon, PVO-NGO/NRMS Cameroon: Yaounde

Embola OK (2001) Traditional Architecture and Cultural Identity of Cameroon. In: Dunlop J, Williams R (eds) Culture and Environment: A Reader in Environmental Education. University of Buea, Buea, pp 158-173

Balgah SN (2001) Exploitation and Conservation of Biological Resources in the Mount Cameroon Region, Cameroon. In: Lambi CM, Eze BE (eds) Readings in Geography. Unique Printers, Bamenda, pp 310-324

CAMPER/USAID (1993) USAID – Cameroon Programme for Environmental Reform. CAMPER, Yaounde

DFID – Department for International Development (2002) Cameroon: Country Strategic Paper. DFID, Yaounde

Essama-Nssah B, Gockowski J (2000) Cameroon Forest Sector Development in a Difficult Political Economy. World Bank, Washington D.C.

Essama-Nssah B, Gockowski J and Kelley L (2002) A New Deal for Cameroon's Forest. In: Uma L (ed) Managing a Global Resource Challenges of Forest Conservation and Development, Vol. 5.Transaction Publishers, New Jersey, pp 137-165

Finance and Development (2003) The World's Forests. IMF, Washington DC.

Fonyam J (2001) The Legal Protection of Forests: A Case Study of Cameroon. In: Dunlop J, William R (eds) Culture and Development. University of Buea, Buea, pp 39-65

Global Forest Watch (2000) An Overview of Logging in Cameroon. World Resources Institute: Washington D.C.

MINEF – Ministry of environment and Forestry (1996) National Environment Management Plan. Main Report, Vol. 1, Yaoundé

Muluh H, Ndoh B (2002) Evolution of the Media in Cameroon. In: Eribo F, Enoh T (eds) Journalism and Mass Communication in Africa: Cameroon. Lexington Books, Maryland, pp 3-16

Ndamukong K (2001) Cameroon Forest: Yesterday, Today and Tomorrow. In: Dunlop J, Williams R (eds) Culture and Environment: A Reader in Environmental Education. University of Buea, Buea pp 27-38

Ndenecho E (2005) Biological Resource Exploitation in Cameroon. Unique Printers, Bamenda

Ndoye O (1998) The Impact of Macro Economic and Agricultural Policies on Forest Conditions in Cameroon. CIFOR, Yaounde

Ngwa NE, Fonjong LN (2002) Actors Options and the Challenges of Forest Management in Anglophone Cameroon. In: GeoJournal 57(2): 95-111

O'Halloran E, Ferrer V (1997) The Evolution of Cameroon's New Forestry Legal, Regulatory, and Taxation System. World Bank, Washington D.C.

Republic of Cameroon (1994) Law No. 94/01 of January 20, 1994 to Lay Down Forestry, Wildlife and Fisheries Regulations

Republic of Cameroon (1995) Decree No. 95/531/PM of August 23, 1995 to Determine the Conditions for Implementation of Forestry Regulations

Tumnde M (2001) Integrating Law and Local Customs in Forest Resource Management around the Mount Cameroon Region. In: Lambi CM, Eze BE (eds) Readings in Geography. Unique Printers, Bamenda, pp 349-369

Wunder S (2000) The Economics of Deforestation. Macmillan Press Ltd, London

17 Agrofuels in Sub-Saharan Africa: Decision-making Criteria for Sustainability

Vincent Onyango

Department of Environmental Planning, Brandenburg University of Technology (BTU), Cottbus, Germany

17.1 Introduction

Agrofuel crops are experiencing increasing interest globally, and recently, in Sub-Saharan Africa (REN21 2010; FAO 2008b). The extent of land-use, investments, scientific research, media coverage and political interest dedicated to agrofuels has increased rapidly (Wade 2008; Biofuelwatch et al. 2007; von Braun and Pachauri 2006). The global production of agrofuels doubled between 2000 and 2005 (UN 2008) and investment reached 100 billion USD by 2010, up from 38.6 billion USD in 2005 (REN21 2010). The drivers for agrofuels include the recent spike in fossil oil prices, global warming and climate change, and the pursuit of rural development and energy security (Mohamed 2007; FAO 2008b). Moreover, the lure to earn money from *Certified Emission Reductions* through the Kyoto Protocol's Clean Development Mechanism may be another impetus to grow agrofuel crops. Growing agrofuel crops in Sub-Saharan African countries appears relatively attractive because both land and labour are inexpensive, reducing capital and working costs, thereby boosting profitability (Knaup 2008). However, controversies and concerns have arisen over the potential of adverse impacts of growing agrofuel crops on the natural environments and socio-economic welfare of Sub-Saharan African countries (Vermeulen and Cotula 2010; ICRISAT 2007; IEA 2007; Biofuelwatch et al. 2007; von Braun and Pachauri 2006).

Following these concerns, Sub-Saharan Africa governments are in the process of establishing agrofuel policies, plans, programmes and projects (PPPPs) that promote sustainable development through effective integration of socio-economic and environmental objectives (see GoK 2008; AFREPREN/FWD 2007; Mohamed 2007). However, the existing agrofuel PPPPs have been criticised as failing to adequately integrate the socio-economic and environmental concerns, which would ensure sustainability of the agrofuels sector, in Sub-Saharan Africa (UNEP 2009a; Biofuelwatch et al. 2007). This has largely been blamed on the lack of 'fit for purpose' decision-making criteria, regarding determining the sustainability of the agrofuels within the African context (UNEP 2009b; GoK/GTZ 2008; Mohamed 2007). Consequently, this has made it especially difficult to make an informed determination on whether to, for example, promote agrofuel crops; under what financial and regulatory framework; to what extent and in which lands/areas; and how to beneficially integrate them into food security and general socio-economic welfare of citizens (UNEP 2009b). In cases where agrofuel PPPPs exist, how the decision-making criteria leading to determining their sustainability were arrived at, remains unclear (UNEP 2009a). This has led to several global and African NGOs, institutions and scientists, urging caution in promoting cultivation of agrofuel crops in Sub-Saharan Africa, until their sustainability is assured, and agrofuel PPPPs made more integrative of the pertinent sustainability issues (GRAIN 2010; UNEP 2009b; FAO 2008a; Oxfam 2008a).

This paper aims to address the problem of determining the sustainability of agrofuels, relevant in the formulation of agrofuel PPPPs, by proposing key decision-making criteria. This is based on the assumption that in order to formulate agrofuel PPPPs that effectively promote sustainability, appropriate decision-making criteria over what is sustainable, is needed. These criteria will serve the purpose of highlighting and interlinking, for consideration during decision-making, the key elements that influence decision-making over sustainability (see Gibson 2006) i.e.: 1) potential adverse impacts from producing agrofuel crops; 2) key concerns, fears and potential for conflict among welfare interests of local peoples; 3) and need to meet socio-economic and environmental objectives, without unjustified prejudice to any one of them. This paper applies the term 'decision-making criteria' to refer to key elements for analyses, on which the determination of sustainability of agrofuel crops shall be based upon.

Since Sub-Saharan African countries have traditionally had weak PPPPs-making frameworks (Collier 2008; Onyango and Schmidt 2007), it is assumed that such decision-making criteria can enhance the quality and evidence base for decision-making. The sustainability agenda is significant to Sub-Saharan Arica for several reasons. For example, the 48 Sub-Saharan Africa countries have over a billion people, many of whom live on less than a dollar a day and rely on subsistence farming (Collier 2008). Of the 33 countries recently identified as facing 'extremely alarming' hunger situations due to the increase in food and energy prices, the majority are in Sub-Saharan Africa (BWI 2008). In addition, the Millennium Development Goals (MDGs), the global agenda for sustainable development, are still uncertain from being achieved (UN 2007b). Therefore, Sub-Saharan Africa interest in not jeopardising the MDGs through unmitigated adverse impacts from the agrofuels sector cannot be overemphasised.

17.2 What are Agrofuels?

Renewable, biodegradable and harmless to the environment if spilled, agrofuels are broadly defined as solid, liquid or gas fuels derived from recent biological material, most commonly plants (Dufey et al. 2007). The term 'agrofuels' is herein preferred to 'biofuels' in order to emphasize their potential to adversely compete with agricultural food crops; and emphasise the intensive, monocultural and industrial ways in which they are produced (Biofuelwatch et al. 2007). Agrofuels can be made from (FAO 2008b):

- Sugar crops e.g. sugarcane, sugar beet, sweet sorghum;
- Starchy crops e.g. maize (corn), wheat, barley, rye, potatoes, cassava;
- Cellulosic materials e.g. switchgrass, *Miscanthus*, willow, poplar, stover;
- Oil crops e.g. rapeseed, oil palm, soybean, sunflower, peanut, *Jatropha;*
- Algae and animal fats.

The most common types of agrofuels are biodiesel and bioethanol. From figure 17.1, it is evident that there has been a rapid and continuing increase in the production of agrofuels, with bioethanol constituting the larger composition by volume. The same rapid increase can be seen in Sub-Saharan Africa (GRAIN 2008). In 2009, the United States and Brazil accounted for 88 percent of global bioethanol production whilst the European Union produced nearly 50 percent of the biodiesel (REN21 2010). Bioethanol is produced mainly by the fermentation of sugarcane or starch (mainly corn), while biodiesel is mainly produced as a result of chemical conversion of fat or oil.

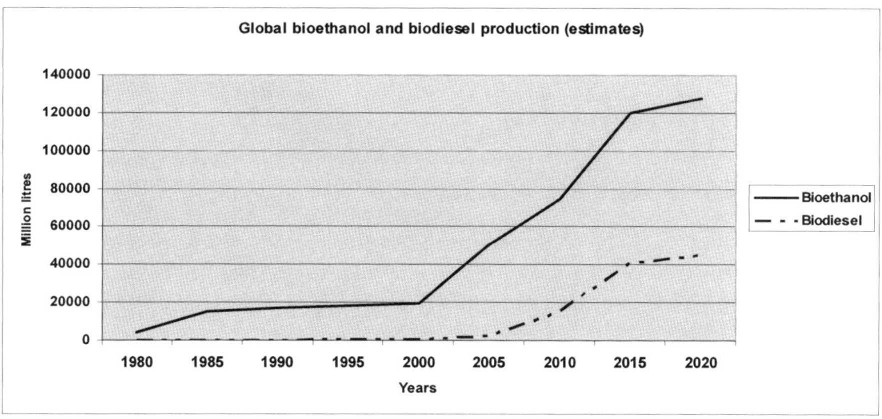

Fig. 17.1. Rapid increase in global production of bioethanol and biodiesel (adopted from: Dufey et al. 2007)

Four broad categories of agrofuels have been identified (UN 2007a) i.e.:

- 'First-generation' agrofuels, commonly biodiesel and bioethanol made from feedstock;
- 'Second generation' agrofuels, mainly cellulosic ethanol made from lignocellulose and other non-food materials, such as waste biomass, stalks of wheat, corn, wood, special energy or biomass crops, such as *Miscanthus*;
- 'Third generation' agrofuels, are low-input/high-yield and derive from algae;
- 'Fourth generation' agrofuels, are made using genetically engineered microorganisms designed to capture large amounts of carbon and efficiently produce fuel.

Currently, only first generation agrofuels are commercially available; and are considered damaging as the feedstock can be used in the animal and human food chains. Additionally, they can directly compete for production factors with food crops (GRAIN 2008; Holt-Gimenez 2007). The other categories of agrofuels are mainly in development and are not yet available at a commercial and global scale (REN21 2010).

17.3 The Concerns over Agrofuels

Several benefits of agrofuels have been stated, albeit overlapping in some aspects, and include the following (Arungu-Olende 2007; ICRISAT 2007; von Braun and Pachauri 2006):

- Potential to reduce demand for fossil fuels, greater energy security, and a sustainable fuel supply for the future;
- Reduced emissions of greenhouse gases and particulates;
- Increased rural development through job creation; higher farmer prices and incomes, alleviating poverty;
- Dampening effect on crude oil prices (Quaiattini 2008);
- Providing more lead time for the world to develop solutions to excess greenhouse gases emissions and global warming.

In contrast, controversies and concerns over the sustainable production of agrofuel crops have also been presented, as follows:

- Demand for agrofuels has resulted in higher food prices, globally and in developing countries, and causing *agflation* i.e. a hike in general prices due to the increase of price of agricultural produce (Learner 2007; Knaup 2008);
- Nearly 290 million more people, mostly in Sub-Saharan Africa, pushed into poverty and hunger by increasing food prices (Oxfam 2008b);
- Nearly 60 million indigenous people at risk of eviction from their lands to make way for agrofuel crops (UN 2007a);
- The complete life cycle of agrofuels produces more greenhouse gases than they reduce (Crutzen et al. 2008; Searchinger et al. 2007; Fargione et al. 2008);
- Agrofuels are not economically viable, as they rely on subsidies and artificial incentives, and their long-term marketability is in doubt (Learner 2007; Knaup 2008).

In addition to the above concerns, first generation agrofuels have been stated to be capable of reliably supplying only a small percentage of our energy requirements (Grunwald 2008). Also pertinent to the Sub-Saharan context, is the concern that the structure of global grains and agrofuels markets are themselves non-sustainable, inequitable and a threat to food security and economic welfare (Oxfam 2008b). This is based on the recognition that more than 50% of the global grain and agrofuel trade is controlled by a cartel of multinational firms, with sub-

Saharan African firms having no influence in the system (Borras Jr et al. 2010; Dauvergne and Neville 2010). Furthermore, the low efficiencies, technologies and participation in global markets, of Sub-Saharan African countries implies that they may not in the long run competitively profit from the agrofuel sector when all costs, e.g. externalities, are factored in (Borras Jr et al. 2010; GRAIN 2010). Some Sub-Saharan African countries have experienced civil unrest over high food prices because of increased demand for agrofuels, consequently threatening national security (RFA 2008; Africanews 2008; Nyamute 2008). Violent evictions of indigenous peoples in order to grow agrofuels, as well as gender, labour and human rights abuses have been documented in Brazil, Argentina, Paraguay, Bolivia and Malaysia (FAO 2008a; Biofuelwatch et al. 2007). It is conceivable that such practices may also occur in Sub-Saharan Africa. Evictions of local populations have already occurred in Uganda, Ghana and Tanzania (Cotula et al. 2009; Africanews 2008). It is within this context that the author argues that:

- the potential adverse impacts of agrofuel sector on the food security and welfares of citizens be predicted, evaluated, mitigated, and where possible, avoided;
- the PPPPs- and decision-making processes be cognizant of the multi-sectoral benefits, costs and trade-offs associated with the production of agrofuel crops (see FAO 2008b; RFA 2008; Arungu-Olende 2007; Dufey et al. 2007).

Therefore, the overriding concern is: what decision-making criteria can integrate the full consideration of the socio-economic and environmental impacts of producing agrofuel crops,on the sustainable devolvement agenda of Sub-Saharan Africa countries?

17.3.1 Weakness of Current Decision-making Context for Agrofuel Crops

While agrofuel production is gaining ground in Sub-Saharan Africa, there remains a lack of formally established set of clear criteria for guiding or determining the sustainability of the agrofuel crops, and consequently, the entire sector (UNEP 2009a; AFREPREN/FWD 2007). Sustainability concerns have mostly been based on lifecycle (net) greenhouse gas emissions and/or lifecycle (net) energy production (REN21 2010); an approach limited in scope if the socio-economic and environmental pillars of sustainability (see Gibson 2006) are to be considered. A literature search by this author did not reveal a more comprehensive list of decisional criteria to determine agrofuels' sustainability under the various competing socio-economic and environmental contexts. However, encouragingly, the government of Kenya drafted a five-year biodiesel policy strategy (GoK 2008), which listed some strategic decisional criteria that provide a starting point. A second weakness of the decision-making context for agrofuel crops in Sub-Saharan Africa comes from the fact that the 'sustainability' of most agrofuel PPPPs is not adequately underpinned by sound evidence or empirical data (UNEP 2009a). For example, policies in Sub-Saharan African countries have already set targets for agrofuels production, although the justification for these numbers is hard to come by. Also, the Kenyan government's policy intends to promote the cultivation of *Jatropha curcas* as a choice species for biodiesel (IRIN 2008), despite the fact that no study has confirmed its suitability (Hunsberger 2010). Furthermore, the Kenya policy identifies 'marginal lands' as priority areas for agrofuels, yet the evidence base to support this choice is not provided. This is in spite of 'marginal and arid lands' being valuable ecosystems in their own right (EcoNexus 2008). A third weakness emanates from the compounding of the above mentioned two. Without fit for purpose decision-making criteria and sound epistemic base for impact assessment, the effectiveness of PPPP tools like Strategic Environmental Assessment (SEA) and Environmental Impact Assessment (EIA) is hampered (Fischer 2007). SEA and EIA are systematic tools of choice that can aid decision-making and the integration of sustainability concerns into PPPPs. However, they rely on clear and explicit decision-criteria to guide their effectiveness (Fischer 2007).

Another weakness in decision-making over agrofuels emanates from the fact that agrofuel crops production and the related PPPPs, represent an emerging industry encumbered with epistemic challenges in determining their sustainability assessments, especially in Africa (Hunsberger 2010; Taylor and Bending 2009). Besides, agrofuel science and technology is relatively unproven (FAO 2008b) and the crops' interactions with local environmental, socio-economic and good governance issues in Sub-Saharan Africa, not empirically well studied (Dufey et al. 2007; EEB 2006). Therefore, adequate and reliable data for formulating decision-making criteria to integrate sustainability concerns is yet to be generated, particularly in Sub-Saharan contexts.

While Sub-Saharan African countries venture into growing agrofuel crops (UNEP 2009a), decision-making criteria over restricted or excluded zones for agrofuel crops would help navigate where and to what scale to grow them. For example, Kenya's predominant areas of land-based conflicts e.g., recurrent food shortages and food insecurity, flooding, land clashes, human-wildlife conflicts, must be cautiously considered when determining the relevant decision criteria for growing agrofuel crops. This is because land is a volatile and emotive issue in most Sub-Saharan countries, and must be planned for with due consideration to mitigate conflicts (Onyango and Gazzola forthcoming). The inadequacy of decision-making criteria perhaps led to the 2008 Kenyan public and environmentalists' court challenge over a $369 million agrofuel project in Kenya's Tana River Delta. The project was opposed by the public on grounds that it threatened the delta's biodiversity; it was not economically viable; and that it would not improve the lives of local residents (Ogodo and Scott 2008). However, since Kenya's legislation requires agrofuel PPPPs to undergo an SEA/EIA, existence of appropriate decision-making criteria can significantly enhance the integration of sustainability concerns into the agrofuel sector.

In another example, in October 2009, the Tanzanian government intervened in the eviction of more than 5,000 rice farmers from their traditional land in order to pave way for growing agrofuel crops (Mande 2009). Yet the government had allowed investors to undertake the agrofuels projects (Mande 2009); and later went ahead to spend $3.1 million USD equivalent to strengthen policy, legal, regulatory and institutional framework to support a sustainable agrofuel industry (Mande 2009). The question arises, pertinent to the paper; could such a situation have been better guided by appropriate decision-making criteria before the projects were approved? In summary, all the above examples depict the lack of clear decision-making criteria for determining the sustainability of agrofuel crops, in various contexts, as a problem.

17.3.2 Proposed Decision-making Criteria

The elaboration of key concerns over decision-making for agrofuels, based on this paper's review of literature, was deemed a justified starting point to distil appropriate decisional criteria. When considered together, these criteria are intended to have the benefit of guiding analyses and capturing the elements that lead to evidence-based determination of the sustainability of agrofuel crops. In other words, they provide a mechanism to integrate socio-economic and environmental concerns into the decisional processes, particularly the questions of if, where, how much and which agrofuel crops are to be grown, and how. The criteria for decision-making may in some cases overlap, and are herein collated to include the following:

1. Pro-poor priorities e.g. rural and agricultural employment and income. This can for example be done by analysing how agrofuel PPPPs will promote the Millennium Development Goals (MDGs).
2. Food security e.g. how will it be affected at local, regional, and national levels? How will this influence susceptibility to civil unrest?
3. Regional balance e.g. what socio-economic pressures will be aggravated or relived by agrofuel plantations in various regions of a country?
4. Land equity e.g. how will landless people be further affected by agrofuel plantations, or how will those with grievances over historical land injustices be affected? Is land grabbing escalated?
5. Livelihood means e.g. how will agrofuel production affect access to livelihoods for both traditional pastoralists and rural farmers? Will their access to local medicines and cultural, seasonal resources be affected?
6. Environmental and biodiversity protection e.g. will wildlife migratory routes be affected? Will key environmental resources be affected?
7. Compatibility with other PPPPs. How will agrofuels impact key developmental goals (MDGs) and other national visions? For example, how will Kenya's Vision 2030 goal of being a middle-income country be affected by agrofuel PPPPs?
8. Consultative and participatory decision-making e.g. are all the local communities and stakeholders consulted and their concerns over agrofuels sustainability taken into consideration?
9. Agricultural characteristic e.g. what are the net beneficial agrofuel crop characteristics such as ability to intercrop, be perennial, be used for multi-purposes or meet certain traditional local community requirements?

10. Climate change e.g. how do agrofuel crops and PPPPs contribute to the climate change agenda?
11. To what extent does the agrofuels sector contribute to nation interest e.g. foreign exchange balance, energy matrix? Where is the balance between socio-economic and environmental objectives?

It is conceived that these criteria will be contextualised and codified within the country's PPPPs assessment frameworks e.g. through SEA/EIA, when deciding on the sustainability of agrofuels. These criteria are 'evidence-based' in two ways. One, they have been distilled from the analyses of evidence found in existing literature. Two, as elements of analyses, they are a bases for generating evidence on which to then base decisions on the sustainability of agrofuels.

17.3.3 Advantages of the Decision-making Criteria

Application of context-specific decisional criteria will lead to several advantages, specifically when determining whether agrofuels have net desirable benefits to a country's sustainable development or not. One, the existence of the decision-making criteria is a basis for efficient, effective and consistent quality of outcome. This promotes predictability and enhances public and investor confidence in the sector. Two, transparency in decision-making will be improved because auditing, review or enforceability of agrofuel decisions is enhanced through existence of known decisions criteria. Three, effectiveness of PPPPs assessment and decision-aiding tools such as SEA and EIA are enhanced, as opposed to where such criteria do not exist. This means that the tools already have decisional criteria to help assess, evaluate, and integrate sustainability issues. Finally, these criteria integrate a wider and comprehensive set of environmental and socio-economic sustainability concerns, including aspects of equity and good governance, as illustrated in sub-section 17.3.2, into the decision-making process. This means that the sustainability agenda is more comprehensively considered within the decision-making process, hence increasing quality assurance. PPPPs assessment, design and licensing can be better guided by these decision-making criteria, in a way that mitigates adverse impacts, and enhances socio-economic and environmental welfare of local populations. This is because they have been distilled as a summary and reflection of the real and practical concerns already being discussed.

17.4 Conclusions and Recommendations

Planning, assessing and making decisions on agrofuel PPPPs that promote socio-economic and environmental welfare of Sub-Saharan African countries has been identified as experiencing challenges. This is because decision-making criteria that integrate the above concerns are yet to be established. Some examples of these have been provided for illustration. This paper has contributed to finding a solution by proposing key decision-making criteria for planning, designing, assessing and approving agrofuel PPPPs, in order to facilitate avoidance and mitigation of potential adverse impacts from agrofuel crops. These criteria are distilled from the literature focusing on their potential impacts on sustainability. Since it is assumed that the examples are representative of many Sub-Saharan Africa countries, the proposed decisional criteria are deemed transferrable within the continent. It is however recommended that such decision criteria only be used as a starting point to develop refined ones for each country context. Constraints that may hinder the establishment of such criteria include effective engagement of competent authorities in formulating them. This might be frustrated by a lack of well-funded research to provide relevant data. Secondly, poor mainstreaming between agrofuel policies and projects, will introduce gaps in the application of the decisional criteria throughout various levels of PPPPs- and decision-making. To remedy this, it is recommended that more effective tiering between higher level and lower level decision-making and planning levels, be prioritised. This can take the form of a strategic decision-making aiding tool like SEA, providing a guiding framework for the application of project EIA. Finally, it is recommended that the decision-making criteria undergo empirical testing, and before being formally integrated into regulatory or SEA/EIA frameworks. Embedding the criteria within a legally enforceable framework would also go a long way in promoting sustainability because it will provide the public with a mechanism to pursue legal recourse in cases of disagreement.

References

AFREPREN/FWD (2007) Renewables in Eastern and Horn of Africa: Kenyan Country Report Occasional Paper No. 29. Nairobi, AFREPREN/FWD & HBF – HA

AFRICAnews (2008) Kenya: food riots loom, published on 27 November 2008 at http://www.africanews.com/site/list_messages/21866, last accessed on 10.12.2010

Arungu-Olende S (2007) Biofuels offer Africa huge potential but pose challenges. Internet address: http://africanagriculture.blogspot.com, last accessed on 10.12.2010

Biofuelwatch, Corporate Europe Observatory, Ecologistas en Acción, EcoNexus, Ecoropa, Grupo de Reflexión Rural, Munlochy Vigil, NOAH (Friends of the Earth Denmark), Rettet Den Regenwald, Carbon Trade Watch & Watch Indonesia (2007) Agrofuels – towards a reality check in nine key areas. Report prepared for the twelfth meeting of the Subsidiary Body on Scientific, Technical and Technological Advice (SBSTTA) of the Convention on Biological Diversity, Paris, 2-6 July 2007. Internet address: http://archive.corporateeurope.org/docs/AgrofuelsRealityCheck.pdf, last accessed on 10.12.2010

Borras Jr. SM, McMichael P, Scoones I (2010) The politics of biofuels, land and agrarian change: editors' introduction. In: Journal of Peasant Studies 37(4): 575-592

BWI – Bread for the World Institute (2008) Agriculture: A Must for the Millennium Development Goals, Background Paper. Bread for the World Institute (BWI), Washington

Collier P (2008) The Bottom Billion: Why the Poorest Countries Are Failing and What Can Be Done About It. Oxford University Press, Oxford

Crutzen PJ, Mosier AR, Smith KA, Winiwarter W (2008) N_2O release from agro-biofuel production negates global warming. In: Atmospheric Chemistry and Physics 8(2): 389-395

Dauvergne P, Neville KJ (2010) Forests, food, and fuel in the tropics: the uneven social and ecological consequences of the emerging political economy of biofuels. In: The Journal of Peasant Studies 37(4): 631-660

Dufey A, Vermeulen S, Vorley B (2007) Biofuels: Strategic Choices for Commodity Dependent Developing Countries. Commodities Issues Series, November 2007. Common Fund for Commodities, Amsterdam

EcoNexus (2008) Agrofuels (Biofuels) and 'Marginal' or 'Idle' Land. Briefing Note Helen Paul, September 2008. Internet address: http://www.econexus.info/topic/agrofuels-biofuels, last accessed on 10.12.2010

EEB – European Environmental Bureau (2006) Biofuels no panacea: EEB urges Commission to keep close watch on wider environmental and social impacts. EEB Press Release, Brussels, 8 February 2006. Internet address: http://www.climnet.org/resources/doc_download/1020-eeb-urges-commission-to-keep-close-watch-on-wider-environmental-and-social-impacts-2006, last accessed on 10.12.2010

FAO – Food and Agriculture Organization of the United Nations (2008a) The right to food and the impact of liquid biofuels (agrofuels). FAO, Rome. Internet address: http://www.fao.org/righttofood/publi08/Right_to_Food_and_Biofuels.pdf, last accessed on 10.12.2010

FAO – Food and Agriculture Organization of the United Nations (2008b) The State of food and Agriculture: biofuels, prospects, risks and opportunities. FOA, Rome. Internet address: ftp://ftp.fao.org/docrep/fao/011/i0100e/i0100e.pdf, last accessed on 10.12.2010

Fargione J, Hill J, Tilman D, Polasky S, Hawthorne P (2008) Land Clearing and the Biofuel Carbon Debt. In: Science 319(5867):1235-1238

Fischer TB (2007) The Theory and Practice of Strategic Environmental Assessment. London, Earthscan

Gibson RB (2006) Sustainability assessment: basic components of a practical approach. In: Impact Assessment and Project Appraisal 24(3):170-182

GoK – Government of Kenya (2008) Strategy for the development of the bio-diesel industry in Kenya, 2008–2012. Ministry of Energy, Renewable Energy Department

GoK/GTZ – Government of Kenya/ Deutsche Gesellschaft für Technische Zusammenarbeit (2008) A roadmap for biofuels in Kenya: opportunities and obstacles, Report prepared by Endelevu Energy and Energy for Sustainable Development Africa

Grunwald M (2008) 'The Clean Energy Scam' TIME Magazine. Published on March 27, 2008. Time Warner Publishing, Amsterdam

GRAIN (2010) An African Call for a Moratorium on Agrofuel Developments. Internet address: http://www.grain.org/agrofuels/?moratoriumen, last accessed on 14.12.2010

Hunsberger C (2010) The politics of Jatropha-based biofuels in Kenya: convergence and divergence among NGOs, donors, government officials and farmers. In: Journal of Peasant Studies, 37(4): 939-962

IEA – International Energy Agency (2007) World Energy Outlook 2006. IEA, Paris

IRIN – Integrated Regional Information Networks (2008) KENYA: Boosting biofuels without compromising food security. Internet address: http://www.irinnews.org/Report.aspx?ReportId=79800, last accessed on 14.12.2010

Knaup H (2008) Africa Becoming a Biofuel Battleground. In: Businessweek Europe, published on September 8, 2008. Internet address: http://www.businessweek.com/print/globalbiz/content/sep2008/gb2008098_506787.htm, last accessed on 14.12.2010

Learner M (2008) Women, Children, and the Global Hunger Crisis: Background Paper, September 2008, No. 198. Bread for the World Institute, Washington

Mande M (2009) Public fury halts biofuel onslaught on farmers. In: The East African, published on October 5, 2009. Internet address: http://www.theeastafrican.co.ke/news/-/2558/667648/-/qy9vngz/-/index.html, last accessed on 14.12.2010

Mohamed FA (2007) Sustainable biofuels production and use, Eastern and Southern Africa regional workshop on biofuels, UNEP, Nairobi 28-29 June 2007. UNIDO, Vienna

Nyamute M (2008) Management of food crisis is a national security issue. In: East African Standard, published on April 22, 2008. East African Standard Publishers, Nairobi

Ogodo O, Scott C (2008) Kenyan courts consider terminating biofuel plans. In: Science and Development Network, published on 5 August, 2008. Internet address: http://www.scidev.net/en/news/kenyan-courts-consider-terminating-biofuel-plans.html, last accessed on 14.12.2010

Onyango V, Schmidt M (2007) Towards a strategic environment assessment framework in Kenya: highlighting areas for further scrutiny. In: Management of Environmental Quality 18(3): 309-328

Oxfam International (2008a) Another Inconvenient truth: How biofuel policies are deepening poverty and accelerating climate change. Oxfam Briefing Paper 114, June 2008. Internet address: http://www.oxfam.org.uk/resources/policy/climate_change/downloads/bp114_inconvenient_truth.pdf, last accessed on 14.12.2010

Oxfam International (2008b) Double-Edged Prices: Lessons from the food price crisis: 10 actions developing countries should take. Oxfam briefing paper 121, October 2008. Internet address: http://www.oxfam.org.uk/generationwhy/cgi/process_comp/photos/2008/10/bp121_double-edged-prices_-final_-13oct08.pdf, last accessed on 14.12.2010

REN21 (2010) Renewables 2010: Global Status Report. REN21 Secretariat, Paris

RFA – Renewable Fuels Agency (2008) Gallagher Review of the indirect effects of biofuel production. Internet address: http://www.renewablefuelsagency.gov.uk/reportsandpublications/reviewoftheindirecteffectsofbiofuels, last accessed on 14.12.2010

Searchinger T, Heimlich R, Houghton RA, Dong F, Elobeid A, Fabiosa J, Tokgoz S, Hayes D, Yu T-H (2008) Use of U.S. Croplands for Biofuels Increases Greenhouse Gases through Emissions from Land Use Change. In: Science 319(5867): 1238-1240

Taylor M, Bending T (2009) Increasing commercial pressure on land: Building a coordinated response: Discussion paper. International Land Coalition, Rome

UN – United Nations (2007a) Sustainable bioenergy: a framework for decision makers. UN-Energy, UN, New York

UN – United Nations (2007b) The Millennium Development Goals 2007. UN, New York

UN – United Nations (2008) Press Conference Launching International Biofuels Forum, 15 January 2008. United Nations Department of Public Information. Internet address: http://www.un.org/News/briefings/docs/2007/070302_Biofuels.doc.htm, last accessed on 14.12.2010

UNEP – United Nations Environment Programme (2009a) Towards sustainable production and use of resources: assessing biofuels. UNEP, Nairobi

UNEP – United Nations Environment Programme (2009b) Integrated Policymaking for Sustainable Development: A Reference Manual, UNEP, Geneva

Vermeulen S, Cotula L (2010) Over the heads of local people: consultation, consent, and recompense in large-scale land deals for biofuels projects in Africa. In: Journal of Peasant Studies 37(4) 899-916

Von Braun J, Pachauri RK (2006) The promises and challenges of biofuels for the poor in Developing Countries. International Food Policy Research Institute, Washington. Internet address: http://www.ifpri.org/sites/default/files/publications/ar05e.pdf, last accessed on 14.12.2010

Part III – Limits to Managing the Environment[1]

Ingmar Lippert

Augsburg University, Chair of Sociology, Augsburg, Germany

Part III investigates some of the limits and contradictions of management of the environment and its resources, through detailed discussions of key dimensions of applied environmental management. This part introduces studies of 1) resource management (rivers as well as recycling), 2) specific techniques drawn on in corporate and public environmental management (suggestion schemes, and respectively, visualisation techniques), and finally, 3) policy discourses (Clean Development Mechanism). The studies presented here are linked by a common thread which recognises that the historicity of environmental management as a social practice requires us to scrutinise its specificity as a practical, social, cultural as well as political achievement. The ascension of science and modernity gave rise to a qualitative change in cultural conceptualisations of the human-nature relationship: nature became an object to be 'managed' by so-called experts. By now, however, environmental management has come under critique in that what it proposes as solutions may simultaneously comprise the causes of environmental problems. First, the means used by environmental management can be identified as instances of modernism, industrialism as well as capitalism. Second, scholars of environmental problems criticise the 'instruments' of environmental 'management' for reproducing the problems, rather than solving them. To examine how environmental problems ought to be approached a critical stance is now seen as essential. Necessarily then, do issues of ideology, epistemology and theory crop up.

Thus, Chapter 18 examines the knowledge drawn on by environmental managers within Corporate Energy Management. This provides a perspective which makes the practices of actors in environmental management an object of study. Chapter 19, on River Management, continues on this line of critique by establishing the interactions between a managed environmental resource, a river, and various people in its context as apt for investigation. The author urges us to reconsider the concept of 'management' itself.

Chapter 20, on Visualising Nuclear Landscapes, provides insight into the minute details of a ubiquitous technique, image production, and its effects. By teasing apart simulations and manipulations, the author foregrounds how phenomenological approaches help to conceptualise the reality of environmental management.

---

[1] For the chapters, presented in this part, we gratefully acknowledge the grant by the UmweltEuro by Brandenburg University of Technology.

In Chapter 21, focusing on how Clean Development Mechanism (CDM) outsources emissions, the author renders a discourse on ecological modernisation and its respective short-comings. Through this angle, an understanding of CDM as externalising, rather than internalising, carbon emissions emerges. Finally, Chapter 22 on Sustaining Waste ascertains the need for analysis to be theoretically informed by problematising the hegemonic practice of recycling. The practical use of theoretically reconceptualising an environmental manager who is setting up a recycling scheme – which sustains, rather than challenges, the mode of resource consumption – is illustrated.

18 Knowledge for Corporate Energy Management - Structural Contradictions and Hope for Change?

Ingmar Lippert

Augsburg University, Chair of Sociology, Augsburg, Germany

18.1 Introduction

'Energy' has been continuously a topic in Western discourses on environmental and technology politics, at the latest since the global oil crises between 1970 and 1980. Potential for private sector innovation to put environmental protection goals into practice is considered significant. Implicit to the aims of energy efficiency and safe energy is the presence of actors who support corporations in reaching these aims. These agents of ecological modernisation, i.e. *environmental managers*, and their practices have rarely been scrutinised. This paper, therefore, aims to make them the object of enquiry – approached from a *Science and Technology Studies* perspective. This article studies the implications for knowledge politics of techno-economic decision-making by such an actor within the energy management at a site of a multinational corporation. Based on ethnographic research at the site the article focuses on an instance of a management tool, corporate suggestion schemes, to mobilise workers' ideas of improving the environmental performance. With this it becomes possible to attend to how corporate agents of ecological modernisation deal with the issue 'energy'. We find that the manager uses specific *forms of knowledge* – adequate to the discourse of ecological modernisation – while, however, sidelining alternative forms. Thus, the latter are lost to sustainable development. It is concluded, that the actors' knowledge practice renders corporate energy management unsustainable. To conceptualise a way out of this dilemma the article draws on theories of grounded utopias.

The global oil crises between 1970 and 1980 provided a discursive environment from which 'energy' emerged as a continuing topic in Western discourses of environmental and technology politics. Actors within this discourse normally consider potential for innovation in the private sector significant to achieve environmental protection goals. These aims are for example energy efficiency and saving energy. This presupposes the presence of actors who support corporations in reaching these aims. Within the environmental management discourse we normally conceptualise these actors, i.e. environmental managers, as acting rationally and grounded in scientific decision-making. Ecological Modernisation Theory, as conceived by e.g. Jänicke (2008) and Mol (2006), helps to conceptualise this rationality. To investigate this normative form of acting, a perspective which focuses on *how actors know* seems apt[1]. Therefore, this article draws on approaches developed within *Science and Technology Studies* (STS) to illustrate how we can focus on knowledge practices of corporate energy management.

If knowledge practices are enacted in the 'social' then we need to expect political implications as well. That is why this article studies the knowledge politics implications of techno-economic decision-making by an actor within the energy management at a site of a multinational corporation. The case which I use to illustrate this discussion is based on ethnographic research. This case provides an instance of a specific kind of management tools, so-called corporate suggestion schemes. In the instance discussed below, this tool was applied to mobilise workers' ideas of improving the corporations' environmental performance. To question the practical implications of this tool I draw on sociologies of human-nature relationships as well as their mediation by science and technology[2]. Fundamental to this approach is the understanding that knowledge is shaped culturally and, thus, a *variety of knowledges* on environments and their relation to societies exist[3]. Relying on this theoretical and conceptual base the paper addresses the question of how to problematise the societal and, following from there, ecological implications of the knowledge of corporate energy managers. While much research exists on organisations' approaches to 'green' themselves rarely can we find studies focussing on the environmental manager herself[4]. This paper aims to contribute to critical, rather than merely affirmative, research on the practices of these managers. This requires breaking with the fundamental norm of research within environmental management, i.e. that principally science is on the right track and environmental problems can be solved with (social) technology, as suggested by Ecological Modernisation Theory (Christoff 1996)[5]. Thus, as a contribution in the critical tradition I aim to point towards structural contradictions in reality. The empirical background of this discussion is an ethnography taking place at five multinationals, including Daimler and Deutsche Telekom inspired by the field of anthropology[6] between 2007 and 2011. My qualitative interpretation is based on field notes and is analysed with TAMS[7].

---

1 I reasoned elsewhere why the investigation of the actual, rather than the presumed, realities of environmental management needs to be postulated and carried out (Lippert 2010).

2 Especially Actor-network theory and Bourdieu's thought influenced this analysis. Cf. e.g. Callon (1981, 1999) Bourdieu (1981, 1992) as well as Shackley and Wynne (1995).

3 Haraway (1991) spread the notion of the plural of knowledge, i.e. knowledges, into a number of disciplines.

4 Cf. Howard-Grenville (2007). She seems to be one of the first who carried out an ethnography of corporate environmental management. See also my other chapter in this book.

5 For recent discussion cf. e.g. Mol and Sonnenfeld (2000), Buttel (2000), Jänicke (2008).

6 See e.g. Malinowski (1922), Thomas (1993), Marcus (1995), Graeber (2004).

7 Cf. Emerson (1995) and Weinstein (2006).

This paper is organised into five further sections. First of all, I shall sketch what I refer to as rationality of environmental management by drawing on Ecological Modernisation Theory, which aims at describing and explaining ecological modernisation as policy and practice. Afterwards I turn to the case which provides the empirical ground for questioning the political implications of using specific forms of knowledge in environmental management practices. After the analysis the article presents a brief theoretical excursion into ways out of the problems analysed and, thus, thinking possibilities of utopia. Finally you will find concluding remarks to emphasise the key contradiction in our case.

18.2 Rationality within Environmental Management

The fundamental claim of the ecological modernisation (EM) thesis is that to reach a balanced relationship between industrialised societies and their environment, these societies need to engage with nature *more technoscientifically and in ways more mediated by the market economy*. Buttel (2000, p. 61) summarises:

> "An ecological modernization perspective hypothesizes that while the most challenging environmental problems of this century and the next have (or will have) been caused by modernization and industrialization, their solutions must necessary lie in more – rather than less – modernization and 'superindustrialization'."

Thus, a better world is envisioned as coming about through making the status quo compatible with environmental needs by continuing the social and economic trajectory, with more of the practices[8] already occurring. The EM thesis construes the global environmental crisis as being transcended (Clark and York 2005, p. 410). The EM discourse postulates innovations[9] which are ecologically less detrimental or even benign both for the realm of material technology as well as social institutions. From a technoscience point of view there is no near end to ecological innovations: Efficiencies are thought to be easily calculable. Technoscientific progress constantly produces knowledge about eco-efficiency and creates artefacts which are seen as less polluting or even contributing to the environment[10]. For example,

---

[8] For example they suggest the continuation of developing 'sustainable technologies' (which everything can be called, i.e. storing recovered carbon dioxide emissions under pressure in the earth (sequestration)).

[9] I use the concept innovation without being familiar with innovation theory. By using 'innovation' I refer to changes which can be seen as stable, relative to the context they are in.

[10] Cf. Buttel (2000, p. 63). Elaborated versions of this kind of technoscience progress literature are limited to life cycle assessments. They tend not to include critical postmodernist contestations such as developed within the field of Science and Technology Studies and Critical Realism, which question the progress ideology (cf. Haraway 1991; Potter and López 2001).

cars are thought to be producible using less and less material and energy input, consuming less petrol and being better recyclable.

Social innovations refer primarily to innovations in management technologies and organisational structures of all kinds. For example it can be seen as an ecological innovation that universities teach industrial ecology, environmental management and environmental sociology[11]. Basically, any instance of implementing (social) technologies[12] which benefit the environment can be seen as an ecological innovation[13]. Important innovations that are widely discussed are the forms of integrating environment as an issue in governmental authorities and businesses[14]. Unsurprisingly, it is always possible to construct *best practice* cases and find institutional learning processes[15]; people today are more aware about environmental issues. Unfortunately, this social ecological innovation does not necessarily and indeed is unlikely to lead to material ecological innovations[16].

Thus, I take, as a rationality of EM, that technoscientific knowledge is used to develop solutions within the hegemonic economic framing – while seeking profits. Industry is perceived to become generally ecologically benign when instances of environmental considerations can be found. This approach is based on assumptions of science being objective, neutral and progressive, disregarding the long history of pointing out the inherent politics of scientific research with (un)intended harmful consequences[17]. In opposition to the latter, critical understanding, EM is carried out within the frame of pragmatism (Prasad and Elmes 2005): "Let's green the organisation as much as possible!" However, the concrete limitations of this are usually not addressed. With this impression of rationality of ecological modernisation let us turn to a case which we use to problematise the knowledge practices of energy management.

---

[11] Major significant instances of management technologies are e.g. procedural, formalised and institutionalised Environmental Management Systems (EMS) or Environmental Impact Assessments (EIA).

[12] I use the concept 'technology' to emphasise that I am talking of social institutions and dynamics which are conceptualised as mechanistic or functionalist by EM. For 'social technologies' see e.g. Bijker (1995).

[13] Of course, we find a debate over whether such instances are merely classified and construed as benefiting the environment or whether they really do (and in the latter case the question occurs whose environment is 'improved').

[14] Cf. Christoff (1996, p. 477), Sonnenfeld and Mol (2006), Søndergård et al. (2004), Mol (2006), Keil and Desfor (2003).

[15] Søndergård et al. (2004).

[16] Cf. Drake et al. (2003), Pellow et al. (2000), White (2006).

[17] Scientific practices and organisations are described as political by a number of people. One could mention e.g. Bakunin (1916), Kuhn (1970), Bourdieu (1990), Haraway (1991).

18.3 The BOTNACO 'Programme'

I encountered the setting during my ethnographic research on agents of ecological modernisation situated in multinational corporations. At a site of a corporation, which I shall name BOTNACO, 1,300 workers were employed performing the mobility industry. Mr. Kunz, who was identified by his business card as an *environmental manager*, told me about a special programme which he designed to run within the corporate suggestion scheme for a limited amount of time. His background was rooted in electrical engineering as well as in chemistry. In terms of energy he was saying: "Actually, [the] energy [issue] is pressing us for years".

We need to conceptualise both the programme and the practices of Kunz within the context of what can be called standardised environmental management: the site was certified with the European Union Eco-management and Auditing Scheme (EMAS) and ISO norm 14001. Both of these norms stipulate extensive documentation of processes which are environmentally relevant as well as continuous environmental improvement. Within this normative context, my research indicates, actors conceptualise saving energy as contributing to sustainable development. To approach sustainable energy management energy is first made calculable; and second, *standardised* calculation procedures are applied[18]. Environmental managers draw on a variety of sources to define local energy management measures, including their own local knowledge as well as workers' knowledge. The programme, to which I shall refer as 'Programme', was devised to mobilise precisely such workers' knowledges of possibilities to protect health and the environment as well as to safe energy. How did the 'Programme' work?

In order to spread the information that the 'Programme' existed Mr. Kunz sent emails to the workers and ordered a poster (Figure 18.1).

The poster declares:

A demand exists for ideas
a. which protect and sustain our environment
b. which help to improve health management for all workers.

The heading indicates a special interest in energy issues. When we met first, the 'Programme' had already taken place. However, the follow-up of it was still going on. During the first conversation Mr Kunz envisaged the follow-up process to complete his aim of mobilising these ideas as quite simple: he drafted the 'Program', got the information out and the workers developed and communicated their ideas through the suggestion scheme. Finally, in the decision-making process, he imagined commenting on the ideas such that decision-makers could make grounded choices. Figure 18.2 visualises the linearity of this process.

[18] These standardised procedures imply, however, that actors are likely to meet discrepancies between ideal assumptions, which are part of the standard, and local conditions.

Fig. 18.1. Getting it out

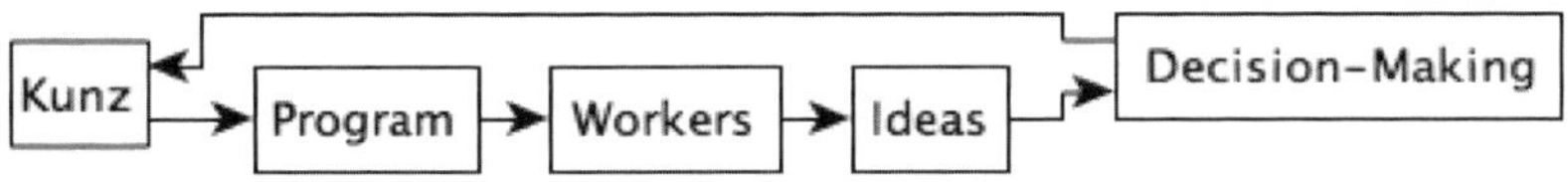

Fig. 18.2. Linear model of the 'Program'

Overall, workers handed in about 60 suggestions. The decision-making thereupon was distributed and the officer for the suggestion scheme defined who would comment on them before the final decision. Because the 'Programme' asked for ideas regarding environmental issues Kunz received the suggestions. For him, the decision whether he should recommend carrying out an idea or not was either straightforward or he had to make some inquiries and negotiate the suggestion with other actors. How did he decide? If his decision was straightforward it was so because the case was self-evident to him. One such case was the idea to install a solar panel. For Kunz this was out of question because at the site another solar panel already existed. From his point of view this case illustrated the lack of knowledge on side of the worker: the worker should have known that solar panels already existed. As the worker did not specify why another panel would be useful, but rather presented a general idea, the environmental manager declined the suggestion. He would have been interested in a suggestion, which would be situated and reasoned from his point of view and which would fit in his frame of interpreting the world. Thus, the idea of the worker was not compatible with Kunz's frame.

Another case concerned saving water. This idea had been declined. The decision upon this idea was heavily contested. Afterwards, several meetings took place to settle the case. While the case was quite straightforward for Kunz "*the [workers] did not want to accept [the decline] and [they] said: 'No! It is possible [to put their idea into practice]; why [do you not see this]?'*". This conflict constituted a problem: Kunz recognised that the *decline is placed in tension with him wanting to motivate the workers* (field note). Overall, then, the 'Programme' brought about problems and additional work. Therefore, they decided, to not run such a 'Programme' again with a specific emphasis on energy.

The significance of the environmental manager's reaction to the ideas of the workers lies within the way ideas are presented and dealt with. A tension exists between Kunz's approach and that of some workers. How can we critically interpret this tension?

18.4 Analysis: Knowledge and Contradictions

To approach this tension within decision-making, this section provides foci on both the subject matter of knowledge in the case as well as its social context. First, let us recall that the 'Programme' was devised to mobilise knowledge to support Mr. Kunz's work to green the corporation. The schemes (of perception and thinking) which he used to evaluate those knowledges which were presented to him were based on diverse sources. Overall, we found: Kunz, himself a trained technician and analytical chemist, drew upon techno-economic knowledge and epistemology to reason about the ideas. In detail, a variety of sources were available to him. First and overarching, he conceptualised environmental issues based on his professional background as well as on professional conferences and contemporary law. Accordingly, on his wall we found a poster with an overview on legal stipulations relevant to his work. Further, he also dealt with magazines, which attended to the environment. The criteria which he used for shaping his advice fit to these forms of knowledge: it was important (1) implicitly, that the ideas are likely to improve the environmental situation, and explicitly that they are feasible in terms of (2) involved technology and (3) temporal and financial implications; he also mentioned (4) life cycle analyses. However, these criteria are all quite 'soft' and when it came down to it; he said "After all, the corporation has to get something out of it, i.e. it has to pay off for the corporation." Thus, the significant question was: is it "financially worth it"?

Kunz also had quite a bit of knowledge about the environmental situation at the production site. Actually we can find that he seemed to take-for-granted that he had the most complete knowledge of the environmental situation at the site (relative to others at the site). This can be seen as a doxic stance as described by Bourdieu: this theoretical approach suggests that actors believe in the presuppositions of a field and by that reproduce its social and economic conditions (Bourdieu 1990). In our case Mr. Kunz had good reasons to believe that he knew best about conditions relevant to sustainable energy management. He already worked for many years at the site – he was even a worker with one of the longest time spans working there. Disposed to such a stance, it can be considered of uttermost difficulty for him to *imagine* that workers may develop an idea, which has both characteristics: a) environmentally useful and b) not conceptualisable within his existing frame of knowing. Furthermore, he had relations to expert-colleagues which can be characterised by co-operation. For him, it was self-evident that together they have the best possible knowledge of the local conditions regarding the environment. Thus, this indicates clearly: his scheme and background of performing knowledge fit well to the rationality of ecological modernisation as described above.

These criteria and his background illustrate his schemes of perception. Both by training and in his practical decision-making he used hegemonic forms of knowledge: technoscience, law, seeking profit, which were shared among his colleagues and stabilised by the corporation. This kind of knowledge should be quantifiable – at least clearly categorisable. If it was not, this would have constituted a problem, not only for him, but – he well knew – also for the corporation. This was the case because his corporation tried to universalise, within its whole structure, the way environmental management was run. Therefore, this organisational habitus (Hård 1994) shaped the practices at our BOTNACO site as well. Kunz would not have been able to easily evade the rationality of the organisation.

When some workers did not know about the situation at the site in the manner he deemed adequate, he conceptualised them as being not informed (case of solar panel). This stance is structured similar to the cognitive *deficit model* discussed within STS[19]. It suggests that laymen have gaps in their scientific knowledge of the world and that they cannot, therefore, adequately conceptualise their environment. The implication of this model being that one needs a funnel to put scientific knowledge into them. Kunz's reaction to the workers' body of knowledge, in line with this, was: *I will "write a piece in the journal, the [BOTNACO] house journal, [about] what kind of things we have here and do, in order ... to prevent such things"*. From his point of view he merely needed to teach them what kind of environmental technologies existed and then they would understand what a proper suggestion is. As he pointed out regarding the suggestion to install another solar panel, such teaching should convey that general suggestions are not proper: *"Obviously this is a rather general suggestion, and actually we cannot put this properly to use"*. This stance illustrates that he, as the environmental manager, has the power to define the terms of the situation. This signifies as well a *hierarchy* between the forms of knowledge, i.e. the general idea vs. the specific suggestion fitting to his ecological modernisation rationality. Like scientific experts knowing better than laymen, the environmental manager knows better than workers. This hierarchy is maintained through the categories in use: workers would allow the expert to define which categories are suitable to analyse a situation. By this process the relations of categories are reproduced. It is not questioned that workers might very well possess useful knowledge to deal with their environment and recognise qualities that are lacking in it.

On the other hand, Kunz also actively negotiated issues which required objective decisions upon them. For example he emphasised that his colleagues, who were part of decision-making, are *human* actors and that therefore he can discuss with them the terms of amortisation of an investment. Thus, practically, he co-constructed objectivity: the objectivity of whether a measure is worth it is socially co-constructed.

Nevertheless, for his identity it seemed to be of importance that he conceptualises himself as an adviser to the site manager and in our case to the suggestion scheme. This advice should be as objective as possible. According to his descriptions, what he and his colleagues had in common was that they developed their decisive advice to the decision-maker based on a shared commitment to rationality and objectivity. The most significant criterion around which their advice was shaped was profitability. It was on these grounds and within these relations in which the environmental manager *constructed* advice.

Let us now turn briefly to some relations in which those workers whose ideas had been declined were situated. Fundamentally, they were the means of the 'Programme'. It was aimed at mobilising their ideas and when they saw the posters and emails they were 'triggered' to develop ideas or make them explicit respectively. The ideas were based on their knowledge of their working environment. When they had a chance to use their knowledge as capital they used it. The suggestion scheme both enabled them to try to 'sell' their ideas and provided a medium for them to communicate the ideas. Thus, they were not merely passively re-

[19] See e.g. Wieser (2002), Lynch (2004), Irwin (2006) and Wynne (1992).

sponding to the poster, but also actively using the 'suggestion scheme' tool for their purposes.

When they recognised that their aim, i.e. gaining from their knowledge, had not been reached that easily they got in touch with the environmental manager. They claimed that their ideas should be judged as acceptable and hence serve them in terms of recognition. In the follow-up to this, several meetings took place to solve the tensions. These provide a chance to illustrate further dimensions of the problem.

18.4.1 Crystallised Conflict: The Meetings

The meetings were attended by Kunz, some of his colleagues and the workers. While the meetings were designed to maintain co-operative stances within the corporation the conflict was not easily solved. The positions which the two groups of actors took were laden with contradictions. On the one hand Kunz (representing the corporate bureaucracy) wanted the workers to be motivated, both in general and specifically through the 'Programme'. He recognised after a while that this had not been realised as to his aims. In conflict with this approach was the stance of him of teaching the workers. This stance makes explicit that he considered their knowledge (too) poor. On the other hand the workers were positioned within a contradiction as well. They wanted to 'sell' their ideas to the corporation, i.e. make them value the ideas and recognise the workers for their contribution. However, while they could not enforce such a recognitive stance by the organisation they still tried to move the organisation towards recognising their ideas.

Thus, between and within both groups structural conflicts existed. So, what was the use of the meetings after all? They took place for (at least) three kinds of reasons. First, Kunz needed them to explain the workers the reasons for declining their ideas. Second, the workers needed them to contest the decision. And third, to have meetings to negotiate can be seen as an act of the organisational habitus. Thus, having meetings satisfies the structural requirements on conflicts within the organisational field.

The latter points again to the relevancy of the main stake within the field: economic profit. The suggestion scheme is aimed at profit and the environmental manager, as well as his colleagues represent the organisational rationality to ensure profits. This interpretation allows the reframing of the position of Kunz and the workers in terms of their stakes.

The job of Kunz (and his colleagues) included improving the environmental management at the site. This should be done as efficiently as possible. The 'Programme' provided the chance for the environmental manager to gain significant new ideas which he could then incorporate into managing environmental issues. However, the 'Program' provided the risk for him as well, that the ideas which were presented to him which could be wearisome to deal with. This might have reduced the efficiency of the management tool. Furthermore, not only that he had to deal with the specific ideas, he was also (co-)responsible for running the 'Programme'. Thus, here is another instance of his stake in terms of managing knowledges. The right choice of the right instruments to manage was part of his job. The fact that he saw the 'Programme' as a failure attests to the relevancy of this choice. For him it was his co-responsibility, which was significant.20 In that respect he decided that the 'Programme' did not run well. His original idea of how it should have generated suggestions did not work well enough (as illustrated in linear, Figure 18.2). Rather, the reality of the 'Program' revealed itself differently to him: Figure 18.3 indicates how the idea, the formal suggestion scheme apparatus and the 'Programme' became background to the more central meetings between Kunz and the workers.

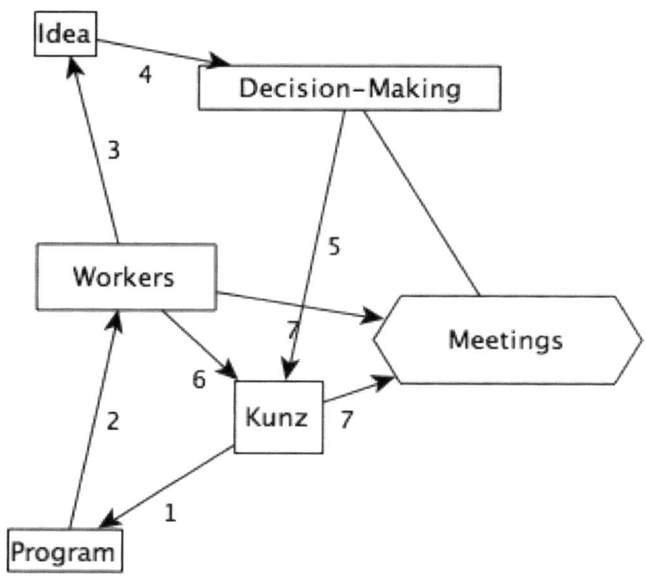

Fig. 18.3. Centrality of Meetings

Thus, for Kunz the 'Programme' was a failure: the turnout of suggestions was not big enough and some even induced considerable excess work. Moreover, he had to believe that the motivation of workers decreased. Hence, the way the reality of the 'Programme' contingently developed was in conflict with his stakes. To improve his position – and from his point of view: the priority of environmental matters as well – a successful 'Programme' would have been better. Could he have acted significantly differently? Possibly; but we cannot know. What we can see, however, is that the way he acted was well grounded in his rationality: the belief in the

[20] Although, the way the instrument worked was contingent, its working was influenced only at the most immediate level by the ideas of the workers and more indirectly by various factors which he also could not control (like the dispositions of the workers, public discourses on the environment, etc.).

neutrality and objectivity of decision-making for sustaining the profits of the corporation. This rationality is required in his position. Other actors expect to put into reality this kind of rationality for dealing with the ideas of the workers. This is at least what he has to assume in his position and he takes-for-granted. Thus, because of both the environmental manager's own background as well as social requirements on him, the field structure is reproduced. Any other agent of ecological modernisation in Mr. Kunz's position would have been disposed to a similar rationality.

For the workers, whose ideas were declined, the situation is structured as follows: The 'Programme' promised to give importance to their ideas. However, this importance is not granted by the experts. To re-construct their self-confidence, for them, it makes sense to argue for the opposite decision. Yet, if such a change of the decision does not happen – which is unlikely because the experts would have to reveal themselves as providing flawed arguments – the worker may still try to put the idea, if practically possible, into practice. This, however, is again unlikely because of the structure of the organisation in question. Workers do not have much incentive to identify with the owners. They do not have a clear stake in the profitability or greening of the corporation; the means of production are owned by others who are also responsible for environmental management. Hence, after having offered their ideas, why should they contribute to unwanted environmental improvements? Thus, for the organisation the idea of the worker is lost.

Overall, then, we find that knowing 'rightly' implies a hierarchy: Mr. Kunz, as techno-scientific and techno-economic expert – along the rationality of ecological modernisation, has superior knowledge relative to workers. This hierarchy became most explicit in his dismissal of the workers' solar panel idea together with the deficit model.

18.4.2 Lost Meanings? Ideas and Suggestions

While analysing the field and the doxic stance of the environmental manager the focus on the structure of the contested content disappeared. However, the structural difference of how the environmental manager constructed the workers' ideas and the needed suggestions reveals an important dimension of the 'Programme'.

During research it seemed that Kunz used the notions of ideas and suggestions interchangeably. However, they have quite different relations to the other elements of the situation. The poster of the 'Programme' asked for ideas while linking the 'Programme' obviously to the suggestion scheme. Those workers who had ideas, which they deemed to fit into what was asked for, accessed the suggestion scheme as a mechanism. This was possible by both material as well as digital forms. Within this mechanism ideas cannot exist – merely suggestions. What does this imply?

A suggestion needs to be clearly categorisable within the organisational division of labour, such that the officer of the suggestion scheme can direct the suggestions to experts. For the environmental manager the suggestions should be oriented towards the criteria which he used. If he was not able to conceptualise the suggestion within these criteria then they had little chance of being approved. Thus, if an idea was not also a successful suggestion it was unlikely to be accepted and turned into reality. The 'Programme' only knew suggestions. If they did not satisfy the implicit standards then they were declined. Thus, whether the workers were aware or not, their ideas were transformed into another social reality by entering them into the mechanism suggestion scheme. The suggestions within the latter were then reviewed by human actors. Independently of how well they fitted to formal requirements, the suggestions provided knowledge.

However, the recipients of the knowledge were not disposed to deal with all knowledges in the same manner, but to select them according to their fit into their objectivist framing. It was this framing which marginalised the specific ideas of the workers. At the same time we can recognise how not only specific ideas but systemically forms of knowing are also disregarded. This resembles Ecological Modernisation Theory (EMT) in that sense that EMT is based on objectively analysing situations and developing solutions. The inherent values and problems of technoscientific knowledges are not considered but reproduced. This corresponds to what Christoff (1996, p. 478) called "a unilinear path to ecological modernity". Alternative forms of human-nature relationships cannot easily find room to evolve under an ecological modernisation paradigm.

To summarise, with this analysis we can recognise two contradictions in the setting: First, the instrument 'Programme' was developed to harvest knowledges. These are needed for effective environmental protection. However, at the same time, certain forms of knowledge are structurally excluded. Knowledges which do not fit to the rationality of ecological modernisation cannot be utilised and may even create conflicts. Second, the ideas are lost not only by excluding them through the suggestion scheme but also because the workers are not disposed to put them otherwise into practice because of their relation to the production site; they neither own the means of production nor are they responsible for the environmental effects of the production.

It is these two forms of hierarchy, among knowledges and the possession of means of production, which sustain unsustainability. With the hierarchy among knowledges embedded into the field and the workers and Kunz positioned to not question this hierarchy, communal learning processes within this kind of field are unlikely. The other form of hierarchy makes it more likely that the workers' ideas are not put into practice by themselves.

Hence, we can see this configuration of the organisational field as constraining the possibility to construct sustainable futures. This is the case even though the environmental manager is good willed and acts very much in the logic of ecological modernisation. At his position within this configuration, he is unlikely to reflexively confront his stance. Therefore, I suggest, to search for possibilities for change in the wider social context. Its actors might reconstruct the configuration of the field, such that alternative futures become more likely. In the following, therefore, we shall turn towards asking how we can conceptualise a way out of the dilemma.

18.5 A Way Out – Based on Determined Negation?

Bourdieu (1998) suggests going for a 'reasoned utopianism' in order to ground the struggle against neoliberalism, an ideology which provides the economic point of reference for ecological modernisation. Rather than focussing on his specific aim, I am interested in how to reason a utopia. In his essay *A Reasoned Utopia and Economic Fatalism* he quotes Ernst Bloch:

> "Bloch describes the 'considered utopian' as one who acts 'by virtue of his fully aware fore-knowledge of the objective trend', the objective, and real, possibility of his 'epoch'; one who, in other words, 'anticipates psychologically a possible reality'."

Drawing on him, Bourdieu argues for a rational utopianism, rather than pure wishful thinking or objectivist automatism. This rational utopianism should be based on science in order to reason both aims and means. Intellectuals (like himself and Ulrich Beck) should collaborate, leading to projects and action. This is what he calls *reasoned utopianism.*

His line of reasoning can be seen as resembling a fragment of the *Frankfurter Schule*, namely the negative dialectics of Adorno and Horkheimer. Demirovic (2005) reads them as proposing that a better future can develop based on *bestimmte Negation*, i.e. determinate negation which is an "immanent criticism [allowing] to wrest truth from ideology" (Zuidervaart 2007). In fact, notions of basing utopianism on real possibilities are widely shared: Karakayali (2004) and Demirovic (2005) describe such utopianism as a specific critique of the here and now. According to Demirovic, directed and radical change only becomes possible by negating instances of the concrete. He juxtaposes this approach to bourgeois utopianism which stabilises capitalism by posing wishes which are not possible to put into practice. The capitalist society digests the latter kind of utopianism well by teaching people that utopianism does not work out, i.e., by giving the impression that bourgeois utopianism is the only form of utopianism. It does not pose a problem for capitalist society to deal with a few dreamers and a radical youth as long as the latter know that their aims cannot become real anyway. He, like Pepper (2005), thus suggests practical utopianism which helps to transgress the boundaries of the hegemonic towards emancipation. Pepper warns against a 'heterotopia' in which utopian thought and fantasies become part of consumerist culture and "are devoid of social change potential" (ibid., p. 18). Rather, he says we need practical utopianism which helps radical movements to experiment with transgressive practices and thought. Echoing the anarchist ideal[21], he argues that such utopianism cannot be based on blueprints for revolutionary change but needs spaces in which alternative paradigms can be developed and tested while grounding them in an analysis of the local and global social and economic realities.

What could this mean for praxis of environmental management? It seems that negating the hierarchical structure of the organisation implies more than merely

[21] Cf. Franks (2006); but see also more theoretical work by May (1994) and a classic relevant to this case, Rocker (1938).

moving some workers up the decision-making ladder (which would be the orthodox Marxist approach). Rather, negating the structure refers to construction of an alternative structure outside of the organisational hierarchy. This would lead to the conducting of experiments towards socially and ecologically sustainable energy management. Indicators of such a development might be workers who organise themselves externally of the dominating organisational hierarchy (maybe with incentives by other societal actors, like labour unions).

18.6 Conclusion

This article investigated a case of corporate energy management in which the environmental manager used a suggestion scheme to mobilise workers' knowledges to improve the energy and environmental performance of the corporation. We found that the hierarchical form of organisation as well as bodies and forms of knowledge reproduced structurally a contradiction: Hierarchies were deemed instrumental for optimising corporate greening, but effectively prevented this optimisation. Thus, we conclude, good environmental management – situated within the framework of ecological modernisation – sticks to hierarchical organisation. And this very kind of organising constitutes a barrier to sustainable development. In our case this became obvious when showing how proper practice within the hegemonic rationality of ecological modernisation assumes superior knowledge by environmental experts.

These experts occupy positions in social space which allow them to decisively shape corporate environmental decision-making. It is their task to know better than so-called 'average' workers about environmental issues. Therefore, if workers – as shown in this case – frame ideas to contribute to sustainable energy management in a way which is not compatible with the rationality of ecological modernisation then their ideas are likely to be lost. We find that the environmental manager uses a *form of knowledge*, which was specific in fitting to the rationality of ecological modernisation. In the course of this, however, alternative forms and by that bodies of knowledge were sidelined and therefore lost to sustainable development. Thus, the manager's knowledge practice renders corporate energy management unsustainable. This micro-level-based analysis is paralleled by the macro take of Blühdorn and Welsh (2007) who argue that we live in an "era of post-ecologism [where] its eco-politics [are] the politics of unsustainability".

Further, this article argues, hope to overcome these contradiction lies in the negation of hierarchies. Rather than bare adjustment to structures of hierarchies, more sustainable approaches to energy management may be found outside the structures identified as problematic, i.e. outside of hegemonic organisational hierarchies. Thus, for affected to contribute to sustainable development it seems adequate to recommend engaging with experiments outside corporate rationality aiming to reconfigure the structure surrounding the organisation, rather than stabilising it. A social structure outside, which would allow for sustainable energy management within the corporation, would be characterised by its recognition of all forms of knowledge – not limited to knowledges compatible with the rationality of hegemonic ecological modernisation. Of course, I recognise, in practice many might want to follow a dual strategy: reform within as well as stepping outside to question the hierarchies and engage with the experiments. Further research, I suggest, should enquire into how to move existing organisations towards recognising their structural weakness embedded in hierarchical organisation and leading to disregarding a variety of bodies and forms of knowledge.

Acknowledgements

Academic knowledge is not produced by individuals but in networks and communities. For the thoughts and discussions which supported me to develop this paper proposal I am especially grateful to Günter Getzinger (IFZ, Inter-University Research Centre for Technology, Work and Culture) and the Research Fellows und Visiting Scholars of the IAS-STS (Institute for Advanced Studies on Science, Technology and Society). Corinna Bath, Verónica Sanz and Torsten Wöllmann provided valuable hints for sketching the argument. Participants of a seminar at the Institute for Social Ecology of Klagenfurt University as well as of the First ERM Alumni Conference (6-8 October 2008) at the Brandenburg University of Technology contributed helpful feedback to the paper. Judith Ancke helped transcribing interviews and critically commented on the final draft. Thanks also to Robert Atkinson for reviewing the paper and his comments on language as well as to Dmitry Palekhov and Vincent Onyango for pursuing the editing of this book. I gratefully acknowledge the funding by Hans-Böckler-Foundation as well as IAS-STS for facilitating my studies and the German National Academic Foundation for their support during the development of this paper.

References

Bakunin M (1916) God and the State. Mother Earth Publishing Association, New York

Bijker W (1995) Handbook of Science and Technology Studies, Chapter Sociohistorical Technology Studies. Sage Publications in Cooperation with the Society for Social Studies of Science, Thousand Oaks, London, New Delhi

Blühdorn I, Welsh I (2007) Eco-politics beyond the paradigm of sustainability: A conceptual framework and research agenda. In: Environmental Politics 16(2): 185-205

Bourdieu P (1981) Men and machines. In: Knorr-Cetina D, Cicourel AV (eds) Advances in social theory and methodology: Toward an integration of micro- and macro-sociologies. Routledge Kegan Paul, Boston, pp. 304-317

Bourdieu P (1990) The scholastic point of view. In: Cultural Anthropology 5(4): 380-391

Bourdieu P (1998) A reasoned utopia and economic fatalism. In: New Left Review I(227): 125-130

Bourdieu P, Wacquant L (1992) An Invitation to Reflexive Sociology. Polity Press, Cambridge

Buttel F (2000) Ecological modernization as social theory. In: Geoforum 31(1): 57-65
Callon M (1999) Some Elements of a Sociology of Translation: Domestication of the Scallops and the Fishermen of Saint Brieuc Bay. In: The Science Studies Reader. Routledge, New York, London, pp. 67-83
Callon M, Latour B (1981) Unscrewing the Big Leviathan: how actors macrostructure reality and how sociologists help them to do so. In: Knorr-Cetina D, Cicourel AV (eds) Advances in social theory and methodology: Toward an integration of micro- and macro-sociologies. Routledge Kegan Paul, Boston, pp. 277-303
Christoff P (1996) Ecological modernisation, ecological modernities. In: Environmental Politics 5(3): 476-500
Clark B, York R (2005) Carbon metabolism: Global capitalism, climate change, and the biospheric rift. In: Theory and Society 34(4): 391-428
Demirovic A (2005) Zur Dialektik von Utopie und bestimmter Negation. In: Kaindl C (ed) Kritische Wissenschaften im Neoliberalismus, Forum Wissenschaft Studien 49. BdWi-Verlag, Marburg, pp. 143-147
Drake F, Purvis M, Hunt J, Millard D (2003) European business, national priorities: Pioneers and laggards of ecological modernization. In: European Environment 13(3): 164-182
Emerson R, Fretz R, Shaw L (1995) Writing Ethnographic Fieldnotes. Chicago Guides to Writing, Editing, and Publishing. The University of Chicago Press, Chicago, London
Franks B (2006) Rebel Alliances: The means and ends of contemporary British anarchisms. AK Press and Dark Star, Edinburgh
Graeber D (2004) Fragments of an Anarchist Anthropology. Prickly Paradigm Press, Chicago
Haraway D (1991) Simians, Cyborgs, and Women, Chapter 9: Situated Knowledges: The Science Question in Feminism and the Privilege of Partial Perspective. Free Association Books, London, pp. 183-201
Howard-Grenville J (2007) Corporate Culture and Environmental Practice: Making Change at a High-Technology Manufacturer. Edward Elgar Publishing, Cheltenham
Hård M (1994) Technology as practice: Local and global closure processes in diesel-engine design. In: Social Studies of Science 24(3): 549-585
Irwin A (2006) The politics of talk: Coming to terms with the 'new' scientific governance. In: Social Studies of Science 36(2): 299-320
Jänicke M (2008) Ecological modernisation: new perspectives. In: Journal of Cleaner Production 16(5): 557-565
Karakayali N (2004) Reading Bourdieu with Adorno: The limits of critical theory and reflexive sociology. In: Sociology 38(2): 351-368
Keil R, Desfor G (2003) Ecological modernisation in Los Angeles and Toronto. Local Environment 8(1): 27-44
Knorr-Cetina K, Cicourel A (eds) (1981) Advances in social theory and methodology: Toward an integration of micro- and macro-sociologies. Routledge & Kegan Paul, Boston
Kuhn T (1970) The Structure of Scientific Revolutions (2 (enlarged) ed.). The University of Chicago Press, Chicago
Lippert I (2010) Fragments of Environmental Management Studies. Der Andere Verlag, Tönning, Lübeck, Marburg
Lynch M (2004) Science as a vacation: Deficits, surfeits, PUSS, and doing your own job. Workshop: Does STS Mean Business

Malinowski B (1922) Argonauts of the Western Pacific: An Account of Native Enterprise and Adventure in the Archipelagoes of Melanesian New Guinea. Studies in economics and political science no. 65. Routledge and Sons, London

Marcus G (1995) Ethnography in/of the world system: The emergence of multi-sited ethnography. In: Annual Review of Anthropology 24: 95-117

May T (1994) The Political Philosophy of Poststructuralist Anarchism. The Pennsylvania State University Press, Pennsylvania

Mol A (2006) Environment and modernity in transitional China: Frontiers of ecological modernization. In: Development and Change 37(1): 29-56

Mol A, Sonnenfeld D (2000) Ecological Modernization around the World: An Introduction. In: Mol A, Sonnenfeld D (eds) Ecological Modernisation Around the World: Perspectives and Critical Debates. Frank Cass, London, Portland, pp. 3-15

Pellow D, Schnaiberg A, Weinberg A (2000) Putting the Ecological Modernization Thesis to the Test: The Promises and Performance of Urban Recycling. In: Mol A, Sonnenfeld D (eds) Ecological Modernisation Around the World: Perspectives and Critical Debates. Frank Cass, London, Portland, pp. 109-137

Pepper D (2005) Utopianism and environmentalism. In: Environmental Politics 14(1): 3-22

Potter G, López J (2001) After Postmodernism: The Millennium. In: López J, Potter G (eds) After Postmodernism: An Introduction to Critical Realism. The Athlone Press, London, New York, pp. 1-16

Prasad P, Elmes M (2005) In the name of the practical: Unearthing the hegemony of pragmatics in the discourse of environmental management. In: Journal of Management Studies 42(4): 845-867

Rocker R (1938) Anarcho-Syndicalism. Phoenix Press, London

Schinkel W (2003) Pierre Bourdieu's political turn? In: Theory, Culture & Society 20(6): 69-93

Shackley S, Wynne B (1995) Mutual construction. Global climate change: the mutual construction of an emergent science-policy domain. In: Science and Public Policy 22(4): 218-230

Søndergård B, Hansen OE, Holm J (2004) Ecological modernisation and institutional transformations in the Danish textile industry. In: Journal of Cleaner Production 12(4): 337-352

Sonnenfeld D, Mol A (2006) Environmental reform in Asia. Comparisons, challenges, next steps. In: The Journal of Environment & Development 15(2): 112-137

Thomas J (1993) Doing Critical Ethnography. A Sage university paper. Sage Publications, Beverly Hills (Calif.)

Weinstein M (2006) TAMS Analyzer: Anthropology as Cultural Critique in a Digital Age. In: Social Science Computer Review 24(1): 68-77

White D (2006) A political sociology of socionatures: Revisionist manoeuvres in environmental sociology. In: Environmental Politics 15(1): 59-77

Wieser B (2002) If the Public Only Knew! On Learning about Genetic Engineering. In: Bammé A, Getzinger G, Wieser B (eds) Yearbook 2002 of the Institute for Advanced Studies on Science, Technology and Society. Profil, München/Wien, pp. 295-311

Wynne B (1992). Misunderstood misunderstanding: Social identities and public uptake of science. In: Public Understanding of Science 1(3): 281-304

Zuidervaart L (2007) Theodor W. Adorno. In: Online Stanford Encyclopedia of Philosophy. Internet address: http://plato.stanford.edu/entries/adorno/, last accessed on 16.12.2010

19 River Management. Technological Challenge or Conceptual Illusion? Salmon Weirs and Hydroelectric Dams on the Kemi River in Northern Finland

Franz Krause

Department of Anthropology, School of Social Science, University of Aberdeen, Scotland

19.1 Introduction

This paper takes the management of the Kemi River in the Finnish province of Lapland as an example for asking what environmental management is or can do, in practice and in theory. It argues that environmental management – if understood as controlling an environmental phenomenon following a ready-made plan – is not a suitable concept for understanding the interactions between the river and the people on its banks. Either, environmental management has to be defined widely as a dialogue between human and non-human actors, or it must be discarded as the illusion of a modernist, positivist ideology that projects static categories on the world. This paper juxtaposes the dams used for salmon fishing and those used in hydroelectricity production on the Kemi River. It illustrates the adaptability of the former to the river's processes and then shows how very different the technology and rhetoric of the latter appears when it comes to relations with the river. In spite of the significantly larger impacts that hydroelectricity production has on the river as a whole, it will be argued that upon a closer look, the operation of the system of power stations has much in common with that of the salmon weirs.

This paper explores to what degree a river can be managed. Observations along the Kemi River, the principal waterway of the Finnish province of Lapland, suggest that in spite of claims to the contrary, no management regime can control the river. Instead, river management has to be understood as a reciprocal engagement between the 'managers' and the 'object' of management. To clarify this, two types of construction that have been built across the flow of the Kemi River over its eventful history will be juxtaposed. Salmon fishing weirs and hydroelectric dams were both intended to regulate and harvest a particular quality of the river – the rising salmon on the one hand, the water's gravity on the other.

While it seems rather obvious how the construction and operation of salmon fishing weirs reflect the reciprocal engagement of its users with the dynamics of the river, hydroelectricity production appears like a brute attempt of controlling the river in a way that comes close to traditional understandings of 'management'. Hydropower is therefore often stylised as a means of effectively controlling the river, both by proponents and adversaries of the technology. This opposition, however, only holds to an extent. Fishing with salmon weirs was in fact highly institutionalised and in many respects managerial. Also, the actual practice of hydroelectricity production reveals that even this form of river use essentially represents a way of negotiating with the flow, the seasonal variations and the unpredictability of the river. River management, if understood as the manipulation of an environmental phenomenon according to a rigid, ready-made plan, emerges as illusionary. All engagement with a river seems to require reciprocal relations with its dynamics. The argument is based principally on ethnographic fieldwork along the Kemi River that the author conducted from August 2007 to September 2008.

The Kemi River catchment comprises the majority of the Finnish province of Lapland into the Gulf of Bothnia (see Figure 19.1) and the histories of the area and the river have been closely entwined[1]. When the region was settled after the last Ice Age, hunters and fisher people exploited the river's banks for habitation and livelihood. Since the 15th century, settlers from Karelia, Southern and Eastern Finland arrived on the scene, using the river as a means of transport through the mostly wooded and swampy area. Towns and villages were established along the river and its flow, waters and ice served a host of purposes, from sanitation and transportation to the provision of fishing grounds.

The exceptionally rich salmon fishery on the Kemi River had, in the Middle Ages, already attracted the attention of the Swedish Crown and the Christian Churches (Vilkuna 1975). Not only were they eager to baptise the people who would gather each year to seize, salt and sell the rising fish; at least as much, they were keen to levy taxes on the catch. Later, when the consolidation of territorial claims became an issue of national interest, the settlement into this peripheral area was encouraged by policies such as exemption from tax or military service for those who would dare to establish a home there. With the onset of industrialisation, factories were built on the river, taking advantage of its power to drive mechanical and later electrical machinery. The predominant industry was – and still is – the wood-processing business, providing timber for construction and small wooden products, but mainly producing pulp and paper. Until less than 20 years ago, the bulk of the logs that had been cut throughout the watershed[2] were floated along the many tributaries into the main course of the Kemi River and from there to the factories that were situated mainly at the river's mouth.

[1] As will become clear throughout the paper, the river is approached analytically as shaped by various influences, including – but not limited to – human actions. Therefore, it can be called a 'hybrid' phenomenon (see Lippert, this volume) or an 'organic machine' to take White's (1995) term.

[2] I use the term 'watershed' in its American connotation, identical to the British 'catchment area' or 'drainage basin'.

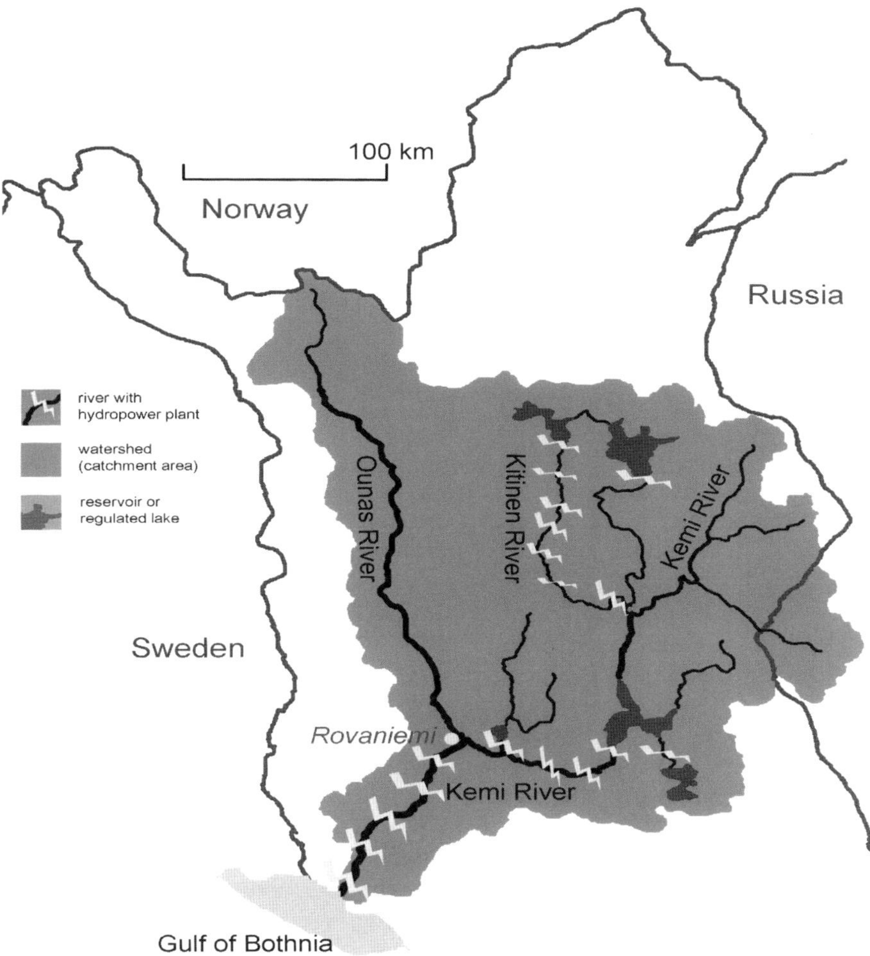

Fig. 19.1. The Kemi River watershed in the Finnish province of Lapland: Over two thirds of the province is drained by this river into the Gulf of Bothnia (Baltic Sea). Most of the salmon fishing took place between Rovaniemi and the mouth of the river. Since the mid 20th century, 18 major hydropower stations have been constructed mostly along the main channel, but also along the tributary Kitinen River. Reservoirs and lakes are used to buffer some of the seasonal variation of the river's discharge. Since 1983, the tributary Ounas River is protected by law against hydropower construction (based on Kemijoki Group 2008, p. 51)

19.2 The Kemi River as a Hydropower Source

Today, the single most prominent use of the Kemi River is the production of hydroelectricity. There are currently eighteen major hydropower plants in the watershed (Figure 19.1), sixteen of which are owned and operated by a single company[3] and a further power station is planned. In addition to the power plants along the course of the river, other plants are situated at lakes and reservoirs, which enable the electricity company to regulate the river's flow both on a daily basis and over the course of the year. The company produces almost one third, 31.4 percent in 2007, of Finland's hydroelectric power, which altogether amounts to roughly 18 percent of the national electricity production (Kemijoki Group 2008, p. 10). More important than the absolute amount of electricity produced, however, is the distinctive feature of hydropower in the overall mix of electricity production: the amount of water that is allowed through the turbines can be instantaneously regulated in order to adjust the production to match the current consumption of energy. While nuclear or coal-powered electricity plants provide high overall output, their production is very slow to adjust and impossible to fine-tune.

From a 'control room', situated in the headquarters of the hydroelectricity company in the provincial capital Rovaniemi, such regulation and fine-tuning is supervised. Adding to the automatic adjustments of the individual turbines to the slightest changes in the electricity network, the engineers[4] in the control room assign distinct production targets to the power plants in the watershed, which, when totalled, meet the overall demand for every individual hour of the day (Figure 19.2). Typically, the turbines are nearly closed down during the night, produce a lot of energy in the morning, slightly reduce the production towards midday, and peak a second time in the afternoon to then decrease production again for the night. At night, electricity production tends to drop off to around ten percent of the daytime maximum. Moreover, less hydroelectricity is produced during the weekends than during weekdays. To what extend the turbines produce electricity is centrally determined from the control room. Although the individual power stations are staffed for part of the day, this is only for monitoring and maintenance work – electricity production is steered from Rovaniemi.

---

[3] In fact, this company has recently taken to steering electricity production even at the two major power stations owned by another company. The electricity output of those two stations is credited to the owning company, but their regulation is achieved in accord with the long chain of other hydropower stations on the river. There are three smaller hydroelectric power stations with minor capacity in the Kemi River watershed, located at lakes on small tributaries. They are owned by different power companies and will be disregarded for the present analysis.

[4] Although I use the term 'engineers' when talking about the personnel in the control room, not all of them are in fact engineers. Two of the senior employees are actually a mathematician and a former electrician, respectively.

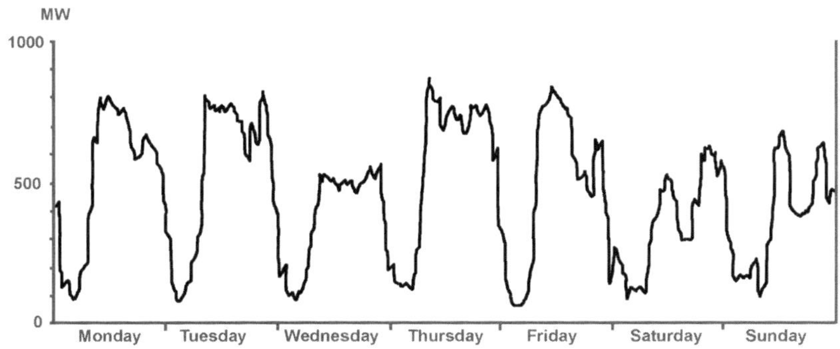

Fig. 19.2. Electricity generation (in megawatts (MW)) of the main hydropower company on the Kemi River during one representative week in September 2007. The pattern shows a stark increase of production in the morning and a sharp decrease during the night of each day, generally with two peaks during each day before midday and in the late afternoon. Hydroelectricity generation on Saturday and Sunday is less than on usual weekdays (based on Kemijoki Group 2008, p. 10)

In order to manage the river in this way, the power company regulates the discharge from all the eighteen major hydroelectric plants every day around the clock. Because the river's surface is frozen for about half a year and precipitation falls as snow which accumulates on the land and on the ice instead of draining into the river, its flow diminishes considerably over the year. Therefore, to continue electricity production all year round – particularly in the cold and dark winter, when demand is high – large reservoirs are filled over the summer and gradually emptied over the winter (Figure 19.3). Because in lakes and reservoirs, only the top layer is frozen over the winter, water can be easily extracted from underneath this ice layer, even at temperatures far below the freezing point. Efficient hydroelectricity generation seem thus to require both short- and long-term regulation, through power plants and reservoirs respectively. Short-term regulation of the river's flow enables the tuning of hydroelectricity production to electricity demand; and long-term regulation of the watercourse attempts to adjust the seasonality of the river to the seasonality of electricity use. To be able to accomplish this task, the engineers in charge have to know and continuously monitor the river very well. For instance they have to be familiar with the amount of time that the water takes to travel from one power station to the next. They can rely on a host of data that is available in their company's control room, but at times some of them prefer to obtain first-hand visual impressions and drive to various parts of the river to take a look themselves.

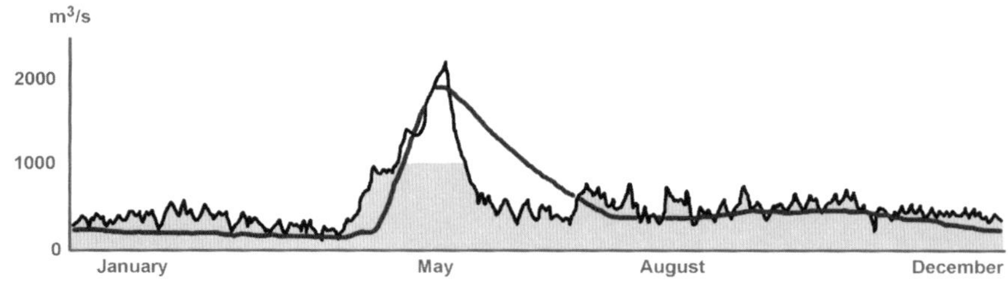

Fig. 19.3. River discharge (in cubic metres per second, m3/s) from one of the hydropower stations on the Kemi River's main channel in 2007. The black line indicates the actual discharge, the shaded area under the curve represents the amount of water that was used for electricity generation. The white area between black line and shaded area stands for the amount of water that was spilled past the turbines during the spring flood, when discharge exceeded the turbines capacity of 1000 m3/s. The grey line indicates the discharge that would occur at the locality without storing flood water in the reservoirs and daily regulating the flow (based on Kemijoki Group 2008, p. 10)

The large-scale harnessing of the Kemi River for hydroelectricity began after the Second World War, when Finland executed major infrastructure projects throughout the country and invested into the economic development of the province of Lapland, which had suffered severely during the war. Hydroelectricity was a major component of the development strategy, along with road construction and the settlement of small farms in the region. After a private company had built two power stations in the watershed, it ran out of money, which prompted the state to set up an institution that was solely meant to develop hydroelectricity on the Kemi River. This state-owned company built power plants along the main course of the river from the early 1950s and constructed large reservoirs during the 1960s. In the 1980s and 90s, the harnessing of water power was extended into a major tributary of the river. Plans to build a further large reservoir on the headwaters of the river were debated for decades until they were ruled out of order by the Finnish Supreme Administrative Court in 2002. Another large tributary had already been placed under natural protection in 1983, banning all constructions for hydroelectricity generation. Under the present legal and technical conditions, there is only a single location on the Kemi River that seems appropriate for the construction of a further power plant. The respective plans exist and hydroelectricity engineers point out that this power station will complete the infrastructure to regulate the entire main course of the river in one 'chain'.

19.3 Salmon Weirs on the Kemi River

When the first hydroelectric dam on the river was finished in 1948, its impacts on the ecology of the river and on the livelihoods of the inhabitants of its banks were regarded as secondary to the goals of national progress and regional development[5] towards which it was seen to contribute. This was in spite of the fact that the dam was situated at the river's mouth and blocked migrating fish from entering the river from the sea. A few years later, the salmon population in the Kemi River – formerly one of the richest of the Baltic Sea – had ceased to exist. Salmon spawn and hatch in the oxygen-rich waters of a fast-running river stretch and swim to the sea as smolts when a few years old. In the sea they live for another couple of years, feeding plentifully and growing big. Then they return to the river where they were born, to spawn there themselves. Once this cycle is permanently broken, it is rather difficult to re-establish a salmon population in a particular river (Karlsson and Karlström 1994).

For centuries, salmon had provided a major source of nutrition and income for the inhabitants of the region, particularly along the lower Kemi River. A brief description of the technology and organisation of the formerly prominent way of salmon fishing on the river will shed light on the very different nature of this type of river management. Salmon fishing was not about managing the water's gravity, but about harvesting a particular quality from the river nonetheless. Salmon fishing weirs provide an illuminating contrast to the hydroelectric dams portrayed above: they were built also to regulate a certain aspect of the river, but interacted with the stream in a somewhat different way.

Each year, when the ice on the river opened in spring, salmon began to swim upstream from the sea and the farmers on the river's banks developed different techniques for catching the valuable and nutritious animals. Probably the most effective and impressive of those was a type of weir that was constructed from the shore far into the river[6] (Figure 19.2). The weir was made from wooden poles that

[5] Finland had just lost a war against the Soviet Union, and with it large territories and a considerable share of its infrastructure, including one third of its hydropower production capacity. The country had to re-settle over ten percent of its population from the ceded areas, and pay large reparations to the Soviet Union. Particularly the province of Lapland was seen as in dire need of infrastructure, as most of its bridges had been blasted and buildings had been burnt by German troops retreating after the Finnish-Soviet armistice in 1944. Hydroelectric stations on the Kemi River were considered a twofold solution: They served both as bridges and for electricity production. Furthermore, they conformed to the view – widely shared among the decision-makers in the far away national capital – that Northern Finland is a store of resources that must be harnessed for national progress and paying reparations (Massa 1994, pp. 200-266).

[6] It is worthwhile noting that these weirs almost completely disappeared from the Kemi River not because of the collapse of the salmon population after 1948, but because of the growing influence of the wood-processing industry throughout Lapland a few decades earlier. The industry was interested in using the entire main channel of the river for loose log floating, which at the time was cheaper than the previous practice of floating in rafts. Only in very few places – usually in secondary river channels – did salmon weirs survive until the construction of the first hydropower plant, after which also those sites had to be abandoned. In the meantime, however, salmon fishing had of course continued employing other techniques, like mobile nets, hooks, etc.

were fixed on the riverbed and connected by further poles above the water surface. Along these poles a net or a layer of brushwood was attached, so that the rising salmon were forced to swim along the weir. Into the weir was built an enclosure in which the salmon were trapped and lifted out of the water with large nets several times a day (Vilkuna 1975).

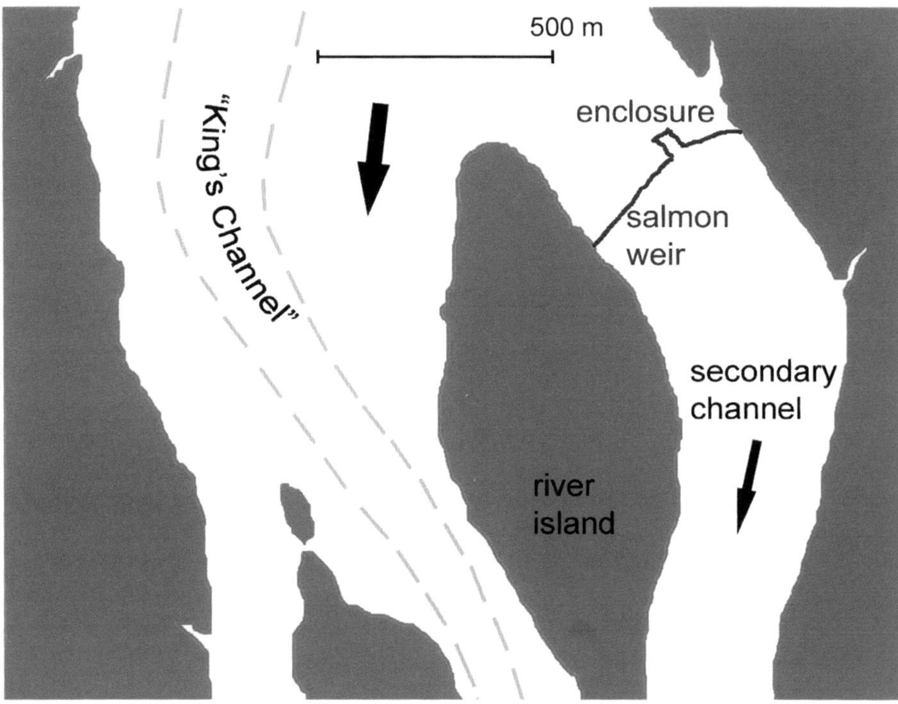

Fig. 19.4. The salmon weir of the village Muurola on the Kemi River in the 19th century: The weir was built across a secondary river channel, making salmon that rose through this channel swim along the weir, which led them into the enclosure where they were trapped. The deepest third of the river, the 'King's Channel' was left open, allowing sufficient numbers of salmon to escape and reproduce (adopted from: Vilkuna 1975, p. 220, Figure 84).

Because of the dimensions of this weir, individual families were not able to build or operate it on their own. Instead, cooperatives were formed that shared the material and labour inputs as well as the catch. During the winter, these cooperatives gathered the necessary construction material and after the spring flood had ceased, they built the weirs into the river. This was a cumbersome and challenging task, because the current was still rather strong at that time of year. Once it was completed, the weir was operated until the salmon stopped rising up the river in late summer. In many places and particularly during the richest catching period in late spring, the weirs were attended to around the clock by small groups from the respective cooperative. Small repairs had to be undertaken constantly and the nets in the enclosure had to be hauled in and maintained. The catch then had to be cleaned and prepared for storage or sale, which mostly meant salting it in large barrels. In order not to compromise the quality of a particular catching place, the weirs were carefully deconstructed each year when the catching season ended. If rocks or pole stumps were left in the river, the water would not flow there the same way in the following year, which might deter salmon from choosing this particular route on their journey up the river.

Only particular places on the river were appropriate for the construction of a weir. These places were of course highly disputed and different arrangements were agreed to over the course of history. The more the interest and influence of the Swedish crown, and later the Russian Tsar and the Finnish State, grew in the region's salmon fishery, and the more the established fisher people saw their privileges jeopardised by newcomers, the more the fishing groups and the distribution of weirs and catching places was institutionalised. Whereas the weirs had been operated by loosely organised groups of inhabitants and seasonal fishermen during the Middle Ages, their organisation was somewhat formalised by the levying of taxes by the church from the 14th century onwards. In the early 17th century, membership in such groups was limited to local land-owners. The maximum catch allowed to a particular fishing family was set proportional to the tax they paid for their lands. In the second half of the 17th century, a system was introduced that rotated the operation of particular weirs on certain catching places among the now closed fishing groups. If a group would have fished at catching place *A* last year, they would move downstream to catching place *B* this year and construct their weir at place *C* next year.

Another important rule concerned the limits of the weirs across the river. One third of the diameter of the stream, where the river was at its deepest, had to be left open. Weirs were not allowed in this channel so that some salmon were always able to escape the nets, reproduce and ensure the durability of the fishery. When the influence of royal fishery regulations increased in the 17th century, this portion came to be known as the King's Channel. But even before, it could happen that upstream fisher people would destroy a weir that they deemed as a violation of this rule. Salmon fishing was – in spite of the abundance of fish – never a very peaceful or harmonious activity: there were continuous quarrels about the position and size of weirs, the ownership of fishing rights and the violation thereof, as well as about the taxation by Crown and Church. Fishing with weirs thus regulated the river, predominantly in terms of its salmon movements, and mediated the relations of the riverside population with the river, particularly in terms of access to benefits – in many ways similar to electricity generation with hydropower dams.

Although weirs represented the most elaborate fishing technique on the Kemi River, it was only one technique among many that were employed according to the time of year, the characteristics of the river at a particular locality and the concomitant behaviour of the salmon (Vilkuna 1975, pp. 35-39). In early spring, when the ice broke and the river flooded, short weirs were built by individual families on the shore in front of their houses. The current was much too rough and the river too broad for the construction of larger weirs. Additionally, the salmon preferred to swim close to the shore because the current was weaker there. Where possible, people fished with a host of different nets, depending on whether they were fishing in a rapid, in a slowly-flowing stretch or close to the shore. When the salmon stopped rising upstream around the end of July, the large weirs were deconstructed and people fished predominantly with dragnets. Even later in the year, stationary nets were used that were spread on the bottom of quiet and shallow pools. When in early autumn the salmon would settle in particular places to spawn, fisher people would use fish forks to catch them. Finally, salmon returning to the sea in late autumn were caught in bow nets placed in rapids where the river would not freeze.

19.4 Degrees of Management

Salmon weirs and hydroelectric dams constitute two particular constructions that have been built across the Kemi River in order to harvest a particular quality from it. The former were meant to make the rising salmon accessible to humans taking advantage of their migration pattern, the latter are made to make accessible the power inherent in the river's water due to the elevation from the sea level and the slope of the stream. Both types of construction can be therefore referred to as 'regulators' of the river and their utilisations display many similarities. The relations of the respective actors with the river seem very different, however. While salmon weirs clearly represent a means of attentive engagement with the river, hydroelectric dams appear to embody an attempt to control it. The former appear to be an expression of the mutual influence of landscape and people; the latter a part of a regime of resource management.

A relation, where one side manages the other, presupposes a certain degree of sovereignty and control over the other side. Only if we are in a position to somewhat impose our ideas on something can we manage it. Imposing ideas on, or applying a ready-made plan to an environmental phenomenon implies that the actor has to command both physical and conceptual power over this phenomenon. On the one hand, the very material dimensions of the environmental event must be controlled; on the other hand, this intervention must concur with a particular image of the environmental phenomenon: what it is like, why it must be managed and how it is likely to react to this intervention.

Hydroelectricity production has often been portrayed as a means of effectively controlling a river. The very architecture and related symbolism of large dams epitomises human mastery over nature (Blackburn 2006, pp. 189-197 on dams in Germany; or Worster 1985 on water engineering in the US American West), or the "technocratic hubris of engineering and its claim to outwit and control nature" (Adams et al. 2004, p. 1932; see also McCully 2001). It is worth the while to investigate how far hydroelectric dams on the Kemi River actually conform to this claim.

The power company, according to this claim, has to control the Kemi River both physically, through dams, reservoirs, channels and floodgates; and conceptually, through pinning it down on maps, in data tables and through diagrams[7]. Hydrological data, precipitation data and available water at any one moment in time and for different scenarios, belong to such conceptual control. The control room in the headquarters of the company sports 26 computer screens, presenting electricity production targets, water levels at different places throughout the watershed, representations of electrical circuits, highly stylised maps of the river and a host of further data depending on the current decision to be made. There are six conventional telephones on the control desk and an additional cordless phone circulates through the room. With this level of information technology and with a watershed broken down into numbers, graphs, tables and single-purpose maps, the Kemi River does appear like a manageable object, a rather complex one indeed, but nevertheless under control.

Leaving the control room and looking at the immense structures of the hydropower stations on the river, this impression remains strong: From the reservoirs on the headwaters to the Bothnian Bay, water passes through up to 15 power stations in a row, flowing along a total of over 35 kilometres of concrete and earthen dams around the stations – not to mention the dozens of kilometres of embankments that have been constructed elsewhere along the river to deal with the hydroelectricity-related changes in the water level. At the power stations, the water falls between seven and 30 metres, thereby turning the huge turbines to generate electricity. Most often, the river is diverted from its former river bed into a canal downstream of the power station, in order to increase its flow away from the dam and thereby maintain a high falling distance ('head') at the power station. Particularly when observed from downstream, the dams and power stations are thoroughly impressive for their size and control of the water, a construction of earth, concrete and steel towers high above, and the wide river upstream is channelled through a single location – the power house – and released downstream sizzling and gurgling in a rather narrow but deep canal. During the spring flood, the engineers in the control room command over 40 flood gates along the river to channel some of its flow around the turbines working at full capacity. One can stand at a hydroelectric plant a few hours drive away from Rovaniemi and watch stunned the opening of such a flood gate, when suddenly a hundred or so cubic metres of water per second cascade from the steel and concrete dam – knowing that this magnificent show is the result of a mouse-click in the headquarters.

Thus, it seems that the hydropower company has achieved a considerable degree of control over the river. From the control room in Rovaniemi, the river's flow can be manipulated in large parts of the watershed and whatever happens of importance along the river seems to be visible on the screens in the control room. Physical and conceptual control of the Kemi River's flow allow the company to 'drive' the river as it suits their needs – mostly defined by the electricity market.

[7] Of course, also salmon fishermen had their own images of the river and information about its characteristics. In fact, they were crucial for successfully constructing and maintaining the salmon weirs. Such 'data', however, were of a somewhat different kind; not abstract and numerical, but grown from personal experiences with the river, the weirs and the fish.

19.5 Controlling a River's Flow?

Physical and conceptual control of a river go hand in hand, an increase in one facilitates an increase in the other; ultimately they really amount to the same thing. Also, physical-conceptual control inevitably changes its object, in this case the river. It first of all makes it a bounded object: it defines what the river is and what it is not; what belongs to the thing to be managed and what does not; and naturally assumes that it is a separate entity from those who manage it. Furthermore, it makes the phenomenon conform to the numbers and other representations that are used to describe and control it. If a map, for instance, depicts a particular layout of the river and the river shifts its course or inundates its surroundings, this is seen as a deviation from the 'real' river and measures are taken to prevent such deviations: more dams are built, flood-protection reservoirs are constructed and an increased number of meteorological stations are operated. Thereby, physical-conceptual control is predisposed to render the river a static thing, both in thinking and in material terms. In addition, resource management presupposes a degree of predictability, because particular actions are intended to yield particular outcomes. Data are gathered to know as much as possible about the river and to be able to predict which effects a management decision will have. Discharge and water level are constantly measured at a great many locations, precipitation and temperatures are assessed and forecast and a database contains the same information for many past decades. Not incidentally, the slogan on the power company's website reads: "Hydro power is generated from countless elements. We know them all."[8] Such an approach sees the river as the sum of a host of different details that only need to be known in order to properly deal with the river. Not only does this present the river as made up from many little, separate elements, it also believes that all of them *can be* known.

River water, however, defies such an approach in many ways. First of all, a river is essentially a flow, not a bounded object. This implies that what are often described as different parts of a whole, are in fact phenomena that could not exist without the other parts. More than from different separate elements, a river is made up from mutually dependent components. The salmon life cycle is only one case in point. The river's flow incorporates its source, the groundwater, adjacent bogs, the sea, the weather and different places, people and their activities. None of them is really a discrete 'thing' on its own. Objectifying the river as a separate entity severs all these relations and makes the very object meaningless (cf. Ingold 2008). Furthermore, trying to control a river is an endeavour against the river itself, because such an attempt can hardly deal with its inherent irregularity; seasonal variations, floods, changes in the course and the continuous processes of erosion and sedimentation make it very difficult to pin down what the river is and even more challenging to control it. The Kemi River's surface is frozen for about half a year and so is the ground around it. During the spring flood, the river's discharge is more that tenfold the amount it carries during a dry summer. And while

---

[8] http://www.kemijoki.fi/Kemijoki/kemijoki.nsf/indexLan2, last accessed on January 15, 2009

its swiftly flowing waters in summer, as well as its thick ice crust in winter provide an inviting arena for a host of activities by the region's inhabitants, the ice floes and frigid waters that make up the river in late spring and autumn are extremely dangerous for human beings.

Therefore it is not surprising that living on and with the Kemi River has for a long time been more of a cyclical process than an advancement in degree of control. Many structures on and across the river have long been – and some still are – temporary. Where a ferry links two parts of a village in the summer, an ice bridge is constructed in the winter, when the ferry is of no use. During the spring flood, neither ice bridge nor ferry connects the two shores, as the ice has been washed downstream and the ice floes on the river, as well as a highly increased discharge, prohibit the operation of a ferry. People cannot cross the river, but instead of getting frustrated about this, they attend to activities around their homes that do not require travelling to the other side. And lucky school children have a reason to miss class. For timber floating, temporary embankments were built over one hundred springs and summers and deconstructed in the fall. Over the winter, a great many bays in the river's shores were used to store the booms from which the structures for timber floating were reassembled anew each spring, when the ice began to weaken. During late spring and summer, the river was first and foremost a road for logs that made their way from the vast inland forests to the industrial centres at the seashore. Salmon weirs are only one more case in point and to the list can be added many more uses of the river. Such arrangements suggest that both social and ecological life is inherently seasonal (cf. Mauss 1979) and our recent obsession with powerful, permanent structures goes against this dynamic.

Hydroelectric dams, however, are essentially meant to control the flow of the river, rather than to flow with it. Dams impound reservoirs and regulate the level of lakes, they attempt to control the annual spring flood, influence the amount of discharge and determine the surface level along the river. Arguably, the hydroelectricity company has attained a considerable degree of control over the Kemi River. The flow of the river can be attuned to the demands of the common electricity market of the Northern European countries[9]. Apparently, the river is made to live according to the rhythms of modern human life – not vice versa.

In order to achieve this degree of control, however, substantial social and ecological costs have been incurred and a host of negative side-effects has been produced. The elevated water level made many shore-based farms unviable, because they depended on the annually flooded fields for hay production in order to feed their cattle over the long winter. With a higher water table, many of these fields became water-logged or were submerged (Massa 1983, pp. 108-125). Continuous changes in the water level, due to the daily fluctuations in energy production, continue to erode the river's banks to a much larger degree than has been the case before dams were built. People living on the river were displaced with them their life-styles and a part of Finnish tradition. Many ecological processes were dis-

[9] Finland, Sweden, Norway and Denmark are linked by a common electricity network and market, NordPool, which means that demands for hydroelectricity from the Kemi River arise not only in Finland, but even, for instance, in Denmark.

turbed, among which the disappearance of salmon[10] was only one, albeit probably the economically most significant. Other locally highly valued fish species, such as grayling and trout, need a river habitat with fast-flowing and oxygen-rich water at least during one crucial stage in their life cycle; exactly these habitats, however, are the very rapids that have to be dammed for hydroelectricity production. The vanishing of grayling and trout leaves the river to other species, that many people consider hardly worthwhile catching. Arguably, this is one of the factors why the inhabitants of the river's banks do not engage with its waters as much as they used to. Another reason for this might be that today the river is – in many places – absent from the acoustic environment: whereas a rapid is constantly present acoustically for the surrounding population, the pool that stretches for kilometres upstream from hydropower stations is mostly inaudible. Furthermore, the regulation of the river's flow regime changed the ice conditions along its course, thereby often compromising popular winter practices such as ice-fishing and moving on frozen watercourses by ski or snowmobile.

19.6 Challenges to Hydroelectricity Production

Regulating the river is necessary to adjust the rhythm of the river to the rhythm of electricity consumption. It has to flow more intensely during morning and afternoon peaks of microwave and electric light use. Its spring flood waters should be contained for electrical heating during the next winter. And – particularly in times where carbon dioxide emissions have to be curbed – every drop of water that is allowed down the river without turning the turbines is a waste of energy, or even a furthering of global warming. People have to manage the river, determine how it flows and thereby decide what is and is not to live there.

But, does the power company actually succeed in such a control? Can its computer systems and concrete masses really determine how the Kemi River flows? To what extent is such a view – that a river can be made to conform to a strategy thought out in a control room or determined by the electricity market – an illusion? In how far can solid structures and hard data control a river? Turning away from the stark impressions of the control room and the armoured concrete structures of the hydropower stations and focussing on the actual tasks of those engineers and other staff who actually make the decisions about how to produce a particular amount of electricity with a current state of the river, helps to qualify this issue. In many ways, of course, these actors do manipulate the river substantially: controlling generator intakes, floodgates and reservoir outlets with just a click on a computer gives them considerable power over some of the river's processes. But naturally there is more to a river than these mechanical structures. The state of the river not only depends on how far floodgates or generator intakes are opened or

[10] Damming the river's mouth led not only to the displacement of salmon, but of other migratory fish species as well, most notably – in terms of local use – white fish and lamprey.

closed, but on a host of other factors as well, over which the power company cannot have any influence: For instance, forests and swamps throughout the watershed keep changing their characteristics as they are deforested and the ground ploughed for reforestation, some areas are ditched to enhance wood or hay harvests, or abandoned ditches are eroding and the landscape reverts to a state as it might have been many decades ago. All this influences how much water is – and other substances are – in the river.

Another factor largely out of reach of the control room managers is the weather: How much it rains or snows, how quickly the snow melts, how much water evaporates or seeps into the ground is something the power company can only react to – not steer or control. Even the intricate forecasting technology that measures – among other things – snow depth, temperature and discharge across the watershed and combines these data with meteorological information to calculate scenarios for the state of the river, is insufficient for actual decision-making. Particularly concerning the marked seasonal variations of the river and its environment over the year, these climatic factors influence the river much beyond the reach of hydroelectricity engineers. Even those members of staff who fully trust in the flow-manipulation machinery are aware that the forming of an ice cover on the river in late autumn and the breaking up of the ice in spring are very sensitive periods, when hydroelectricity production must be subordinated to more pressing issues on the river. In autumn, it is important that a stable ice cover forms on the river as quickly as possible. On the one hand, this has to do with the demands of the riverside population, who are interested in using the river ice for ice-skating, skiing, snowmobiling and even playing 'ice golf', alongside the ice bridges that enable transport across the river in some places. On the other hand however, a reliable ice cover is essential for the very functioning of the hydropower stations. A continuous ice cover, preferably with some snow on top, acts as an insulator between the water in the river and the air above. The water will then never quite reach the freezing point, even if air temperature reaches minus 30 degrees Celsius or colder, which is not infrequent in a Lappish winter. If this ice cover is not continuous, however, the air will cool the river water below the freezing point, where it forms so-called 'frazil ice', small ice crystals in the water that readily stick to any surface the water touches. Thus, not only can the flow of the river be hampered when this frazil ice accumulates around rocks in the river bed, but it can also seriously damage hydropower facilities, like the turbine's rotor blades, should it enter a power station. Frazil ice forms particularly in river stretches with fast water movement, such as rapids, but also in calmer stretches, if no ice cover has formed due to continuous and pronounced changes in the water level – as created by hydropower generation. Therefore, in order to preserve infrastructure and good relations with the neighbours, manipulation of the river in late autumn is a very delicate matter for the hydropower company.

Similar observations apply in spring: When the snow melts and the river swells to a tenfold volume of its winter flow, the ice crust breaks up and heavy ice floes float down the river. The amount of water starkly exceeds the capacity of the turbines, so that floodgates have to be opened at the dams, to channel a large portion of the river water around the hydropower stations. On the one hand, because water is so abundant during the flood, the turbines run continuously at full capacity, generating a large amount of electricity every day. On the other hand, because of the increased water volume in the river, the head at the individual power stations is reduced; hence they produce less energy per unit of water. Furthermore, by this continuous production, some of the regulatory capacity of hydroelectricity is lost. The special – and also financially highly priced – feature of hydropower, to balance out the daily variations in electricity demand by instantaneously adjusting production, is mostly absent during the flood. A rather complicated task at this time of year for hydroelectric engineers is to keep the water level along the river within the limits specified by their power plant operation licences. Every licence for running a hydroelectricity plant states exactly, how high or low the water table may be above its dam (Holm 1991, pp. 116-120) – during flood times, these limits are even more difficult to keep than during the rest of the year.

The most dreaded event during the spring flood, for hydroelectric engineers and other river-dwellers alike, is the formation of an 'ice dam', that is, the conglomeration of ice floes across the river, jamming its flow and causing the water upstream to rise. The water level during flood times is already exceptionally high, but when an ice dam forms and accumulates sufficient further ice floes, the water can rise to a level that inundates and damages not only roads and auxiliary buildings like barns and saunas, but also people's homes. Ice dams are prone to form on shallow river stretches with rocks close to the surface, like in rapids and on particularly narrow points along its course. Furthermore, they can occur when an upstream section of the river has already discharged its ice cover, while there is still solid ice on a downstream part, so that the floes get stuck on the edge of the persisting ice crust. This used to happen only rarely on the Kemi River, because its upstream sections lie northwards and north-eastwards from the downstream river, in colder regions thus, where the spring flood would set in later. Since the construction of hydroelectric infrastructure on the river, however, the latter kind of ice dam has become a real threat, because the ice cover does not readily leave the pools upstream of the power stations, where the current is slow. Thus, the power company tends to get blamed for many damages associated with the spring flood and ice dams. Arguably, during spring the river controls the hydroelectricity engineers more than they control the river, as their main occupation seems to consist of averting damages to their infrastructure and public image.

Such rather concrete threats are not the only factors limiting the hydroelectricity engineers' grip on the river. Changing climate patterns, for instance, make the reliance on data that has been collected over the decades less meaningful. Observations from the past are unlikely to be indicative of what happens in the future. Mild winters, wet summers and various unpredictable and extreme weather events are prone to considerably change how the river is – and can be – dealt with. This results in more of an 'experimenting' with the river, than a well thought out managing of it. For instance, it is projected that in the near future, precipitation in late autumn will increasingly be in the form of rain – instead of snow – which enlarges the river's volume. At this time of year, however, the reservoirs throughout the watershed are usually full to the brim, because they are anticipated to store as much water as possible for the winter. Therefore, there will be the risk of an 'autumn flood', albeit with less overall discharge than in spring, but also with reduced capacities to mitigate it, as the reservoirs, that serve to buffer the peak of the flood discharge in spring, cannot be resorted to.

19.7 Dealing with a Flowing River

Such future scenarios, as well as the description of challenges around river ice, might give the impression that hydroelectricity engineers would be particularly worried during autumn and spring, or regarding the future. I have, however, not found this to be the case. Quite on the contrary, these periods of increased attention blend in smoothly with their work throughout the rest of the year. When dealing with the Kemi River, anything can happen – anytime. Part of a generator might suddenly break, some electrical equipment might malfunction, or a few rainy days might raise the water level at a particular reach to unforeseen heights. Even if nothing unforeseen happens, the engineers' grip on the river is never totally fast: no matter what they do, the river flows and if their dams are not opened according to this constant stream of water, reservoirs and river will overflow. The control room staff knows this and knows just as well that engaging with a river requires much more than sitting in the control room watching screens and pushing buttons. A leading figure of this staff, for instance, proposes to supplement the numerical data constantly flowing into the computers with more visual and acoustic information from the power stations. For example, it can be decisive to actually see the ice floes upstream from a power station, in order to sensibly decide how to work the flood gates so that potential damage is averted. Similarly, installing microphones at the turbines should enable engineers to find out what is going on at the particular plant more readily than – or at least complementary to – merely figures about electrical currents and circuits.

During winter, two members of staff regularly drive along the river throughout the municipality of Rovaniemi in order to get a first-hand impression of the quality of ice cover. This is particularly relevant during late autumn and early winter, when the ice is forming. For the public image of the hydropower company, the stretch of the river around Rovaniemi is especially important, as about one third of the entire population of the province of Lapland lives in this area. Here, direct observations of the river's surface can be more significant than data tables and computer models. If – as has been the case for several weeks during the rather mild winter of 2007-08 – the ice cover is too fragile or features too many open spots, all the hydroelectricity engineers can do, is to not manage the river very much at all: allowing the river to flow evenly and slowly is the best recipe for the formation of stable ice.

Also during spring, in order to better estimate the extent of the coming flood, hydroelectricity producers do not rely on figures and models retrievable on the screens in the control room. The same two members of staff who drive along the river in the winter embark upon a reconnaissance flight over the fringes of the watershed in spring. During the flight in a tiny propeller plane they closely watch and photograph the amount of snow and water in the landscape, estimating from their observations the amount of water that will descend the river during spring, as well as gauging approximately when this will happen, or over which period of time. A moderate amount of snow, melting quickly during a sudden heat spell, can cause a much larger flood than a huge amount of snow that melts slowly because of low temperatures.

A further fact that precludes a genuine 'management' of the Kemi River is that the hydroelectricity producers' lives are interwoven with the river in many ways that have little to do with hydropower. They all live close to it and spend a considerable part of their leisure time at, on and in the river. Some even grew up along the river. The hydroelectricity company owns a number of cabins on the Kemi River and its tributaries, which employees can, and often do, utilize. Hydroelectricity producers thus know and experience the river not merely as a power resource, but also by fishing, skiing, swimming and living with it. Many of the engineers' ideas about the river do not come from books or hydroelectricity production, but from their childhood and leisure time experiences. To an extent, the river has become part of the engineers' personalities. Therefore, it is unlikely that the Kemi River figures in their work merely as an object of management.

Focussing on the practices of hydroelectricity production, instead of solely on the immensity of the dams and data employed, a rather different image emerges than that of a subjugation of the river. The people working in the power company have to know the river exceptionally well and they must constantly negotiate the energy demands of the electricity market with the actual state of the river. This relation is not adequately described with the concept of 'control'. Even 'management' – if understood as the manipulation of an environmental phenomenon according to a predefined plan – captures the reality of hydroelectric production only partially. In fact, hydroelectricity producers do not manage the river any more than the river manages them.

19.8 Conclusion: The Limits of River 'Management'

What is thus to be made of river management? Is it possible at all? Or does the very logic of a river – its flow, its seasonal variation and its unpredictability – preclude the idea of management, if not understood as a reciprocal relation of engagement? Is it useful to further the ideal of river management by increasing the amount of structures and data to tighten the grip on an ephemeral flow? Or would a fundamentally different approach do the river more justice – and thereby also work better?

Arguably, the actual practice of hydroelectricity production – as opposed to the ideal to which it is often stylised by both proponents and adversaries – can serve as a point of departure for thinking about such an alternative. With its pronounced elements of negotiating with the dynamics of the river, this practice is – at closer inspection – much more similar to that of constructing and maintaining the other type of cross-river construction, the salmon weir: These weirs were not built to stop or fundamentally alter the river, neither were they constructed to cover the entire diameter of the flow. The flow had to continue, otherwise they were ineffective. They were constructed annually, when the conditions on the river were right, not triggered by an external signal such as the calendar date or a price increase. Later in the season they were carefully deconstructed again, trying not to compromise the quality of the fishing site. Other fishing methods were employed in other places along the river and during other phases in the season; the weirs were not designed to do all the fishing. Finally, measures were in place to ensure the sustainability of the activity, such as the closure against over-exploitation, the identification of specific fishing sites and leaving the King's Channel open. Of course, these two technologies cannot be simply equated; because they regulate and harvest different aspects of the river, their impact on the entire watershed has been very different, as has been their scale. However, both of them have to deal with the basic characteristics of a river in order to harvest something from its flow. This reveals more parallels than initially obvious.

Ideas and technology are two sides of the same coin. A barrier that harvests the river selectively and adapts to its varying characteristics presupposes a conceptual base that varies significantly from that of modernist environmental management11, which sets out to subdue and control environmental phenomena conceptually and physically. The example of the Kemi River shows that such control can hardly be entirely possible. Salmon weirs and hydroelectric dams both harvest a particular quality of the river and the operators of both types of construction have to know and respond to the river's dynamics. Even though hydropower development on the Kemi River has been, and to some extend still is, driven by modernist visions of harvesting controllable natural resources to suit particular needs, the actual operation of the system of power stations does not comply with the ideal of management as controlling a phenomenon in order to execute a ready-made plan.

Thus, if not even a technology that commands almost one million cubic metres of reinforced concrete, data collected during many decades throughout an immense area and a group of highly educated and experienced staff – if not even such a technology controls the Kemi River, the idea of river management in the traditional sense seems to be a conceptual illusion. A river cannot be managed, by imposing a rigid, predefined plan, but an engagement with its flow is always a reciprocal relation. This is not to claim that a river cannot be dealt with or used for human interests at all. Since it emerged after the last Ice Age, the Kemi River has always been used by humans and probably will be for a long time to come. But such uses have been – and necessarily will be – based on reciprocal engagement with the river's flowing characteristics. Only thus can they work.

[11] For a critical evaluation of environmental modernisation, see Chapter 18.

References

Adams W, Perrow M, Carpenter A (2004) Conservatives and champions: river managers and the river restoration discourse in the United Kingdom. In: Environment and Planning A 36(11): 1929-1942

Blackbourn D (2006) The Conquest of Nature. Water, Landscape, and the Making of Modern Germany. W.W. Norton, New York

Holm J (ed) (1991) Voimaa koskesta. Suomen vesivoiman rakentamisen vaiheita. Helsinki: Suurpadot – Suomen Osasto ry

Ingold T (2008) Bindings against boundaries: entanglements of life in an open world. In: Environment and Planning A 40(8): 1796-1810

Karlsson L, Karlström Ö (1994) The Baltic salmon (*Salmo salar L.*): its history, present situation and future. In: Dana 10: 66-85

Kemijoki Group (2008) Annual Report 2007. Kemijoki OY, Rovaniemi

Massa I (1983) Ihminen ja Lapin luonto. Lapin luonnonkäytön historiaa. Suomen Antropologinen Seura, Helsinki

Massa I (1994) Pohjoinen luonnonvalloitus. Suunnistus ympäristöhistoriaan Lapissa ja Suomessa. Gaudeamus, Helsinki

Mauss M, Beuchart H (1979) Seasonal variations of the Eskimo. A study in social morphology. Routledge and Kegan Paul, London

McCully (2001) Silenced Rivers. The Ecology and Politics of Large Dams.Zed Books, London

Vilkuna K (1975) Unternehmen Lachsfang. The Finnish Literature Society, Helsinki

White R (1995) The Organic Machine. The Remaking of the Columbia River. Hill and Wang, New York

Worster D (1985) Rivers of Empire. Water, Aridity, and the Growth of the American West. Oxford University Press, Oxford

20 Visualising Nuclear Landscapes: Visual Simulation in the Licensing for Finnish Nuclear Facilities

Hannah Strauss

Thule Institute, University of Oulu, Finland

20.1 Introduction

This chapter discusses the use of visual techniques for project simulation in planning procedures as part of the reflection on environmental management practices in Part III of this book. The problem that such simulation techniques attempt to solve is the perception of environmental changes, such as the construction and operation of nuclear power plants, before they are realised. The purpose of this chapter is to introduce phenomenological theories to the discussion of visualisation techniques in order to achieve a more critical understanding of management practices. It will be argued that sophisticated technologies, as employed in the licensing of nuclear power plants in Finland (section 20.2), enable realistic views on the changes in landscape while the implications of their increasingly prominent role in planning are discussed very little. Managerial approaches (section 20.3) enthusiastically highlight the possibilities for producing suggestions in a format that "everybody can understand" (section 20.4). However, it is argued in this article that personal perception of landscapes cannot be modelled by simulations, which are therefore of limited use when it comes to assessment of possible changes and informed decision-making. Phenomenological approaches (section 20.5) highlight the short-sightedness of environmental management practices. In the licensing procedure of nuclear facilities in Finland, visual simulations are employed rather often, while the frequent use of manipulated images is as such not subject to scrutiny. In this respect, a free hand is granted to the project developer, who naturally aims at a smooth assessment process and positive outcomes. Moreover, and despite showing the projected changes in the landscape, Finnish companies deliver a certain kind of image of nature conservation and social responsibility. The chapter concludes with comments and recommendations that could help improve the use of visualisation techniques in the Finnish licensing procedure (section 20.6).

20.2 Licensing of Nuclear Facilities in Finland and the Use of Visual Simulations

Finland is the first European nation to build a new nuclear power plant for more than a decade. In addition to four existing units, a fifth unit is scheduled to start operation in 2012. Finland employs a world-wide unique licensing procedure for nuclear facilities, demanding a decision on the project by the Government and ratification of governmental decisions by the Parliament. Developers of nuclear facilities must provide an environmental impact assessment report in their application for a decision-in-principle. The candidate municipality retains an absolute veto right, and is to be consulted before a decision-in-principle is made. In order to ensure an unbiased process, the applicant is allowed to make investment decisions and publish a call for bids only after both Government and Parliament have decided positively on the project. Construction license and operation license must be applied for separately. In 2000, the Finnish Government decided on a final repository for highly radioactive waste, and became thus the first democratic nation to make this decision. Construction of the repository is underway, and disposal of spent fuel will begin around the year 2020.

Currently, applications for three further nuclear power plants or plant units are being prepared. In their environmental impact assessment reports, three companies – Teollisuuden Voima (2008), Fortum Power and Heat (2008), and Fennovoima (2008) – each suggest the building of a 1600 Megawatts plant or plant unit. Under the growing threat of climate change, political debates indicate a rather positive standing towards the expansion of nuclear power in Finland, and approval of at least one application seems likely. Additionally, the joint company responsible for the disposal of radioactive waste, Posiva, is preparing an application for the extension of the final repository in order to deal with the waste produced by the plant currently under construction (Posiva 2008). With every licensed power plant unit, disposal of waste produced during the unit's lifetime must be assessed and applied for separately.

Negotiations between power companies and local communities take place during the obligatory environmental impact assessment under supervision of the Ministry for Employment and the Economy and the Radiation and Nuclear Safety Authority STUK. Regional environment centres are asked to engage in the licensing procedure. Further, the Ministry of the Environment organises public hearings in the candidate municipalities. Guiding competences remain with the Ministry for Employment and the Economy and STUK, which both actively pursue the development of nuclear power.

During recent environmental impact assessments, all four companies requested help from one major Finnish energy consultant, Pöyry Energy. The assessments are usually organised by a company-consultant working group, and most involved consultants work on all four projects. This is highly visible in the publications, such as the environmental impact assessment programmes and reports. This paper will especially focus on one aspect of these reports, the visual simulation of nuclear power plants during environmental impact assessments. Images referred to in this paper are available in publication and for download (see list of references).

The consultant's long-standing expertise in energy consultancy provides companies with a certain set of proven practices. Presentations of assessments are thus rather similar across nuclear power projects. The consultant, for instance, suggests participatory elements for the assessment, and advises on the write-up of the report. Assessment reports of all three companies present an identical structure to the reader. Each report introduces a separate project logo. All issues are published in several languages and they look highly professional. Full-page aesthetic pictures require much of the publications' length. In Fortum's environmental impact assessment report (2008) there are 30 full-page photographs taken by a local photographer. Throughout the assessment procedure, visual presentations of the proposed project are distributed by the developer in environmental impact assessment programmes and reports, newspapers, leaflets, websites, exhibitions and oral presentations. With the help of computer software, the new unit or plant is fitted into photographs (aerials) of the considered site. Production of (manipulated) images, printing and binding costs must be considerably high, and are thus only affordable to major companies (cf. Al-Kodmany 1999; Lange 2001).

The reader of these publications is confronted with a peaceful, beautiful, healthy environment and happy people (see especially Fennovoima's online presentation). It is suggested that nuclear power facilitates protect nature without restrictions to comforts and living standards. The look of programmes and reports often resembles that of a sales magazine. A member of Finland's Green Party called the efforts of one developer concerning an earlier project a "commercial blitz" (Andersson 2002, p. 81).

In regard to project simulation, manipulated images look highly realistic and the observer is encouraged to imagine the effects of project implementation. Usually the picture shows the completed power plant from the sea side, from a bird's eye perspective. All developers provide pictures of candidate sites in summer time, decorated by clear blue skies. The horizon is visible in the picture, as is a wide area of the sea, and the power plant itself takes up only a little part of the whole image. The bird's eye perspective comes close to features of maps or GPS, and therefore enables an almost holistic view of the scene. However, for assessing the impacts of project implementation this view is also restrictive. It does not, for instance, allow an assessment of heights, and it is not clear how much of the plant is visible from different perspectives on the ground or at sea level. Fennovoima (2008, pp. 240ff.) is the only company to provide one additional picture for each candidate site where the power plant is simulated from a sea level perspective. Further, the presentation of the completed plant in summer time does not allow an assessment of effects of discharges into the sea water and thus effects on sea ice and fishing, nor does it allow an assessment of the visual landscape with leafless trees and snow on the ground. In general, many of the issues residents are concerned about are hard to imagine with the help of a manipulated photograph, such as increases in traffic, presence of around two thousand foreign workers, changes in the municipality's image and identity, and increasing municipal dependency on the company. The construction site, which will prevail for some years, is not subject to visual presentation.

The given visualisations invite us to engage in the assessment in certain ways. We can conclude that manipulated and polished pictures direct attention towards visual assessment of the completed project, and at the same time deliver messages of nature conservation and social responsibility. Thus, the aerial view from the sea with clear blue skies and a visible horizon transports meanings that go beyond landscape assessment in regard to impacts of a single project. Moreover, the picture describes the energy company in heroic terms, where new lands are approached and new frontiers reached.

Finland employs a strong "polluter-pays"-principle, and it is mainly the developer who is in charge of carrying out the environmental impact assessment. Coordinating authorities are supposed to encourage nuclear development and do not take a critical stance towards assessment procedures concerning possible biases. Local and regional authorities have restricted themselves to the observation of assessments rather than active engagement. Thus, certain biases in the set up of the assessment including the making and presentation of simulations are easily identified. Since the environmental impact assessment report will be the main document for the following debates and decisions on the project, an analysis of the use of images is necessary. This article therefore focuses on scrutinising the possible benefits and restrictions born by the use of imaging technologies. We will start our analysis by reviewing the expectations and functions assigned to visual project simulation by practitioners and scientists as stated in major management journals (e.g. *Landscape and Urban Planning*, *Environment and Planning*) and monographs. Despite their eagerness to employ imaging technologies, many authors have voiced concerns about the use of images in assessment procedures, since biases are quite often obvious. Moreover, theories of perception do not agree that the high expectations of practitioners could be met by using imaging technologies. Based on a literature review, managerial aims to facilitate smooth procedures with the help of manipulated images and underlying assumptions about visual perception will be contrasted with phenomenological theories about the perception of the environment.

20.3 Practical uses of Imaging Technologies in Environmental Planning

Lange (2001) exemplifies the purpose of using imaging technologies by stating that planning disciplines "want to be better understood by the public" (Lange 2001, p. 179). The notion of improving the "understanding of people" has been described as the cognitive deficit model in research on public understanding of science. In the deficit perspective, it is assumed that people have a lack of knowledge which can be supplemented. Having received such lessons people are supposed to make the right decisions (see Wieser 2002, Lynch 2004, Irwin 2006 and Wynne 1992).

However, Lange (2001) points out constraints in the use of the produced images, in that "even the best simulation is only a representation of the real world. A virtual walk-through is not the same and will never be the same as a real walk in nature" (Lange 2001, p. 179). Nevertheless, Lange argues, visualisation techniques could support "better and more informed decisions about the spatial organisation of the landscape" (Lange 2001, p. 180) and facilitate "improved communication among experts and lay persons, i.e. among planners and the persons affected by planning" (ibid.). A critical point for Lange and other scholars is the timing of image distribution, since at that time project simulations were only published after public negotiations and environmental impact assessments took place. Lange argues that project simulation should be available from the start of the procedure (Lange 1994: 103). In the case of nuclear power licensing in Finland, manipulated images have been distributed through websites, bulk mail and newspapers from an early stage of the assessment procedure. In the case of the company Fennovoima, several candidate sites have been assessed, and all sites have been clipped in separate images. However, there have been no opportunities for residents to influence the choice of a site or the choice of plant design.

Al-Kodmany (1999) presents a rather different approach developed in small-scale urban planning. Al-Kodmany (1999, p. 38) agrees that "visualization is the key to effective public participation because it is the only common language to which all participants – technical and non-technical – can relate"[1]. However, he refers to a rather different use of imaging technology, when simulations are a result of collaborative planning rather than a pre-produced sketch to be fed into the process at some point of time. In his study, Al-Kodmany reviews several different visualisation methods applied in a collaborative planning scheme. He concludes that interactive planning with different methods (GIS, artist's free-hand sketches, and photo-manipulation using computer imaging) required a range of sometimes expensive technological devices, and their failures often slowed down the creative process. Nevertheless, seeing their own suggestions become visible almost immediately after proposing them encouraged residents to continue participation. Al-Kodmany concludes, "[t]he designs that were created by the planners and designers reflected the community's wishes and respected their cultural heritage" (Al-Kodmany 1999, p. 45). Notwithstanding these potential benefits, few project developments may be able or willing to include a procedure as presented by Al-Kodmany due to time, cost and personnel constraints.

1 Merlau-Ponty (1989) discusses how blind people perceive the environment. In contrast to Al-Kodmany (1999), who does not mention the possibility of not being able to see, Merleau-Ponty uses the example of blind persons to support his argument of interacting senses.

20.4 Expectations and Concerns towards the Use of Imaging Technologies

Practitioners in planning have been enthusiastic about the possibilities visual simulation has to offer in regard to decision making.

> "People are good at understanding images, but they are bad at understanding information presented in other forms" (Lange 1994, p. 111)

Although more than a decade has passed since Lange expressed his view his claim still dictates practices in environmental planning such as the licensing procedure for nuclear facilities in Finland, where reports are stylised and comparable to sales magazines. Lange's phrase indicates the rhetorical power of images, and that they work differently compared to texts. The effects of visual representation have been described from a more critical perspective by Barry (1997) in regard to advertisement. Barry notes that "consumers read visual language more quickly and easily than verbal language" and that they "block out negative messages in favour of positive messages" (Barry 1997, p. 277). The manipulated images of nuclear power companies aim at similar effects, since the developer strives for implementation of the project.

In a more recent publication Cosgrove (2008) is concerned with the role of images in 20th century environmentalism and discusses how we read them. "The pictorial image veers towards the affective and sensuous rather than syllogistic and analytic, and in more than merely its aesthetic aspect. Further, the eye engages a picture as a whole, working across its surface in nonlinear (thus nonhistorical) fashion." (Cosgrove 2008, p. 1864) Cosgrove adds that certain combinations of "line, form, composition, colour and tone generate immediate sensual and aesthetic responses" (Cosgrove 2008, p. 1864). The composition suggested by the developer does not only deliver aesthetic values, but engages the viewer to understand at once what is otherwise only possible by endless reading through texts and interpreting cartographic material.

Aerial views from the seaside including distant horizons and a rather small power plant evoke certain sensations. Since very few residents have ever had the possibility to look at the locality from 200 metres above the sea, and are used to look at their environment from rather different angles, presented pictures aim to produce a good "gestalt"[2]. Van den Berg (2006) explains how expectations on compositions of images have developed over centuries:

> "Histories of photography [...] tell and show us to what extent photographers, since the very first beginnings of photography, have tried to imitate painted representations of nature that have been developed by painters since the 15th century. The German noun 'Vorbild' reflects two dimensions of this relation: on the one hand, it means the preced-

[2] Gestalt psychology discusses perception from a phenomenological perspective. It assumes the cognitive organisation of visual impressions in regard to good shapes (*"gestalt"*). However, this theory has been criticised for being descriptive rather than explanative.

ing, the pre-existing picture and, on the other, it has a normative reading since the model claims to be followed." (Van den Berg et al. 2006, p. 43)

Due to the long process of production, painted representations are not just understood as representing an instant view of the landscape, but that much thought was devoted towards rules of composition. Regarding photography, the composition work is usually not given as much consideration, although we can expect most residents in western societies to know about possibilities to digitally manipulate pictures due to the distribution of home user manipulation software.

The training of landscape architects devotes much time to the teaching of aesthetic values, which are assumed to be measurable and usually studied in psychological surveys (cf. Daniel 2001). Reflection on decisions concerning the choice of locality, viewpoint, focus, and thus the discussion of ethical questions, is scarce. In that respect Sheppard (2001, p. 183) suggests "developing a code of ethics" and thereby establishing some sort of "guidance for crystal ball gazers". He concludes that the aim should be the production of an "honest and neutral visual representation of the expected landscape" (Sheppard 2001, p. 196). Therefore, he suggests five principles as a code of ethics for the use of visualisation technology, including accuracy, representativeness, visual clarity, interest, and legitimacy. Concerning representativeness, Sheppard claims that visualisations "should represent typical or important views/conditions of the landscape" (Sheppard 2001, p. 194). E.g. residents could be consulted to identify important viewpoints. In terms of "interest", the author states that "the visualization should engage and hold the interest of the audience" (Sheppard 2001, p. 194); however, current technologies are likely to produce over-stimulation and to carry metaphors. Further, errors and degrees of uncertainty should be disclosed. Sheppard's evaluation of incorporating ethics into the training of practitioners is yet pessimistic (2001, p. 192), especially because many of those producing visualisations never participated in any training and acquired their skills through self-education.

Following the approaches by Lange and Al-Kodmany, visualisation techniques enable stakeholders (and developers in the latter case) to understand difficult data on projects in the planning stage. As an expert in imaging software, Lange is especially concerned with the question of how to provide ever more realistic views on the landscape and claims that images should feed into the planning procedure at an early stage. Al-Kodmany's study showed the benefits of producing project simulations in collaboration with residents. These two approaches of using imaging technology in environmental planning are thus diverse. However, we can consider Lange's idea of feeding manipulated images into the planning procedure at an early stage as a normal case. This raises the question how images are actually produced if they are not a result of collaborative planning.

In her ethnographic studies, Büscher (2006) observes practitioners producing photographic material for visual manipulation. She describes the difficulties practitioners face when trying to identify and capture viewpoints suitable for the purpose of manipulation and how perception of the target area is bound to movement around the place. In the first case of her study, landscape architects and visualisation specialists preliminarily decided on possible viewpoints from maps and aerial photographs (from here on referred to as aerials). For instance aerials were understood to provide only limited information of the place, since they do not give indication of height (ibid. 286). Practitioners then got to know the place by moving around the site in order to take pictures for visual manipulation. Büscher's second case presented in the same article reveals strategies used and problems faced by a landscape architect when actually figuring out the exact site for a windmill with the help of maps and GPS. Her discussion of findings reflects on the practitioner's movement around the place with reference to theories of environmental perception. However, in her ethnographic analysis Büscher is restricted to describing how practitioners gain a sense of place and she does not reflect on further implications of the work by landscape architects such as aesthetic judgements, in this case the decisions on views and the consequences of presenting certain views (but not others) in the planning procedure.

20.5 Perception of the Environment

Theories of perception in environmental management often relate to psychological or physical approaches with regard to bodily functions, usually limiting the description to visual perception. Aesthetic value judgements are observed as difficult, but still possible, to measure, and thus can be used as transferable indicators. In concurrence with this understanding, views of a landscape, such as provided by aerials, can be manipulated following certain culturally shaped aesthetic values. Another approach acknowledged in environmental management is the "theory of optic flow and affordance" (Bell 2001, p. 207) developed by Gibson in 1979, also known as the ecological theory of perception. Following this approach, and according to Bell's interpretation, we perceive our environment based "on our moving through a landscape so that it 'flows' around and past us" (Bell 2001, p. 207), thereby enhancing our spatial understanding. Consequently, Bell argues, visualisation tools should focus on producing a three-dimensional simulation "where we appear to be moving through the landscape" (Bell 2001, p. 210). Projected benefits would be great: "This [visualisation] technique also enables people to experience the landscape more fully and from whatever viewpoint they wish to choose for themselves, rather than one decided for them by the planner" (Bell 2001, p. 210).

Although Bell's presentation acknowledges the shortcomings of two-dimensional views, as introduced by aerials, there are different shortcomings in his understanding, as phenomenological theories of perception will show below. Nevertheless, it may be considered as a common reflection on environmental perception as proclaimed by technology enthusiasts. Bell (2001) assumes that it is possible to produce value-neutral visual representations. Sheppard (2001, p. 188) on the contrary argues, "[e]ven with the best intentions, any two preparers, using the same software and the same base-data, are likely to produce very different visualizations". Another shortcoming of Bell's argumentation is the interpretation of the "flow of the environment", bluntly translated into the need for three-dimensional simulation.

In the following paragraphs we will reflect on these approaches to environmental perception with the help of Merleau-Ponty's (1989) and Ingold's (2000) analyses. In the year 1945 Merleau-Ponty first published his analysis in which he relates the theory of perception to a theory of the body. It is not only bodily functions that enable perception, but the moving body in the environment perceiving with all its senses and with the awareness of its own body moving through the place.

> "Our own body is in the world as the heart is in the organism: it keeps the visible spectacle constantly alive, it breathes life into it and sustains it inwardly, and with it forms a system. When I walk round my flat, the various aspects in which it presents itself to me could not possibly appear as views of one and the same thing if I did not know that each of them represents the flat seen from one spot or another, and if I were unaware of my own movements, and of my body as retaining its identity through the stages of those movements. I can of course take a mental bird's eye view of the flat, visualize it or draw a plan of it on paper, but in that case too I could not grasp the unity of the object without the mediation of bodily experience, for what I call a plan is only a more comprehensive perspective: it is the flat 'seen from above', and the fact that I am able to draw together in it all habitual perspectives is dependent on my knowing that one and the same embodied subject can view successively from various positions." (Merleau-Ponty 1989, p. 203)

The view from somewhere is contrasted with the view from nowhere, produced by someone who has experienced different perspectives and who remembers these (see also Ingold 2000, p. 191)[3]. This idea has later been adopted by Gibson, who interprets perception of the environment as a constant flow, and the moving body as constituent of perception (1979). Gibson (2002) argued that the possibility of moving around from one point of observation to the next differentiates space from environment. "The points of geometrical space are abstract fictions, whereas the points of observation in an environment are the positions where an observer might be stationed." (Gibson 2002, p. 85) Another notion, again picked up by Gibson, is the affordances of environment and a person's attention to it. A person's attention is directed towards certain things in its environment. People perceive the environment differently, because they received a "different education of attention" (Ingold 2000, p. 190). Ingold illustrates this argument through the example of a novice hunter who "travels through the country with his mentors, and as he goes, specific features are pointed out to him" (2000, p. 189), which (s)he would not have noticed otherwise. Further, the landscape is constituted of past events and people having dwelled in it, thereby leaving "something of themselves" (Ingold 2000, p. 189). "To perceive the landscape is therefore to carry out an act of remembrance, and remembering is not so much a matter of calling up an internal image, stored in the mind, as of engaging perceptually with an environment that is itself pregnant with the past" (Ingold 2000, p. 189).

---

[3] Haraway (1991) criticises the common understanding of perception from a slightly different angle by stating that neutral vision is impossible, and interprets the adoption of a god-eye perspective as masculinist domination. Haraway further argues that vision is both bodily and socially shaped (see also Chapter 23 on sustaining waste in this book).

Ingold further argues that in perceiving a landscape we assemble a list of tasks that must be completed; in that we see a garden which needs to be maintained, corn to be harvested, and houses to be built. These perceived tasks, and active engagement in the following, are "the constitutive acts of dwelling". Ingold terms this ensemble of tasks the "taskscape" (Ingold 2000, p. 194ff.), which is not a stable condition, but underlies temporal alteration. Following Merleau-Ponty, the perception of the environment is not restricted to visual fields, and requires the moving body with all its senses. Vision, sound and colours, smells and touches all relate to perception.

> "It has been wrongly asserted that the edges of the visual field always furnish an objectively stable point. Once again, the edge of the visual field is not a real line. Our visual field is not neatly cut out of our objective world, and is not a fragment with sharp edges like the landscape framed by the window. We see as far as our hold on things extends, far beyond the zone of clear vision, and even behind us. When we reach the limits of the visual field, we do not pass from vision to non-vision: the gramophone playing in the next room, and not expressly seen by me, still counts in my visual field." (Merleau-Ponty 1989, p. 277)

Practitioners of environmental management may argue that an environment, including its specific smells and sounds, could be simulated with some sort of future technology, as for instance performed in the science fiction TV series Star Trek. In three-dimensional simulations on board of a space ship members of the "next generation" are able to rebuild their favourite environments in a highly realistic manner for leisure purposes.

Driven by the idea that people could make better informed decisions about changes in their local environment, planners today aim at ever more realistic simulation in order to facilitate "real experiences". However, we can object that experiences of simulated and existing environment cannot enable similar perceptions, since a person would be aware of the artificiality. Further, it is hard to imagine that people would be able to spend a longer period of time in the simulated environment, experience seasonal changes, to permanently dwell in it, work with it, and use it without being aware of it, in the sense of an "attentive involvement" (Ingold 2000, p. 207). What is more, perception of a familiar environment might not be feasible. The producers of simulations may direct their attention towards very specific details in the target environment, whereas residents would probably depict a different set of features. Landscape architects moving around a particular site in order to get "good views" and take pictures for visual simulation perceive the environment by spending time in it. However, their "taskscape" and therefore their attention towards particular things differ from residential taskscapes and their particular attentive involvement.

Büscher's ethnographic study on the work of landscape architects concludes by referring to Ingold (2000) that landscape architects were provided with "views from nowhere" through maps and plans, but that in their work preparing the visual simulation of projects they gained a "view from somewhere" (Büscher 2006, p. 294). Practitioners therefore get to know the candidate location as other visitors to the place would. Büscher describes landscape architects as being emphatic in employing some kind of imagined local perspective to the field. However, the meaning of the place, with regard to seasonal and historical changes, and different activities ("taskscape") does not unfold to the landscape architect and the resident in the same way.

20.6 Conclusions and Recommendations

Visual simulations receive a high status in environmental planning; however, expectations are revealed to be unrealistic. As shown in this article, an ordinary perception of the target environment and changes within it cannot be achieved by the manipulation of images. A better or even full understanding of prospected changes – which is a declared goal of practitioners – and consequently informed evaluation and decision-making turns out to be a fallacy. Phenomenological approaches show that it is our own bodily movement and successive discovery of things in the landscape that will form our perception of the environment, which unfolds historical traces and certain tasks, depending on the individual's personal needs and experiences. Further, the flow of perception is not restricted to sight, but employs all our bodily senses, including smell and taste, touch and hearing. As the notion of flow indicates, perception is governed by temporality and not an instant moment of time, condensed in a picture. In addition, the environment is always viewed from somewhere, knowing that things can be explored successively. On the contrary phenomenologists argue that aerial views or maps do not offer a view from somewhere, but a view from nowhere,.

In the licensing of nuclear facilities in Finland, visually manipulated aerial views are employed rather often during environmental impact assessments. Only in the latest environmental impact assessment report of one developer have a couple of simulated views from the ground been introduced. However, the use of images and visual simulations of power plants is not reflected upon by involved actors. On the contrary, we can assume a strong demand for visual material by decision makers and the public, and we can sense why so little attention is drawn to quality control of current practices.

The analysis of Finnish nuclear power projects has further shown that visually manipulated images of landscapes have metaphorical character, and that they aim to presenting beauty rather than reality. International research provides evidence that although biases in project simulation have been identified by many scholars, their reflection is seldom part of practical training. Ethics and guidelines are called for (see Sheppard 2001), but technologies tend to develop faster than these can be elaborated.

From a phenomenological viewpoint we can argue that the goals of visual assessments cannot be achieved. Finnish residents will not be able to imagine the projected changes and impacts on their livelihoods by looking at simulated nuclear power plants on paper. Ever more sophisticated technologies may not depict impacts on movement in the vicinity of the power plant, changes in the sound (e.g. construction noise, absence of birds) and smell (released e.g. by chemical substances during construction), touch (e.g. sensing the fragile sea ice during winter) and taste (e.g. of fishes drawn to the warm discharge waters of a power plant). Visual simulations are thus more of use in rather abstract assessments of landscapes and visual representations for tourism purposes and the like.

As a general conclusion of this article, practices like the use of visualisations in the licensing of nuclear power plants in Finland do not only need further guidance in training, supervision in practice, and thus ethical reflection throughout application, but also a critical evaluation of what visual simulations can offer in regard to a "better understanding by local people", and which priority should be assigned to their use in a planning procedure when compared to other methods of assessment. It is likely that technology enthusiasm in environmental management continues to overlook the pitfalls in focussing on visual assessment which does not enable the user to *perceive* environmental changes in advance. Thus, it is less an informed decision-making promoted by environmental managers, but the delivery of a positive image about a company's activities and consequently a smooth siting process. Alternative approaches such as presented by Al-Kodmany (1999) should not be expected to enable citizens to perceive or understand "better", however, collaborative production of visual representations allows individual interpretation and engagement. Instead of being swamped with beautiful images, people could directly participate in the process of visualisation, learn about uncertainties and contingency, observe experts dealing with computer failures and explore their environment on foot in the quest for a "good view" of their environment (as those landscape architects in Büscher 2006). Practitioners would aim at an "attentive involvement" (Ingold 2000, p. 207) of residents in the assessment rather than the distribution of finalised information.

In order to achieve such a participatory development of visualisation, I propose the following points for consideration.

- Environmental legislation should specify assessment practices in general, in particular regarding the use of visual material and visual simulations.
- Industries should be encouraged to commit themselves to a more reflective use of visual material and to provide open information with regard to the production and aims of simulations.
- Main documents like the environmental impact assessment programme and report should include a section disclosing information on visual material, such as a description of the uncertainty and arbitrariness of visual simulations.
- Authorities should supervise the assessment procedure and guarantee quality control.
- Decision makers should be made aware of current practices and possible biases in the documents they are dealing with.
- Public participation should be aimed at with regard to the making of visual material. If this is not feasible due to technical and time constraints, an information campaign could put the production and use of simulations and aesthetic photographs into a wider and reflective context.

Although these points refer to the Finnish case study, recommendations may be generalised and applied to other country cases and international environmental impact assessment practices.

References

Al-Kodmany K (1999) Using visualization techniques for enhancing public participation in planning and design: process, implementation, and evaluation. In: Landscape and Urban Planning 45(1): 37-45

Barry A (1997) Visual Intelligence. Perception, Image, and Manipulation in Visual Communication. SUNY Press, New York

Bell S (2001) Landscape pattern, perception and visualisation in the visual management of forests. In: Landscape and Urban Planning 54(1-4): 201-211

Van den Berg A, de Vries D, Vlek C (2006) Images of Nature, Environmental Values and Landscape Preference: Exploring their Interrelationships. In: Van den Born RJG, de Groot W, Lenders RHJ (eds) Visions of Nature: A Scientific Exploration of People's Implicit Philosophies Regarding Nature in Germany, the Netherlands and the United Kingdom. LIT Verlag, Berlin, pp. 43-60

Büscher M (2006) Vision in motion. In: Environment and Planning 38(2): 281-299

Cosgrove D (2008) Images and imagination in 20th-century environmentalism: from the Sierras to the Poles. In: Environment and Planning 40(8): 1862-1880

Daniel TC (2001) Whither scenic beauty? Visual landscape quality assessment in the 21st century. In: Landscape and Urban Planning 54(1-4): 267-281

Fennovoima Oy (2008) Environmental Impact Assessment Report for a Nuclear Power Plant. Fennovoima Ltd, Helsinki

Fortum Power and Heat Oy (2008) Supplementing the Loviisa Nuclear Power Plant with a Third Unit. Environmental Impact Assessment Report. Fortum Power and Heat Oy, Helsinki

Gibson JJ (2002 [1972]) A Theory of Direct Visual Perception. In: Noë A, Thompson E (eds) Readings in the Philosophy of Perception. Bradford, London

Gibson JJ (1979) The ecological approach to visual perception. Houghton Mills, Boston

Haraway DJ (1991) Simians, Cyborgs, and Women: the Reinvention of Nature. Routledge, New York

Ingold T (2000) The Perception of the Environment. Essays on livelihood, dwelling and skill. Routledge, London

Irwin A (2006) The Politics of Talk: Coming to Terms with the 'New' Scientific Governance. In: Social Studies of Science 36(2): 299–320

Lange E (1994) Integration of computerized visual simulation and visual assessment in environmental planning. In: Landscape and Urban Planning 30(1-2): 99-112

Lange E (2001) The limits of realism: perception of virtual landscapes. In: Landscape and Urban Planning 54(1-4): 163-182

Lynch M (2004) Science as a vacation: Deficits, surfeits, PUSS, and doing your own job. Paper for workshop "Does STS Mean Business?", Oxford Saïd Business School

Merleau-Ponty M (1989) Phenomenology of Perception. Routledge, London

Posiva Oy (2008) Expansion of the Repository for Spent Nuclear Fuel. Environmental Impact Assessment Programme. Posiva Oy, Helsinki

Sheppard SRJ (2001) Guidance for crystal ball gazers: developing a code of ethics for landscape visualization. In: Landscape and Urban Planning 54(1-4): 183-199

Teollisuuden Voima Oyj (2008) Environmental Impact Assessment Report. Extension of the Olkiluoto Power Plant by a Fourth Unit. Teollisuuden Voima Oyj, Helsinki

Wieser B (2002) If the Public Only Knew! On Learning about Genetic Engineering. In: Yearbook 2002 of the Institute for Advanced Studies on Science, Technology & Society. Profil, München, pp. 295-311

Wynne B (1992) Misunderstood misunderstanding: Social identities and public uptake of science. In: Public Understanding of Science 1(3): 281-304

21 Outsourcing Emissions: Clean Development Mechanism (CDM) as Ecological Modernisation

Anup Sam Ninan

Bremen International Graduate School of Social Sciences (BIGSSS), Bremen, Germany

21.1 Introduction

Ecological Modernisation (EM), which emerged as a major theoretical perspective in environmental sociology and politics during the last decades of the twentieth century, addresses the advanced industrial development and the ecological crises associated with it. Besides playing a significant role in the discussions on state, production and consumption within the environmental social science academia, the perspective is highly influential in both strategic environmental planning by governments and the restructuring of production by manufacturers (Mol and Spaargaren 2005; Murphy 2000).

Closely integrated to the neoliberal ideas of economic organisation, the Ecological Modernisation 'theory' aims to analyse how contemporary industrialised societies deal with environmental crises (Mol and Sonnenfeld 2000). As an 'improved' synonym for Sustainable Development, EM proposes that environmental problems can be sufficiently dealt within the framework of continued modernisation of capitalism and the application of modern experimental sciences (Buttel 2000) and presumes that economic growth and environmental protection can be symbiotic. It is claimed that the malleability of EM with the institutions and technological capabilities of industrial capitalism, particularly in the wake of the political challenge posed by radical environmentalism, is a significant aspect behind its emerging prominence (Buttel 2000). As an approach that presupposes unplanned social change (Mol 1995) EM identifies economic actors and entrepreneurs as among the most important constituents who bring forth transformation (Murphy 2000) even though the perspective upholds the need for macro economic structural changes. However, the discursive realm of EM can not be restricted to the ecological and economic interrelations, rather it revolves around the economic, political and social processes that integrate the ecological phenomena to modernisation process (Mol 1995). As a whole, the proponents argue that EM is ultimately a *political-sociological* perspective and, an advanced theory of EM

> "must ultimately (be) a theory of politics and the state- that is, a theory of the changes in the state and political practices (and a theory of the antecedents of these changes) which tend to give rise to private eco-efficiencies and overall environmental reforms" (Buttel 2000, p. 58).

This article examines Clean Development Mechanism (CDM) of the United Nations Framework Convention on Climate Change (UNFCCC) as a prescriptive illustration of EM perspective and argues that the increasing counterpoints raised against CDM, both as systemic flaws and as potholes of implementation, are inherent to EM framework. This article, set within the backdrop of calls for explicit environmental governance, discusses the formulation of CDM in conjunction with the basic tenets of EM before looking in to the criticisms pitted against the CDM. Subsequently, it elaborates how certain fundamental presumptions of EM can produce such outcomes.

21.1.1 CDM in Global Environmental Governance

Environmental Governance, defined broadly as attempts by governing bodies or combinations thereof to alleviate recognised environmental dilemmas (Davidson and Frickel 2004), varies drastically in the formulation of the issues, organisation of governing bodies and prescription of solutions at different scales, particularly in geopolitical frames. A very significant trend in the late 20th-century environmental governance, according to Davidson and Frickel (2004), is the framing of environmental problems and solutions in the global context. The prominent features of this emergent shift include, but are not restricted to, a) new forms of institutionalising the environment, b) the emergence of transnational institutions, c) the legitimation of science and expertise in environmental discourse, and, d) the polarity between north and south in articulating environmental problems and devising solutions. These often mutually inclusive features permeated through multivalent forms of interplay between diverse actors on different platforms constitute the discursive terrain of present-day global environmental governance.

21.1.2 Emergent Global Environmental Governance

The first feature of global environmental governance is the perforation of scales. The emergent practices of institutionalising environment began to appear with the perforation of erstwhile (predominantly national) scales leading to new forms of scalar configurations and scalar politics (Amin 2002; Bulkeley 2005). At one level, this led to reframing the 'moral- technocratic construction of global environmental change' (Taylor and Buttel 1992) by prioritising the focal attention on specific environmental issues. At a different level, it altered the ways of *how* institutionalising is done. The market based environmental regulatory instruments in the case of EM measures (Sonnenfeld and Mol 2002) or the specific ways of constructing new geographies of environmental conservation (Zimmerer 2006) are examples of this process.

Secondly, the global environmental governance is marked with the emergence of transnational institutional arrangements, particularly as a result of the 1980s and 1990s spurt of interest in global environmental problems and the capacity of global frameworks for solving them. In this context, organizations, groups, and governments began to think of desirable environmental futures in new ways (Buttel 2003). These institutional mechanisms are networks with organizational parameters for dealing with knowledge claims. They also have policies and specific norms. They function on the basis of legitimacy claims codified through operational procedures and instruments (Ninan 2009). Simultaneously, these institutional mechanisms co-construct the political space for transnational movements as response to their activities.

Thirdly, science and expertise play a special role in the emergent global environmental governance. Besides having a central role in defining what is counted as an environmental problem, scientific expertise plays a central role in the governance of the networks. It is viewed that any reconstruction of science and politics in environmental governance must be a multifaceted process wherein both scientific and social are bound together in interpretations and actions,

> "jointly reinforced by the formulation of problems, the tools available, the audiences being addressed and enlisted to act, the support (financial and otherwise) elicited, and so on" (Taylor and Buttel 1992, p. 413).

The fourth significant feature of the global environmental governance is the north-south tensions in the framing of environmental problems and political priorities. The northern and southern countries differ very much on how and what to perceive as significant knowledge claims and the modalities on how to form institutional mechanisms. These differences of perceptions have often culminated in polemic negotiation between parties[1].

21.1.3 Emergence of Climate Change Regime

Though there have been scientific warnings since at least the 19th century, when colonial environmentalists pointed towards the significant implications of climate variations (Grove 1996)[2]; the organised international efforts to mitigate global warming – a process wherein excessive presence of green house gases (GHGs) in the atmosphere results in a progressive increase in temperature on earth's atmosphere with detrimental implications – only started in the late 1970s. The World Meteorological Organization's (WMO) first World *Climate Conference* in 1979 expressed its concern over anthropogenic 'regional and *even global changes*' of

[1] See Johnson 2003; Kulkarni 2003. See also Agarwal and Narain (1999) for elaboration of this point within the climate change discussions and negotiations.

[2] I am grateful to Ingmar Lippert for bringing in Grove's references to climate change.

climate (emphasis added). The US National Academy of Sciences' (NAS) *Ad Hoc Study Group on Carbon Dioxide and Climate Report* in the same year and NAS' assessment report called *Changing Climate* in 1983 also had major international impacts on policy initiatives. Consequently, the *Conference on the Assessment of the Role of Carbon Dioxide and of Other Green House Gases in Climate Variation and Associated Impacts* was held in 1985 in Villach (Austria). Sponsored by United Nations Environmental Programme (UNEP), WMO and the International Council of Scientific Unions (ICSU), the conference brought together 89 scientists from 23 countries across the world to form an international panel interfacing science and policy. To pursue the recommendations of the Villach conference, follow up studies and conferences were held. The Toronto conference in 1988 called *the World Conference on the Changing Atmosphere: Implications for the Global Security* marked the beginning of high level political debate on the risks of anthropogenic climate change (van der Sluijs et al. 1998). It recommended 20% reduction in the worldwide CO_2 emissions by 2005 (from a 1988 benchmark). Simultaneously, independent of the Toronto Conference, the WMO established the Intergovernmental Panel on Climate Change (IPCC) with the support of the UNEP in 1988 to assess the scientific, technical and socio-economic aspects of anthropogenic climate change. In 1990, the scientific Working Group of IPCC brought out a comprehensive report that was accepted by the second *World Climate Conference in Geneva* as a vital scientific basis for international negotiations on climate change. The said efforts culminated in the conception of the UNFCCC, which was adopted in 1992 at Rio de Janeiro and came in to force in 1994. It remains as one of the most widely supported international environmental agreements with 193 countries currently party to it.

The decision making body of the UNFCCC is the Conference of the Parties (CoP), which meets annually. The major agreement reached at the third CoP in Kyoto in 1997, called the Kyoto Protocol and operational since February 2005, under the broader framework of UNFCCC, forms the legal basis for international climate change mitigation policies and programmes. The Protocol stipulates the mechanisms of regulation to operationalise the GHG[3] abatement process through specific commitments and other functional requirements. The mechanism, which is intended to stabilize atmospheric GHG concentration to prevent detrimental anthropogenic effects to the climate, is based on the scientific understanding that industrially advanced countries (termed as the Annex 1 countries in the parlance of the Protocol) bear the historical responsibility for the present state of excess concentration. Consequently, Annex 1 countries ought to devise legally binding commitments to reduce their carbon emissions. These commitments are in the form of controlling emissions to within stipulated permitted levels of emission over a period of time. While the countries with commitments to limit GHG emissions are directed to meet their targets mainly through national measures, the Protocol has created three market-based mechanisms as additional means of meeting

[3] GHGs regulated under the Kyoto Protocol are Carbon dioxide (CO_2), Methane (CH_4), Nitrous oxide (N_2O), Hydrofluorocarbons (HFCs), Perfluorocarbons (PFCs) and Sulphur hexafluoride (SF_6).

the targets transterritorially, primarily to attain these targets 'cost-effectively'. As an effect, it is mainly through these mechanisms that the climate change regime operationalises the functional requirements of mitigation in a major way. These mechanisms constitute what has been referred to as the carbon market (MacKenzie 2008) and has evolved to be the key tool for reducing emissions worldwide with transactions worth 30 billion USD in 2006.

These instruments, called the Flexible Mechanisms, aim at reducing GHG emissions and are defined on the basis of the geographical location of the parties. Through these instruments the parties engage in collaborative actions resulting in emission reduction as defined by the scientific and policy norms of the Protocol. By fusing the scientific understanding that the GHG emissions, or the reduction of emissions anywhere on earth, affect the atmosphere uniformly with the economic rationale of differential operational costs across the different parts of the globe, the climate change regime constructed a tradable commodity in emission reductions so that the different actors in the regime could transact particular values of emission 'currencies' across the market. These units, over the 2008-2012-commitment period, expressed as levels of allowed emissions, or 'assigned amounts' are calculated in terms of tonnes of CO_2 -equivalent emissions.

Among the flexible mechanisms, the Emissions Trading (ET) is an instrument, used between the parties with commitments to accepted targets, for limiting emissions over the said commitment period. Through ET, the Protocol permits those countries with emission units to spare to sell this excess capacity to countries that have exceeded their targets. The Joint Implementation (JI) is a project-based mechanism directly linked to the carbon market that enables industrialized countries to carry out joint implementation projects with other developed countries. The JI is based on discrete emission reduction units that could be credited to an investor country for reduction projects realised in a host country based on actual, project-based avoidance, reduction, or sequestration of GHGs. Third among the flexible mechanisms – the CDM – forms a transterritorial instrument between the developed and the developing countries. Like JI, CDM is a project-based mechanism and involves investment in projects that reduce emissions in developing countries. The CDM is intended to make the GHG abatement process economically more feasible for developed countries, while simultaneously assisting developing countries to set a sustainable development trajectory through investments and technology transfer. With the emission targets for the first commitment period (2008-2012) set and different institutional and operational mechanisms in place, large number of CDM projects[4] have already begun to generate *Certified Emission Reductions* (CERs) – the exchange unit of CDM projects as per the Protocol – and CERs are being transferred across the territories.

---

[4] As of on December 12, 2008, there are 1261 registered CDM projects across the different developing countries. Among them, India has the largest number with 375 projects, followed by China and Brazil with 323 and 146 projects respectively. Among the investor parties, UK and Northern Ireland invested in 475 projects followed by Switzerland with 350 projects. Scale wise, the large projects are only marginally higher (with 54.64%) than the smaller projects though the CER potential is far higher with the large projects.

21.2 Clean Development Mechanism and Ecological Modernisation

Proceeding from the previous section, this part of the article seeks to comprehend how the CDM can be understood in terms of EM. First, it considers the viewpoints of Huber (2008) regarding Kyoto mechanisms and then proceed to explicate that CDM can be seen as a prescriptive illustration of EM by showing how the central notions of CDM are keeping abreast with the key propositions of EM.

21.2.1 Huber on Kyoto Mechanisms

Joseph Huber, who is considered to be the founder of EM perspective, in a recent article (Huber 2008) dealing with the theory and policies of EM, puts forth the role of 'pioneer countries' in the global diffusion of environmental innovations. He presents six theses in this direction:

- Advanced technology as the pivotal component of EM;
- Stringent regulation as the most important precondition for eco-innovation;
- The significant role of the lead markets of pioneer countries in environmental innovation;
- The notable preponderance of pioneering countries over the global environmental regimes;
- The central role of internationally active companies in the creation and global diffusion of eco-innovations, and;
- The difficulties involved in trickling down the environmental innovations (including leapfrogging and tunnelling-through) to 'the hierarchy of world-system'.

While Huber's article focuses specifically on the role of pioneer countries in global diffusion of environmental innovations, it is significant beyond its immediate purview on at least two grounds. First, it clearly throws light on the direction of scientific exploration within EM and the emerging convictions (like the role of pioneering countries, regulation, international companies etc) within the perspective. Second, and important with regard to this article, it highlights the specific ways in which disciplinary boundaries are negotiated and constructed. The basic argument against Huber here is that, though the idea of CDM is in accordance with the underlying arguments of EM, it is put aside (perhaps) on the basis of this rather recent thesis of preferring 'pioneer' countries to global regimes. This does not, however, mean to argue that the role of the nation-state or the national cultures in ecological sensitivity were insignificant in EM. Nevertheless, here the emphasis is on the depiction of contrasting postures of national and transnational regulatory mechanisms. While this could be an issue of emphasis when addressing theoretical understanding and specific sociopolitical processes between the first and second-generation literature within the EM perspective (Mol and Sonnenfeld 2000), it is necessary to deal with this translation process more clearly. It should be noted that Huber's specific case, as stated earlier, is not directly concerned with the case of Kyoto Mechanisms. Rather it is explained as part of an illustration of the preponderance of national regulation and national markets over the international environmental regimes in environmental policy and technological innovation. However, it is interesting to consider his rendering of the Kyoto Mechanisms in general, to depict CDM as a prescriptive illustration of the EM perspective.

Huber primarily points out that the impact of this UN-organised multilevel approach to global environmental governance is more formative than effective, as it is neither being supported by the newly industrialised countries, nor ratified by all advanced countries; even those who did ratify have implemented it poorly. On the eco-innovation front, Kyoto mechanisms are particularly uncertain in their effects as they lack an explicit innovation strategy on how to curb GHGs – whether by consumer sufficiency approach, by increasing the eco-efficiency within the existing production mechanisms or by improving metabolic consistency of production and products. With regard to instruments like ET, JI and CDM, Huber opines that while these economic instruments are thought to foster allocative efficiency, their effects on technological innovation are not clear. He contends that the differential national reduction targets set by the Kyoto Protocol do not represent general performance standards. Further he points out that the free granting of emission rights along with many exemptions made in the process of implementing ET is counter productive. Similarly diverse political conditions, institutional arrangements and the real world experiences in the cases of JI and CDM lead to the break down of the model-worlds of the economists.

21.2.2 CDM within EM Framework

Notwithstanding Huber's points, which are particularly appropriate with regard to eco-innovations strategies, this part of the article proposes to take up the case of one of the Kyoto instruments – CDM – to argue that the underlying premises of CDM are intrinsically fused to EM in conceiving the problem and devising the solutions.

Basis on Liberal Capitalism and Market Mechanisms

One of the underlying tenets of the EM perspective, particularly articulated in the first generation literature, is the emphasis on the institutional capacity of capitalist liberal democracies to reform their impact on the natural environment to achieve improved ecological outcomes (Buttel 2000). According to the EM perspective, capitalism is sufficiently flexible to incorporate ecologically sustainable practices. It postulates that the urge to modernise is an inherent compulsion in capitalist market economies that leads to a continuous acceleration of technological innovation. The task of EM is to change the direction of these technological innovations into an ecologically sensitive path so as to facilitate 'ecological-economic "win-win" solutions' (Jänicke 2008, p. 558).

The Kyoto instruments are the quintessence of a prescriptive assimilation of EM ideals, with its emphasis on commodified nature and technological mediation in environmental relations, where the linkage of economic rationale and non-environmental goals are synchronised (Glover 1999). As an essential feature of the ongoing transformation in environmental governance, the increased role of market-based regulatory instruments is argued to facilitate an interplay of market actors and political institutions that allows environmental considerations, requirements and interests to become increasingly institutionalised in the economic domain (Sonnenfeld and Mol 2002).

Method of Problem Identification and Conceptualisation

As indicated in section 21.2 of this article, the identification and problematisation of climate change as part of the UNFCCC regime is very much a rigorous scientific project. While the exercises of negotiating different knowledge claims can itself be a highly contested process with diverse representations (Boehmer-Christiansen 2003; Ninan 2008), it is on the basis of certain specific scientific understanding that instruments like CDM emerge. The scientific and institutional emergence of CDM does not specifically contradict with the framework of EM either in terms of knowledge claims or methods of problem identification. Both EM as a framework and CDM as an instrument are mediated through the special relationship between environmental science and politics, as Taylor and Buttel (1992) argue, whereby a certain course of action is facilitated over others in the problems chosen, categories used, relationships investigated and confirming evidence required. As they further maintain, politics, in climate change as in any other *global* environmental problems, is not merely simulated by scientific findings, but *woven into* science.

Technological Optimism

While the proponents of EM reiterate that it does not represent a 'technomaniac attitude', the reliance on technology and emphasis on technological advancement is one of the essential theses of EM (Huber 2008; Jänicke 2008; Murphy 2000)[5]. EM is understood as a

> "readaptation of industrial society within the global geo and biosphere by modern means such as scientific knowledge base and advanced technology in order to upgrade the earth's carrying capacity and make development more sustainable" (Huber 2008, p. 360).

---

[5] Though York and Rosa (2003) tend to suggest that technological optimism of EM has become more subtle as time passed by, even the very recent literature from the major exponents demonstrate that they still throw their weight behind technological optimism while recognising that technological practice as a socially embedded process (Huber 2008).

On the same lines, the conception of CDM is fundamentally based on the optimism that mitigation of, and adaptation to climate variations can be achieved through technological solutions. It envisions that the systematic deployment of environment-friendly solutions in the form of cleaner technologies in the existing system of production processes and in the augmentation of the same in industrial proliferation through a network of actors can effectively address the climate change problem. It is very much in line with the approach of EM that focuses on environmental improvements through resource efficient innovation (Jänicke 2008), particularly the incremental improvement of technology. Incremental improvement, according to Jänicke (2008), denotes the application of cleaner technologies for different dimensions of efficiencies such as material intensity, energy intensity, transport intensity, surface intensity and risk intensity whereas the radical innovation is understood as the market introduction of a new technology that enhances the life cycle of a product. Thus, CDM is in harmony with EM with regard to its technological optimism coupled with its inherent predisposition to the potential of industrial capitalism to overcome the environmental problems created as part of the industrialisation process.

The form of technological optimism in EM, particularly that of super-industrialisation, is very close to technological determinism, which considers technology as value neutral autonomous process with an innate capacity for logical progression, thereby black-boxing the social processes that construct technology – a point that is thoroughly challenged by the Science and Technology Studies (STS) on the basis of the contextually and ideologically contingent nature of knowledge and instrument creation.

Commodification of Nature

The commodification of nature is one of the essential operational prerequisites for EM. Drawing from Mol's 'economization of ecology' as an introduction to economic concepts, mechanisms and principles to environmental policy, Murphy identifies that this process may involve

> "placing an economic value to nature with the general aim of encouraging economic actors to take the environment into consideration" (Murphy 2000, p. 3).

This goes in line with another postulate of EM where environment can be seen as an increasingly autonomous arena of decision making (Buttel 2000). The proposition for commodification of nature in the EM perspective is derived from the fundamental conviction that the market can be more effective and efficient than the state in dealing with ecological problems. On the other hand, in reference to Kyoto mechanisms, it is argued that by creating economic and emission-reduction accreditation schemes the climate change regime has sought to create market tools for trading the commodity of GHG emissions, which points to the capitalistic identification of new resources and the commodification of the atmospheric commons (Glover 1999). This is one of the ways in which, as referred to by Sonnenfeld and Mol (2002), environment is institutionalised in the economic domain.

Negation of Radical Change and Politics

Closely linked to the neoliberal economic understanding, EM eschews radical political options from its schemata by emphasising the macro structural changes that bring forth transformation in the relation between state and society. Buttel (2000) points out that the rise of EM has more to do with its role as a response to the radical environmental politics of 1980s that stood for overhauling capitalist industrialism through deindustrialisation, decentralisation and localisation by advocating significant decreases in fossil energy usage, reversal of tropical forest destruction and biodiversity loss and by demanding for strict regulation etc. Thus, while the negation of radical politics is inherent to EM, its overarching faith in the prevailing forms of liberal capitalism to lead to sustainable environmental practices by merging the economic and ecological rationalities forecloses the possibility of any radical systemic changes from within its purview. By adhering to the market instruments to address climate change mitigation, Kyoto mechanisms very much stand within the basic understanding of EM and do not incorporate the possibility of any radical change in the interplay of ecological and economic actors or in the framing of climate politics (directly).

Regulatory Issues

While the proponents of EM consider that the 'command-and-control' model of state regulation is outmoded, inflexible and inefficient (Buttel 2003), stringent regulation is argued, particularly of late, to be an important precondition for the emerging technological regimes (Huber 2008). They envisage *smart regulation* where knowledge embedded instruments is intrinsically part of the emerging regulatory capitalism (Jänicke 2008). At the same time there is a plea to reinvent and strengthen the role of government to establish rigorous environmental standards for industrial innovation in the context of multilevel governance (Jänicke 2008; Murphy 2000). The national targets of the Kyoto mechanism that combine the demanding, calculable and dialogue oriented policy style economic instruments at one level with the broad but integrated actor configuration in a framework at another, according to Jänicke (2008), is an advanced and sophisticated policy approach to EM.

21.2.3 Clean Development Mechanism as Ecological Modernisation

The previous parts of this section attempted to contextualise how the principal presumptions of CDM concurrent with the theoretical premises of the EM perspective. Though Huber (2008) shows his scepticism about the Kyoto mechanisms by citing them to be formative (rather than effective) and marred with operational limitations, in principle, it can be argued that CDM as an instrument of climate change mitigation conceptually emanates from the discursive boundaries of EM framework. Huber's contentions discussed above, as clearly indicated, rather revolve around the practical schemes of implementation beside the supremacy he attaches to the *national* endeavours of environmental standards setting and spearheading innovation policies. The next section delves into a critical review of CDM in the light of EM to probe whether these issues of contention can be defined exclusively within the operational limitations of the transnational regimes.

21.3 A Critical Review of CDM

This section looks into a few of the contentions raised about the systemic and functional aspects of CDM to find how these issues are located within the larger setting of the emergent form of environmental governance in general and EM in particular. Though mostly articulated either as systemic limitations or operational flaws, in a closer analysis it can be found that these issues are not as clearly distinguishable as they are often made out to be, particularly because the process of noncompliance (in the case of operational flaws) itself is very much ingrained in the system. Most of these issues ranging from the potential and real outcomes of CDM, questions about the categories and definitions, emphasis on production processes, issues around incremental change and pollution to technification of politics, began to crop up simultaneously with the emergence of the CDM regime and remained with varying hues as CDM evolved.

21.3.1 Outcomes of CDM

The CDM, as an instrument in the climate change regime is, politically and economically, a significant mechanism beyond its immediate functions of creating carbon credits and facilitating sustainable development. Wara (2007) and Werksman (2002), for instance, consider that engaging developing nations in the climate regime was one of the major political stumbling blocks in the initial phase of climate negotiations and that CDM has become an effective means of engaging the global South into the process. However, the same process is not uniformly understood unilaterally as it is also viewed as a relationship between unequal parties even to the extent that it is denoted as 'carbon colonialism' (Agarwal and Narain 1995; Bachram 2004). At the same time, on a more concrete level, the twin objectives of the exchange of carbon credits and facilitation of sustainable development themselves have generated diverse reactions.

CDM as a Market Instrument

The suitability CDM as a market instrument is challenged on conceptual and operational grounds. Primarily, as Wara (2007) points out, despite being one of the major vehicles of emission reduction, CDM is considered to be highly inadequate to deal with the scientifically projected amounts of emission reduction. It is indicated that the Kyoto mechanism as a whole is performing below its own targets (Christoff 2006). The estimated annual emission reduction through the CDM projects, which amounts to 278 million tonnes of CO_2-equivalent GHGs, is a small fraction of the annual global CO_2 emissions, calculated as 26 billion tonnes in 2003 (Wara 2007). If the timescales for negotiations and implementation is also taken into account, it is argued that at least thirty Kyoto Protocols are required to address the climate change problem as it is understood today (Malakoff 1997). However, beyond its limitations with regard to the inadequacy of scale, the points raised about the mechanism and its operational parameters are varied and significant. The creation of a market instrument to tackle climate change variations is questioned on the basis of the capability of the market to enable sustainable environmental relations, particularly from an environmental justice perspective where the critics argue that issues of equity, access to resources, balanced distribution etc are beyond the operational priorities of markets (Bachram 2004; Roberts and Parks 2007; Byrne and Glover 2000). Even within the functional parameters of the CDM procedures the market induced reformulation of projects concentrated on specific GHGs, as in the case of HFC-23, has distorted the very market process (Wara 2007; 2008). Furthermore, there is another set of contradictions that is pointed out in the process of market formulation where there are no clear demarcations that distinguish consultants, verifiers and monitors, who in turn can be the same set of actors (Bachram 2004; CSE 2005). The proliferation of private actors in the central governance of CDM projects raises not only questions about accountability, but the diffusion of political authority as well (Lövbrand et al. 2007).

Kulkarni (2003) argues similarly, that relying on the market mechanisms to deal with mitigation in the form of carbon credits results in environmental stewardship mostly around end-of-the-pipe solutions where sustainability and equity could be compromised globally with investments made in the quickest and easiest emissions reduction options. Moreover, it is argued that market is not a level playing ground among the stakeholders, where the dominant players, mostly the powerful buyers, can set the terms of trade (Nelson and Jong 2003). The criticisms against the operational parameters of the clause of *additionality*[6], particularly, for instance in the case of carbon sinks where a generations old rainforest would not qualify the emission credits while a monoculture plantation can qualify (Bachram 2004), run on the same lines where the market become instrumental in defining the terms of inclusion and exclusion.

CDM as a Channel for Sustainable Development

The CDM as a vehicle for sustainable development is problematised mainly on two grounds. Firstly, since the concept of sustainable development generally encompasses a variety of meanings and strategies in development discourses (Hopwood et al. 2005; Luke 2005; Redclift 2005), the conception and definition of sustainable development in CDM projects are subjected to variety of mediations in definitions, tools and analyses. Further, the different actors in different locations in the same regime could define sustainability or regime requirements within their

[6] Additionality is a clause wherein the emission reduction is calculated as the amount of planned reduction from the baseline counterfactual rate in the absence of the project.

local contexts that need not necessarily subscribe to the larger understanding of sustainability (CSE 2005; Kim 2004).

Secondly, in operational contexts, CDM as an instrument that combines the dual objectives of attaining cost effective GHG reductions for the advanced industrial countries and accomplishing sustainable development in developing countries, is referred to both as a source of synergy and conflict (Olsen 2005). There is a trade-off happening between these twin objectives (Lövbrand et al. 2007) where the actors exert different strategies to appropriate the mechanism according to their interests. After reviewing quite a few studies that deal with this conflict, Olsen (2005) points out that the aim of cost-effective GHG reductions overruns the sustainability priorities significantly. The projects with higher social equity features are progressively decreasing not only because of the higher investment/operational costs but also due to the lower volume of carbon credits they generally fetch. This market pressure in turn leads the host countries and their DNA (Designated National Authority) to define[7] competitively lower standards for sustainable development criteria within their territorial limits to attract more CDM investments. Thus, the sustainability standards are set as per the prevailing market situations of the carbon transactions, due to the global scope of CDM and the wider choice of location for the investors (Olsen 2005).

21.3.2 Analytical Categories and Definitions of Problems

While conceiving the problem and operationalising the remedial courses, the climate change regime has constructed an elaborate network of actors and charted out the specific modalities of interaction. These network prescriptions and categories in turn regulate and govern the actors by placing them in specific locations of specific significance. The issues around the analytical categories and problem definitions have been some of the widely contentious domains in the case of CDM. However, the difficulties with analytical categories and definitions of problems can be rather broad (see Grundmann 2006; Pielke Jr. 2005; van der Sluijs et al. 1998).

National Emissions against per Capita Emissions

Emissions measured on the basis of the country levels, and not on the basis of per unit of population, is an issue argued to be disproportionate and against the values of equity and ecological justice (Agarwal and Narain 1999; Byrne et al. 1998). Byrne et al. (1998) argue for a per capita emission-based stabilization objective that they consider to be equitable as every individual has a common share in the potential emission to the common atmosphere. While the present emission levels show a huge disparity between people belonging to different regions, the problem

[7] DNA of the specific developing country is the agency to define the specified sustainability standards that are applicable to that particular country.

is still deeper on the basis of reference points on which the disparities are accounted even within a region or in a production or exchange system.

Developed and Developing Countries Categories

The categorisation of developed and developing countries poses several inherent problems with regard to the CDM's operational guidelines. The arrangement is problematic because of the inherent spatial organization and standards of the regime wherein the North-South dichotomy obfuscates the differential vulnerability, accessibility and adoption capabilities among the different countries/regions in the South (Kulkarni 2003), and Central and East European Countries (Muhovic-Dorsner 2005) and overlooks the broader categories, classes or communities within a category. There are studies that demonstrate how some categories of population, particularly the affluent sections in developing countries emit on a par with the highest emitters in the advanced world and hide behind the poor without conceding to any restrictions (Ananthapadmanabhan et al. 2007). Again, with regard to investment pattern, as cautioned by Agarwal and Narain (1999), the ongoing trend of CDM indicates that the more advanced among the developing countries are drawing more resources and effectively exacerbating the disparities among the developing nations. As an instrument stemmed from EM, the transterritoriality of the climate change regime may also foster the analytical complexity of CDM further, since some regions may lack the cultural endowments of industrially advanced western societies that Cohen (1998) attributed to EM.

Category of emission units

The general standard of emission units, as in the form of CER in CDM, is calculated as CO_2 equivalents and has the inherent predisposition to classify emissions of all kinds in to a standard technical category without taking into account the broader production, distribution and consumption practices, differential access to resources and prevailing inequalities in production and distribution processes. Thus, there can be a mismatch between *luxury emissions* by some with the *survival emission* of others, which is one of the long-standing contentions of the developing countries (Agarwal and Narain 1995).

Environment as against Development

The framing of the climate change varies among the different actors at different levels of the regime and they integrate themselves to the regime through ascribing contextual values to their specific acts (Kim 2004). As Olsen (2005) suggests, there exists a well-explored line of conflict between north and south; in the north the focus on climate change as a global environmental problem whereas in the south it is more focused on as a development problem. Consistent to that are the approaches devised to tackle the focal issues too. The priorities of the nation-states with regard to CDM can inherently pose a conflict of interests where the twin objectives of the mechanism could be tilted accordingly.

21.3.3 Emphasis on Production and Related Issues

The climate change regime in general, and its instruments like CDM as a whole, emphasizes intervention in practices that mostly encompass production. The regime, set according to the understanding of EM, overtly presupposes that the sphere of intervention for ecological sustainability is logically centralised around the production practices. The discussion on consumption in EM revolves around the agency of the citizen-consumers for greening of consumption (eg. Spaargaren and Mol 2008) which tends to delink the structural processes in which the consumption is embedded. EM mostly renders the different aspects around consumption, access to products, equity in resource allocation etc to lesser significance. Consequently, this perpetuates the existing hierarchies in political and economic arrangements of resource utilisation and sets aside the complex processes of production and exchange.

It also presumes that the action performed at a specific point of the process entail direct correlation to sustainable practices and detaches the network of processes in which this specific action could be embedded. As York and Rosa (2003) argue, EM does not ensure that the industries or the firms, that are reducing their direct impact on the environment, are not facilitating the expansion of negative impacts by other industries or firms. Furthermore, the emphasis on production processes focuses on the achievement of a high degree of end-use efficiency that, as suggested by Kulkarni (2003) by citing the experience of the developed countries, need not necessarily mitigate the emissions. Rather, these processes intensify the demand and dependence on the prevailing systems of production. Similarly, the transfer of technologies to developing countries can induce overall increase in emissions as the technologies could engender life style changes that demand increased resources or energy consumption (Kulkarni 2003). Thus, a CDM project can potentially be detrimental to its own objectives within the current parameters of operation.

21.3.4 Commodification of Atmosphere

The operational aspects of the climate change regime commodify atmosphere through technically mediated standards, which give rise to two immediate issues of analysis. Firstly, commodification embeds the atmosphere in new economic relations and opens a domain for the market to operate within parameters that are rooted in the 'politics of market design' (MacKenzie 2008). It is argued that by creating economic and emission-reduction accreditation schemes, the Kyoto mechanisms have sought to create market tools for trading the commodity of GHG emissions, which points to the capitalistic identification of new resources and the commodification of the atmospheric commons (Glover 1999).

Secondly, commodification of the atmosphere is symbiotically connected to technification of politics in the climate change regime, where representation of collective interests is entrusted to experts or large organizations alongside the states (which in turn rely on experts). The carbon market tends to marginalize the non-corporate, non-state and non-expert contributions toward climate stability (Lohmann 2006). However, the effective engagement of other stakeholders is confined not only because the performance standards are set in scientific terms that are decipherable only to experts; it is also because of, as Lövbrand et al. (2007) identify, the arena in which local stakeholders may provide input, which is generally confined to host governments and DOEs(Designated Operational Entities), is mediated on a technical level.

One of the operational translations of commodification of atmosphere is the institutionalization of emission in the form of cap and trade scheme, where the polluters are effectively entitled to pollute at permissible levels. By making carbon fungible (MacKenzie 2008), wider possibilities of exchange become possible; where, as Bachram (2004) argues, a polluter can invest in emission reduction projects and earn credits, keep the unused credits for future or sell them to another polluter in the open market. On the other hand, a emitter can exceed the 'allowed emissions' by purchasing additional credits. Thus, the process of *outsourcing emissions* does not inherently ensure aggregate emission reduction.

21.3.5 Problem of Incremental Change

The climate change regime and its instruments facilitate incremental changes rather than radical alterations in addressing the mitigation of climate variations. The process does not curtail the ongoing industrial practices; rather, it focuses to augment the current practices. Thereby, it is argued that it leaves a possibility of perpetuating slow and continuous pollution through environmentally friendly technologies (MacKenzie 2008).

As the incremental changes within the larger framework do not alter the existing systems of production, distribution or consumption that are at present designed based on a high reliance on fossil fuels, it is also argued that the emphasis on clean-coal technologies could lead to a locking in with the fossil fuel economy (Kulkarni 2003). On the other hand, the option to externalize emissions from the industrialized countries through CDM projects may result in the intensification of ongoing operations, which could result in worse cumulative emissions. Similarly, Kulkarni (2003) further points out that the cheaper abatement of emissions elsewhere may prompt firms in developed countries to avoid any action at home, and in effect the abatement in the developed countries is nullified by the increasing emissions at home.

21.4 Conclusion: CDM as Outsourcing Pollution

The article is an overview of the current discussions about CDM in the light of the EM perspective to see how this emergent mechanism in the climate change regime illustrates one of the prominent trends in the present direction of environmental governance. In the initial part, it analysed how CDM as an instrument for GHG abatement conceptually emanates from within the discursive boundaries of the EM framework on the basis of its roots in liberal capitalism and technological optimism. This is beside the identical methods of problem conceptualization and the orientation towards politics and regulatory issues. In this context, the following part indicates how most of the aspersions made on CDM are inherent to the EM perspective itself, with both systemic and operational aspects intertwined within.

While the commodification of atmosphere has far reaching implications; from the very initial analyses onwards, CDM is observed to be subverting its sustainability objectives by its role as a market instrument. Similarly, EM's preoccupation with production practices as a main domain of operation enables mechanisms like CDM to quarantine themselves from other potential effects that the processes can have on other points in the product cycle or in another industry. At the same time, the overwhelming reliance on incremental change, and negation of radical solutions, may result in more environmentally disastrous outcomes in the long run. On the other hand, CDM's analytical categories and problem-definitions, both on functional and theoretical postulates, entail systematic methods of inclusion and exclusion, whereas it explicitly upholds the 'level playing ground' of market and 'objectivity' of science.

Externalising emissions, as similar to other capitalist production or consumption processes, from its location of generation is one the fundamental features of GHG abatement efforts of the climate change regime. This process of *outsourcing pollution* is mostly formulated through technoscientific mechanisms and operationlised through transterritorial market instruments like CDM. The complexities involved in the politics of market and science make the process of outsourcing pollution a locus of multiple negotiations and appropriations of diverse interests. In this process, as noted in the previous sections, EM and its operational manifestations like CDM are inherently predisposed to certain specific ways of dealing with environmental problems, which may ingrain socio-political values antithetical to equity and justice on different geographical and political scales.

Acknowledgments

The comments and suggestions made by both Ingmar Lippert and Rosmin Mathew were immensely valuable and I am thankful to them. However, the responsibility for the possible shortcomings in the paper is strictly mine.

References

Agarwal A, Narain S (1995) Global Warming in an Unequal World: A Case of Environmental Colonialism. In: Conca K. et al. (eds) Green Planet Blues: Environmental Policy from Stockholm to Rio. West View, Boulder, pp. 157-160

Agarwal A, Narain S (1999) How Poor Nations can help to Save the World. In: Munasinghe M, Swart R (eds) Climate Change and its Linkages with Development, Equity and Sustainability. Proceedings of the IPCC Expert Meeting held in Colombo, Sri Lanka, 27-29 April 1999. LIFE/RIVM/World Bank, pp. 191-214

Amin A (2002) Spatialities of Globalisation. In: Environment and Planning A 34(3): 385-399

Ananthapadmanabhan G, Srinivas K, Gopal V (2007) Hiding Behind the Poor. Greenpeace India, New Delhi

Bachram H (2004) Climate Fraud and Carbon Colonialism: the New Trade in Greenhouse Gases. In: Capitalism/Nature/Socialism 15(4): 1-16

Boehmer-Christiansen S (2003) Science, Equity, and the War against Carbon. In: Science, Technology and Human Values 28(1): 69-92

Bulkeley H (2005) Reconfiguring Environmental Governance: Towards a Politics of Scales and Networks. In: Political Geography 24(8): 875-902

Buttel FH (2000) Ecological Modernization as Social Theory. In: Geoforum 31(1): 57-65

Buttel FH (2003) Environmental Sociology and the Explanation of Environmental Reform. In: Organization and Environment 16(3): 306-344

Byrne J, Glover L (2000) Climate Shopping: Putting the Climate Up for Sale. TELA Publications Series, Melbourne

Byrne J, Wang YD, Lee H, Kim JD (1998) An Equity and Sustainability-based Policy Response to Climate Change. In: Energy Policy 26(4): 335-343

Christoff P (2006) Post-Kyoto? Post-Bush? Towards an Effective 'Climate Coalition of the Willing'. In: International Affairs 82(5): 831-860

Cohen MJ (1998) Science and the Environment: Assessing Cultural Capacity for Ecological Modernization. In: Public Understanding of Science 7(2): 149-167

CSE – Centre for Science and Environment (2005) Black as the Carbon They Deal in. In: Down To Earth Vol. 14, No. 12, Society for Environmental Communications, New Delhi

Davidson DJ, Frickel S (2004) Understanding Environmental Governance: A Critical Review. In: Organization and Environment 17(4): 471-492

Glover L (1999) Atmosphere for Sale: Inventing Commercial Climate Change. In: Bulletin of Science, Technology and Society 19(6): 501-510

Grove RH (1996) Green imperialism: Colonial Expansion, Tropical Island Edens and the Origins of Environmentalism, 1600-1860. Cambridge University Press, Cambridge

Grundmann R (2006) Ozone and Climate: Scientific Consensus and Leadership. In: Science, Technology and Human Values 31(1): 73-101

Hopwood B, Mellor M, O'Brien G (2005) Sustainable Development: Mapping Different Approaches. In: Sustainable Development 13(1): 38-52

Huber J (2008) Pioneer Countries and the Global Diffusion of Environmental Innovations: Theses from the Viewpoint of Ecological Modernisation Theory. In: Global Environmental Change 18(3): 360-367

Jänicke M (2008) Ecological Modernization: New Perspectives. In: Journal of Cleaner Production 16(5): 557-565

Johnson K (2001) Brazil and the Politics of the Climate Change Negotiations. In: The Journal of Environment and Development 10(2): 178-206

Kim JA (2004) Sustainable Development and the Clean Development Mechanism: A South African Case Study. In: Journal of Environment and Development 13(3): 201-219

Kulkarni JS (2003) A Southern Critique of the Globalist Assumption about Technology Transfer in Climate Change Treaty Negotiations. In: Bulletin of Science, Technology and Society 23(4): 256-264

Lohmann L (2006) Carbon Trading: A Critical Conversation on Climate Change, Privatisation and Power. Development Dialogue, no. 48. The Dag Hammarskjöld Centre, Uppsala

Lövbrand E, Nordqvist J, Rindefjäll T (2007) Everyone Loves a Winner – Expectations and Realisations in the Emerging CDM Market. Amsterdam Conference on the Human Dimensions of Global Environmental Change, May 24-26 2007

Luke TW (2005) Neither Sustainable nor Development: Reconsidering Sustainability in Development. In: Sustainable Development 13(4): 228-238

MacKenzie D (2008) Making Things the Same: Gases, Emission Rights and the Politics of Carbon Markets. In: Accounting, Organizations and Society 34(3-4): 440-455

Malakoff D (1997) Thirty Koyotos needed to control warming. In: Science 278(5346): 2048

Mol APJ, Sonnenfeld DA (ed) (2000) Ecological Modernization around the World: Perspectives and Critical Debates. Frank Cass, London

Mol APJ, Spaargaren G (2005) From Additions and Withdrawals to Environmental Flows: Reframing Debates in the Environmental Social Sciences. In: Organization and Environment 18(1): 91-107

Mol APJ (1995) The Refinement of Production: Ecological Modernization Theory and the Chemical Industry. Van Arkel, Utrecht

Muhovic-Dorsner K (2005) Evaluating European Climate Change Policy: An Ecological Justice Approach. In: Bulletin of Science Technology Society 25(3): 238-246

Murphy J (2000) Ecological Modernisation. In: Geoforum 31(1): 1-8

Nelson KC, Jong BD (2003) Making Global Initiatives Local Realities: Carbon Mitigation Projects in Chiapas, Mexico. In: Global Environmental Change 13(1): 19-30

Ninan AS (2009) Technopolitical Mediations in the Climate Change Regime: STS takes on Hot Air. In: Bammé A, Getzinger G, Wieser B (eds) Yearbook 2008 of the Institute for Advanced Studies on Science, Technology and Society. Profil, Munich/Vienna, pp. 277-295

Olsen KH (2005) The Clean Development Mechanism's Contribution to Sustainable Development. ReNED Conference, October 27, 2005

Pielke Jr. RA (2005) Misdefining "Climate Change": Consequences for Science and Action. In: Environmental Science and Policy 8(6): 548-561

Redclift M (2005) Sustainable Development (1987–2005): An Oxymoron Comes of Age. In: Sustainable Development 13(4): 212-227

Roberts JT, Parks BC (2007) A Climate of Injustice: Global Inequality, North-South Politics, and Climate Policy. MIT Press, Cambridge

Sonnenfeld DA, Mol APJ (2002) Globalization and the Transformation of Environmental Governance: An Introduction. In: American Behavioral Scientist 45(9): 1318-1339

Spaargaren G, Mol APJ (2008) Greening Global Consumption: Redefining Politics and Authority. In: Global Environmental Change 18(3): 350-359

Taylor PJ, Buttel FH (1992) How do we Know we have Global Environmental Problems? Science and the Globalization of Environmental Discourse. In: Geoforum 23(3): 405-416

van der Sluijs J, van Eijndhoven J, Shackley S, Wynne B (1998) Anchoring Devices in Science for Policy: The Case of Consensus around Climate Sensitivity. In: Social Studies of Science 28(2): 291-323

Wara M (2007) Is the Global Carbon Market Working? In: Nature 445(8): 595-596

Wara M (2008) Measuring the Clean Development Mechanism's Performance and Potential. In: UCLA Law Review 55(6): 1759-1803

Werksman J (2002) The Clean Development Mechanism: Unwrapping the 'Kyoto Surprise'. In: Review of European Community and International Environmental Law 7(2): 147-158

York R, Rosa EA (2003) Key Challenges to Ecological Modernization Theory: Institutional Efficacy, Case Study Evidence, Units of Analysis, and the Pace of Eco-Efficiency. In: Organization and Environment 16(3): 273-288

Zimmerer KS (2006) Cultural Ecology: At the Interface with Political Ecology- the New Geographies of Environmental Conservation and Globalization. In: Progress in Human Geography 30(1): 63-78

22 Sustaining Waste – Sociological Perspectives on Recycling a Hybrid Object

Ingmar Lippert

Augsburg University, Chair of Sociology, Augsburg, Germany

Abbreviations

ANT	Actor-network theory
EM	Ecological Modernisation
EMT	Ecological Modernisation Theory
OPP	Obligatory Passage Point

22.1 Introduction

Recycling is a concept, normally taken-for-granted within academic approaches to environmental management. Recognising that recycling should be preceded by reduction of waste and re-use, the science of recycling usually addresses its object as an activity which needs optimising, rather than questioning. My take on recycling differs from the standard one: I focus on possibilities to conceptualise an agent who was responsible for implementing a recycling scheme for her[1] organisation. By way of drawing on sociological theories (especially Bourdieu's theory of practice and Actor-network theory) I point to significant problems in approaching sustainability. The empirical data consists of ethnographic field work which illustrates societal implications of thinking about transforming organisations towards sustainable conduct: by constructing a recycling scheme the waste manager of the organisation ensures that the organisation does not move towards reducing or altering resource consumption. Rather, she stabilises an unsustainable trajectory and inhibits societal transformation even beyond her organisation. Thus, sociological theory allows for problematising and better grasping of the societal implications and limitations of environmental management.

In this paper I am concerned with an everyday set of activities to protect the environment: recycling. Recycling is a ubiquitous social practice which in general

[1] In order to break with the ascribed masculinity of agency, this paper refers to agents in general as female, while the case study revolves around a male actor.

is taken-for-granted as contributing to ecological sustainability. Western environmentalists, both governments and many grassroots activists, share the common sense of 'the more recycling, the better'. However, recycling is merely *one* moment of materialised social relations between humans and things, in Western societies characterised by capitalist production and consumption. The aim of this paper, then, is to focus on the social context of this very moment and, therefore, we ask: how can social theory be of help to problematise environmental management practices and technologies, including their social and environmental implications? To make this practically relevant I focus on theories that may illuminate the role of the actor, i.e. the environmental manager. By far the most influential discourse on recycling seems to be *Ecological Modernisation*. Its paradigm is one of greening the state and industry by more efficient industrial production enabled by all-encompassing capitalist markets. However, both critical academics as well as ecologically oriented social movements argue that, in fact, the hegemonic paths of greening are sustaining 'unsustainability' (Blühdorn and Welsh 2007). To uncover the relevancy of social relations embedded in recycling practices I draw on a case of an environmental manager of a small organisation who set up a recycling network for a nightclub. I encountered this case during ethnographic research on environmental managers in Germany, Austria and the UK between 2006 and 2008. The method used, ethnography, is increasingly deemed useful for research on (environmental) management[2].

Three theoretical approaches serve to frame this set of practices which bring about a recycling network. First, the hegemonic approach to conceptualise greening of organisations, *Ecological Modernisation Theory*, enables us to understand how recycling can easily be thought of as use- and meaningful. Second, *Actor-network theory*, a relational method developed to scrutinise the enacting of science and technology, illuminates the social context in which recycling is socially and materially constructed as necessary and which is embedded within recycling. Third, a Bourdieusian approach, i.e. one drawing on the writings of the French sociologist *Pierre Bourdieu*, problematises the societal conditions under which recycling is use- and meaningful. This engagement with conflicting theoretical approaches, a kaleidoscope of social theory, allows us to question everyday waste and one of the prime technologies to handle it, i.e. recycling.

By sketching this kaleidoscopic view it becomes possible to imagine the complexity of recycling reality. A single theoretical approach alone would risk drawing too nice and neat a picture of recycling. In the following, therefore, I will outline the case and, thereafter, apply the three theoretical perspectives to it to illustrate the myriad social aspects of recycling. The discussion of these perspectives points us to limits of manageability. Finally, by way of summarising, the conclusion argues that recycling may sustain unsustainability both materially and socially. Thus, inspired by Keller (1998, p. 290), recycling emerges as a useful object to question the social technologies which Western societies are based upon.

[2] Cf. e.g. Howard-Grenville et al. 2008, Hassard et al. 2007.

22.2 Situating Recycling in Practice

The practice of recycling is intrinsically linked to the creation and management of waste. Societies of all kinds, cultures and ages had to deal with both the disposal of no-longer needed materials and the gathering of those bits which could be used directly or after processing (Keller 1998, p. 61)[3]. By now, it seems common sense in policy discourse that "industrial operations should be encouraged that are more efficient in terms of resource use, that generate less pollution and waste [as well as on those] that are based on the use of renewable [...] resources" (Brundtland et al. 1987, p. 213). Corporations claim to green themselves and in the course of that they introduce recycling schemes. However, the limits of recycling remain to be scrutinised. To situate the limits of managing recycling in the social[4] a case seems adequate.

The case revolves around Julian Berger whom I met in 2006 during my ethnographic fieldwork. I spent a day with Julian[5] at one of my frequent meetings with students and staff involved in 'greening' universities – somewhere in Western Europe[6]. Julian was employed by the student union of his university to co-ordinate environmental projects and the environmental management of the union. Before this part-time job he had been taking a course dealing with environmental issues. His work consisted, amongst other things, of communicating with authorities and firms to organise recycling within the university and other facilities within the union. At the same time he was responsible for the recycling of the union office waste. Other topics he dealt with were energy saving and mobility.

I joined Julian at his work to study his practices. For his work he was constantly communicating with others: he needed them to fulfil his tasks, he tried to convince them, they directed him and he served them. Julian was telling me that it was his aim to implement structures within the student union that would help it to become 'green'. During this day it became obvious to me that he was part of many social relations. He made this explicit by talking about what he was doing: "(I)

---

[3] For a definition of recycling see Simonis et al. (2003, p. 167).

[4] Within the paper, 'the social' is not conceived of as a sphere, neatly separated from other spheres. Rather, the social signifies the all encompassing presence of societal relations, practices mediating between us, involved in all human reality including the knowing of any kind of reality.

[5] During this day I undertook ethnographic fieldwork (Agar 1980; Thomas 1993; Burawoy 1998; Graeber 2004) which was part of an engagement with Julian lasting about 10 months. My prime role was being an observer, and occasionally I helped Julian to carry out his tasks. All data from this day is based on field notes. My use of field notes has been inspired by Emerson, Fretz, and Shaw (1995). The analysis aimed at problematising an instance of his practices and do neither represent Julian's intentions nor the wider micro-political setting in which he acted.

[6] I have been involved with 'greening' universities from 2001 till 2007. In this time I met all kinds of university members who dealt with this issue in Austria, Belgium, Germany and the UK.

force him to have an appointment with me", but also "people are avoiding (me)". These relations were a significant medium to achieve his tasks. What were 'his tasks'? Actually, I found it was not easy to differentiate between the tasks he set for himself and the ones his job required. Or, did his job require him to set his own tasks?

In the early afternoon we went through the offices of the student union to gather materials and bring them to recycling points. At one of the points he recognised that the recycling container was 'polluted' with matter which was not supposed to be there. So he got the matter out and brought it somewhere else. Was this a required task? It probably was not part of his job description, but of his stance towards environmental issues: Julian had – and used his – *agency* to change this detail to improve the environmental situation. Later that day he was talking with his boss about energy saving in one of the clubs of the union. The boss made clear where Julian's agency ended: "night clubs (are) designed to waste energy". Four years later, Julian remarked in a written comment on this paper: "Exactly! It is not the remit of an environmental manager to close down the organisation for which he works for".

In my analysis of the day I became particularly interested in Julian's agency in setting up a recycling network. He had the task to organise glass recycling for one of the facilities of the student union; a task which he approached by getting in touch with recycling companies. From them he learned that the amount of glass 'waste' was not enough for the recycling companies and hence they would not come 'just' for the student union facility. In this situation he could have said: "Well, I don't get enough glass and therefore recycling does not work." Instead, however, he got in touch with other producers of glass 'waste', pubs, and managed to get them into a joint glass recycling scheme. In Bourdieu's terms (which I will sketch below) he would do this if it is reasonable to him. Whether something is reasonable depends on the situation consisting of inner stances and external circumstances. I aim to open up whether his setup of the recycling scheme can be considered as Ecological Modernisation (EM). The rationale of Julian's action will remain unknown. What we can investigate, however, is how he used the agency he had at hand. Hence, we shall turn towards approaches of social theory to describe his action, what it encompasses and its limits.

22.3 A Kaleidoscope of Social Theory

The aim of this section is to introduce three perspectives which seem useful to problematise limits of managing the environment. On the one hand Ecological Modernisation Theory is good at sketching the rationality underlying hegemonic discourses and practices of environmental management. On the other hand the partially conflicting perspectives of Pierre Bourdieu and Actor-network theory allow situating management practices in their relations. I do not give full analyses of either of these theories[7]. Rather, I aim at *illustrating* a possibility to problematise Julian's construction of the recycling network.

22.3.1 The Green Lenses of Ecological Modernisation Theory

Julian's job, greening an organisation, is normally considered by sociologists as within the paradigm of Ecological Modernisation. Ecological Modernisation is conceptualised by sociology as Ecological Modernisation Theory[8] – and EMT prevails[9]. Here goes the story-line:

Modern industrial societies created and experience ecological crises. The idea that 'greening' the institutions of industrial society can solve the global ecological crisis[10] has been called Ecological Modernisation (EM). The theorists Arthur Mol, Gert Spaargaren, Martin Jänicke and Joseph Huber[11] suggest(ed) that industrial societies provide a *role model* for mitigating and preventing further deepening of the crisis. Their approach became widely known as Ecological Modernisation Theory (EMT). EM claims that industrialised societies can reach a balanced relationship with nature by engaging with the latter *more techno-scientifically and in ways more mediated by the market economy.*

This claim, however, is also the focus of fundamental critique. According to critics the claim can be categorised as ideological because it is sustained by techno-corporate élites without taking into account well-known critiques which convincingly point out that the ecological crisis has been created systematically and inherently by those structures which EM aims to modernise. Thus, a slight 'greening' of the economic order, i.e. capitalism, cannot constitute a suitable substitute for abolishing this economic order as it also fundamentally constitutes an ecological order in which profit is always more important than nature[12].

Nevertheless, EM as a rationality, i.e. people believing in and practising it, exists. Julian provides a case of someone who believes that EM is part of solving the environmental crisis. Opponents of EM, however, recognise that EM fails to understand what is necessary for the realisation of 'green' goals for all. Therefore,

---

7 For a more detailed discussion of the theories in relation to the case see Lippert (2010).

8 Cf. York and Rosa (2003).

9 Cf. e.g. Blühdorn and Welsh (2007), Jänicke (2008).

10 Summaries of the ecological crisis can be found e.g. in Carvalho (2001, p. 70), Haque (2000, pp. 5-8) and Dingler (2003, p. 4).

11 Sonnenfeld and Mol (2006), Mol (2006), Jänicke (2004), Mol (2001), Mol and Sonnenfeld (2000a), Mol (2000)

12 This has been shown by many academics, i.e. Benton (2001) and Pepper (1984). More specifically, see the critique known as the Treadmill of Production thesis (e.g. Schnaiberg, Pellow, and Weinberg 2000), the concept of Passive Revolutions by Gramsci (as in Li and Hersh 2002) and the theory of Metabolic Rift (von Liebig, Marx and Foster) together with the Jevons Paradox (as in Clark and York 2005).

they suggest that a solution to the crisis needs to be searched outside of either capitalism, industrialism or both[13].

The social existence of EM and its work in and on reality are reason enough to look more closely at what EM rationality assumes. Two claims can be identified: (a) reactive technologies are and ought to be substituted by proactive technologies and (b) the government shall enable the market to allocate environmental goods *efficiently*. Implementing these moves would lead to *win-win solutions*. The EM rationality goes together with the discourse of Sustainable Development. The latter can be seen as a form of EM and has become the key discourse through which environmental problems are discussed since the 1990s[14].

EMT reflects upon EM and asserts that nature and capitalism (including its institutions) can and are in the process of being *reconciled*. Proponents of EMT argue (wrongly) that the environment is becoming autonomous from the economic sphere[15]. ‘Green’ states – they are postulated by EMT – cannot become a reality without abolishing the capitalist mode of production. The trap into which EMT falls is that it construes instances of tiny considerations of the environment as ‘green societies’ becoming true[16]. Such instances might be analytically distinct from ignoring the environment altogether but are clearly not enough to change the essence of capitalism[17]. The gain of EMT is that it provides a quite good conceptualisation of the rationality of EM. The theory implies that EM has agents who put it into practice. Unfortunately, EMT does not explicitly theorise its individual agents, i.e., the individual meaningful actions.

Does Julian’s construction of the recycling network fit into the rationality of EM? We find that Julian in fact enlarged what one could conceptualise as a green market; he drew other business actors into the recycling market in order to comply with his task. Thus, this aspect of construction meets the rationality of EM. Furthermore, this way of constructing a recycling network not only increases the market but also approaches the recycling issue qualitatively in market terms. With EM we can conceptualise the situation preceding recycling as one in which the material ‘glass waste’ was not integrated as a resource into the market[18]. EM suggests that such waste merely has to be processed (technically) and henceforth can be brought into use again. Thus, the construction of the recycling network also constitutes an approach to solving problems technically. Overall, then, Julian did a good job in terms of EM: he reformed his organisation (such that it started recycling) and induced similar changes in other organisations (integrating them into

[13] See e.g. Enzensberger (1996) or Pepper (2005).

[14] Cf. i.e. Redclift and Benton (1994), Benton (1996), von Weizäcker (1999), Mol (2001).

[15] See e.g. Mol (2000) vs. Pellow et al. (2000).

[16] Schnaiberg, Pellow and Weinberg (2000, p. 15)

[17] Marx (1968, see especially Chapter 4 and 5) showed that capitalism is inherently expansive and exploitive. More recently this has been re-discussed by i.e. Li and Hersh (2002, p. 196) as well as Clark and York (2005, pp. 406-407).

[18] The history of glass had included re-use and recycling. In the situation preceding Julian's activities, glass along with all other materials out of place were transported to landfills.

the network) both on the base of integrating waste materials into the market and rendering waste into resources through a technical process. Thus, EMT conceives Julian's recycling network as useful to society and its environmental effects as meaningful to Julian himself.

22.3.2 A Fresh and Flat Perspective through Actor-network Theory

Latour, Callon and Law study science and technology as *actor-networks*. Their approach is usually called Actor-network theory (ANT)[19]. Fasten your seat belts! ANT uses lots of concepts which need to be introduced. Crucial to this approach is that they break, like Haraway (1991), with the culture/nature dualism. In ANT an actor can be anything that acts, i.e., human beings, institutions, and hybrid objects, i.e., those which are shaped by society through technology or discourse (consider e.g. a genetically modified animal). This claim is necessary for Actor-network theorists in order to avoid false assumptions about which actor has how much power. Thus, their approach is based on an ontology[20] which does not discriminate between humans and non-humans. For ANT, all those who act or are subject or object of relations of representation are called *actants*; and they are mapped principally in symmetry. The actor-network is not assumed to be asymmetrical from the outset. Rather, who has power is a matter of empirical study. Power derives from networks which actants control. What does this mean?

Key authors of ANT, Callon and Latour, agree with many sociologists that the fundamental problem of society is agent's interest in more power (1981, p. 293). In order to win, i.e., to increase power, an actant, say Julian, aims to arrange other actants such that they provide power to him. This activity is called *enlistment*. How does this work? Julian would put elements into a black box, such that they are not considered anymore by other actants. An element can be anything. ANT proposes, he "makes other elements dependent upon [himself] and translates their will into a language of [his] own" (ibid., p. 286). Actants are constantly engaged in controversies and struggle. The use of ANT is to investigate how controversies are black-boxed and by that the actants who sits "on top of the box" (ibid., p. 297) gains power[21].

The process of *translation* is of prime importance to ANT. ANT, as studying translation (Law 1992), identifies "the simultaneous production of knowledge and construction of a network of relationships in which social and natural entities mu-

[19] In this account I am focussing on Callon and Latour (1981), Woolgar (1991), Law (1992), Callon (1995), Strathern (1996), Callon (1999) and am informed by Fairhead and Leach (2003), Michael (2000) as well as Bijker (1995). Law and Hassard (1999) became aware of many short-comings of ANT meanwhile and sophisticated it significantly. Within the scope of this paper I focus on original formulations of ANT.

[20] *Ontology* refers to what is. Different ontologies make different assumptions about that. Cf. Mutch (2002, p. 485).

[21] Strathern (1996, p. 523) points us to the fractal logic within the box: networks can be traced into depth without limits.

tually control who they are and what they want" (Callon 1999, p. 67). According to ANT, to gain power Julian has to establish himself as an *Obligatory Passage Point* (OPP) such that others need him. He would construct *obstacle-problems* for others, i.e., make them believe a) that they have a certain aim, b) that such an obstacle-problem is in their way and c) that he is/provides the solution. Thus, by constructing an obstacle-problem one creates problems for others. In this process entities/elements/actants are *enlisted.* To enlist them they need to be interested. To bring this about Julian interposes himself between their obstacle-problem and their aim. To actually mobilise actants one creates new, rather than pre-existing, roles in which they are put. This is called *enrolment.* Callon (1999) postulates that the actants need to be willing to be enrolled[22]. If Julian, who enrols other actants, is successful and establishes himself as an OPP then he can represent the others. In his representation he construes himself as speaking and acting for the others. If the others do not participate in these processes they become dissidents and, by that, destabilise the network which Julian aims to construct. The processes which are necessary to construct the network successfully, i.e., to shape other actants such that they support a network, are called translation. With this Callon refers to two aspects of the processes: a) the other actants are displaced and b) the constructor, i.e., Julian establishes himself as a spokesperson. Through translation "social and natural worlds progressively take form" (1999, p. 81). To exercise the sociology of translations it is necessary to provide a "symmetrical and tolerant description" (ibid), starting with a clean slate (Law 1992), of complex socio-natural processes and by that one explains how *some* obtain the right to represent. Of course the constructor is in conflict with other actants who also want to gain power. Hence, to become stronger a constructing agent needs to enrol others and disassociate the black boxes of others such that the agent can enlist their elements. Callon (1995) points out that translation is not about truth. What ANT does seems to be a translation of the strategies of the actants. Let us see how this analytical approach works in practice. ANT takes all interaction between written marks (inscriptions), technical devices and embodied skills as translation.

This is, taking an ANT perspective, how Julian tried to construct a glass-recycling scheme: First, Julian established himself as an OPP by construing glass waste as an obstacle-problem. By this move he connected all actants, i.e., himself, the glass waste, the recycling company, his boss, the club, other glass waste producers and a governmental authority. He pointed out to them that the glass waste constitutes an obstacle-problem for them (problematisation) and hence they should

[22] In his famous study *Some Elements of a Sociology of Translation: Domestication of the Scallops and the Fishermen of Saint Brieuc Bay*, Callon (1999) looks at a situation in which scientists try to make themselves necessary to problems which a fishermen's community supposedly has. In the course of his study we come across several actants: fishermen, scientists, and scallops. According to his sociology of translation, for enrolment to be successful the scallops need to want to be enrolled: "To negotiate with the scallops is to first negotiate with the currents" (1999, p. 74). Thus, he suggests that the scientists try to communicate with natural objects (which he, of course, sees as social). I will criticise this later on.

move into an advantaged position by dealing with the glass waste. These advantages were construed by pointing out what was at stake for each actant: For example, the recycling company could earn money and needed to pass the obstacle-problem 'glass waste as potential source for profits', the authority could reach its environmental policy goals better by giving financial support for recycling of 'glass waste'. By showing this, Julian established himself as representing their interests: he translated his interests into theirs with the result that his organisation of the glass recycling scheme constituted acting and speaking on their behalf. Thus, Julian tried to enrol the other actants in order to get his job done. ANT says that Julian's enrolment had the aim to black-box the actants. Actors outside, then, would take the black box for-granted, rather then questioning its configuration. This implies he controlled the actor-network 'glass recycling' consisting of several human and non-human entities. It included 'glass' as a *hybrid* of culture and materiality. This means, with ANT, 'glass' emerges as an entity which was significantly shaped by humans. Human actors: first construe glass through a socially shaped process of understanding and recognition and second inscribe culture on the materiality of glass. Some of the relevant actants and their relations are shown in Figure 22.1. To summarise, Julian's aim was the translation of actants and the establishment of himself as a spokesperson[23]. The ANT reading suggests that he negotiated with all the actants and that each of them either wanted to participate in this actor-network or not.

The main problem with ANT is its construal of agents and agency. Many have pointed out that not all entities are actors[24]. Indeed when Callon (1981, p. 299) claims that "(i)t is no more difficult to send tanks into Kabul than to dial 999" it becomes obvious that their analysis of power is not in touch with reality: it is neither possible for me to send tanks into Kabul nor can I imagine how my cup of tea, which helps me a lot in writing this text, should be able to dial 999. Hence, ANT cannot convince totally. Nevertheless, ANT helps to recognise *how significant entities can be as conditions under which we act.* For analysis we need to appreciate this approach to break up 'taken-for-grantedness' regarding the relevancy of materials.

The discussion of Julian's set up of the recycling scheme reveals how it is meaningful to see it as a network which was stabilised through the various humans involved and their material and virtual products. While Julian emerged as acting as a key person to co-configure and stabilise the recycling network, with ANT we have to wonder: how is the agency to alter the network configured? If ANT's interpretation of agency is too broad then we need to move on to another sociological approach which may problematise the agency we have in affecting realities.

---

[23] In order to construct this overall translation aim he also engaged with 'minor' translations like: *job task* to *email 1* to *Governmental authority* to *Public/private organisation* to *communication 1* to *Recycling company* to *collecting glass waste*. The length of this paper does not permit to open this black box as well.

[24] Cf. e.g. Sibeon (1999, p. 322).

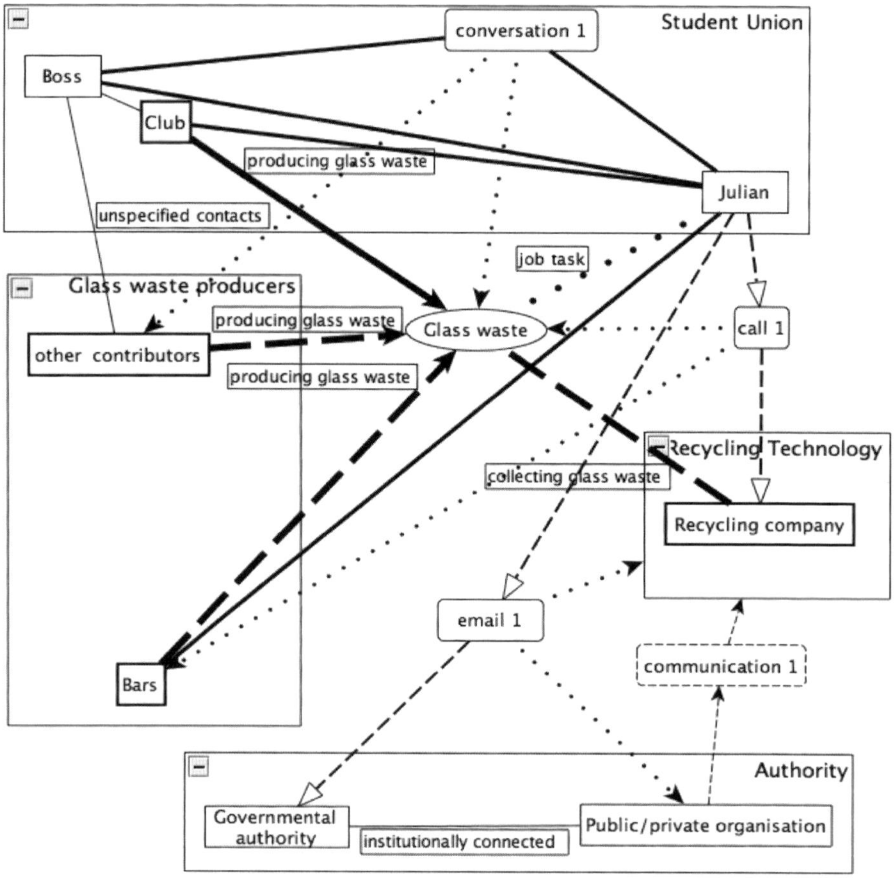

Fig. 22.1. An ANT mapping of actants and relations. *Notes:* thinnest dashed lines: wished-for relations; dotted lines with black ending arrow: references to something; medium dashed lines with white ending arrow: observed communication; thick lines (dashed indicates 'wished-for'): material connections with glass; simple black lines: existing contacts (redrawn from Lippert (2010, p. 76))

22.3.3 Considering Agency of Environmental Managers with Pierre Bourdieu

In order to discuss whether Julian could act otherwise, I introduce the approach of Bourdieu[25]. It is apt to use Bourdieu because he transcends the dichotomy between structure and agency. Thus, by following his thinking we are likely to find results which are not bound to the dualist framing – in the sense that either the agent can

[25] To introduce his approach to social theory I draw on Bourdieu (1989), Bourdieu and Wacquant (1992), Bourdieu (2001).

solve all problems or only structural change will help. Rather, we will develop an understanding of how humans influence others both directly and indirectly. His account is similar to that of Giddens (1986).

Bourdieu uses an open set of concepts to theorise members of society and their agency. He views us as existing in social space, a *field* which comprises all social relations. We are positioned in this field. We cannot know any absolute position but must imagine our positions relative to each other[26]. What we can enquire about is the relation between our positions. The forms of relations are manifestations of our access to the *capital* which is relevant in the field. Through this also power relations are expressed. At my position in the field I encounter the world from this very standpoint. Nobody can have a Godeye's view. Standing at my social position I repeatedly experience similar situations: as a researcher I repeatedly come across situations in which I discuss with so-called experts. These repeating experiences, which are based on situations which vary but have some common characteristics, form my *habitus*. The concept habitus refers to a system of preferences, perceptions and practices which shape and channel how we go through the world.

How can we apply this approach to the day with Julian? The student union in which Julian worked was a social field in which a kind of capital was decisive. The position of Julian within the field, his access to capital and his relative power, influenced, rather than determined, his practices. His position let him repeatedly experience similar situations, which formed his habitus. This, along with his relative position, shaped the way Julian used capital, acted and perceived the world. Let me explain the relation of field to habitus and its implications for agents and for questioning Ecological Modernisation practices in depth.

Fundamental to an understanding of Bourdieu (1989, p. 15) is his "intention [...] to overcome" the opposition between *objective* and *subjective* structures which "stand in dialectical relationship" (1988, p. 782). The objective can influence people independent of their consciousness and will. An example of objective structures would be the upward mobility of peasant women through marriage in Béarn, Bourdieu's childhood village in southwestern France, in the 1960s (2004, p. 589). Subjective structures are those through which we perceive the world and make sense of it, e.g. the dualisms black/white, female/male. He puts forward that to understand actors we need to grasp them in terms of both kinds of structure. Thus, the social fields which we move in comprise both objective reality as well as agents' perception of it.

Such a social field can be imagined like a game. The players know the rules; they take them and what is at stake for-granted. Only those with the characteristics (i.e. access, knowledge of rules, etc.) can participate in the game, be an agent of the field, try to win what is at stake. Rather than talking about interest, Bourdieu uses the concept *illusio* to refer to such an attitude of an agent to the game in which the agent is trapped and lost. This happens when the stake is important to the agent and is not questioned. Bourdieu uses the concept of capital to refer to what is at stake. The capital of a field allows the player to exercise significant in-

[26] I recognise, of course, that social positions are always contested and changing: positioning is an ongoing process.

fluence in the field. Capital is anything which allows such an influence. Therefore players compete over all kinds of capital. Thus, the field structure can be described in terms of the distribution of capital, which refers to the same as the relations between players. Therefore, Bourdieu constructs fields as independent from individual access to capital: as long as the distribution of capital has effects on us, we are part of the field. If a capital is no longer effective, we are in a different field. Within the field, the capital lends power to the agent, over rules and regularities, over material and incorporated means of (re-) production. Hence, a field is much more dynamic than a game: Based on some, but never a complete and objective[27], form of understanding their position players can try to increase their capital as well as to alter the rules or to change the boundaries (2006, p. 129). These moves can be actualised, e.g. by introducing access barriers like certificates, or incorporating others with a different set of capital such that one's relative position is changed. To describe agents we need to understand their position relative to those of others, i.e. to describe the relations between agents who show the structure of the field. How would such a field look in Julian's case?

From my ethnographic field notes it is possible to draw together the field 'work'. Some of the effective forms of capital in it were: (a) institutionalised hierarchy (i.e. the boss could order Julian around), (b) means for getting the work done (this included material means, like a computer, as well as Julian's motivation) and (c) constructions of the *raison d'être* of work (the student union paid Julian as an environmental expert who, therefore, had some power to define what the work was about). Thus, several forms of capital were effective in this field, which implies that there were complex and multiple relations between the positions. These capitals were somehow distributed. Julian had some control, his boss had control and the environmental discourse had significant effects as well. At each position in the field, actors had different access to capital and hence developed a different habitus, specific to the position.

While the field is constructed through objective relations the agents experience it subjectively. The habitus mediates the objective with the subjective. Usually we meet situations which are normal to us, which shapes our perceptions and our practices. By experiencing situations which are alike, and usually they are because of our relative position in the social field, we repeat the experiences, repeat using the same categories successfully, again and again. Under this condition what were singular perceptions and rational practices become a scheme of dealing with the world. This sense is durable and can be conveyed even over generations. With this, the habitus enables us to deal with situations and is actualised situationally. Thus it is a system of potentialities and virtualities. What happens in a situation is not predictable; while most experiences are repeating and thus being strengthened, we can also experience new and different situations. Through learning and reflecting the habitus changes. Thus, it is an open and historical product at the same time. "It is durable but not eternal!" (Bourdieu)[28] Thus, our habitus is contingent.

[27] Thus, for Bourdieu so-called rational choice or a rational actor does not exist (Bourdieu 1988, p. 782).

[28] In: Bourdieu and Wacquant (1992, p. 133)

Reflexivity allows the distancing of oneself from habitus. Habitus is most constraining when the actor is not acting consciously[29]. Enlightening reflexivity can thus help to change how one is influenced by dispositions. This means that Bourdieu conceptualises action as neither mechanistic reaction nor deliberate, free and rationally planned moves. The field influences our moves and at the same time we influence the field. An actor can *emancipate* themselves through reflection and changing their practices. Nevertheless, this subjective acting is societal and therefore unlikely to *easily* change.

Relevant to the patterning of our perception, then, is Bourdieu's idea that the field configures the habitus. The habitus then, helps to understand and create the field as a meaningful world in which investing is worthwhile. The world is shaped by human actors and thus, the social world exists both as habitus and field as well as in things, bodies and minds both within and external of actors. The social world becomes part of the actor and produces the categories which the actor uses to understand the world and therefore the world seems self-evident to the actor. This is relevant in two respects: First, all interactions are also power-relations and if power-relations are not recognised we will be unconscious accomplices in actualising theses relations. Second, if our perception of the world is never all encompassing but relative to our position, which makes us take at least parts of the world as self-evident – a *doxic* stance, then one cannot speak of the actor as using strategies referring to purely intentionally and rationally acting. Bourdieu uses the concept 'strategy' to refer to practice which makes sense, thus is reasonable or rational, in certain constellations of the field[30]. Habitus explains why people are not necessarily stupid although they do not make conscious plans all the time. The habitus is a conditioning to deal with the situations which the agent is *likely* to meet. The concept helps to explain why dispositions/tastes are so durable.

To illustrate, let us visit Julian's work place, get an idea about what he was doing and how he talked about his work: In the beginning he told me about a meeting he would have later the day, "[t]he rest of the time [he] would be phoning and responding to emails"[31]. And in fact, he called a number of actors, looked up contact information on his computer (e.g. visiting a governmental website). Several times he got in touch with authorities. One time he let an official know that his "job is contingent on having *'these things in place'*[32]". In this situation he referred to the environmental management system of the university.

[29] This implies that actors can act more or less consciously. The less conscious an actor is of her actions, contexts, her habitus and the field structure, the more grip the habitus has on her (acts).

[30] Some might wonder how Bourdieu conceptualises reason. For him, the economy of practices relates to any kinds of ends and functions. Practices can serve these functions or meet these ends without being consciously reasoned; nevertheless they can be reasonable.

[31] From a fieldnote

[32] Quote from Julian

Overall, we find that Julian took things for-granted, he followed routines and one can find patterns of how he perceived the world. Some of his routine activities were as follows: he perceived the world much through the computer and used it to organise information; he had to rely heavily on authorities for his work and seemed to take this for-granted; and furthermore, he perceived it as necessary to do the recycling of the student union offices and he carried it out routinely, although he did not enjoy doing it. This means, doing recycling (whatever this means, a care for the environment or just getting the job done) was more reasonable for him than not doing it. As already pointed out, communicating was of high importance to him. He communicated a lot, using all kinds of technologies. In terms of his work's content, his work place organisation included several items which carried messages like "making business sense of climate change" and an environment & money leaflet. As it was his work place organisation, these items could be interpreted to express content which he took-for-granted to be relevant. In terms of schemes of perception it was striking that he interpreted it as worrying when a communication partner forgot his name: *"Adam. Why is she calling me Adam? That's a bit worrying"*[33]. He had the perception that people avoided him and that he needed to use force to make people actually interact with him. Listen to this: *"people are avoiding you"*, *"you have only a certain time chasing people"*, *"force him* [the person he is calling] *to have an appointment with me"*[34]. With Bourdieu, Julian's perceptions and motivation can be considered part of his habitus. The latter makes much sense in terms of Julian's position in the field: he was working in an environmental job with little in the way of job requirements. Much competition existed for such jobs. Hence, if he was not motivated and did not sustain his motivation it was likely that he would have been replaced. At the same time, fitting to his position in an 'unpolitical' context[35] was his acceptance of mainstream propaganda on environmental issues (like the "business sense of climate change")[36]. To play the game of Ecological Modernisation well it was probably more than just helpful to be convinced of its value and being committed allows a seemingly strong position in the field. His habitus was to see small institutional improvements of 'greening' as significant successes and for this reason he contributed pragmatically his own resources to his work – sometimes even beyond job requirements and at other times against his liking.

To sum up, while thinking with Bourdieu emerges as an apt method of situating an environmental manager in terms of her habitus it remains to be discussed in more depth how technology and materiality can influence the actor.

---

[33] Quote

[34] Quotes

[35] Officially, his job was executive, rather than political. The student union had an officer who was responsible for environmental politics.

[36] If he had ethical/political problems with this message it seems it would have been easily possible for him to dispose it: taking away a sticker, commenting it, hiding it.

22.4 Discussion: Limits to Manageability in a Hybrid Field

Bourdieu (1981, p. 307) urges us to disclose how powerful agents conceal the struggles within their field. As alluded to above, such a stance implies breaking with sticky notions of the everyday and questioning how we could construct our object usefully. Let us take a closer look at whether or not the suggested *epistemological break* can be used for analysing glass recycling. To do this, let us return to Figure 22.1. If we look at it we find the central item ‘glass waste’. While Bourdieu does not emphasise the role of material items, Actor-network theory renders them as potentially decisive actants. For our theory to be actually useful for conceptualising environmental management it is doubtless relevant to discuss how a Bourdieusian approach can account for technology and materials which influence social action.

Sterne (2003) focuses on this very issue. He suggests that technology is part of the habitus, i.e., part of the way we move, a socially organised form of movement. Reading Sterne implies a move towards conceptualising technology relationally. What does this mean? In the relational logic things exist relative to each other rather than having absolute characteristics. Schinkel (2003, pp. 78-79) sees this logic as having critical potential: Bourdieu’s “analyses are *unmasking* and *demythologizing*. This is a direct consequence of his anti-essentialism”[37]. If one takes this anti-substantialist, non-naturalising stance one contradicts those who believe in the essence of things and their natural meanings. The non-naturalising stance assumes that one deconstructs these meanings as ideology/ignorance. Using such a relationalist approach Sterne suggests:

> “Technologies are socially shaped along with their meanings, functions, and domains and use. Thus, they cannot come into existence simply to fill a pre-existing role, since the role itself is co-created with the technology by its makers and users. More importantly, this role is not a static function but something that can change over time for groups of people.” (2003, p. 373)

This moves Sterne to view technologies as points at which practices *crystallise*.

> “They are structured by human practices so that they may in turn structure human practices. They embody in physical form particular dispositions and tendencies – particular ways of doing things.” (ibid., p. 377)

Thus, using Bourdieu, one can construe technology as ontologically non-special. Therefore I suggest conceptualising our habitat as *hybrid*. It is both given and socially constructed, technologically and textually. Sterne (2003, p. 386) brings out “technologies (as) just particularly visible sets of crystallised subsets of practices, positions and dispositions in the habitus. They are merely one sort of ‘sedimented history’.”

This hybridisation take on Bourdieu and how to use his work for analysing technologies, provides the ground on which to revisit Julian’s construction of a recycling network. By considering technology as part of habitus, rather than some-

[37] I read essentialism as a synonym of substantialism.

thing ontologically different, a new understanding of Figure 22.1 develops: we are seeing habitus, positions, dispositions and fields. Recycling is a technology which is habitus. Whose habitus is it? The technology, as sedimented history, is shared. Recycling is an artefact of the social technology at which practices crystallise. The practices which crystallise are distributed over various fields, which we can analytically differentiate, i.e., the work field of Julian, the field of the recycling business and politics, the field of capitalism in general. If we look at what, according to ANT, is the common obstacle-problem, glass waste, then the Bourdieusian approach opens novel perspectives: What *is* 'glass waste'? How can we break with the substantialist, sticky idea of the everyday that 'glass waste' is simply glass waste? By applying the notion of habitus to it, we can construct glass waste as part of habitus. The habitus refers to embodied schemes of perceptions and practices. 'Glass waste' (of a night club) is part of our practices of drinking. Agents drink and produce 'glass waste'; in the night club agents are disposed to drink. The habitus generates drinking and putting the bottle somewhere. 'Glass waste' is something we habitually deal with. It is sedimented history, a cultural product of how one normally deals with empty bottles. Around the artefact 'glass waste' practices crystallise which are attuned to the game of drinking, to the position of drinking in the social field 'night club'.

What is Julian faced with and what is he doing? He is organising a recycling technology. By organising recycling he works on the symptom, i.e., an instance of the habitus of the drinking folk. He can 'carry away' as much glass as he wants (by using the shared recycling practices which are taken-for-granted in his field) and, yet, 'glass waste' will not change. To change 'glass waste', one needs to approach its cause, the habitus which generates practices which produce 'glass waste'. Of course, these practices are distributed. 'Glass waste' is not only part of the drinking folk's habitus but also of Julian's, the re-sellers', sellers', producers' and of all the other intermediaries' habitus. Herewith it comes into view that 'glass waste' was part of relations which extended from, in this case, the night club to Julian's office to the global sources of silicon dioxide molecules which were needed for producing glass and to firms which encompassed world-wide cultures of drinking as well as to all those who shared and reproduced the culture of drinking. Julian was situated amongst all these relations. To approach one of them and their relations, i.e. those who drink and put the bottle somewhere, we must not substantialise them. Also, the everyday idea of 'drinking folk' is tenacious. To tackle the 'glass waste' problem one would need to consider changing the fields which stabilise a kind of habitus, which generates practices of producing 'glass waste'. The Bourdieusian take presents the case as a relational issue: a focus on changing symptoms of multiple relations, as in 'glass waste', does not promise changing the relations themselves.

Are then, Julian's management practices determined through the structure of the social field? We find that Julian creates constrains for himself and his organisation through an organisational policy document on 'environmental conduct'. By co-designing such a document he aimed to bring about objective products at which his desired practices would legitimately crystallise. Thus, Julian had some agency and his practices were not totally determined. Nevertheless, whilst he designed such constraints for his organisation others, within the organisation as well as without, i.e. state bureaucracies and public discourses on the environment, constructed constrains for him. Julian was faced with many relations which affected his work practices and his position provided little power to influence them. In our case, the symptom 'glass waste' was a site at which various constraints intersected; to name but a few: economic, cultural, legal and organisational. This site was stabilised through these multiple relations and it was not easy to alter them. Any 'greening' exercise will have to deal with such constraints.

Comparing this discussion with thoughts presented above makes obvious that the construction of a recycling network is not clearly a ground for developing a sustainable human-nature relationship. Rethinking the case – with Bourdieu, Actor-network theory as well as Ecological Modernisation Theory in mind – indicates that recycling naturalises 'glass waste' and that this technological so-called solution carries the taken-for-grantedness of waste and therefore processes it in a proper EM rationality. This rationality produces a lock-in of having to have more, rather than less, glass waste. The recycling network has to ensure sufficient glass waste to sustain itself. However, for humans involved it seems rational in order to ensure having sufficient waste to ensure rather more than less waste produced. Thus, this analysis suggests that *in the course of Ecological Modernisation practices, unsustainability can be sustained.*

Having recognised this, we should now turn the critique to consider where change could come from. This requires consideration of both the tendency of change and the inert character of social order. By using Sterne's work we recognised that the 'world-making' which Bourdieu (1989) refers to can be extended, in that we make the world by both construing and constructing it[38] – symbolically and materially. However, this 'we' needs to be differentiated. The power of world-making is unequally distributed. Some have more access to forms of capital than others. Consider 'glass waste'. It was part of many actors' habitus. 'Glass waste' served as a crystallisation site of many habitus, i.e. of Julian's, the recycling company's agents', the bottle producers' as well as the 'drinking folk's'. Among these actors the bottle producers, I assume, have most agency in shaping the social phenomenon 'glass waste', albeit they have no monopoly in it. In a market economy the consumer has some say and in our example the agents of the social technology recycling can transform the phenomenon as well. Needless to say, neither the material glass nor its constituting entities, like silicon dioxide molecules, have agency in how they become the site of history being objectified; the real/actual aspects of glass merely effectuate how the social can be inscribed on it (Sayer 2000); my cup of tea has effects, rather than agency, on me writing this paper. However, the same aspects of glass structure not only the room for configurations of habitus but also wider fields. If glass became scarcer, it would become expensive and recycling might be substituted by returnable bottles. Of course, a bottle and the specific fabrication of glass are a hybrid between the social and the natural and through them agency can be exercised. An analysis which construes 'glass waste' as a given, naturalises it.

[38] Cf. Fairclough et al. 2002

The construction of a glass-recycling scheme by Julian constructed a world in which more glass was needed, rather than less. Such symbolical and material naturalising, a co-construction of the social and the natural (Irwin 2001), goes hand in hand with drinking. The 'glass waste' was a site at which several habitus intersected – among them drinking. "Drinks construct the world as it is" (Douglas 1987), Julian's 'glass waste' presupposed drinking in bars and drinks are central to Western European cultures. Agency can be increased as well as limited with drinks. To illustrate: for Julian, drinks, as objectified history, allowed him to become a central actor in devising a social technology. Julian's agency was constrained by his culture, in which recycling had become a ritual, and at the same time he co-constructed a culture of drinking which sustained his job. Nevertheless, such agents have some say in – and beyond – their job. In the case provided in this paper Julian could have easily turned the issue of 'glass waste' in a political problem and by that might have allowed other actors, i.e., political green agents, to participate in interpreting and thereby shaping the issue. Thus, if a critical understanding of the issue is developed it is more likely that sustainable pathways will be recognised and, hopefully, used.

22.5 Concluding Thoughts

In this paper I told a partial story about Julian Berger, who co-ordinated environment-related activities for his organisation, and visited his construction of a recycling network. His story is woven into an introduction to two major bodies of social theory: Actor-network theory and Bourdieu's thought. Together, it became possible to problematise the Ecological Modernisation practices of Julian Berger as well as to highlight limits of manageability. Thus, the paper shows possibilities of how social theory can be of help in the study of environmental management. We learned that in the course of constructing a recycling network actually a social lock-in was created; rather than ending up with a social structure (of the recycling network) in which reduction of waste or alternative consumption patterns became the focus the actual network required the production of *enough* waste. If the production of waste decreases more waste will be required to sustain the recycling network!

Furthermore, we found a variety of social implications of the network. Both approaches, ANT and Bourdieu, stress relationality. With this emphasis we demonstrated that the management practices are embedded in a variety of relations – material as well as social. The recycling network was designed to be successfully embedded in a variety of hegemonic relations – amongst them capitalist and technological ones. This complies very well with the paradigm of Ecological Modernisation which states that problems are approached by way of integrating them into capitalist market mechanisms and finding technical solutions. The construction of the recycling network meets these postulations. As we have shown, however, it is precisely the stabilisation of the material and social relations which renders the network a problem. Hence, the story of Julian Berger illustrates how the set-up of a recycling network can lock a social network into a trajectory of 'unsustainability' (Blühdorn and Welsh 2007).

To sum up: recycling naturalises, rather than reduces, 'glass waste'. That is to say, it stabilises the symptom of multiple relations which go hand in hand with diverse problems: environmental destruction (using up more resources) and economic exploitation (through capitalist relations). Both these problems are silenced through the naturalisation of 'glass waste'. This should provoke further thought. Of course, it can be seen as a mishap that we live in a contradictory world in which the theoretical insights about 'glass waste' cannot be easily put into practice and I recognise that the recycling practices are interlocked with wider environmental policies and culture. The agency to change recycling is distributed within and among social fields. Various agents, including Julian Berger, take part in shaping the issue. I identified 'glass waste' as a site at which history has been and is being objectified. Therefore, an analysis of (glass) waste would see the wasted objects as social. To deal with them, solutions are needed which take into account the historical, social and political dimensions. These dimensions are integral, rather than external, to the objects. Thus, waste is socionatural – *attention to the waste problem requires including, not merely adding, critical takes on the society of which waste is part of.*

What needs doing now – a task for further research as well as for practical experiments by environmental managers – is to investigate how agents can counter the unsustainable trajectory of Western capitalist consumerism and production. Such questioning should aim at a negation of *practices* which produce undesired social and ecological effects. This focus on practices goes beyond only considering *ideas*[39]. To turn this conclusion into the positive and being inspired by Pepper (2005), I propose that practitioners engage with experiments to change the social situations which hitherto resulted in more, rather than less, waste (Krivtsov et al. 2004). For such an aim they would surely find as partners researchers and other social agents who are aware of social and ecological justice and the problems with unsustainable ecological modernisation practices.

22.6 Postscript

Four years afterwards, Julian provided a friendly comment on the preceding analysis[40]. He stressed the meanings his practices had at that time. His prime aim was one of "instituting a social norm" of "good housekeeping" within the organisation. This was supposed to induce a sense which would lead "to further recycling of other waste streams". He assured the reader that implementing the recycling scheme did not increase the amount of waste. As a trickle down effect, Julian

---

[39] Practices have to change and the change of ideas might be only a tiny step of the path to that. In that respect see Howard-Grenville (2005, p. 573) who discusses the ideas which environmental managers hold and how they seem to be stable.

[40] The quotes in this part are sourced from his written comments on this article.

hoped that recycling would "open doors to new commercial opportunities which would constitute green jobs rather than the norm which is to base useful work on extractive highly damaging industries".

Acknowledgments

Knowledge is produced in networks. First of all, I am much obliged to Julian Berger for welcoming me in his working environment. I am especially grateful to Brian Wynne for supervising me during the production of the original paper concerning this case. Furthermore I thank my PhD supervisor Christoph Lau for encouraging me to continue to work on the case and the research fellows of the Institute for Advanced Studies on Science, Technology and Society (IAS-STS) as well as the participants of the workshop *Environmental Management: More of the Same or Time for Change? – Confronting the Manageability Paradigm* (at Brandenburg University of Technology, January, 11-13, 2008) for providing feedback to earlier versions of this paper. Specifically, Helen Jackson, Torsten Wöllmann, Franz Martin Krause and Hannah Strauss provided me with valuable comments. Robert Atkinson provided helped to translate this paper into a more accessible language for scholars of environmental management. I gratefully acknowledge the funding by the German National Academic Foundation, Hans-Böckler-Foundation as well as IAS-STS for facilitating my studies.

References

Agar M (1980) The Professional Stranger: An Informal Introduction to Ethnography. Studies in Anthropology. Academic Press, Orlando

Benson D, Hughes J (1983) The Perspective of Ethnomethodology. Longman, London, New York

Benton T (ed) (1996) The Greening of Marxism. Democracy and Ecology. The Guilford Press, New York, London

Benton T (2001) Why are sociologists naturephobes? In: López J, Potter G (eds) After Postmodernism: An Introduction to Critical Realism. The Athlone Press, London, New York, pp. 133-145

Bijker W (1995) Sociohistorical Technology Studies. In: Jasanoff S, Markle G, Petersen J, Pinch T (eds) Handbook of Science and Technology Studies. Sage Publications in Cooperation with the Society for Social Studies of Science, Thousand Oaks, London, New Delhi, pp. 229-256

Blühdorn I, Welsh I (2007) Eco-politics beyond the paradigm of sustainability: A conceptual framework and research agenda. In: Environmental Politics 16(2): 185-205

Bourdieu P (1981) Men and machines. In: Knorr-Cetina K, Cicourel A (eds) Advances in social theory and methodology: Toward an integration of micro- and macro-sociologies. Routledge & Kegan Paul, Boston, pp. 304-317

Bourdieu P (1988) Vive la crise!: For heterodoxy in social science. In: Theory and Society 17(5): 773-787
Bourdieu P (1989) Social space and symbolic power. In: Sociological Theory 7(1): 14-25
Bourdieu P (1998) Practical Reason. Polity Press, Cambridge
Bourdieu P (2001) Meditationen: Zur Kritik der scholastischen Vernunft. Suhrkamp, Frankfurt am Main
Bourdieu P (2004) The peasant and his body. In: Ethnography 5(4): 579-599
Bourdieu P Wacquant L (1992) An Invitation to Reflexive Sociology. Polity Press, Cambridge
Bourdieu P Wacquant L (2006) Reflexive Anthropologie. Suhrkamp, Frankfurt am Main
Brundtland G, Agnelli S, Al-Athel S, Casanova P, Chidzero B, Padika L, Hauff V, Lang I, Shijun M, do Botero M, Singh N, Nogueira-Neto P, Okita S, Ramphal S, Ruckelshaus W, Sahnoun M, Salim E, Shaib B, Sokolov V, Stanovnik J, Strong M, MacNeill J (1987) Our Common Future/World Commission on Environment and Development. Oxford University Press, Oxford
Burawoy M (1998).The extended case method. In: Sociological Theory 16(1): 4-33
Callon M (1995) Four Models for the Dynamics of Science. In: Jasanoff S, Markle G, Petersen J, Pinch T (eds) Handbook of Science and Technology Studies. Sage Publications in Cooperation with the Society for Social Studies of Science, Thousand Oaks, London, New Delhi, pp. 29-63
Callon M (1999) Some Elements of a Sociology of Translation: Domestication of the Scallops and the Fishermen of Saint Brieuc Bay. In: Biagioli M (ed) The Science Studies Reader. Routledge, New York, London, pp. 67-83
Callon M, Latour B (1981). Unscrewing the Big Leviathan: how actors macrostructure reality and how sociologists help them to do so. In: Knorr-Cetina K, Cicourel A (eds) Advances in social theory and methodology: Toward an integration of micro- and macro-sociologies. Routledge & Kegan Paul, Boston, pp. 277-303
Carvalho G (2001) Sustainable development: Is it achievable within the existing international political economy context? In: Sustainable Development 9: 61-73
Christoff P (1996) Ecological modernisation, ecological modernities. In: Environmental Politics 5(3): 476-500
Clark B, York R (2005) Carbon metabolism: Global capitalism, climate change, and the biospheric rift. In: Theory and Society 34: 391-428
Dingler J (2003) Postmoderne und Nachhaltigkeit. Eine diskurstheoretische Analyse der sozialen Konstruktion von nachhaltiger Entwicklung. Ökom, München
Douglas M (ed) (1987) A distinctive anthropological perspective. In: Douglas M (ed) Constructive Drinking: Perspectives on Drink from Anthropology. Cambridge University Press, Cambridge, pp. 3-16
Emerson R, Fretz R, Shaw L (1995) Writing Ethnographic Fieldnotes. The University of Chicago Press, Chicago, London
Enzensberger H (1996) A Critique of Political Ecology. In: Benton T (ed) (1996) The Greening of Marxism. Democracy and Ecology. The Guilford Press, New York, London, pp. 17-4
Fairclough N, Jessop B, Sayer A (2002) Critical realism and semiosis. In: Journal of Critical Realism 5(1): 2-10
Fairhead J, Leach M (2003) Science, Society and Power: Environmental knowledge and policy in West Africa and the Caribbean. Cambridge University Press, Cambridge
Garfinkel H (1967) Studies in Ethnomethodology. Blackwell, Malden

Giddens A (1986) The constitution of society: outline of the theory of structuration. University of California Press, Berkeley
Graeber D (2004) Fragments of an Anarchist Anthropology. Prickly Paradigm Press, Chicago
Graham S, Thrift N (2007) Out of Order: Understanding Repair and Maintenance. In: Theory, Culture & Society 24(3): 1-25
Haque M (2000) Environmental discourse and sustainable development: Linkages and limitations. In: Ethics and the Environment 5(1): 3-21
Haraway D (1991) Simians, Cyborgs, and Women. Free Association Books, London
Hassard J, McCann L, Morris J (2007) At the sharp end of new organizational ideologies. Ethnography and the study of multinationals. In: Ethnography 8(3): 324-344
Howard-Grenville J (2005) Explaining Shades of Green: Why Do Companies Act Differently on Similar Environmental Issues? In: Law & Social Inquiry 30(3): 551-581
Howard-Grenville J, Nash J, Coglianese C (2008) Constructing the license to operate: Internal factors and their influence on corporate environmental decisions. In: Law & Policy 30(1): 73-107
Irwin A (2001) Sociology and the Environment. Polity Press, Cambridge
Jänicke M (2004) Industrial transformation between ecological modernisation and structural change. In: Jacob K, Binder M, Wieczorek A (eds) Governance for Industrial Transformation. Proceedings of the 2003 Berlin Conference on the Human Dimensions of Global Environmental Change, Berlin, pp. 201-207
Jänicke M (2008) Ecological modernisation: new perspectives. In: Journal of Cleaner Production 16(5): 557-565
Jasanoff S, Markle G, Petersen J, Pinch T (eds) (1995) Handbook of Science and Technology Studies. Sage Publications in Cooperation with the Society for Social Studies of Science, Thousand Oaks, London, New Delhi
Keller R (1998) Müll, die gesellschaftliche Konstruktion des wertvollen: Die öffentliche Diskussion über Abfall in Deutschland und Frankreich. Westdeutscher Verlag, Opladen
Knorr-Cetina K, Cicourel A (eds) (1981) Advances in social theory and methodology: Toward an integration of micro- and macro-sociologies. Routledge & Kegan Paul, Boston
Krivtsov V, Wäger P, Dacombea P, Gilgen P, Heaven S, Hilty L, Banks C (2004) Analysis of energy footprints associated with recycling of glass and plastic — case studies for industrial ecology. In: Ecological Modelling 174: 175-189
Law J (1992) Notes on the Theory of the Actor Network: Ordering, Strategy and Heterogeneity. Internet address: http://www.lancaster.ac.uk/fss/sociology/papers/law-notes-on-ant.pdf, last accessed on 02.11.2006
Law J, Hassard J (eds) (1999) Actor Network Theory and after. Blackwell, Oxford, Malden
Li X, Hersh J (2002) Understanding capitalism: Crises and passive revolutions. In: Competition & Change 6(2): 193-212
Lippert I (2010) Agents of Ecological Modernisation. Der Andere Verlag, Tönning, Lübeck, Marburg
Marx K (1968) Das Kapital. Dietz Verlag, Berlin
Michael M (2000) Reconnecting Culture, Technology and Nature: From society to heterogeneity. Routledge, London, New York
Mol A (2000) The environmental movement in an era of ecological modernisation. In: Geoforum 31(1): 45-46

Mol A (2001) Globalization and Environmental Reform. The Ecological Modernization of the Global Economy. The MIT Press, Cambridge, Massachusetts

Mol A (2006) Environment and modernity in transitional China: Frontiers of ecological modernization. In: Development and Change 37(1): 29-56

Mol A, Sonnenfeld D (2000a) Ecological Modernization Around the World: An Introduction. In: Mol A, Sonnenfeld D (eds) Ecological Modernisation Around the World: Perspectives and Critical Debates. Frank Cass, London, Portland, pp. 3-16

Mol A, Sonnenfeld D (eds) (2000b) Ecological Modernisation Around the World: Perspectives and Critical Debates. Frank Cass, London, Portland

Mutch A (2002) Actors and networks or agents and structures: Towards a realist view of information systems. In: Organization 9(3): 477-496

Pellow D, Schnaiberg A, Weinberg A (2000) Putting the Ecological Modernization Thesis to the Test: The Promises and Performance of Urban Recycling. In: Mol A, Sonnenfeld D (eds) Ecological Modernisation Around the World: Perspectives and Critical Debates. Frank Cass, London, Portland, pp. 109-137

Pepper D (1984) The Roots of Modern Environmentalism. Croom Helm, London, Sydney, Dover (New Hampshire)

Pepper D (2005) Utopianism and environmentalism. In: Environmental Politics 14(1): 3-22

Redclift M, Benton T (eds) (1994) Social Theory and the Global Environment. Routledge, London, New York

Sayer A (2000) Realism and Social Science. Sage Publications, London, Thousand Oaks, New Dehli

Schinkel W (2003) Pierre Bourdieu's political turn? In: Theory, Culture & Society 20(6): 69-93

Schnaiberg A, Pellow D, Weinberg A (2000) The Treadmill of Production and the Environmental State. Internet address: http://www.northwestern.edu/ipr/publications/papers/2004 /schnaiberg/17_%TreadmillEnvirState.pdf, last accessed on 16.02.2007

Sibeon R (1999) Anti-reductionist sociology. In: Sociology 33(2): 317-334

Simonis U, Altner G, Böhm N, Göll E, Löffler K, Pilardeaux B, Siebenhüner B, Volkery A (2003) Öko-Lexikon. CH Beck, München

Sonnenfeld D, Mol A (2006) Environmental reform in Asia. Comparisons, challenges, next steps. In: The Journal of Environment & Development 15(2): 112-137

Sterne J (2003) Bourdieu, technique and technology. In: Cultural Studies 17(3/4): 367-389

Strathern M (1996) Cutting the network. In: The Journal of the Royal Anthropological Institute 2(3): 517-535

Thomas J (1993) Doing Critical Ethnography. Sage Publications, Beverly Hills (Calif.)

von Weizäcker E (ed) (1999) Das Jahrhundert der Umwelt. Vision: Öko-effizient leben und arbeiten. Campus-Verlag, Frankfurt am Main, New York

Woolgar S (1991) Configuring the user: the case of usability trials. In: Law J (ed) A Sociology of Monsters: Essays on Power, Technology and Domination. Routledge, London, New York, pp. 57-99

York R, Rosa E (2003) Key challenges to ecological modernization theory. In: Organization & Environment 16(3): 273-288

23 An Indicator-based Approach to Environmental and Resource Management in a Globalised World

Gerhard Wiegleb

Chair of General Ecology, Brandenburg University of Technology (BTU), Cottbus, Germany

23.1 Introduction

On 19 June 1999, 31 European ministers of education from 29 countries, among them ministers of all current EU member states (except Cyprus) as well as representatives of Switzerland, Norway and Iceland, signed the so-called 'Bologna Declaration'[1]. They agreed to create a unified European Higher Education Area by the year 2010. The Bologna Declaration is thus a precursor of the Lisbon Strategy, published one year later in 2000,[2] according to which the European Union should become the *"most competitive and dynamic knowledge based economic area of the world"*[3] by the year 2010.

The aims of Bologna[4] are: the implementation of a system of easily understandable and comparable academic degrees; the distribution of a Europe-wide Diploma Supplement, a uniform description of academic degrees and qualifications; the implementation of a two-tiered system of study programmes (undergraduate/graduate); the implementation of a credit point system to foster mobility; the overcoming of mobility obstacles for students, teachers, scientists, and administrative personnel; better comparability of quality management approaches; and the advancement of the necessary European dimension in the university sector.

Based on the Bologna Declaration, governments of all Bologna states subsequently made further decisions in order to promote the 'Europeanization' of the

---

[1] German version see http://www.bmbf.de/pub/bologna_deu.pdf.

[2] Europäischer Rat (Lissabon), Schlussfolgerungen des Vorsitzes v. 23./24.03.2000, see http://www.europarl.europa.eu/summits/lis1_de.htm.

[3] See before named, point I.5.

[4] Bologna declaration (see 1), p. 3ff.

university system. In the year 2001, the Prague Communiqué[5] added three aims to the declaration: life-long learning should be advanced, the European higher education area should be made more attractive, and it should be opened for the participation of students. Two years later the Berlin Communiqué[6] added some details to the general declarations, e.g. for national quality controlling. In 2005 the Bergen Communiqué[7] drew a balance of the achievements so far (speaking of "considerable progress") and set up further aims to be reached by 2010 concerning improvement of study structure and recognition of international acknowledgement of course achievements. In 2007 a London meeting decided that employability of graduates should be improved as well (a detailed overview of the Bologna process is found in Wiegleb et al. 2009).

We can summarise that several concepts mentioned in the official texts need operationalisation, in particular with respect to the questions: What is it that defines an improved study structure? What is it that makes an institution competitive on the higher education market? And what is it that makes former graduates employable on a globalised job market? How do topics addressed in research and practical training of ERM students reflect real world environmental problems? Do students actively participate in their scientific and professional career formation? These questions are being tentatively answered by analysing the internationalisation process at BTU Cottbus.

23.2 Materials and Methods

The first part of the paper is based on the evaluation of various internal documents at BTU Cottbus, which were compiled in the context of two important evaluation procedures:

- Reaccreditation of the ERM Bachelor and Master programmes in 2009/2010, carried out by the accreditation agency ACQUIN.
- International audit of BTU, carried out by an international panel under the guidance of HRK (German Conference of University Rectors).

In addition, inquiries carried out in the framework of an Alumni+ programme (funded by DAAD) and a graduate placement study carried out with the help of INCHER (see Flöther 2010) were used.

The second part is based on an assessment of a series of books, which have been published by Springer Publishing (Schmidt et al. 2004, Schmidt et al. 2006, Schmidt et al. 2011, this volume) and the observation of self-organized alumni activities on BTU campus (ERM Board of Students 2010).

---

[5] See http://www.bmbf.de/pub/prager_kommunique.pdf , or http://www.ond.vlaanderen.be/hogeronderwijs/Bologna/documents/MDC/PRAGUE_COMMUNIQUE.pdf.

[6] See http://www.bmbf.de/pub/berlin_communique.pdf.

[7] See http://www.bmbf.de/pub/bergen_kommunique_dt.pdf.

23.3 The Bologna Process at BTU Cottbus

At BTU Cottbus internationalisation started in 1998 with the implementation of the ERM Bachelor programme, followed by the Master programme in 1999. New regulations for all Bachelor and Master Programmes offered at BTU were introduced in 2004[8] and since 2009 all courses at BTU are offered under the new system. Diploma degrees are no longer awarded. This is to be regarded as a spin-off effect of the early implementation of the ERM courses.

Since then ERM has become a recognised consecutive study programme all over the world. Eight international study programmes are offered at BTU and 476 international students are enrolled (as of 2010). One programme is offered as joint degree with four other universities (Eurohydroinformatics and Water Management). With the introduction of the ERM PhD-programme in 2004, the implementation of new PhD regulations with a focus on science-oriented accompanying studies and the publication of the above mentioned series of books the focus has shifted from teaching and education to the integration of scientific research. The ERM PhD programme was among the first structured PhD programmes in Germany and can be regarded as trend setting for the future development of graduate studies (see Mersch and van Rebber 2010).

23.3.1 Study Structure in International Programmes

Quality indicators of an international study programme are summarised in Table 23.1. Likewise the estimated degree of fulfilment is indicated in column 2. The formal requirements of the Bologna process are all met by the ERM programmes. This is true for the ECTS credit system, bilingual transcripts, diploma supplement and online documentation of the syllabus (module descriptions[9]). However, even though all classes are given in the English language, the English proficiency of some teachers is still being criticised by students during regular course evaluations.

Table 23.1. Quality indicators international study programmes at BTU

Indicator	Degree of fulfilment
ECTS credit system fully implemented	***
All mandatory courses in English	***
Bilingual transcripts	***
Diploma supplement	***
Online-documentation of syllabus	***
Excellent language proficiency of teachers	**

*** good, ** satisfying, * to be improved

[8] Available under http://opus.kobv.de/btu/volltexte/2007/215/pdf/abl151_05.pdf

[9] Available under http://www.zv.tu-cottbus.de/moveron/admin/portal.php

23.3.2 Integration into the European Higher Education Market

Indicators of integration of BTU and competitivity of BTU graduates in the European higher education market are listed in Table 23.2. The ultimate criterion of success of an academic institution is the placement of graduates in recognised Master and PhD programmes in Germany and abroad. We know that our students are widely distributed among higher graduate study courses at other universities, both in Germany and abroad. BTU is also well established with respect to national accreditation of its study courses and the quality of its partner universities, even though partner universities have been changing substantially since 1998. The number remained relatively constant (around 20) while there was a strong turnover. On the other hand the state of the exchange of scientific personnel and the number of joint and double degree programmes are unsatisfying.

Table 23.2. Competitivity indicators of BTU on the European higher education market

Indicator	Degree of fulfilment
Placement of graduates in recognized Master and PhD programmes	***
Number of accredited international study programmes	***
Quality of partner universities (full semester in English)	***
Number of incoming students from abroad	**
Joint research projects with partner universities	**
Number of foreign students holding scholarship	**
Number of graduates from abroad within the described period of study	**
Number of international post docs and scientists at BTU	*
Worldwide exchange of scientific personnel	*
Double and joint degrees with universities abroad	*

*** good, ** satisfying, * to be improved

23.3.3 Employability of BTU Graduates

Another major criterion for academic success is the employability of graduates, of which an overview is shown in Table 23.3. Some criteria such as international topics in class are only prerequisites, while others like placement in academic positions in Germany and elsewhere are real indicators. Despite the fact that some prerequisites are not fully satisfying, the main indicators are very convincing. Both in practical fields and in academia our students are very successful. As to practical fields, we know that most alumni are employed in larger companies. Large companies tend to be more international than small companies, administrative bodies such as environmental agencies, and even NGOs. Thus having international experience (one semester abroad) and being able to communicate in several languages are major advantages of our graduates which are appreciated by large companies.

Table 23.3. Indicators for international employability of BTU graduates

Indicator	Degree of fulfilment
Professional success of graduates in relevant practical fields	***
Professional success in academic positions, in particular in home countries	***
Proportion of international topics in classes	**
English proficiency of students	**
Number of B.Sc./M.Sc. theses written abroad	**
Number of international guest lecturers	*

*** good, ** satisfying, * to be improved

23.4 Change of Research Topics in ERM Books

So far only formal aspects have been discussed, but also the development of important issues deserves some investigation. The shift in interest is documented in a series of books, which have been published by Springer Publishing (Schmidt et al. 2004, Schmidt et al. 2006, Schmidt et al. 2011, this volume). All books are based on achievements of PhD students as presented during a workshop on Current Development in Environmental Management.

23.4.1 Topics in ERM

Table 23.4 shows an overview of topics addressed in the above named series of books.

Table 23.4. Relevant topics addressed in ERM books (n = number of articles)

Topic	SEA book 2004	EIA book 2006	Implementation book 2011
Legislation	20	1	1
Planning theory and assessment	14	8	1
Biodiversity	2	1	-
Water resource management	2	-	1
Waste management / landfills	1	1	1
Mining	1	1	-
Landscape planning and land use	1	2	-
Soil protection	1	1	-
Dams and reservoirs	1	2	-
Water quality management	1	2	-
Transport and infrastructure	1	1	-
Energy management	1	-	4
Urban planning	1	-	-
Agriculture	1	-	-
Waste water	-	2	1

Table 23.4. (cont.)

Health / disease control	-	2	-
Ecotoxicology	-	2	-
Air pollution	-	2	-
Renewable energies	-	1	4
Forest management	-	1	1
Governance	-	1	-
Recycling	-	1	
Tourism	-	1	-
Marine pollution	-	1	-
Noise abatement	-	1	-
Nano technology	-	1	-
Clean development mechanisms	-	-	2
Corporate environmental management	-	-	2
Renewable raw materials	-	-	2
Ecosystem services	-	-	1
Nuclear energy	-	-	1

In 2004 (Schmidt et al. 2004), there was a strong emphasis on theoretical aspects such as legislation, implementation of laws into policies and programmes, and planning theory. The latter category comprises papers on assessment and decision-support methods. In the 2006 book (Schmidt et al. 2006), papers dealing with assessment and decision-making in general were more and more replaced by concrete case studies and applications in the real world. In the 2011 book (Schmidt et al., this volume) almost no theoretical papers can be found. Most papers are based on own research or practical experience and deal with a variety of environmental issues. Energy related issues such as energy management, renewable energies and clean development mechanisms have a definite majority.

23.4.2 Geographical Distribution of ERM Research

In Table 23.5 an overview of the geographical distribution of ERM topics is given. This distribution is not only reflecting the geographical origin of ERM students, but is overlaid by current trends.

In 2004 there was still a strong focus on German research issues. Interest in German topics has declined since then. In 2006 a slight majority of issues related to German neighbour countries and Central European trans boundary issues can be observed. In 2010 geographical emphasis has shifted to rising economies (G 20 states) such as Brazil and India, while continent comparisons were also carried out. Research topics now come from all continents and often take a globalised viewpoint. This is also indicated by the agenda of the latest self-organized alumni workshop (ERM Board of Students 2009).

Table 24.5. Distribution of ERM research topics by country (n = number of articles)

Country	SEA book 2004	EIA book 2006	Implementation book 2011
Germany	9	7	2
Portugal	1	1	-
Spain	-	1	-
Belgium	-	1	-
Italy	-	1	-
Poland	2	2	-
Finland	-	1	2
Sweden	1	1	-
UK	1	3	-
Austria	-	1	-
Czech Republic	-	1	-
Latvia	-	1	-
Estonia	-	1	-
Ukraine	1	1	1
Turkey	-	1	1
European trans boundary	3	3	-
Azerbaijan	-	1	-
Yemen	2	-	-
India	-	-	2
China	-	1	1
Thailand	1	-	1
Morocco	1	-	-
Kenya	1	1	-
Cameroon	1	-	1
Ghana	1	1	-
Sub-Saharan Africa	-	-	1
Canada	-	1	-
USA	-	1	-
Mexico	1	-	-
Brazil	1	-	4
New Zealand	-	1	-
Australia	-	-	1
Intercontinental comparison	-	-	3

24.5 Discussion and Conclusions

The improved study structure at BTU, as codified in the framework regulations for Bachelor and Master Courses at BTU is the basis of success. This study structure has been extended from Bachelor to Master and PhD and makes the university understandable for students coming from abroad. Competitivity is based on a mixture of aspects, both formal ones (accreditation, network of partner universities) and aspects related to the qualification and motivation of students and teachers. Success on the globalised job market is influenced by a variety of factors. Besides languages proficiency the input of international information by students and teaching personnel plays a major role.

Topics addressed in research and practical training of ERM students truly reflect real world environmental problems. Any check of current issues in textbooks of environmental management or a simple Google search would show that all major environmental issues are being dealt with. These issues not only span the totality of the challenges but the whole globe. Thus one might say that ERM follows a universal approach rather than simply a globalised one. Students themselves actively participate in their scientific and professional career formation by travelling abroad, independently selecting research topics, coming together for alumni workshops, and cooperatively issuing books with a universal environmental dimension.

From the preceding we can conclude that at BTU Cottbus 'internationalisation' is not only a nice label, but the concept has been filled with content both on the levels of teaching and research. The scope of ERM clearly goes beyond the European framework. Instead all emerging economies and many states struggling for enforcement of a functioning legal system including environmental regulations are included in the problem catalogue of ERM.

Acknowledgement

I thank Prof. M. Schmidt for the invitation to co-edit this volume and valuable discussions on indicator-based assessment. I thank N. Zechel, N. Wolfeil, F. Schulz and K. Golz for providing the data basis for tables 23.1-4.

References

ERM Board of Students (2009) Mind the Gap. Announcement of Alumni workshop. Internet address: http://board.erm.tu-cottbus.de, last accessed on 06.01.2011

Flöther C (2010) Follow me: Was kommt nach der Uni? Internet address: http://www.uni-kassel.de/wz1/pdf/Kurz_KS_JG2007.pdf, last accessed on 06.01.2011

Mersch B, van Rebber F (2010) Die Meister sterben aus. duzMagazin 03/2010:10-11

Schmidt M, Glasson J, Emmelin L, Helbron H (eds) (2006) Standards and Thresholds for Impact Assessment. Springer, Berlin, Heidelberg

Schmidt M, João E, Knopp L (eds) (2004) Implementing Strategic Environmental Assessment. Springer, Berlin, Heidelberg

Schmidt M, Onyango V, Palekhov D, Wiegleb G (2011) Implementing Environmental and Resource Management. Springer, Berlin, Heidelberg

Wiegleb G, Küchenhoff B, Kullick S. (2009) Internationalität und Hochschulen. In: Knopp L, Peine FJ, Nowacki K, Schröder W (eds) Hochschulen im Umbruch. Cottbuser Schriften für Hochschulrecht und Hochschulpolitik 1, pp. 81-108

Subject Index